FORTY YEARS FOR LABRADOR

BOOKS BY SIR WILFRED T. GRENFELL

FORTY YEARS FOR LABRADOR

BY
SIR WILFRED GRENFELL
K.C.M.G., M.D. (OXON.), F.R.C.S., F.A.C.S.

WITH ILLUSTRATIONS

BOSTON AND NEW YORK
HOUGHTON MIFFLIN COMPANY
The Riverside Press Cambridge
1932

The Riverside Press
CAMBRIDGE · MASSACHUSETTS
PRINTED IN THE U.S.A.

TO
MY WIFE

PREFACE

A BIOLOGIST, watching one animal in his vivarium to see how
an experiment turns out, expects to arrive nearer the truth as
time elapses and the end draws near. Just so, spectators
watching a runner in a race get more and more interested as
the last lap approaches and the goal looms in sight. Then the
runner's achievement is easier to appraise. Life's struggle,
moreover, becomes increasingly interesting now that philosophers again permit us to regard results as dependent upon
causes which are under the control of the individual runner to
a very large extent.

The title of this new record has been changed, to suggest
that this is the last lap, and that deductions from the facts
may be expected to be more mature and therefore more worth
while, provided they are honest. The consciousness of having
to live alongside the first venture into autobiography involved
a kind of vivisection; for to have to tell the truth about one's
real self carries with it the inescapable reproach of nudism,
however salutary that may be for one's spiritual welfare, or
however interesting to others. This effort is more like a 'last
testament'; and it is easier for a doctor to see the reasonableness of offering to a school of anatomy that which he cannot
take with him, and which should be more useful for dissecting
than for any other purpose.

The purpose of this book is the same as that of its predecessor, 'A Labrador Doctor,' written many years ago in response
to the persuasion of friends, as a record of a humble com-
petitor in the race of life who was pledged to the utmost of his
ability to carry the colours of the Christian theory into
practice. To endeavour to foist the story of any one com-
petitor onto the attention of a busy world would be unpardon-
able were it not for the generous insistence of a still larger circle
of friends that the record be brought as closely up to date as
the writer of any autobiography can expect to bring it —
though the picture, of course, cannot be completed this side
the Great Divide.

Naturally, the records of childhood and youth must stand unchanged. Otherwise the entire book has been rewritten, with the better perspective and, one hopes, the generally accorded riper wisdom of age. The last chapter, on my religious life, has been this time entitled 'Salaam,' in order to carry all the old English meaning which the word 'farewell' bore — 'God be with you till we meet.'

Many new activities have been undertaken since the old book, 'A Labrador Doctor,' appeared. Many new ventures have been entered upon and new methods devised to carry to the down-and-out brother, in ways he cannot mistake as being messages of love, that reflection of Divine love which, wherever it has been intelligently exhibited, has remade man, and through him is remaking this world. The years have left such ineffaceable convictions of the truth of this that I have at last accumulated the conceit which encourages me not merely to send a new edition to the press, but a new book.

As for this effort in the North, what is it? Is it dead or alive? If growth is a sign of life, I venture to believe that this record of the past nearly fifteen years since my pen was laid down will show that the work has more than its pristine vitality, and is just now entering upon a new era of enlarged service.

But for the hundreds of colleagues who have so self-effacingly 'lent more power to my elbow,' the work would never have been possible at all. They are far too numerous for me to record their names or their service individually here; but their imprint is indelible, both in our hearts and on the lives of the fishermen.

To my wife, who was willing to leave all the best which the civilized world can offer to share my life, both on this lonely shore and in the infinitely more difficult and prosaic task of working for the Coast in the world outside, I want to dedicate this book. Like its predecessor, it would never have come into being but for her.

W. G.

CONTENTS

ILLUSTRATIONS

*Many of the illustrations are from
photographs by Professor F. C. Sears*

FORTY YEARS FOR LABRADOR

FORTY YEARS FOR LABRADOR

∵

CHAPTER I

ON THE SANDS OF DEE

I MUST admit to forty years at the helm — 1932 — 1892 = 40.
Mathematics is the one and only science which can prove anything. Today I like to hear that some philosophers are courageous enough to question even that. But even accepting the
hypothesis, what of it? Why not regard today as the commencement of my second forty years?

Fifteen years have elapsed since 'A Labrador Doctor' was
written. As I looked through the index, I was amazed to
notice how many friends mentioned in it are among the so-
called 'dead.' A photograph suggested to me today how like
the colour of my own hair has become to that of its winter environment; and for the last four years there have been increasing signs of wear in the faithful old pump. Truly, it is time
which stays. It is we who fly.

Much as the majority of mankind would like to revise the
records of their early days, those records have to stand. The
eagerness to get a story all at once has made serials unpopular
in this tabloid age. Yet life cannot help being a serial; and if
parts of the early pages of this story are already familiar to
my readers, I can only hope that the desire to know what happened next, the longing which used to send me as a boy running to meet the postman on the mornings when 'My Magazine' was due, may kindle some of the same reaction in my
friends.

When we sense the approaching shadow of the inevitable
'last chapter,' the fact impresses itself upon us increasingly
that the only thing which even a Crœsus can take with him
off the stage, which he did not bring onto it, is that same
record which, alas, like the laws of the Medes and Persians,
'altereth not.'

FORTY YEARS FOR LABRADOR

.·.

CHAPTER I

ON THE SANDS OF DEE

I MUST admit to forty years at the helm — 1932 — 1892 = 40. Mathematics is the one and only science which can prove anything. Today I like to hear that some philosophers are courageous enough to question even that. But even accepting the hypothesis, what of it? Why not regard today as the commencement of my second forty years?

Fifteen years have elapsed since 'A Labrador Doctor' was written. As I looked through the index, I was amazed to notice how many friends mentioned in it are among the so-called 'dead.' A photograph suggested to me today how like the colour of my own hair has become to that of its winter environment; and for the last four years there have been increasing signs of wear in the faithful old pump. Truly, it is time which stays. It is we who fly.

Much as the majority of mankind would like to revise the records of their early days, those records have to stand. The eagerness to get a story all at once has made serials unpopular in this tabloid age. Yet life cannot help being a serial; and if parts of the early pages of this story are already familiar to my readers, I can only hope that the desire to know what happened next, the longing which used to send me as a boy running to meet the postman on the mornings when 'My Magazine' was due, may kindle some of the same reaction in my friends.

When we sense the approaching shadow of the inevitable 'last chapter,' the fact impresses itself upon us increasingly that the only thing which even a Crœsus can take with him off the stage, which he did not bring onto it, is that same record which, alas, like the laws of the Medes and Persians, 'altereth not.'

To be born on the twenty-eighth of February is not altogether without its compensations. It affords a subject of conversation when you are asked to put your name in birthday books. It is evident that many people suppose it to be almost an intrusion to appear on that day. However, it was perfectly satisfactory to me so long as it was not the twenty-ninth. Still, I used at times to be oppressed by the danger, so narrowly missed, of growing up with undue deliberation.

The event occurred in 1865 in Parkgate, near Cheshire, England, whither my parents had moved to enable my father to take over the school of his uncle. I was always told that what might be called boisterous weather signalled my arrival. Experience has since shown me that that need not be considered a particularly ominous portent in the winter season on the Sands of Dee.

It is fortunate that the selection of our birthplace is not left to ourselves. It would most certainly be one of those small decisions which would later add to the things over which we worry. I can see how it would have acted in my own case. For my paternal forbears are of Cornish extraction — a corner of our little Island to which attaches all the romantic aroma of the men, who, in defence of England, 'swept the Spanish Main,' and so long successfully singed the King of Spain's beard, men whose exploits never fail to stir the blood of Englishmen, and among whom my direct ancestors had the privilege of playing no undistinguished part. On the other hand, my visits thither have — romance aside — convinced me that the restricted foreshore and the precipitous cliffs are a handicap to the development of youth, compared with the broad expanses of tempting sands, which are closely associated with another kinsman, whose songs have helped to make them famous, Charles Kingsley.

My mother was born in India, her father being a colonel of many campaigns, and her brother an engineer officer in charge during the siege of Lucknow till relieved by Sir Henry Havelock. At the first Delhi Durbar no less than forty-eight of my cousins met, all being officers either of the Indian military or civil service.

To the modern commercial mind the wide sands are a stumbling-block. Silting up with the years, they have closed

THE SANDS OF DEE

the river to navigation, and converted our once famous Roman city of Chester into a sleepy, second-rate market-town. The great flood of commerce from the New World sweeps contemptuously past our estuary, and finds its clearing-house under the eternal, assertive smoke-clouds which camouflage the miles of throbbing docks and slums called Liverpool — little more than a dozen miles distant. But the heather-clad hills of Heswall and the old red sandstone ridge, which form the ancient borough of the 'Hundred of Wirral,' afford an efficient shelter from the insistent taint of out-of-the-worldness.

Every inch of the Sands of Dee was dear to me. I learned to know their every bank and gutter. Away beyond them there was a mystery in the blue hills of the Welsh shore, only cut off from us children in reality by the narrow, rapid water of the channel through the sands, that we called the 'Deep.' Yet they seemed so high and so far away! The people there spoke a different language from ours, and all their instincts seemed diverse. Our own humble neighbours lived by the seafaring genius which we ourselves loved so much. They made their living from the fisheries of the river mouth; and scores of times we children would slip away and spend the day and night with them in their boats.

I was still quite a small boy, when a terrible blizzard struck the estuary while the boats were out, and for twenty-four hours one of the fishing craft was missing. Only a lad of sixteen was in charge of her — a boy whom we knew and with whom we had often sailed. All our family were away from home at the time except myself; and I can still remember the thrill I experienced when, as representative of the 'Big House'! I was taken to see the poor lad, who had been brought home at last, frozen to death.

The men of the opposite shores were shopkeepers and miners. Somehow we knew that they couldn't help it. The nursery rhyme about 'Taffy was a Welshman; Taffy was a thief,' because familiar, had not led us to hold any unduly inflated estimate of the Welsh character. One of my old nurses did much to redeem it, however. She had undertaken the burden of my brother and myself during a long vacation, and carried us off bodily to her home in Wales. Her clean little cottage stood by the side of a road leading to the village school of the State Mining District of Festiniog. We soon learned that the local boys resented the intrusion of the two English lads, and they so frequently chased us off the village green, which was the only playground offered us, that we at last decided to give battle. We had stored up a pile of slates behind our garden wall, and, luring the enemy to the gates by the simple method of retiring before their advance, we saluted them with artillery fire from a comparatively safe entrenchment. To my horror, one of the first missiles struck a medium-sized boy right over the eye, and I saw the blood flow instantly. The awful vision of David and Goliath flashed across my terror-stricken mind, and I fled incontinently to my nurse's protection. Subsequently, by her adroit diplomacy, we were not only delivered from justice, but gained the freedom of the green as well.

Far away up the estuary came the great salt-water marshes which seemed so endless to our tiny selves. There was also the Great Cop, an embankment miles long, intended to reach 'from England to Wales,' but which was never finished because the quicksand swallowed up all that the workmen could pour into it. Many a time I have stood on the broken end, where the discouraged labourers had left their very shovels and picks and trucks and had apparently fled in dismay, as if convicted of the impiousness of trying to fill the Bottomless Pit. To my childish imagination the upturned wheelbarrows and wasted trucks and rails always suggested the banks of the Red Sea after the awful disaster had swept over Pharaoh and his host. How the returning tide used to sweep through that, to us, fathomless gulch! It made the old river seem ever so much more wonderful, and ever so much more filled with adventure.

Many a time, just to dare it, I would dive into the very cauldron, and let the swirling current carry me to the grassy sward beyond — along which I would run till the narrowing channel permitted my crossing to the Great Cop again. I would be drying myself in the sunshine as I went, and all ready for my scanty garments when I reached my clothing once more.

Then came the great days when the heavy nor'westers

howled over the Sands — our sea-front was exposed to all the power of the sea right away to the Point of Ayr — the days when they came in with big spring tides, when we saw the fishermen doubling their anchors, and carefully overhauling the holding-gear of their boats, before the flooding tide drove the men ashore, powerless to do more than watch them battling at their moorings like living things — the possessions upon which their very bread depended. And then this one would sink, and another would part her cable and come hurtling before the gale, until she crashed right into the great upright blocks of sandstone which, riveted with iron bands to their copings, were relied upon to hold the main road from destruction. Sometimes in fragments, and sometimes almost entire, the craft would be slung clean over the battlements and be left stranded high and dry on our one village street, a menace to traffic, but a huge joy to us children.

The fascination of the Sands was greatly enhanced by the numerous birds which at all times frequented them, in search of the abundant food which lay buried along the edges of the muddy gutters. There were thousands of sandpipers in enormous flocks, mixed with ring plovers, knots, dunlins, and turnstones, which followed the ebb tides and returned again in whirling clouds before the oncoming floods. Black-and-white oyster-catchers were always to be found chattering over the great mussel patches at low water. With their reddish bills, what a trophy a bunch of them made as we bore them proudly home over our shoulders! Then there were the big long-billed curlews. What a triumph when one outwitted them! One of my clearest recollections is discovering a place to which they were flighting at night by the water's edge; how, having no dog, I swam out for bird after bird as they fell to my gun — shooting some before I had even time to put on my shirt again; and my consequent blue-black shoulder which had to be carefully hidden next day. There were wild ducks, too, to be surprised in the pools of the big salt marshes.

From daylight to dark I would wander, quite alone, over endless miles, entirely satisfied to come back with a single bird, and not in the least disheartened if I got none. All sense of time used to be lost, and often enough the sandwich and biscuit for lunch forgotten, so that I would be forced occasionally to resort to a solitary public house near a colliery on our side of the water for 'tea-biscuits,' all that they offered except endless beer for the miners. I can even remember, when very hard-driven, crossing to the Welsh side for bread and cheese.

These expeditions were made barefoot as long as the cold was not too great. A diary that I essayed to keep in my eighth year reminds me that on my birthday, five miles from home in the marshes, I fell head over heels into a deep hole, while wading out, gun in hand, after some oyster-catchers which I had shot. The snow was still deep on the countryside, and the long trot home was never quite forgotten. My grief, however, was all for the gun.

There was always the joy of venture in those dear old Sands. The channels cut in them by the flowing tides ran deep, and often intersected. Moreover, they changed with the varying storms. The rapidly rising tide, which sent a bore up the main channel as far as Chester, twelve miles above us, filled first of all these treacherous waterways, quite silently, and often unobserved. To us, taught to be as much at home in the water as on the land, they only added spice to our wanderings. They were nowhere very wide, so, by keeping one's head and being able to swim, only our clothes suffered by it, and they, being built for that purpose, did not complain.

One day, however, there was great excitement. The tide had risen rapidly in the channel along the parade front, and the shrimp fishermen, who used push-nets in the channels at low tide, had returned without noticing that one of their number was missing. Word got about just too late, and already there was half a mile of water, beyond which, through our telescopes, we could see the poor fellow making frantic signals to the shore. There was no boat out there, and, a big bank intervening, there seemed no way to get to him. Watching through our glasses, we saw him drive the long handle of his net deep into the sand and cling to it, while the tide rose speedily around him. Meanwhile, a whole bevy of his mates had rowed out to the bank, and were literally carrying over its treacherous surface one of their clumsy and heavy fishing punts. It was a veritable race for life; and never have I watched one with keener excitement. We actually saw his post give way and wash downstream with him clinging to it, just before his friends got near. Fortunately, drifting with the spar, he again found bottom, and was eventually rescued, half full of salt water. I remember how he fell in my estimation as a seaman — though I was only a boy at the time.

There were four of us boys in all, of whom I was the second. My next brother Maurice died when he was only seven, and the fourth, Cecil, being five years younger than I, left my brother Algernon and myself as the only real companions for each other. Moreover, an untoward accident, of which I was the unwitting cause, left my younger brother unable to share our play for many years. Having no sisters, and scarcely any boy friends, in the holidays, when all the boys in the school went home, it might be supposed that my elder brother and I were much thrown together. But as a matter of fact such was not the case, for our temperaments being entirely different, and neither of us having any idea of giving way to the other, we seldom or ever found our pleasures together. And yet most of the worst scrapes into which we fell were coöperative affairs. Though I am only anxious to shoulder my share of the responsibility in the escapades, my brother possessed any genius to which the family could lay claim, in that as in every other line. He was my father over again, while I was a second edition of my mother. Father was waiting to get into the sixth form at Rugby when he was only thirteen years old. He was a brilliant scholar at Balliol, but had been compelled to give up study and leave the University temporarily owing to brain trouble. He never published anything, but would reel off brilliant short poems or essays for friends at a moment's notice. I used always to remark that, in whatever company he was, he was always deferred to as an authority in anything approaching classics. He could read and quote Greek and Latin like English, spoke German and French fluently, while he was an excellent geologist, and Fellow of the Geographical Society.

Some of my brother's poems and hymns have been published; his vesper hymns and wedding hymn are widely used. He has also published a Spanish grammar, a Greek lexicon, a book of unconventional prayers for boys, an excellent shortened version of the Psalms for boys' choirs — an infinite advance for boys on the long and wearisome versions I hated so much in my own youth. His 'Red Book of Spelling' and international school spelling competitions, and his copy-books and emphasis for inducing legible handwriting have been real contributions to us today. While at Oxford, my brother ran daily, with some friends, during one 'eights week' a cynical comic paper called 'The Rattle,' to boost some theories he held and which he wished to enforce, and also to 'score' a few of the dons to whom he objected. This would have resulted in his being asked to retire for a season from that seat of learning at the request of his enemies had not our beloved provost routed the special cause of the whole trouble, who was himself contributing to a London society paper, by replying that it was not to be wondered at if the scurrilous rags of London found an echo in Oxford. Moreover, a set of 'The Rattle' was ordered to be bound and placed in the college archives, where it may still be seen.

My father having a great deal of responsibility and worry during the long school terms, as he was not only head master, but owned the school as well, which he had purchased from his great-uncle, used to leave almost the day the holidays began and travel abroad with my mother. This accounts for the very unusual latitude allowed to us boys in coming and going from the house — no one being anxious if now and again we did not return at night. The school matron was left in charge of the vast empty barracks and we had the run of play-field, gymnasium, and everything else we wanted. To outwit the matron was always considered fair play by us boys, and on many occasions we were more than successful.

One time, when we had been acquiring some new lines of thought from some trashy boys' books of the period, we became fired with the desire to enjoy the ruling passion of the professional burglar. Though never kept short of anything, we decided that one night we would raid the large school storeroom while the matron slept. As always, the planning was entrusted to my brother. It was, of course, a perfectly easy affair, but we played the whole game 'according to Cavendish.' We let ourselves out of the window at midnight, glued brown paper to the window-panes, cut out the putty, forced the catch, and stole sugar, currants, biscuits, and I am ashamed to say port wine — which we mulled in a tin can over the renovated fire in the matron's own sanctum. In the morning the remnants were turned over to fishermen friends who were passing alongshore on their way to catch the early tide.

I had no share in two other of my brother's famous escapades, though at the time it was a source of keen regret, for we were sent to different public schools. But we heard with pride how he had extracted phosphorus from the chemical laboratory and, while drawing luminous ghosts on the wall for the benefit of the timorous, had set fire to the large dormitory and the boys' Sunday clothing neatly laid out on the beds, besides burning himself badly. Later he pleaded guilty to beeswaxing the seat of the boys in front of him in chapel, much to the detriment of their trousers and the destruction of the dignity of Sunday worship.

During the time that my parents were away, we never found a moment in which to be lonely, but on one occasion it occurred to us that the company of some friends would add to our enjoyment. Why we waited till my father and mother departed, I do not know, but I recall that immediately they had gone we spent a much-valued sixpence in telegraphing to a cousin in London to come down to us for the holidays. Our message read: 'Dear Sid. Come down and stay the holidays. Father has gone to Aix.' We were somewhat chagrined to receive the following day an answer, also by wire: 'Not gone yet. Father.' It appeared that my father and mother had stayed the night in London in the very house to which we had wired, and Sid, having to ask his father's permission in order to get his railway fare, our uncle had shown the invitation to my father. It was characteristic of my parents that Sid came duly along, but they could not keep from sharing the joke with my uncle.

During term-time some of our grown-up relatives would occasionally visit us. But alas, it was only their idiosyncrasies which used to make any impression upon us. One, a great-uncle, and a very distinguished person, being Professor of Political Economy at Oxford, was a great friend of the famous Dr. Jowett, the chancellor. He was the only man we knew who ever, at any time, stood up long to my father in argument. It was only on rare occasions that we witnessed such a contest, but I shall never forget one which took place in the evening in our drawing-room. My great-uncle was a small man, rather stout and pink, and almost bald-headed. He grew so absorbed in his arguments, which he always delivered walking up and down, that on this occasion, coming to an old-fashioned sofa, he stepped right up onto the seat, climbed over the back, and went straight on with his remarks.

Whether some of our pranks were suggested by those of which we heard, I do not remember. One of my father's yarns, however, always stuck in my memory. For once, being in a very good humour, he told us how when some distinguished old lady had come to call on his father — a house master with Arnold at Rugby — he had been especially warned not to interrupt this important person, who had come to see about her son's entering my grandfather's 'House.' It so happened that quite unconsciously the lady in question had seated herself on an old cane-bottomed armchair in which father had been playing, thus depriving him temporarily of a toy with which he desired to amuse himself. He never, even in later life, was noted for undue patience, and, after endeavouring in vain to await her departure, he somehow secured a long pin. Armed with this he crawled from behind under the seat, and by discreetly probing upwards, succeeded suddenly in dislodging his enemy.

Our devotions on Sunday were carried out in the parish church of the little adjoining village of Neston, there being no place of worship of the Established Church in Parkgate. In term-time we were obliged to go morning and evening to the long services, which never made any concessions to youthful capacities. So in holiday-time, though it was essential that we should go in the morning to represent the House, we were permitted to stay home in the evening. But even the mornings were a time of great weariness, and oft-recurrent sermons on the terrible fate which awaited those who never went to church, and the still more untoward end which was in store for frequenters of dissenting 'meeting-houses,' failed to awaken in us the respect due to the occasion.

Usually on the way to church we had to pass by those who

dared even the awful fate of the latter. It was our idea that
to tantalize us they wore especially gorgeous apparel, while
we had to wear black Etons and a top hat — which, by the
way, greatly annoyed us. One waistcoat especially excited
our animosity, and from it we conceived the title 'speckle-
belly,' by which we ever afterwards designated the whole
'genus nonconformist.' The entrance to the chapel (ours was
the Church!) was through a door in a high wall over which we
could not see; and my youthful brain used to conjure up un-
righteous and strange orgies, which we felt must take place
in those precincts which we were never permitted to enter.
Our Sunday Scripture lessons had familiarized us thoroughly
with the perverse habits of that section of the Chosen People
who *would* serve Baal and Moloch, when it obviously paid
so much better not to do so. But although we counted the
numbers which we saw going in, and sometimes met them
coming out, they seemed never to lessen perceptibly. On this
account our minds, with the merciless logic of childhood,
gradually discounted the threatened calamities.

This must have accounted for the lapse in our own conduct,
and a sort of comfortable satisfaction that the Almighty contented Himself in merely counting noses in the pews. For
even though it was my brother who got into trouble, I shall
never forget the harangue on impiety that awaited us when a
most unchristian sexton reported to our father that the pew
in front of ours had been found chalked on the back, so as to
make its occupants the object of undisguised attention from
the rest of the congregation. As circumstantial evidence also
against us, he offered some telltale squares of silver paper,
on which we had been cooking chocolates on the steam pipes
during the sermon.

At fourteen years of age my brother was sent to Repton,
to the house of an uncle by marriage — an arrangement which
has persuaded me never to send boys to their relatives for
training. My brother's pranks were undoubtedly many, but
they were all boyish and legitimate ones. After a time, however, he was removed at his own request, and sent to Clifton,
where he was head of the school, and the school House also,
under Dr. Percival, the late Bishop of Hereford. From there
he took an open scholarship for Oxford.

It was most wisely decided to send us to separate schools, and therefore at the age of fourteen I found myself at Marlborough — a school of nearly six hundred resident boys, on entering which I had won a scholarship.

CHAPTER II

AT MARLBOROUGH COLLEGE

MARLBOROUGH 'COLLEGE,' as we in England designate a large University preparatory school, is situated in Wiltshire, in a perfectly beautiful country, close to the Savernake Forest — one of the finest in all England. Everything and everybody was strange to me on my arrival. Some Good Samaritan, hearing that I was bound for a certain House, allowed me to follow him from the station to the inn — for a veritable old inn it was. It was one of those lovely old wayside hostels along the main road to the west, which, with the decline of coaching days, found its way into the market and had fallen to the hammer for the education of youth. The building formed the end of a long avenue of trees and was approached through high gates from the main road. It was flanked on the east side, somewhat inharmoniously, by other houses which served as school-rooms, dining-hall, chapel, racquets and fives courts, studies, and other dwelling-houses. The whole was entirely enclosed so that no one could pass in or out, after the gates were shut, without ringing up the porter from his lodge and having one's name taken as being out after hours. At least it was supposed that no one could, though we boys soon found that there were more ways than one leading to Rome.

The separate dwelling-houses were named A, B, and C. I was detailed to C House, the old inn itself. Each House was again divided into three, with its own house master, and its own special colour and badges. Our three were at the time 'Sharps,' 'Upcutts,' and 'Bakers.' Our particular division occupied the second floor, and was reached by great oak staircases, which, if you were smart, you could ascend at about six steps at a time. This was a special desideratum, because, until you reached the fifth form, according to law you ascended by the less direct back stairway.

Our colours were white and maroon, and our sign a bishop's mitre. This effigy I still find scribbled all over the few book relics which I have retained. The emblem, when borne subsequently on my velvet football cap, proved to be the nearest I was ever to approach to that dignified insignia.

My benefactor, on the night of my arrival, having done more for me than a new boy could expect of an old one, was whirled off in the stream of his returning chums long before I had found my resting-place. The dormitory to which I at last found myself assigned contained no less than twenty-five beds, and seemed to me a veritable wilderness. If the coaches which used to stop here could have ascended the stairs, it might have accommodated several. The room most nearly like it which I can recall is the great dining-hall of an old manor, into which the knights in armour rode on horseback to meals, that being far less trouble than removing one's armour. More or less amicably I obtained possession of a bed in a good location, under a big window which looked out over the beautiful gardens below. I cannot remember that I experienced any of those heart-searchings or forebodings which sentiment deplores as the inevitable lot of the unprotected innocent.

One informal battle during the first week with a boy possessed of the sanctity of having come up from the lower school, and therefore being an 'old boy,' achieved for me a greater privilege than the actual decision perhaps entitled one to enjoy, namely, being left alone. I subsequently became known as the 'Beast,' owing to my belligerent nature and the undue copiousness of my hair.

The fact that I was placed in the upper fourth form condemned me to do my 'prep' in the intolerable barrack called 'Big School'—a veritable bear-garden to which about three hundred small boys were relegated to study. Order was kept by a master and a few monitors, who wandered to and fro from end to end of the building, while we were supposed to work. For my part, I never tried it, partly because the work came very easy to me, while the 'repetition' was more readily learned from a loose page at odd times like dinner and chapel, and partly because, winning a scholarship during the term, I was transferred to a building reserved for twenty-eight such privileged individuals until they gained the further distinction of a place in the House classroom, by getting their transfer into the fifth form.

Besides those who lived in the big quad there were several houses outside the gates, known as 'Out-Houses.' The boys there fared a good deal better than we who lived in college, and I presume paid more highly for it. Our meals were served in 'Big Hall,' where the whole four hundred of us were fed. The meals were exceptionally poor; so much so that we boys at the beginning of term formed what we called brewing companies, which provided as far as possible breakfasts and suppers for ourselves all term. As a protection against early bankruptcy, it was our custom to deposit our money with a rotund but popular school official, known always by a corruption of his name as 'the Slug.' Every Saturday night he would dole out to you your deposit made on return from the holidays, divided into equal portions by the number of weeks in the term. Once one was in the fifth form, brewing became easy, for one had a right to a place on the classroom fire for one's kettle or saucepan. Till then, the space over gas stoves in Big School being strictly limited, the right was only acquired *vi et armis*. Moreover, most of the fourth-form boys and the 'Shells,' a class between them and the fifth, if they had to work after evening chapel, had to sit behind desks around the house classroom facing the centre, in which as a rule the fifth-form boys were lazily cooking and devouring their suppers. Certain parts of those repasts, like sausages, we would import ready cooked from the 'Tuck Shop,' and hence they only needed warming up. Breakfast in Big School was no comfort, and personally I seldom attended it. At dinner and tea, however, one had to appear, and remain till the doors were opened again. It was a kind of roll-call; and the penalty for being late was fifty lines to be written out. As my own habits were never as regular as they should have been, whenever I was able to keep ahead I possessed pages of such lines, neatly written out during school hours and ready for emergencies. On other occasions I somewhat shamefacedly recall that I employed other boys, who devoted less time to athletics than was my wont, to help me out — their only remuneration being the 'joy of service'!

The great desire of every boy who could hope to do so was to excel in athletics. This fact has much to commend it in such an educational system, for it undoubtedly kept its devotees from innumerable worse troubles and dangers. All athletics were compulsory, unless one had obtained permanent exemption from the medical officer. If one was not chosen to play on any team during the afternoon, each boy had to go to gymnasium for drill and exercises, or to 'flannel' and run around the Aylesbury Arms, an old public house three quarters of a mile distant. Any breach of this law was severely punished by the boys themselves. It involved a fives batting — that is, a birching carried out with a hardwood fives bat — after chapel in the presence of the House. As a breach of patriotism, it carried great disgrace with it, and was very, very seldom necessary.

No punishments ever touched the boys one tenth part as much as those administered by themselves. On one occasion two of the Big School monitors, who were themselves notorious far more for their constant breaches of school law than for their observance of it, decided to make capital at the expense of the sixth form. One day, just as the dinner-bell rang, they locked the sixth-form door, while a conclave was being held inside. Though everyone was intended to know to whom the credit belonged, it was understood that no one would dream of giving evidence against them. But it so happened that their voices had been recognized from within by one of the sixth-form boys — and bullies and unpopular though the culprits were, they would not deny their guilt. Their condign punishment was to be fives-batted publicly in Big School — in which, however, they regained very considerable popularity by the way they took a spanking without turning a hair, though it cost no less than a dozen bats before it was over.

The publicity of Big School was the only redemption of such a bear-garden, but that was a good feature. It served to make us toe the line. After tea, it was the custom to have what we called 'Upper School Boxing.' A big ring was formed, boxing-gloves provided, and any differences which one might have to settle could be arranged there. There was more energy than science about the few occasions on which I appeared personally in the ring, but it was an excellent safety-valve and quite an evolutionary experience.

The exigency of having to play our games immediately after noon dinner had naturally taught the boys at the head of athletic affairs that it was not wise to eat too much. Dinner was the one solid meal which the college provided, and most of us wanted it badly enough when it came along, especially the suet puddings which went by the name of 'bollies' and were particularly satisfying. But whenever any game of importance was scheduled, a remorseless card used to be passed round the table just after the meat stage, bearing the ominous legend, 'No bolly today.' To make sure that there were no truants, all hands were forced to 'Hooverize.' Oddly enough, beer in large blue china jugs was freely served at every dinner. We called it 'swipes,' and boys, however small, helped themselves to as much as they liked. Moreover, as soon as the game was over, all who had their House colours might come in and get swipes served to them freely through the buttery window. Both practices, I believe, have long since fortunately fallen into desuetude.

To encourage the budding athlete there was an excellent custom of classifying not only the players who attained the first team; but beyond them there were 'the Forty' who wore velvet caps with tassels, 'the Sixty' who wore velvet caps with silver braid, 'the Eighty,' and even 'the Hundred' — all of whom were posted from time to time, and so stimulated their members to try for the next grade.

Like every other school there were bounds beyond which one might not go, and therefore beyond which one always wanted to go. Compulsory games limited the temptation in that direction very considerably; and my own breaches were practically always to get an extra swim. We had an excellent open-air swimming-pool, made out of a branch of the river Kenneth, and were allowed one bathe a day, besides the dip before morning chapel, which only the few took and which did not count as a bathe. The punishment for breaking the rule was severe, involving a week off for a first offence. But one was not easily caught, for even a sixth-former found hundreds of naked boys very much alike in the water and the fact of anyone having transgressed the limit was very hard to detect. Nor were we bound to incriminate ourselves by replying to leading questions.

Late for Gates was a more serious crime, involving detention from beloved games — and many were the expedients

to which we resorted to avoid such an untoward contingency.
I remember well waiting for an hour outside the porter's
view, hoping for some delivery wagon to give me a chance to
get inside. For it was far too light to venture to climb the
lofty railings before prep time. Good fortune ordained, however, that a four-wheel cab should come along in time, containing the parents of a 'hopeful' in the sick-room. It seemed
a desperate venture, for to run the gate was a worse offence
than being late and owning up. But we succeeded by standing
on the off step, unquestioned by the person inside, who guessed
at once what the trouble was, and who proved to be sport
enough to engage the porter while we got clear. Later on a
scapegrace who had more reason to require some by-way than
myself revealed to me a way which involved a long détour
and a climb over the laundry roof. Of this, on another occasion, I was sincerely glad to avail myself. One of the older
boys, I remember, made a much bolder venture. He waited
till dusk, and then boldly walked in through the masters'
garden. As luck would have it, he met our form master, whom
we will call Jones, walking the other way. It so happened he
possessed a voice which he knew was much like that of another
master, so simply sprinting a little, he called out, 'Night,
night, Jones,' and got by without discovery.

Our chapel in those days was not a thing of beauty; but
since then it has been rebuilt (out of our stomachs, the boys
used to say) and is a model work of art. Attendance at chapel
was compulsory, and no 'cuts' were allowed. Moreover,
once late, you were given lines, besides losing your chapel
half-holiday. So the extraordinary zeal exhibited to be
marked off as present should not be attributed to religious
fervour. The chapel was entered from quad by two iron
gates, with the same lofty railings which guarded the entrance
on each side. The bell tolled for five minutes, then was silent
one minute, and then a single toll was given, called 'stroke.'
At that instant the two masters who stood by the pillars
guarding each gate, jumped across, closing the gates if they
could, and everyone outside was late. Those inside the open
walk — the length of the chapel that led to the doors at the
far end — then continued to march in.

During prayers each form master sat opposite his form, all

of which faced the central aisle, and marked off those present. Almost every morning half-dressed boys, with shirts open and collars unbuttoned, boots unlaced, and jumping into coats and waistcoats as they dashed along, could be seen rushing towards the gate during the ominous minute of silence. There was always time to get straight before the mass of boys inside had emptied into chapel; and I never remember a gatemaster stopping a boy before stroke for insufficiency of coverings. Many were the subterfuges employed to get excused, and naturally some form masters were themselves less regular than others, though you never could absolutely count on any particular one being absent. Twice in my time gates were rushed — that is, when stroke went, such crowds of flying boys were just at the gate that the masters were unable to stop the onslaught, and were themselves brushed aside or knocked down under the seething mass of panic-stricken would-be worshippers. On one of these occasions we were forgiven — stroke was ten seconds early; and on the other, a half-holiday was stopped, as one of the masters had been injured. To trip one's self up and get a bloody nose, or possibly a face scratched on the gravel, and then a sick cut from the kindly old school doctor, was one of the more common ways boys discovered of saving their chapel half — when it was a very close call.

The school surgery was presided over in my day by a much-beloved old physician of the old school, called Fergus, which cognomen the boys had so long ago corrupted into Fungi that many a lad was caught mistakenly addressing the old gentleman as Dr. Fungi — an error I always fancied he rather appreciated.

By going to surgery you could very frequently escape evening chapel — a very desirable event if you had a big brew coming off in classroom, for you could get things cooked and have plenty of room on the fire before the others were out. But one always had to pay for the advantage, the old doctor being very much addicted to potions. I never shall forget the horrible tap in the corner, out of which cough mixture flowed as 'a healing for the nations,' but which, nasty as it was, was the lowest price at which one could purchase the cut. Some boys, anxious to cut lessons, found that, by putting a little soap in one's eye, that organ would become red and watery. This art they practised so successfully that sometimes for weeks they would be forbidden to do lessons on account of eye-strain. They had to use lotions, eye-shades and every spectacle possible, but all to no avail. Sometimes they used so much soap that I was sure the doctor would suspect the bubbles.

I had two periods in sick-room with a worrying cough, where the time was always made so pleasant that one was not tempted to hasten recovery. Diagnosis, moreover, was not so accurate in those days as it might have been, and the dear old doctor took no risks. So at the age of sixteen I was sent off for a winter to the South of France, with the diagnosis of congestion of the lungs.

One of my aunts, a Miss Hutchinson, living at Hyères in the South of France, was delighted to receive me. With a widowed friend and two charming and athletic daughters, she had a very pretty villa on the hills overlooking the sea. My orders — to live out-of-doors — were very literally obeyed. In light flannel costumes we roamed the hills after moths and butterflies, early and late. We kept the frogs in miniature ponds in boxes covered with netting, providing them with bamboo ladders to climb, and so tell us when it was going to be wet weather. We had also enclosures in which we kept bands of trapdoor spiders, which used to afford us intense interest with their clever artifices. To these we added the breeding of the more beautiful butterflies and moths, and so, without knowing what we were learning, we were taught many and valuable truths of life. There were horses to ride also, and a beautiful *plage* to bathe upon. It was always sunny and warm, and I invariably look back on that winter as spent in paradise. I was permitted to go over with a young friend to the Carnival at Nice, where, disguised as a clown, and then as a priest, with the abandon of boys, we enjoyed every moment of the time — the world was so big and so wonderful. The French that I had very quickly learned, as we always spoke it at our villa, stood me on this occasion in good stead. Better still, I happened, when climbing into one of the flower-bedecked carriages parading in the *bataille des fleurs* — which, being in costume, was quite the right thing to do — to find that the owner was an old friend of my family, one Sir William Hut. He at once carried me to his home for the rest of the Carnival, and, of course, made it doubly enjoyable.

A beautiful expedition, made later in that region which lives in my memory, was to the gardens at La Mortola, just over the Italian border, made famous by the frequent visits of Queen Victoria to them. They were owned by Sir Thomas Hanbury, whose wife was my aunt's great friend.

The quaintness of the memories which persist longest in one's mind often amuse me. We used, as good Episcopalians, to go every Sunday to the little English Church on the rue des Palmiers. Alas, I can remember only one thing about those services. The clergyman had a peculiar impediment in his speech which made him say his *h*'s and *s*'s, both as *sh*. Thus he always said 'shuman' for 'human,' and invariably prayed that God might be pleased to 'shave the Queen.'

About the middle of the winter I realized that I had made a mistake. In writing home I had so enthusiastically assured my father that the place was suiting my health that he wrote back that he thought in that case I might stand a little tutoring, and forthwith I was despatched every morning to a Mr. B., an Englishman, whose house, called the Hermitage, was in a thick wood. I soon discovered that Mr. B. was obliged to live abroad for his health, and that the coaching of small boys was only a means to that end. He was a good instructor in mathematics, a study which I always loved, but he insisted on my taking Latin and French literature, for neither of which I had the slightest taste. I consequently made no effort whatever to improve my mind, a fact which did not in the least disturb his equanimity. The great interest of those journeys to the Hermitage were the fables of La Fontaine — which I learned as 'repetition' and enjoyed — and the enormous numbers of lizards on the walls, which could disappear with lightning rapidity when seen, though they would stay almost motionless, waiting for a fly to come along, which they then swallowed alive. They were so like the stones one could almost rub one's nose against them without seeing them. Each time I started, I used to cut a little switch for myself and try to switch them off their ledges before they vanished. The attraction to the act lay in that it was almost impossible to accomplish. But if you did, they scored a bull's-eye by incontinently discarding their tails, which made them much harder to catch next time, and seemed in no way to incommode them, though it served to excuse my conscience of cruelty. At the same time I have no wish to pose as a protector of flies.

Returning to Marlborough School the following summer, I found that my father, who knew perfectly the thorough groundwork I had received in Greek and Latin, had insisted on my being given a remove into the lower fifth form *in absentia*. Both he and I were aware that I could do the work easily; but the form master resented it and had already protested in vain. I believe he was a very good man in his way, and much liked by those whom he liked. But alas, I was not one of them; and never once, during the whole time I was in his form, did I get one single word of encouragement out of him. My mathematical master, and 'stinks,' or chemical master, I was very fond of, and in both those departments I made good progress.

The task of keeping order in a chemistry class of boys is never easy. The necessary experiments divert the master's eye from the class and always give opportunity for fooling. Added to this was the fact that our stinks master, like many scientific teachers, was far too good-natured, and himself half-enjoyed the diversion which his experiments gave. When obliged to punish a boy caught *flagrante delicto*, he invariably looked out for some way to make it up to him later. Thus, on one occasion, in most righteous anger, just as if a parenthesis to the remark he was making, he interposed, 'Come and be caned, boy. My study, twelve o'clock.' When the boy was leaving, very unrepentant after keeping the appointment, in the same parenthetical way the master remarked, 'Go away, boy. Cake and wine, my room, five o'clock' — which proved eventually the most effective part of the correction.

To children there always appears a gap between them and grown-ups as impassable as that which Abraham is made to describe as so great 'that they who would pass to and fro cannot.' As we grow older, we cease to see it, but it exists all the same. Sometimes grown-ups are apt to grudge the time and trouble put into apparently transient pleasures. A trivial strawberry feast, given to children on our dear old lawn under the jasmine and rose-bushes, still looms as a happy memory of my parents' love for children, punctuated by the fact that though by continuing a game in spite of warning I broke a window early in the afternoon and was banished to the nursery as advised, my father forgave me an hour later, and himself fetched me down again to the party.

To teach us independence, my father put us on an allowance at a very early age, with a small bank account, to which every birthday he added five pounds on our behalf. We had no pony at that time, indeed had not yet learned to ride, so our deposits always went by the name of 'pony money.' This was an excellent plan, for we did not yet value money for itself, and were better able to appreciate the joy of giving because it seemed to postpone the advent of our pony. However, when we were thought to have learned to value so sentient a companion and to be likely to treat him properly, a Good Samaritan was permitted to present us with one ever afterwards to be counted one of our most cherished friends. To us, she was an unparalleled beauty. How many times we fell over her head, and over her tail, no one can record. She always waited for you to remount, so it did not much matter; and we were taught that great lesson in life, not to be afraid of falling, but to learn how to take a fall. My own bent, however, was never for the things of the land, and though gallops on the Dee Sands, and races with our cousins, who owned a broncho and generally beat us, had their fascination, boats were the things which appealed most to me.

Having funds at our disposal, we were allowed to purchase material and, under the supervision of a local carpenter, to build a boat ourselves. To this purpose our old back nursery was forthwith allocated. The craft which we desired was a canoe that would enable us to paddle or drift along the deep channels of the river and allow us to steal upon the flocks of birds feeding at the edges. Often in memory I enjoy those days again — the planning, the modelling, the fitting, the setting-up, and at last, the visit of inspection of our parents. Alas, stiff-necked in our generation, we had insisted on straight lines and a square stern. Never shall I forget the indignation aroused in me by a cousin's remark, 'It looks awfully like a coffin.' The resemblance had not previously struck either of us, and father had felt that the joke was too dangerous a one to make and had said nothing. But the pathos of it was that we now saw it all too clearly. My brother explained that the barque was intended to be not 'seen.' Ugliness was almost desirable. It might help us if we called it the Reptile, and painted it red — all of which suggestions were followed. But still I remember feeling a little crestfallen, when, after launching it through the window, it lay offensively resplendent against the vivid green of the grass. It served, however, for a time, ending its days honourably by capsizing a friend and me, guns and all, into the half-frozen water of the lower estuary while we were stalking some curlew. I had to run home dripping. My friend's gun, moreover, having been surreptitiously borrowed from my cousin's father, was recovered the following day, to our unutterable relief. Out of the balance of the money spent on the boat, we purchased a pin-fire, breech-loading gun, the pride of my life for many days. I was being kept back from school at the time on account of a cold, but I was not surprised to find myself next day sitting in a train, bound for Marlborough, and 'referred once more to my studies.'

A little later, my father, not being satisfied, took me away to read with a tutor for the London matriculation, in which I received a first class.

A large boarding-school in England is like a miniature world. One makes many acquaintances, who change as one gets pushed into new classes, so at that state one makes few lasting friends. Those who remain till they attain the sixth form and make the school teams probably form more permanent friendships. I at least think of that period as one when one's bristles were generally up, and, though many happy memories linger and I have found that to be an old Marlburian is a bond of friendship all the world over, it is the little oddities which one remembers best. I have the greatest love for the old school.

A new scholarship boy had one day been assigned to the closed corporation of our particular classroom. To me he had many attractions, for he was a genius both in mathematics and chemistry. We used to love talking over the problems that were set us as voluntary tasks for our spare time; and our united excursions in those directions were so successful that we earned our class more than one 'hour off' as rewards for the required number of stars given for pieces of work. My friend had, however, no use whatever for athletics. He had never been from home before, had no brothers and five sisters, was the pet of his parents, and naturally somewhat of a square plug in a round hole in our school life. He hated all conventions, and was always in trouble with the boys, for he entirely neglected his personal appearance, while his fingers were always discoloured with chemicals, and he would not even feign an interest in the things for which they cared. I can remember him sitting on the foot of my bed, talking me to sleep more than once with some new plan he had devised for a self-steering torpedo or an absolutely reliable flying machine. He had received the sobriquet of 'Mad G.,' and there was some justice in it from the opposition point of view. I had not realized, however, that he was being bullied — on such a subject he would never say a syllable — till one day as he left classroom I saw a large lump of coal hit him square on the head and a rush of blood follow it that made me hustle him off to surgery. Scalp wounds are not so dangerous as they are bloody to heads as thick as ours. His explanation that he had fallen down was too obvious a distortion of truth to deceive even our kindly old doctor. But he asked no further question, seeing that it was a point of honour. The matter, however, forced an estrangement between myself and some of my fellows that I realized afterwards was excellent for me. Forthwith we moved my friend's desk into my corner of the room which was always safe when I was around, though later some practices of the others to which I took exception led to a combination which I thought of then as that made by the Jews to catch Paul, and which I foiled in a similar way, watchfully eluding them when they were in numbers together, but always ready to meet one or two at a time. The fact that I had just taken up racquets impressed it on my memory, for considering the classroom temporarily unsafe for prep work, I used that building as a convenient refuge for necessary study. It would have been far better to have fought it out and taken, if unavoidable, whatever came to me — had it been anywhere else I should probably have done so. But the classroom was a close corporation for Foundation scholars, and not one of my chums had access to it to see fair play.

My friendship for Mad G. was largely tempered by my own love for anything athletic, and eccentricities paid a very heavy price among all boys. Thus, though I was glad to lend my protection to my friend, we never went about together — as such boys as he always lived the life of hermits in the midst of the crowd. I well remember one other boy, made eccentric by his peculiar face and an unfortunate impediment of speech. No such boy should have been sent to an English public school as it was in my day. His stutter was no ordinary one, for it consisted, not in repeating the first letter or syllable, but in blowing out both cheeks like a balloon and making noises which resembled a back-firing motor engine. It was the custom of our form master to make us say our repetition by each boy taking one line, the last round being always expressed — that is, unless you started instantly the boy above you finished, the next boy began and took your place. I can still see and hear the unfortunate J. getting up steam for his line four or five boys ahead of time, so that he might explode at the right moment; which desirable end, however, he but very rarely accomplished, and never catching up, he used, like the man in the parable, always to 'begin with shame to take the lowest place.' Sometimes the master in a merciful mood allowed us to write a line, but that was risky, for it was considered no disgrace to circumvent him, and under those circumstances it was easy for the next boy to write his own and then yours, and pass it along if he saw you were in trouble.

There was, and I think with some reason, a pride among the boys on their appearance on certain occasions. It went by the name of good form. Thus, on Sundays at morning chapel, we always wore a button-hole flower if we could. My dear mother used to post me along a little box of flowers every week — nor was it by any means wasted energy, for not only did the love for flowers become a hobby and a custom with many of us through life, and a help to steer clear of sloppiness in appearance, but it was a habit quite likely to spread to the soul. Beyond that, the picture of my mother, with the thousand worries of a large school of small boys on her hands, finding time to gather, pack, address, and post each week with her own hands so fleeting and inessential a token of her love, has a thousand times arisen to my memory, and led me to consider some apparently quite unnecessary little labour of love as being well worth the time and trouble. It is these deeds of love — not words, however touching — that never fade from the soul.

Form is a part of the life of all English schools, and the boys think much more of it than sin. At Harrow you may not walk in the middle of the road as a freshman; and in American schools and universities, such regulations as the 'fence' laws at Yale show that they have emulated and even surpassed us in these. It was, however, a very potent influence, and we were ridiculously sensitive about breaches of it. Thus, on a certain prize day my friend Mad G., having singularly distinguished himself in his studies, his parents came all the way from their home, at great expense to themselves, to see their beloved and only son honoured. I presume that, though wild horses would not drag anything out of the boy at school, he had communicated to them the details of some little service rendered. For to my horror I was stopped by his mother, whom I subsequently learned to love and honour above most people, and actually kissed while walking in the open quad — strutting like a peacock, I suppose, for I remember feeling as if the bottom had suddenly fallen out of the earth. The sequel, however, was an invitation to visit their home in North Wales for the Christmas holidays, where there was rough shooting — the only kind I really cared for — boating, rock-climbing, bathing, and the companionship of as lovely a family as it was possible to meet anywhere. Many a holiday afterwards we shared together, and the kindness showered upon me I shall never be able to forget, or, alas, return; for my dear friend Mad G. has long ago gone to his rest, and so have both his parents, whom I loved almost as my own.

We were taught that the only excuse that made the taking of animal life honourable was for some useful purpose, like food or study or self-preservation. Several cases of birds stuffed and set up when we were fourteen and sixteen years of age still adorn the old house. Every bit had to be done by ourselves, my brother making the cases and I the rock work and taxidermy. The hammering-up of sandstone and granite, to cover the glue-soaked brown paper that we moulded into rocks, satisfied my keenest instinct for making messes, and only the patience of old-time domestics would have 'stood for it.' My brother specialized in birds' eggs, and I in butterflies and moths. Later we added seaweeds, shells, and flowers. Some of our collections have been dissipated; and, though we have not a really scientific acquaintance with either of these kingdoms, we acquired a hail-fellow-well-met familiarity with all of them, which has enlivened many a day in many parts of the world as we have journeyed through life. Moreover, though purchased pictures have other values, the old cases set on the walls of one's den bring back memories that are the joy and solace of many lonely moments later in life — each rarer egg, each extra butterfly picturing some day or place of keen triumph, otherwise long since forgotten. Here, for instance, is a convolvulus hawk father found killed on a mountain in Switzerland; there an Apollo I caught in the Pyrenees; here a red burnet with a five eyes captured as we raced through the bracken on Clifton Downs, and there are purple emperors lured down to meat baits in the Surrey Woods.

Many a Sunday at school have I stolen into the great forest, my butterfly net under my coat, to try and add a new specimen to my hoard. We were always supplied with good key-books, so that we should be able to identify our specimens, and also to search for others more intelligently. One value of my own specialty was that for the moths it demanded going out in the night, and the thrills of out-of-doors in the beautiful summer evenings, when others were fugging in the house or had gone to bed, used actually to make me dance around on the grass. The dark lantern, the sugaring of the tree-stems with intoxicating potions, and the subsequent excitement of searching for specimens, fascinated me utterly.

CHAPTER III

WHITECHAPEL AND WALES

IN 1883, my father became anxious to give up teaching and to confine himself more exclusively to the work of a clergyman. With this in view he contemplated moving to London where he had been offered the chaplaincy of the huge London Hospital. I remember his talking it over with me, and then asking if I had any idea what I wanted to do in life. It had never occurred to me to look forward to a profession; except that I knew that the heads of tigers, deer, and all sorts of trophies of the chase which adorned our house came from soldier uncles and others who hunted them in India, and I had always thought that their occupation would suit my taste admirably. It never dawned on me that I would have to earn my bread and butter. I had never seen real poverty in others, for all the fisherfolk in our village seemed to have enough. I hated dress and frills, and envied no one. At school, and on the Riviera, and even in Wales, I had never noticed any want. It is true that a number of dear old ladies from the village came in the winter months to our house once or twice a week to get soup. They used to sit in the back hall, each with a round tin can with a bucket handle. These were filled with hot broth, and the old ladies were given a repast as well before leaving. As a matter of fact, I very seldom actually saw them, for that part of the house was entirely cut off by large double green-baize covered doors. But I often knew that they must have been there, because our Skye terrier, though fed to overflowing, usually attended these séances, and doubtless, while the old ladies were occupied with lunch, sampled the cans of soup which stood in rows along the floor. He used to come along with dripping whiskers which betrayed his excursion, and the look of a connoisseur in his large round eyes — as if he were certifying that justice had been done once more in the kitchen.

While I was in France the mother of my best chum in school had been passing through Marseilles on her way home from India, and had most kindly taken me on a jolly trip to Arles,

Avignon, and other historical places. She was the wife of a famous missionary in India. She spoke eight languages fluently, including Arabic, and was a perfect *vade mecum* of interesting information.

About the time of my father's question, my friend's mother was staying in Chester with her brother-in-law, the Lord Lieutenant of Denbighshire. It was decided that, as she was a citizeness of the world, no one could suggest better for what profession my peculiar talents fitted me. The interview I have long ago forgotten, but I recall coming home with a confused idea that tiger-hunting would not support me, and that she thought I ought to become a clergyman, though it had no attraction for me, and I decided against it.

None of our family on either side, as far as I can find out, had ever practised medicine. My own experience of doctors had been rather a chequered one, but at my father's suggestion I gladly went up and discussed the matter with our country family doctor. He was a fine man, and we boys were very fond of him and his family, his daughter being our best girl friend. He had an enormous practice, in which he was eminently successful. The number of horses he kept, and the miles he covered with them, were phenomenal to my mind. He had always a kind word for everyone, and never gave us boys away, though he must have known many of our pranks played in our parents' absence. The only remaining memory of that visit was that the old doctor brought down from one of his shelves a large jar, out of which he produced a pickled human brain. I was thrilled with entirely new emotions. I had never thought of man's body as a machine. That this weird, white, puckered-up mass could be the transmitter of all that made man, that it controlled our physical strength and growth and our responses to life, that it made one into Mad G. and another into me — why, it was absolutely marvellous. It attracted me as has the gramophone, the camera, the automobile, and the airplane.

My father saw at once on my return that I had found my real interest, and put before me two alternative plans, one to go to Oxford, where my brother had just entered, or to join him in London and take up work in the London Hospital and University, preparatory to going in for medicine. I chose the

latter at once — a decision I have never regretted. I ought to
say that business as a career was not suggested. In England,
especially in those days, these things were more or less hereditary. My forbears were all fighters or educators, except for an
occasional statesman or banker. Probably there is some
advantage in this plan.

Most of the subjects for the London matriculation were
quite new to me, especially English, but with the fresh incentive and new vision of responsibility I set to work with a will,
and soon had mastered the required subjects sufficiently to
pass the examination with credit. But I must say here that
Professor Huxley's criticisms of English public school teaching
of that period were none too stringent. I wish with all my
heart that others had spoken out as bravely, for in those days
that wonderful man was held up to our scorn as an atheist and
iconoclast. We spent years of life and heaps of money on our
education, and came out knowing nothing of the special
subjects which fit us for everyday life, except that which we
picked up incidentally.

When I followed my father to London, I was not familiar
with one word of botany, zoölogy, physics, physiology, or
comparative anatomy, or any natural science whatever.
About the universe which I inhabited I knew as little as I did
about cuneiform writings. Except for my mathematics and
a mere modicum of chemistry, I had nothing on which to base
my new work. Students coming from Government free
schools, or almost anywhere, had a great advantage over men
of my previous education; I did not even know how to study
wisely. Again, as Huxley showed, medical education in London was so divided, there being no teaching university, that
the curriculum was ridiculously inadequate. There were still
being foisted upon the world far too many medical men of the
type of Bob Sawyer.

Our hospital was the largest in the British Isles, and in the
midst of the poorest population in England, being located in
the famous Whitechapel Road, and surrounded by all the
purlieus of the East End of the great city. Patients came
from Tilbury Docks to Billingsgate Market, and all the river
haunts between, from Shadwell, Deptford, Wapping, Poplar,
from Petticoat Lane and Radcliffe Highway, made famous by

crime and by Charles Dickens. They came from Bethnal Green, where queens and their courts once dwelt, but now the squalid and crowded home of poverty; from Stratford and Bow, and a hundred other slums.

The hospital had some nine hundred beds, which were always so full that the last surgeon admitting to his wards constantly found himself with extra beds poked in between the regulation number through sheer necessity. It afforded an unrivalled field for clinical experience and practical teaching.

Looking back, I am grateful to my *alma mater*, and have that real affection for her that every loyal son should have. But even that does not conceal from me how poor a teaching establishment it was. Those who had natural genius, and the advantages of previous scientific training, who were sons of medical men or had served apprenticeships to them, possibly did not suffer so much through its inefficiency. But men in my position suffered quite unconsciously a terrible handicap, and it was only the influences for which I had nothing whatever to thank the hospital that saved me from the catastrophes which overtook so many who started with me.

To begin with, there was no supervision of our lives whatever. We were flung into a coarse and evil environment, among men who too often took pride in their shame, just to sink or swim. Not one soul cared which you did. I can still remember numerous cases where it simply meant that men paid quite large sums for the privilege of sending the sons they loved direct to the devil. I recall one lad whom I had known at school. His father lavished money upon him, and sincerely believed that his son was doing him credit and would soon return to share his large practice and bring to it all the many new advances he had learned. The reports of examinations successfully passed he fully accepted; and the non-return of his son at vacation times he put down to professional zeal. It was not till the time came for the boy to get his degree and return that the father discovered that he had lived exactly the life of the prodigal in the parable, and had neither attended college nor attempted a single examination of any kind whatever. It broke the father's heart and he died.

Examinations for degrees were held by the London University or the Royal College of Physicians and Surgeons, never by the hospital Schools. The former were practically race committees; they did no teaching, but when you had done certain things, they allowed you to come up and be examined, and if you got through a written and *viva voce* examination, you were inflicted on an unsuspecting public licensed to kill — often only too literally so.

It is obvious on the face of it that this could be no proper criterion for so important a decision as to qualifications; special crammers studied the examiners, their questions, and their teachings, and luck had a great deal to do with success. While some men never did themselves justice in examinations, others were exactly the reverse. Thus I can remember one resident accoucheur being 'ploughed,' as we called it, in his special subject, obstetrics — and men to whom you would not trust your cat getting through with flying colours.

First you had to be signed up for attending courses of lectures on certain subjects. This was simply a matter of tipping the beadle, who marked you off. I personally attended only two botany lectures during the whole course. At the first some practical joker had spilled a solution of carbon bisulphide all over the professor's platform, and the smell was so intolerable that the lecture was prorogued. At the second, some wag let loose a couple of pigeons, whereupon everyone started either to capture them or stir them up with pea-shooters. The professor said, 'Gentlemen, if you do not wish to learn, you are at liberty to leave.' The entire class walked out. The insignificant sum of two and sixpence secured me my sign-up for the remainder of the course.

Materia medica was almost identical; and while we had better fortune with physiology, no experiments and no apparatus for verifying its teachings were ever shown us.

Our chemistry professor was a very clever man, but extremely eccentric, and his class was pandemonium. I have seen him so frequently pelted with peas when his head was turned as to force him to leave the amphitheatre in despair.

There was practically no histology taught and little or no pathology. Almost every bit of the microscope which I did was learned on my own instrument at home. Anatomy, however, we were well taught in the dissecting-room, where we could easily obtain all the work we needed. But not till Sir

Frederick Treves became our lecturer in anatomy and surgery was it worth while doing more than pay the necessary sum to get signed up.

On the other hand, we had to attend in the dispensary, actually to handle drugs and learn about them — an admirable rule. Personally I went once, fooled around making eggnogg, and arranged with a considerate druggist to do the rest that was necessary. Yet I satisfied the examiners at the College of Physicians and Surgeons and those of the London University at the preliminary examination for Bachelor of Medicine — the only ones which they gave which carried questions in any of these subjects.

In the athletic life of the University, however, I took great interest, and was secretary in succession of the cricket, football, and rowing clubs. I helped remove the latter from the old river Lea to the Thames, to raise the inter-hospital rowing championship and start the united hospitals' rowing club. I found time to row in the inter-hospital race for two years and to play on the football team in the two years of which we won the inter-hospital football cup. A few times I played with the united hospitals' team; but I found that their ways were not mine, as I had been taught to despise alcohol as a beverage and to respect all kinds of womanhood. For three years I played regularly for Richmond — the best of the London clubs at the time — and subsequently for Oxford, being put on the team the only term I was in residence. I also threw the hammer for the hospital in the united hospitals' sports, winning second place for two years. Indeed, athletics in some form occupied every moment of my spare time.

It was in my second year, 1885, that, returning from an outpatient case one night, I turned into a large tent erected in a purlieu of Shadwell, the district to which I happened to have been called. It proved to be an evangelistic meeting of the then famous Moody and Sankey. It was so new to me that, when a tedious prayer-bore began with a long oration, I started to leave. Suddenly the leader, who I learned afterwards was D. L. Moody, called out to the audience, 'Let us sing a hymn while our brother finishes his prayer.' His practicality interested me, and I stayed the service out. When I left, it was with a determination either to make religion a real

effort to do as I thought Christ would do in my place as a
doctor, or frankly abandon it. That could only have one issue
while I still lived with a mother like mine. For she had always
been my ideal of unselfish love. Later, I went down to hear
the brothers J. E. and C. T. Studd speak at some subsidiary
meeting of the Moody campaign. They were natural athletes,
and I felt that I could listen to them. I could not have listened
to a sensuous-looking man, a man who was not a master of his
own body, any more than I could to the precentor, who, coming to sing the prayers at college chapel dedication, I saw get
drunk on sherry which he abstracted from the banquet table
just before the service. Never shall I forget, at the meeting of
the Studd brothers, the audience being asked to stand up if
they intended to try and follow Christ. It appeared a very
sensible question to me, but I was amazed how hard I found it
to stand up. At last one boy, out of a hundred or more in
sailor rig, from an industrial or reformatory ship on the
Thames, suddenly rose. It seemed to me such a wonderfully
courageous act — for I knew perfectly what it would mean to
him — that I immediately found myself on my feet, and went
out feeling that I had crossed the Rubicon, and must do
something to prove it.

We were Church of England people, and I always attended
service with my mother at an Episcopal church of the evangel-
ical type. At her suggestion I asked the clergyman if I could
in any way help. He offered me a class of small boys in his
Sunday School, which I accepted with much hesitation. The
boys, derived from houses in the neighbourhood, were as smart
as any I have known. With every faculty sharpened by the
competition of the street, they so tried my patience with their
pranks that I often wondered what strange attraction induced
them to come at all. The school and church were the property
of a society known by the uninviting title of the 'Episcopal
Society for the Promotion of Christianity Among the Jews.'
It owned a large court, shut off from the road by high gates,
around which stood about a dozen houses — with the church
facing the gates at one end of a pretty avenue of trees. It was
an oasis in the desert of that dismal region.

One instance of a baptism I have never forgotten. I was
then living in the court, having hired a separate house under

the trees after my father had died and my mother had moved to Hampstead. In such a district the house was a Godsend. One Sunday I was strolling in the court when the clergyman came rushing out of the church and called to me in great excitement, 'The Church is full of Jews. They are going to carry off Abraham. Can't you go in and help while I fetch the police?' My friend and I, therefore, rushed in as directed to a narrow alleyway between high box pews which led into the vestry, into which 'Abraham' had been spirited. The door being shut and our backs put to it, it was a very easy matter to hold back the crowd, who probably supposed at first that we were leading the abduction party. There being only room for two to come on at once, 'those behind cried forward, and those in front back,' till after very little blood spilt, we heard the police in the church whereupon the crowd at once took to flight. I regret to say that we expedited the rear-guard by football, rather than strictly Christian, methods. His friends then charged Abraham with theft, expecting to get him out of his place of refuge and then trap him, as we were told they had a previous convert. We therefore accompanied him personally through the mean streets, both to and fro, spoiling for more fun. But they displayed more discretion than valour, and to the best of my belief he escaped their machinations.

My Sunday-School efforts did not satisfy me. The boys were few, and I failed to see any progress. I joined a young Australian of my class in hospital in holding services on Sunday nights in half a dozen of the underground lodging-houses along the Radcliffe Highway. He was a good musician, so he purchased a fine little portable harmonium, and whatever else the lodgers thought of us, they always liked the music. We used to meet for evening tea at a place in the famous Highway known as The Stranger's Rest, outside of which an open-air service was always held for the sailors wandering up and down the docks. At these a few ladies would sing; and after the meetings a certain number of the sailors were asked to come in and have refreshments. There were always some who had spent their money on drink, or been robbed, or were out of ships, and many of them were very fine men.

A single story will illustrate the good points which some of these men displayed. My hospital chief, Sir Frederick Treves, had operated on a big Norwegian, and the man had left the hospital cured. As a rule such patients do not even know the name of their surgeon. Some three weeks later, however, this man called at Sir Frederick Treves's house late one dark night. Having asked if he were the surgeon who had operated on him and getting a reply in the affirmative, he said he had come to return thanks, that since he left hospital he had been wandering about without a penny to his name, waiting for a ship, but had secured a place on that day. He proceeded to cut out from the upper edge of his trousers a gold Norwegian five-kronen piece which his wife had sewed in there to be his standby in case of absolute need. He had been so hungry that he had been tempted to use it, but now had come to present it as a token of gratitude — upon which he bowed and disappeared.

The underground lodging-house work did me lots of good. It brought me into touch with real poverty — a very graveyard of life I had never surmised. The denizens of those miserable haunts were men from almost every rank of life. They were shipwrecks from the ocean of humanity, drifted up on the last beach. There were large open fireplaces in the dens, over which those who had any food cooked it. Often, while the other doctor or I was holding services, the other would have to sit down on some drunken man to keep him from making the proceedings impossible; but there were always some who gathered around and really enjoyed the singing.

There was always a narrow passage from the front door to the staircase which led down into those huge underground basements. The guardians had a room inside the door, with a ticket window, where they took tuppence or possibly fourpence from the boarders for their night's lodging. At about eleven o'clock a 'chucker-out' would go down and clear out all the 'gentlemen' who had not paid in advance for the night. This was always a very melancholy period of the evening, and in spite of our hardened hearts, we always had a score against us there. That, however, had to be given in person, for there were plenty among our audiences who had taken special courses in imitative calligraphy. I.O.U.'s on odd bits of paper were a menace to our banking accounts till we sorrowfully abandoned that convenient way of helping often a really deserving case.

In those houses, somewhat to my astonishment, we never once received any physical opposition. Some considered us harmless and gullible imbeciles; but the great majority were still able to see that it was an attempt, however poor, to help them. Drink, of course, was the chief cause of the downfall of most; but, as I have already said, there were cases of genuine, undeserved poverty — like our sailor friend, overtaken with sickness in a foreign port.

One poor creature, in the last stage of poverty and dirt, proved to be an honours man in Oxford. We looked up his record at the University. He assured us that he intended to begin again a new life, and we agreed to help. We took him to a respectable, temperance lodging-house, paid for a bed, a bath, and a supper, and purchased a good second-hand outfit of clothing for him. We were wise enough only to give this to him after we had taken away his own while he was having a bath in the tub. We did not give him a penny of money, fearing his lack of control. Next morning, however, when we went for him, he was gone — no one knew where. We had the neighbouring saloons searched, and soon got track of him. Some 'friend' in the temperance house had given him sixpence. A barman offered him whiskey, his hands trembled so that he could not lift the glass to his mouth, and the barman kindly poured it down his throat. We never saw him again.

My growing experience had shown me that there was a better way to the hearts of my Sunday-School boys than merely talking to them. Like myself, they worshipped the athlete, whether he were a prize-fighter or a big football player. There were no Y.M.C.A.'s or other places for them to get any physical culture, so we arranged to clear our dining-room every Saturday evening, and give boxing lessons and clubs and parallel-bar work — the ceiling was too low for the horizontal. The transformation of the room was easily accomplished. The furniture was very primitive, largely our own construction, and we could throw out through the window every scrap of it except the table, which was soon adapted. We also put up a quoit pitch in our garden.

This is no place to discuss the spiritual influences of 'the noble art of boxing.' Personally I have always believed in its value; and my Sunday-School class soon learned the graces of fair play, how to take defeat and to be generous in victory. They began at once bringing pals whom my exegesis of Scripture would never have lured within my reach. We ourselves began to look forward to Saturday night and Sunday afternoon with an entirely new joy. We all learned to respect and so to love one another more — indeed, lifelong friendships were developed and that irrespective of our hereditary affiliations. The well-meaning clergyman, however, could not see the situation in that light, and declining all invitations to come and sample an evening's fun instead of condemning it unheard, or I should say unseen, he delivered an ultimatum which I accepted — and resigned from his school.

My Australian friend was at that time wrestling with a real ragged school on the Highway on Sunday afternoons. The poor children there were street waifs and as wild as untamed animals. So, being temporarily out of a Sunday job, I consented to join him.

Our schoolroom this time owed no allegiance to any one but ourselves. If the boys were allowed in a minute before there was a force to cope with them, the room would be wrecked. Everything movable was stolen instantly opportunity arose. Boys turned out or locked out during session would climb to the windows and triumphantly wave stolen articles. On one occasion, when I had chucked out a specially obstreperous youth, I was met with a shower of mud and stones as I passed through a narrow alley on my return home. The police were always at war with the boys, who annoyed them in similar and many other ways. I remember two scholars whose eyes were blacked and badly beaten by a 'cop' who happened to catch them in our doorway, as they declared, 'only waiting for Sunday School to open.'

With the night work at the lodging-houses, we used to combine a very aggressive total abstinence campaign. The saloon-keepers as a rule looked upon us as harmless cranks, and I have no doubt were grateful for the leaflets we used to distribute to their customers. These served admirably for kindling purposes. At times, however, they got ugly, and once my friend, who was in a saloon talking to a customer, was trapped and whiskey poured into his mouth. On another occasion I noticed that the outer doors were shut and a couple of men backed up against them while I was talking to the bartender over the counter, and that a few other customers were closing in to repeat the same experiment on me. However, they greatly overrated their stock of fitness and equally underrated my good training, for the scrimmage went all my way in a very short time.

If I told my football chums (for in those days I was playing hard) of these adventures in a nether world, they invariably wanted to come and coöperate; but I have always felt that reliance on physical strength alone is only like war — an insurance of failure. Only unselfish love can win in the end. At this time also at Saint Andrew's Church, just across the Whitechapel Road from the hospital, the clergyman was a fine athlete and good boxer. He was a brother of Lord Wenlock and was one night returning from a service in the Highway when he was set upon by footpads and robbed of everything, including the boots off his feet. Meanwhile, Jack the Ripper was also giving our residential section a most unsavoury reputation.

My long vacations at this time were taken on the sea. My brother and I used to hire an old fishing smack called the Oyster which we rechristened the Roysterer. This we fitted out, provisioned, and in her put to sea with an entirely untrained crew, and without even the convention of caring where we were bound so long as the winds bore us cheerily along. My brother was generally cook — and never was there a better. We believe still that he would have made a mark in the world as a chef, from his ability to satisfy our appetites and cater to our desires out of so ill-supplied a galley. We always took our departure from Anglesea. We carried our fishing gear with us, and thus never wanted for fresh food. We could replenish our bread, milk, butter, and egg supply at the numerous small ports at which we called. The first year the crew consisted of my brother and me — skipper, mate, and cook between us — and an Oxford boating friend as second mate. For a deckhand we had a young East London parson, whom we always knew as 'the Puffin' because he so closely resembled that particular bird when he had his vestments on. We sailed first for Ireland, but the wind coming ahead we ran instead for the Isle of Man. The first night at sea the very tall undergraduate as second mate took the 12 P.M. to 4 A.M. night watch. The tiller handle was low, and when I gave him his course at midnight before turning in myself, he asked me if it would be a breach of nautical etiquette to sit down to steer, as that was the only alternative to directing the ship's course with his ankles. No land was in sight and the wind had died out when I came on deck for my 4 A.M. to 8 A.M. watch. I found the second mate sitting up rubbing his eyes as I emerged from the companion hatch.

'Well, where are we now? How is her head? What's my course?'

'Don't worry about such commonplace details,' he replied. 'I have made an original discovery about these parts that I have never seen mentioned before.'

'What's that?' I asked innocently.

'Well,' he replied, 'when I sat down to steer, the course you gave brought a bright star right over the topmast head and that's what I started to steer by. It's a perfect marvel what a game these heavenly bodies play. I just shut my eyes for a second and when next I opened them the sun was exactly where I had left that star' — and he fled for shelter.

It is a wonder that we ever got anywhere, for we had not so much as a chronometer watch, and in spite of a decrepit sextant even our latitude was often an uncertain quantity. However, we made the port of Douglas, whence we visited quite a part of the historic island. As our parson was called home from there, we wired for and secured another chum to share our labours. Our generally unconventional attire in fashionable summer resorts was at times quite embarrassing. Barelegged, bareheaded, and 'tanned to a chip,' I was carrying my friend's bag along the fashionable pier to see him off on his homeward journey, when a lady stopped me and asked me if I were an Eskimo, offering me a job if I needed one. I suppose the job was in a sideshow.

We spent that holiday cruising around the island. It included running ashore off the north point of land and nearly losing the craft; and also in Ramsey Harbour a fracas with the harbour authorities. We had run in that night on top of the full spring tide. Not knowing the harbour, we had tied up to the first bollard and gone incontinently to sleep. We were awakened by the sound of water thundering on top of us, and rushing up found to our dismay that we were lying in the mud, and a large sewer was discharging right on to our decks. Before we had time to get away or clean up, the harbour master, coming alongside, called on us to pay harbour dues! We stoutly protested that as a pleasure yacht we were not liable and intended to resist to the death any such insult. He was really able to see at once that we were just young fellows out for a holiday, but he had the last word before a crowd of sight-seers who had gathered on the quay above us.

'Pleasure yacht, pleasure yacht, indeed!' he shouted as he rode away. 'I can prove to any man with half an eye that you are nothing but one of them old coal or mud barges.'

The following year the wind suited better the other way. We were practically all young doctors this time, the cook being a very athletic chum in whose rooms were collected as trophies, in almost every branch of athletics, over seventy of what we called silver 'pots.' As a cook he proved a failure except in zeal. It didn't really interest him, especially when the weather was lively. On one occasion I reported to the galley, though I was the skipper that year, in search of the rice-pudding for dinner — Dennis, our cook, being temporarily indisposed. Such a sight as met my view! Had I been superstitious I should have fled. A great black column the circumference of the boiler had risen not less than a foot above the top rim, and was wearing the iron cover jauntily on one side as a helmet. It proved to be rice. He had filled the saucepan with dry rice, crowded in a little water, forced the lid on very tight, and left it to its own devices!

We visited Carnarvon, Harlech, and other castles, lost our boat in a breeze of wind off Dynllyn, climbed Snowdon from Pwllheli Harbour, and visited a dozen little out-of-the-world harbours that one would otherwise never see. Fishing and shooting for the pot, bathing and rowing, and every kind of healthy out-of-doors pleasure was indulged in along the road of travel — and all at no cost.

At one little seaport a very small man not over five feet high had married a woman considerably over six. He was an idle, drunken rascal, and I met her one day striding down the street with her intoxicated little spouse wrapped up in her apron, feebly protesting.

One result of these holidays was that I told my London boys about them, using one's experiences as illustrations, till suddenly it struck me that this was shabby Christianity. Why shouldn't these town cagelings share our holidays? Thirteen accompanied me the following summer. We had three tents, an old deserted factory, and an uninhabited gorge by the sea, all to ourselves on the Anglesea coast, among people who spoke only Welsh. Thus we had all the joys of foreign travel at very little cost.

Among the many tricks the boys 'got away with' was one at the big railway junction at Bangor, where we had an hour to wait. They got into the baggage-room and stole a varied assortment of labels, which they industriously pasted over those on a large pile of luggage stacked on the platform. The subsequent tangle of destinations can better be imagined than described. I have never put much value on 'labels' since that day.

Camp rules were simple — no clothing allowed except short blue knickers and gray flannel shirts, no shoes, stockings, or caps except on Sundays. The uniform was provided and was as a rule the amateur production of numerous friends, for our finances were strictly limited. The knickers were not particularly successful, the legs frequently being carried so high up that there was no space into which the body could be inserted. Everyone had to bathe in the sea before he got any breakfast. I can still see ravenous boys staving off the evil hour till as near midday as possible. No one was allowed in the boats who could not swim, an art which they all quickly acquired. There was, of course, a regular fatigue party each day for the household duties. We had no beds, but slept on long, burlap bags stuffed with hay. A very favourite pastime was afforded by our big lifeboat, an old one hired from the National Lifeboat Society. The tides flowed very strongly alongshore, east on the flood tide and west on the ebb. Food, fishing-lines, and a skipper for the day being provided, the old boat would go off with the tide in the morning, the boys had a picnic somewhere during the slack-water interim, and came back with the return tide.

When our numbers grew, as they did to thirty the second year, and nearly a hundred in subsequent seasons, thirty or more boys would be packed off daily in that way, and yet we never lost one of them. If they had not had as many lives as cats, it would have been quite another story. The boat had sufficient sails to give the appearance to their unfamiliar eyes of being a sailing vessel, but the real work was done with twelve huge oars, two boys to an oar being the rule. At nights they used to come drifting homeward on the returning tides singing their dirges, like some historic barge of old.

An annual expedition was to the top of Mount Snowdon, the highest in England or Wales. It was attempted by land and water. Half of us tramped overland in forced marches to the beautiful Menai Straits, crossed the suspension bridge, and were given splendid hospitality and good beds on the straw of the large stables at the beautiful country seat of a friend at Trevorth. Here the boat section who came around the island were to meet us, anchoring their craft on the south side of the Straits. Our second year the naval division did not turn up, and some had qualms of conscience that evil might have overtaken them. Nor did they arrive until we by land had conquered the summit, travelling by Bethesda and the famous slate quarries, and returning for the second evening to Trevorth. We then found that they had been stranded on the sands in Red Wharf Bay, so far from the shore that they could neither go forward nor back; had thus spent their first night in a somewhat chilly manner in old bathing-machines by the land-wash, and supped off the superfluous hard biscuit which they had been reserving for the return voyage. They were none the worse, however, our genial host making it up to them in an extra generous provision and a special evening entertainment. One of my smartest boys (a Jew by nationality, for we made no distinctions in election to our class), in recounting his adventures to me next day, said: 'My! Doctor, I did have some fun kidding that waiter in the white choker. He took a liking to me, so I let him pal up. I told him my name was Lord Shaftesbury when I was home, but I asked him not to let it out, and the old bloke promised he wouldn't.' The 'old bloke' happened to be our host, who was always in dress-clothes in the evening, which was the only time we were at his house.

These holidays drew us very closely together; and to make

the boys feel it less a charitable affair, everyone was encouraged to save up his railway fare and as much more as possible. By special arrangement with the railway and other friends, and by very simple living, the per capita charges were so much reduced that many of the boys not only paid their own expenses, but even helped their friends. The start was always attended by a crowd of relatives, all helping with the baggage. The father of one of my boys was a costermonger, and had a horse that he had obtained very cheap because it had a disease of the legs. He always kept it in the downstairs portion of his house, which it entered by the front door. It was a great pleasure to him to come and cart our things free to the station. The boys used to load his cart at our house, and I remember one time that they made him haul unconsciously all the way to the big London terminal at Euston half our furniture, including our coal boxes. His son, a most charming boy, made good in life in Australia and bought a nice house in one of the suburbs for his father and mother. I had the pleasure one night of meeting them all there. The father was terribly uneasy, for he said he just could not get accustomed to it. All his old pals were gone, and his present neighbours' tastes and interests made a great gulf between them. I heard later that, as soon as his son left England again, the old man sold the house, and returned to the more congenial associations of a costermonger's life, where I believe he, like his pony, died in harness.

The last two years of my stay in London being occupied with resident work at hospital, I could not find time for such far-off holidays, and at the suggestion of my chief, Sir Frederick Treves, himself a Dorsetshire man, we camped by permission of our friends, the owners, in the grounds of Lulworth Castle, close by the sea.

One of the great attractions of the new camping-ground was the exquisite country and the splendid coast, with chalk cliffs over which almost anyone could fall with impunity. Lulworth Cove, one of the most picturesque in England, was the summer resort of my chief, and he being an expert mariner and swimmer used not only very often to join us at camp, but always gave the boys a fine regatta and picnic at his cottage. Our water polo games were also a great feature here, the water being warm and enabling us easily to play out the games. There are also numerous beautiful castles and country houses all the way between Swanage and Weymouth, and we had such kindness extended to us wherever we went that every day was a dream of joy to the lads. Without any question they acquired new visions and ideals through these experiences.

CHAPTER IV

'THE LONDON'

HAVING finished my second year at hospital and taken my preliminary examinations, including the scientific preliminary, and my first Bachelor of Medicine for the University of London degree, I had advanced to the dignity of 'walking the hospitals,' carried a large, shining stethoscope, and spent much time following the famous physicians and surgeons around the wards.

Our first appointment was clerking in the medical wards. We had each so many beds allotted to us, and it was our business to know everything about the patients who occupied them, to keep accurate 'histories,' and to be ready to be quizzed or queried by our resident house physician or our visiting consultant on the afternoon when he made his rounds, followed by larger or smaller crowds of students according to the value which was placed upon his teaching. I was lucky enough to work under the famous Sir Andrew Clark, Mr. Gladstone's physician. He was a Scotchman greatly beloved, and always with a huge following, to whom he imparted far more valuable truths than even the medical science of those days afforded. His constant message, repeated and repeated at the risk of wearying, was: 'Gentlemen, you must observe for yourselves. It is your observation and not your memory which counts.'

Compared with the methods of diagnosis today, those of that day were very limited, but Sir Andrew's message was the more important, showing the greatness of the man, who, though at the very top of the tree, never for a moment tried to convey to his followers that his knowledge was final, but that any moment he stood ready to abandon his position for a better one. On one occasion, while he was in one of the largest of our wards (one with four divisions and twenty beds each), he was examining a lung case, while a huge class of fifty young doctors stood around.

'What about the sputum, Mr. Jones?' he asked. 'What have you observed coming from these lungs?'

'There is not much quantity, sir. It is greenish in colour.'

'But what about the microscope, Mr. Jones? What does that show?'

'No examination has been made, sir.'

'Gentlemen,' he said, 'I will now go to the other ward, and you shall choose a specimen of the sputum of some of these cases. When I return, we will examine it and see what we can learn.'

When he returned, four specimens awaited him, the history and diagnosis of the cases being known only to the class. The class never forgot how, by dissolving and boiling, and with the microscope, he told us more from his examination of each case than we knew from all our other information. His was real teaching, and reminds one of the Glasgow professor who, in order to emphasize the same point of the value of observation, prepared a little cupful of kerosene, mustard, and castor oil, and, calling the attention of his class to it, dipped a finger into the atrocious compound and then sucked his finger. He next passed the mixture around to the students who all did the same with most dire results. When the cup returned and he observed the faces of his students, he remarked: 'Gentlemen, I am afraid you did not use your powers of obsairvation. The finger that I put into the cup was no' the same one that I stuck in my mouth.'

On changing over to the surgical side in the hospital, we were employed in a very similar manner, only we were called 'dressers,' and under the house surgeon had all the care of a number of surgical patients. My good fortune now brought me under the chieftaincy of Sir Frederick Treves, the doyen of teachers. His great message was self-reliance. He taught dogmatically as one having authority, and always insisted that we should make up our minds, have a clear idea of what we were doing, and then do it. His ritual was always thought out, no detail being omitted, and each person had exactly his share of work and his share of responsibility. It used greatly to impress patients, and he never underestimated the psychical value of having their complete confidence. Thus, on one occasion asking a dresser for his diagnosis, the student replied:

'It might be a fracture, sir, or it might be only sprained.'

'The patient is not interested to know that it might be measles, or it might be toothache. The patient wants to know what is the matter, and it is your business to tell it to him or he will go to a quack who will inform him at once.'

All his teachings were, like Mark Twain's, enhanced by such over-emphasis or like Christ's own, by hyperbole. He could make an article in the 'British Medical Journal' on Cholecystenterostomy amusing to a general reader, and make an ordinary remark as cutting as an amputation knife. He never permitted laxity of any kind in personal appearance or dress, or any imposing on the patients. His habit of saying openly exactly what he meant made many people fear, as much as they respected, him.

One incident recurs to my mind which I must recount as an example when psychology failed. A Whitechapel 'lady,' suffering with a violent form of delirium tremens, was lying screeching in a strait-jacket on the cushioned floor of the padded room. With the usual huge queue of students following, he had gone in to see her, as I had been unable to get the results desired with a reasonable quantity of sedatives and soporifics. It was a very rare occasion, for cases which did not involve active surgery he left strictly alone. After giving a talk on psychical influence, he had the jacket removed as 'a relic of barbarism,' and in a very impressive manner, looking into her glaring eyes and shaking his forefinger at her, he said: 'Now you are comfortable, my good woman, and you will sleep. You will make no more disturbance whatever.' There was an unusual silence. The woman remained absolutely passive, and we all turned to follow the chief out. Suddenly the 'lady' called out, 'Hi, Hi' — and some perverse spirit induced Sir Frederick to return. Looking back with defiant eyes she screamed out, 'You! You with a faice! You do think yerself —— —— clever, don't yer?' The situation was promptly relieved by his bursting into a genuine fit of laughter.

Among other celebrated men who were admired and revered was Mr. Hurry Fenwick on the surgical side, for whom I had the honour of illustrating in colours his prize Jacksonian essay. Any talent for sketching, especially in colours, is of great value to the student of medicine. Once you have sketched a case from nature, with the object of showing the peculiarity of the abnormality, it remains permanently in your mind. Besides this, it forces you to note small differences; in other words, it teaches you to 'obsairve.' Thus, in the skin department I was sent to reproduce a case of anthrax of the neck, a rare disease in England, though all men handling raw hides are liable to contract it. The area had to be immediately excised; yet one never could forget the picture on one's mind. On another occasion a case of genuine leprosy was brought in, with all the dreadful signs of the disease. The macula rash was entirely unique so far as I knew, but a sketch greatly helped to fix it on one's memory. The poor patient proved to be one of the men who was handling the meat in London's greatest market at Smithfield. A tremendous hue and cry spread over London when somehow the news got into the paper, and vegetarianism received a temporary boost which in my opinion it still badly needs for the benefit of the popular welfare.

Truly one has lived through wonderful days in the history of the healing art. The first operations which I saw performed at our hospitals were before Lord Lister's teaching was practised; though even in my boyhood I remember getting leave to run up from Marlborough to London to see my brother, on whom Sir Joseph Lister had operated for osteomyelitis of the leg. Our most famous surgeon in 1880 was Sir Walter Rivington; and today there arises to memory the picture of him, clad in a blood-stained, black velvet coat, and, without any attempt at or idea of asepsis, removing a leg at the thigh. The main thing was speed, although the patient was under ether, and in quickly turning round the tip of the sword-like amputation knife, he made a gash in the patient's other leg. The whole thing seemed horrible enough to us students, but the surgeon smiled, saying, 'Fortunately it is of no importance, gentlemen. The man will not live.' Amputations practically always went septic then.

Then came the day when everyone worked under clouds of carbolic steam, which fizzed and spouted from large brass boilers over everything; and then the time when everyone was criticizing the new, young surgeon, Treves, who was daring to discard it, and getting as good results by scrupulous cleanliness. His aphorism was, 'Gentlemen, the secret of surgery is the nailbrush.' Today, with blood examinations, germ cultures, sera tests, X-rays, and a hundred added improvements, one can say to a fisherman in far-off Labrador arriving on a mail steamer, and to whom every hour lost in the fishing season spells calamity, 'Yes, you can be operated on, and the wound will be healed, and you will be ready to go back by the next steamer, unless some utterly unforeseen circumstance arises.'

A little later my father's health began to fail in London, the worries and troubles of a sensitive clergyman's work among the poor creatures who were constantly passing under his care utterly overwhelming him. We agreed that a complete change of thought was necessary, and he and I started for a fishing and sight-seeing tour in Norway. Our steamer was to sail from the Tyne, and we went up to Newcastle to catch it. There some evil fiend persuaded my father to go and consult a doctor about his illness. Thus, while I waited at the hotel, my father became persuaded that he had some occult disease of the liver and must remain in Newcastle for treatment. However, I happened to be treasurer of the voyage, and for the first time asserting my professional powers, insisted that I was family physician for the time, and turned up in the evening with all our round-trip tickets and reservations taken and paid for. In the morning I had the trunks packed and conveyed aboard, and we sailed together for one of the most enjoyable holidays I ever spent. We travelled much afoot and in the little native carriages called 'stolkjaerre,' just jogging along, staying anywhere, fishing in streams, and living an open-air life, which the increasing flood of tourists in after years has made much less possible.

My father's death a year later made a great difference to me, my mother removing to live with my grandmother at Hampstead, as it was too lonely and not safe for her to live alone in East London. Twice our house had been broken into by burglars. The second occasion was in open daylight during the hour of evening service on a Sunday. Only the maids would have been in the house had I not been suffering from two black eyes contracted during the Saturday's football game. Though I had accompanied the others out, I had decided that my appearance might have led to misinterpretations in church, and returned unnoticed. The men escaped by some method which they had discovered of scaling a high fence, but I was close behind following them through the window by which they had entered. Shortly afterward I happened to be giving evidence at the Old Bailey on one of the many cases of assault and even murder where the victims had been brought into hospital as patients. London was ringing with the tale of a barefaced murder at Murray Hill in North London, where an exceedingly clever piece of detective work, an old lantern discovered in a pawnbroker's shop in Whitechapel — miles away from the scene of the crime — was the means of bringing to trial four of the most rascally looking villains I ever saw. The trial preceded ours, and we had to witness it. One of the gang had turned Queen's evidence to save his own neck. So great was the hatred of the others for him and the desire for revenge that even in the court they were handcuffed and in separate stands. Fresh from my own little fracas, I learned what a fool I had been, for in this case also the deed was done in open daylight and the lawn had tight wires stretched across it. The young son, giving chase as I did, had been tripped up and shot through the abdomen for his pains. He had, however, crawled back, made his will, and was subsequently only saved by a big operation.

The giving of expert evidence on such occasions was the only opportunity which the young sawbones had of earning money. True, we got only a guinea a day and expenses while thus in court, but we learned a lot about medical jurisprudence, a subject which always greatly interested me. It was no uncommon sight either at 'The London,' or 'Poplar,' at both of which I did interne work, to see a policeman always sitting behind the screen at the foot of the patient's bed. One man, quite a nice fellow when not occupied in crime, when furiously drunk had killed his wife and cut his own throat. By the curious custom of civilization all the skill and money which the hospital could offer to save a most valuable life was as usual devoted to restoring this man to health. He was weaned slowly back from the grave by special nurses and treatment, till it began to dawn upon him that he might have to stand his trial. He would ask me if I thought he would have to undergo a long term, for he had not been conscious of what he was doing. As he grew better, and the policeman arrived to watch him, he decided that it would probably be quite a long time. He had a little place of his own somewhere, and he used to have chickens and other presents sent up to fellow patients, and would have done so to the nurses, only they could not receive them. I was not personally present at his trial, but I felt really sorry to hear that they hanged him.

Many of these poor fellows were only prevented from ending their own lives by our using extreme care. The case of one wretched man, driven to desperation, I still remember. 'Patient male; age forty-five; domestic trouble — fired revolver into his mouth. Finding no phenomena of interest develop, fired a second chamber into his right ear. Still no symptoms worthy of notice. Patient threw away pistol and walked to hospital.' Both bullets had lodged in the thick parts of his skull, and, doing no damage, were left there. A subsequent note read: 'Patient today tried to cut his throat with a dinner-knife which he had hidden in his bed. Patient met with no success.'

Another of my cases which interested me considerably was that of a professional burglar who had been operated upon in almost every part of the kingdom, and was inclined to be communicative, as the job which had brought him to hospital had cost him a broken spine. Very little hope was held out to him that he would ever walk again. He was clear of murder, for he said it was never his practice to carry firearms, being a nervous man and apt to use them if he had them and got alarmed when busy burglaring. He relied chiefly on his extraordinary agility and steady head to escape. He and a friend had been detailed by the gang to the job of plundering one of a row of houses. The plans of the house and of the enterprise were all in order, but some unexpected alarm was given and he fled upstairs, climbed through a skylight onto the roof, and ran along the gables of the tiles, not far ahead of the police, who were armed and firing at him. He could easily have escaped, as he could run along the coping of the brick parapet without turning a hair, but he was brought up by a narrow side street on which he had not counted, not having anticipated, like cats, a battle on the tiles. It was only some twelve to fifteen feet across the gap, and the landing on the other side was a flat roof. Taking it all at a rush he cleared the street successfully, but the flat roof, black with ages of soot, proved to be a glass skylight, and he entered a house in a way new even to him. His falling on a stone floor many feet below accounted for what he characterized 'his unfortunate accident'! After many months in bed, the man took an unexpected turn, his back mended, and with only a slight leg paralysis he was able to return to the outside world. His long suffering and incarceration in hospital were accepted by the law as his punishment, and he assured me by all that he held sacred that he intended to retire into private life. Oddly enough, however, while on another case, I saw him again in the prisoner's dock and at once went over and spoke to him.

'Drink this time, Doctor,' he said. 'I was down on my luck and the barkeeper went out and left his till open. I climbed over and got the cash, but there was so little space between the bar and the wall that with my stiff back I couldn't for the life of me get back. I was jammed like a stopper in a bottle.'

Among many interesting experiences, one especially I shall never forget. Like the others, it occurred during my service for Sir Frederick Treves as house surgeon, and I believe he told the story. A very badly burned woman had been brought into hospital. Her dress had somehow got soaked in paraffin and had then taken fire. Her terribly extensive burns left no hope whatever of her recovery, and only the conventions of society kept us from giving the poor creature the relief of euthanasia, by some cup of laudanum negus. But the law was interested. A magistrate was brought to the bedside and the husband sent for. The nature of the evidence, the meaning of an oath, the importance of the poor creature acknowledging that her words were spoken 'in hopeless fear of immediate death,' were all duly impressed upon what remained of her mind. The police then brought in the savage, degraded-looking husband, and made him stand between two policemen at the foot of the bed, facing his mangled wife. The magistrate, after preliminary questions, asked her to make her dying statement as to how she came by her death. There was a terrible moment of silence. It seemed as if her spirit were no longer able to respond to the stimuli of life on earth. Then a sudden rebound appeared to take place, her eyes lit up with a flash of light, and even endeavouring to raise her piteous body, she said, 'It was an accident, Judge. I upset the lamp myself, so help me God': and just for one moment her eyes met those of her miserable husband. It was the last time she spoke.

Tragedy and comedy ran hand in hand even in this work. Saint Patrick's Day always made the hospital busy, just as Christmas was the season for burned children. Beer in an East London 'pub' was generally served in pewter pots, as they were not easily broken. A common head injury was a circular scalp cut made by the heavy bottom rim, a wound which bled horribly. A woman was brought in on one Saint Patrick's Day, her scalp turned forward over her face and her long hair a mass of clotted blood from such a stroke, made while she was on the ground. When the necessary readjustments had been made and she was leaving hospital cured, we asked her what had been the cause of the trouble. ''Twas just an accidint, yer know. Sure, me an' another loidy was just havin' a few words.'

On another occasion late at night, we were called out of bed by a cantankerous, half-drunken fellow whom the night porter could not pacify. 'I'm a regular subscriber to this hospital, and I have never had my dues yet,' he kept protesting. A new drug to produce immediate vomiting had just been put on the market, and, as it was exactly the treatment required, we gave him an injection. To our dismay, though the medicine is in common use today, either the poison which he had been drinking or the drug itself caused a collapse followed by head symptoms. He was admitted, his head shaved and icebags applied, with the result that next day he was quite well again. But when he left, he had, instead of a superabundance of curly, auburn hair, a polished white knob oiled and shining like a State House at night. We debated whether his subscription would be as regular in future, though he professed to be profoundly grateful.

The intimacy which grew up between some of my patients and myself showed me (which I never could otherwise have understood) the seamy side of life in great cities, its terrible tragedies and pathos, and how much good there is in the worst, how much need of courage, and what vast opportunities lie before those who accept the service of man as their service to God. It proved to me how infinitely more needed are unselfish deeds than orthodox words.

My parents having gone, it became necessary for me to find lodgings — which I did, 'unfurnished,' in the house of a Portuguese widow. Her husband, who had a good family name, had gone down in the world and had disappeared with another 'lady.' The eldest son, a mathematical genius, had been able to pay his way through Cambridge University by the scholarships and prizes which he had won. One beautiful little dark-eyed daughter of seven was playing in a West End Theatre as the dormouse in 'Alice in Wonderland.' She was second fiddle to Alice herself, also, and could sing all her songs. Her pay was five pounds a week, poor enough for the attraction she proved, but more than all that of the rest of the family put together. The 'dormouse' used to come up and say her parts for my benefit and that of occasional friends, and was so modest and winsome, and her earnings so invaluable to the family, that then and there I came to the conclusion that the drama was an essential part of art, and that those who were trying to elevate and cleanse it, like Sir Henry Irving, whose son I had met at Marlborough, must have the support of a public who demanded clean plays and good conditions both in front and behind the curtain.

My new lodgings being close to Victoria Park afforded the opportunity for training if one were unconventional. To practise throwing the sixteen-pound hammer requires rough ground and plenty of space, and, as I was scheduled for that at the inter-hospital sports, it was necessary to work when not too many disinterested parties were around. Even an East-Ender's skull is not hammer-proof, as I had seen when a poor woman was brought into hospital with five circular holes in her head, the result of blows inflicted by her husband with a hammer. The only excuse which the ruffian offered for the murder was that she had forgotten to wake him, he had been late, and lost his job.

A number of the boys in my class were learning to swim. There was only one bathing-lake and once the 'waters were troubled' we drew the line at going in to give lessons. So we used to meet at the gate at the hour of opening in the morning, and thus be going back before most people were moving. Nor did we always wait for the park keeper, but often scaled the gates and so obtained an even more exclusive dip. Many an evening we would also 'flannel,' and train round and round the park, to improve one's wind before some big event. For diet at that time I used oatmeal, milk, and eggs, and very little or no meat. It was cheaper and seemed to give me more endurance. Moreover, the real value of money was dawning on me.

Victoria Park is one of those open forums where every man with a sore spot goes out to air his grievance. On Sundays there were little groups around the trees where orators debated on everything from a patent medicine to the nature of God. Charles Bradlaugh and Mrs. Annie Besant were associated together in iconoclastic efforts against orthodox religion, and there was so much truth in some of their contentions that they were making no little disturbance. Hanging on their skirts were a whole crowd of ignorant, dogmatic atheists, who published a paper called 'The Freethinker,' which, while it was a villainous and contemptible rag, appealed to the passions and prejudices of the partially educated. To answer the specious arguments of their propaganda an association known as the Christian Evidence Society used to send out lecturers. One of them became quite famous for his clever arguments and answers, his ready wit, and really extensive reading. He was an Antiguan, a black man named Edwards, and had been a sailor before the mast. I met him at the parish house of an Episcopal clergyman of a near-by church, who, under the caption of Christian Socialism, ran all kinds of social agencies that found their way to the hearts of the people. His messages were so much more in deeds than in words that he greatly appealed to me, and I transferred my allegiance to his church, which was always well filled. I particularly remember among his efforts the weekly parish dance. My religious acquaintances were apt to class all such simple amusements in a sort of general category as 'works of the Devil,' and turn deaf ears to every invitation to point out any evil results, being satisfied with their own statement that it was the 'thin edge of the wedge.' This good man, however, was very obviously driving a wedge into the hearts of many of his poor neighbours who in those days found no opportunity for relief in innocent pleasures from the sordid round of life in the drab purlieus of Bethnal Green.

Exactly opposite the hospital was Oxford House, only two minutes distant, which combined definite doctrinal religion with social work. Being an Oxford effort it had great attractions for me. Moreover, right alongside it in the middle of a disused sugar refinery I had hired the yard, converted it into a couple of lawn-tennis courts, and had run a small club. There I first met the famous Dr. Hensley Henson, now Bishop of Hereford, and also the present Bishop of London, Dr. Winnington-Ingram — a good all-round athlete. He used to visit in our wards; and as we had a couple of fives courts, a game which takes little time and gives much exercise, we used to have an afternoon off together, once a week, when he came over to hospital. Neither of these splendid men was a dignitary in those days, or I am afraid they would have found us medicals much more stand-offish. We liked both of these men because they were unconventional and good sports, and especially in that they were not afraid to tackle the atheist's propaganda in the open. I have seen Dr. Henson in Whitechapel debating alone against a hall full of opponents and with fairness and infinite restraint. Moreover, I have seen Dr. Ingram doing just the same thing standing on a stone in the open park. It may all sound very silly when one knows that by human minds, or to the human mind, the Infinite can never be demonstrated as a mathematical proposition. But the point was that these clergy were proving that they were real men — men who had courage as well as faith, who believed in their message. Christ Himself showed His superb manhood by just such speaking out.

Far and away the most popular of the Park speakers was the Antiguan. His arguments were so clever it was obvious that he was well and widely read. His absolute understanding of the crowd and his witty repartee used frequently to cause his opponents to lose their tempers, and that was always their undoing. The crowd as a rule was very fair and could easily distinguish arguments from abuse. Thus, on one Sunday the debate was as to whether nature was God. The atheist representative was a loud-voiced demagogue, who when angry betrayed his Hibernian origin very markedly. Having been completely worsted and the laugh turned against him, he used the few minutes given him to reply, in violent abuse, ending up that 'ladies and gentlemen did not come out on holidays to spend their time being taught English by a damned nigger.'

'Sir,' Edwards answered from the crowd, 'I am a British subject, born on the island of Antigua, and as much an Englishman as any Irishman in the country.'

Edwards possessed an inexhaustible stock of good-humour, and his laugh could be heard halfway across the Park. As soon as his turn came to mount the stone, he got the crowd so good-natured that they became angry at the interruptions of the enemy, and when someone suggested that if nature were that man's God, the near-by duckpond was the natural place for him, there was a rush for him, and for several subsequent Sundays he was not in evidence. Edwards was a poor man, his small salary and incessant generosity left him nothing for holidays, and he was killing himself with overwork. So we asked him to join us in the new house which we were fitting up in Palestine Place. He most gladly did so and added enormously to our fun. Unfortunately, tuberculosis long ago got its grip upon him, and removed a valuable life from East London.

It was a queer little beehive in which we lived in those days, and a more cosmopolitan crowd could hardly have been found; one young doctor who has since made his name and fortune in Australia; another in whose rooms were nearly a hundred cups for prowess in almost every form of athletics, and who has also 'made good' in professional life, besides several others who for shorter or longer periods were allotted rooms in our house. Among the more unusual was C. M., a Brahmin from India, a priest in his youth, who had been brought back to England by some society to be educated in medical missionary work, but whom for some reason they had dropped. For a short time a clever young Russian of Hebrew extraction who was studying for the Church helped to render our common-room social engagements almost international affairs.

It so happened that there was at that time in hospital under my care a patient known as 'the Elephant Man.' He had been starring under that title in a cheap vaudeville, had been seen by some of the students, and invited over to be shown to and studied by our best physicians, and to be cared for kindly for the rest of his life. The poor fellow was really exceedingly sensitive about his most extraordinary appearance. The disease was called 'leontiasis,' and consisted of an enormous overdevelopment of bone and skin on one side. His head and face were so deformed as really to resemble a big animal's head with a trunk. My arms would not reach around his hat. A special room in a yard was allotted to him, and several famous people came to see him, among them Queen Alexandra, then the Princess of Wales, who afterward sent him an autographed photograph of herself. He kept it in his room, which was known as the 'Elephant House,' and it always suggested Beauty and the Beast. Only at night could the man venture out-of-doors, and it was no unusual thing in the dusk of nightfall to meet him walking up and down in the little courtyard. He used to talk freely of how he would look in a huge bottle of alcohol — an end to which in his imagination he was fated to come. He was of a very cheerful disposition and pathetically proud of his left side, which was normal. Very suddenly one day he died — the reason assigned being that his head fell forward and choked him, being too heavy for him to lift up.

In 1886 I passed my final examinations and duly became a member of the College of Physicians and of the Royal College of Surgeons of England; and sought new fields for change and rest, where also I could use my newly acquired licence to my own, if to no one else's benefit.

CHAPTER V

OFF THE DOGGER BANKS

AMONG the patients who came to the London Hospital, there were now and again fishermen from the large fishing fleets of the North Sea. They lived out, as it were, in floating villages, sending their fish to market every day by fast cutters. Every two or three months, as their turn came round, a vessel would leave for the home port on the east coast, being permitted, or supposed to be permitted, a day at home for each full week at sea. As the fleets kept the sea summer and winter, and the boats were small, not averaging over sixty tons, it was a hazardous calling. The North Sea is nowhere deeper than thirty fathoms, much of it being under twenty, and in some places only five. Indeed, it is a recently sunken and still sinking portion of Europe, so much so that the coasts on both sides are constantly receding, and when Heligoland was handed over by the English to the Kaiser, it was said that he would have to keep jacking it up, or soon there would be none left. Shallow waters exposed to the fierce gales which sweep the German Ocean make deep and dangerous seas, which readily break and wash the decks of craft with low freeboard, such as the North Sea vessels are obliged to have, in order to get boats in and out to ferry their fish to the cutter.

There being no skilled aid at hand, the quickest way to get help in cases of accident used to be to send an injured man to market with the fish. Often it was a long journey of many days, simple fractures became compound, and limbs and faculties were often thus lost. It so happened that Sir Frederick Treves had a love for navigating in small sailing-craft, and had recently made a trip among the fishing fleets. He told me that a small body of men, interested in the religious and social welfare of the deep-sea fishermen, had charted a small fishing-smack, and sent her out among the fishermen to hold religious services of a simple, unconventional type, in order to afford the men an alternative to the grog vessels when fishing was slack, and to carry first aid, the skipper of the vessel being taught ambulance work. They wanted, however, to get a young doctor to go out, who cared also for the spiritual side of the work. His advice to me was to go and have a look at it. 'If you go in January, you will see some fine seascapes, anyhow. Don't try it in summer when all the old ladies go there for a rest.'

I therefore applied to go out the following January; and that fall, while working near the Great London docks, I used often to look at the tall East Indiamen, thinking that I soon should be aboard just such a vessel in the North Sea. It was dark and raining when my train ran into Yarmouth, and a dripping, stout fisherman in a blue uniform met me at that then unattractive and ill-lighted terminus. He had brought a forlorn 'growler' or four-wheel cab. Climbing in we drove a mile or more along a deserted road, and drew up at last apparently at the back of beyond.

'Where is the ship?' I asked.

'Why, those are her topmasts,' replied my guide, pointing to two posts projecting from the sand. 'The tide is low and she is hidden by the quay.'

'Heavens!' I thought; 'she's no tea clipper, anyhow.'

I climbed up the bank and peered down in the darkness at the hull of a small craft, a little larger than our old Roysterer. She was just discernible by the dim rays of the anchor light. I was hesitating as to whether I should not drive back to Yarmouth and return to London, when a cheery voice on deck called out a hearty welcome. It broke the spell and I had my cabby unload my bags on the bank. As his wheels rumbled away into the rain and dark, I felt that my cables were cut. Too late to save me, the cheery voice shouted, 'Mind the rigging, it's just tarred and greased.' I was already sliding down in jerks, caused by my sticking to it as I went. Small as the vessel was, she was absolutely spotless. Her steward, who cooked for all hands, was smart and in a snow-white suit. The contrast of between-decks and that above was very comforting, though my quarters were small. The crew were all stocky, good-humoured, and independent. Democratic as East London had made me, they impressed me very favourably, and I began to look forward to the venture with real pleasure.

Drink was the worst enemy of these men. The quay sides of

the fishermen's quarters teemed with low saloons. Wages were even paid off in them or their annexes, and grog vessels, luring men aboard with cheap tobacco and low literature, plied their nefarious calling among the fleets. They were the death, body and soul, of many of these fine specimens of manhood. Many is the time I have pitied those who manufacture and sell alcoholic drink to make a few sordid dollars.

Thirty years ago we were more conventional than today, and I was much surprised to learn from our skipper that we were bound first to Ostend to ship four tons of tobacco, sent over from England for us in bond, since he might not take it out consigned to the high seas. In Belgium, however, no duty was paid. The only trouble was that our vessel, to help pay its expenses, carried fishing gear, and as a fishing vessel could not get a clearance for trading even in Belgium. Our nets and beams, therefore, had to go out to the fishing grounds in a friendly trawler, while we passed as belonging to the mercantile marine during the time we took on our cargo.

So bitter was the cold that in Ostend we got frozen in and were able to skate up the harbour. We had eventually to get a steamer to go around us and smash our ice bonds, when we were again ready for sea. During the next two months we saw no land except Heligoland and Terschelling — or Skilling, as the fishermen called it — far away in the offing. Nor was our deck once clear of ice and snow during the whole time.

Our duty was to visit as many fleets as we could, and arrange with some reliable vessel to take a stock of tobacco for the use of their special fleet. The ship was to carry about six feet of blue bunting on her foretopmast stay, a couple of fathoms above her bowsprit end, so that all the fleet might know her. She was to sell the tobacco at a fixed price that just covered the cost, and undersold the 'coper' or grog vessel by fifty per cent. She was to hoist her flag for business every morning, while the small boats were out boarding fish on the carrier, and was to lie as far to leeward of the coper as possible so that the men could not go to both. Nineteen such floating dépôts were eventually arranged for, with the precaution that if any one of them had to return to port, he should bring no tobacco home, but hand over his stock and accounts to a reliable friend.

These deep-sea fisheries were a revelation to me. It was amazing to find over twenty thousand men and boys afloat — the merriest, cheerfullest lot which I had ever met. They were hail-fellow-well-met with everyone, and never thought of deprivation or danger. Clothing, food, conventions were all subordinated to utility. In efficiency and for their daring resourcefulness in physical difficulties and dangers, they were absolutely in a class by themselves, embodying all the traits of character which make men love to read the stories of the buccaneers and other seamen of the sixteenth century.

Each fleet had its admiral and vice-admiral, appointed partly by the owner, and partly by the skippers of the vessels. The admiral directed operations by flags in the daytime and by rockets at night, thus indicating what the fleet was to do and where they were to fish. Generally he had the fastest boat, and the cutters hunting for the fleet always lay just astern of the admiral, the morning after their arrival. Hundreds of men would come for letters, packages, to load fish or to get the news of what their last consignment fetched in the market. Moreover, a kind of Parliament was held aboard the cutter every morning, to consider policies and hear complaints.

At first it was a great surprise to me how these men knew where they were, for we never saw anything but sky and sea, and not even the admirals carried a chronometer or could work out a longitude; while only a small percentage of the skippers could read or write. They all, however, carried a sextant and could by rule of thumb find a latitude roughly. But that was only done at a pinch. The armed lead was the fisherman's friend. It was a heavy lead with a cup on the bottom filled fresh each time with sticky grease. When used, the depth was always called out by the watch, and the kind of sand, mud, or rock which stuck to the grease shown to the skipper. 'Fifteen fathoms and coffee grounds — must be on the tail end of the Dogger. Put her a bit more to the westward, boy,' he would remark, and think no more about it, though he might have been three or four days looking for his fleet and not spoken to a soul since he left land. I remember one skipper used to have the lead brought down below, and he could tell by the grit between his teeth after a couple of soundings which way to steer. It sounds strange even now, but it was so universal, being just second-nature to the men who from boyhood had lived on the sea, that we soon ceased to marvel at it. Skippers were only just being obliged to have certificates. These were obtained by *viva voce* examinations. You would sometimes hear an aspiring student, a great black-bearded pirate over forty-seven inches around the chest, and possibly the father of eight or ten children, as he stamped about in his watch keeping warm, repeating the courses — 'East end of the Dogger to the Horn. S.E. by E.½E. and W. point of the island [Heligoland], to Borkum, S.S.E.'

Whatever they did, they did hard. One of the admirals, being a thirsty soul, and the grog vessels having been adrift for a longer while than he fancied, conceived the fine idea of holding up the Heligoland saloons. So one bright morning he hove his fleet to under the lee of the island and a number of boats went ashore, presumably to sell fish. Altogether they landed some five hundred men, who held up the few saloons for two or three days. As a result subsequently only one crew selling fish to the island was allowed ashore at a time. The very gamble of their occupation made them do things hard. It was a dangerous task to throw out a small boat in half a gale of wind, fill her up with heavy boxes of fish, and send her to put these over the rail of a steamer wallowing in the trough of a mountainous sea.

It was on these very days, when less fish was sent to market, that the best prices were realized, and so there were always a number of dare-devils, who did not care if lives were lost so long as good prices were obtained, and their own record stood high on the weekly list of sales, which was forwarded to both owners and men. I have known as many as fourteen men upset in one morning out of these boats; and the annual loss of some three hundred and fifty men was mostly from this cause. Conditions were subsequently improved by the Board of Trade, who made it manslaughter against the skipper if any man was drowned boarding fish, unless the admiral had shown his flags to give the fleet permission to do so. In those days, however, I often saw twenty to thirty boats tied up alongside the cutter at one time, the heavy seas every now and again rolling the cutter's rail right under water, which, when she righted again, might come up under the keels of some of the boats and tip them upside down. Thus, anyone in them was caught like a mouse under a trap or knocked to pieces trying to swim among the rushing, tossing boats.

As a rule, we hauled the net at midnight. This was always a fresh source of wonder, for the trawl was catholic in its embrace, and brought up anything that came in its way. To emphasize how comparatively recently the Channel had been dry land, many teeth and tusks of mammals who used to roam its now buried forests were given up to the nets by the ever-shifting sands. Old wreckage of every description, ancient crockery, and even a water-logged old square-rigger that must have sunk years before were brought one day as far as the surface by the stout wire warp. After the loss of a large steamer called the Elbe, many of the passengers who had been drowned were hauled up in this way; and on one occasion great excitement was caused in Hull by a fisher lad from that port being picked up with his hands tied behind his back and a heavy weight on his feet. The defence was that the boy had died and was thus buried to save breaking the voyage — supported by the fact that another vessel had also picked up the boy and thrown him overboard again for the same reason. But some thought otherwise, and more especially as cruelty to these boys was not unknown.

These lads were apprenticed to the fishery masters largely from industrial or reformatory schools. They had no relations to look after them, and often no doubt gave the limit of trouble and irritation. On the whole, however, the system worked well, and a most excellent class of capable seamen was developed. At times, however, they were badly exploited. During their apprenticeship years they were not entitled to pay, only to pocket money, and yet sometimes the whole crew including the skipper were apprentice and under twenty-one years of age. After that they were fitted for no other calling but to follow the sea, and had to accept the master's terms. There were no fishermen's unions, and the men, being very largely illiterate, were often left victims of a peonage system in spite of the Truck Acts. The master of a vessel has to keep discipline, especially in a fleet, and the best of boys have faults and need punishing while on land.

These skippers themselves were brought up in a rough school; and those who fell victims to drink and made the acquaintance of the remedial measure of our penal system of that day were only further brutalized by it. Religion scarcely touched the majority, for their brief periods of leave ashore were not unnaturally spent in having a good time. To those poisoned by the villainous beverages sold on the sordid grog vessels, no excess was too great. Owners were in sympathy with the Mission in trying to oust the coper, because their property, in the form of fish, nets, stores, and even sails, was sometimes bartered on the high seas for liquor. On one occasion during a drunken quarrel in the coper's cabin one skipper threw the kerosene lamp over another lying intoxicated on the floor. His heavy wool jersey, soaked in kerosene, caught fire. He rushed for the deck, and then, a dancing mass of flames, leaped overboard and disappeared.

Occasionally skippers devised punishments with a view to remedying the defects of character. Thus, one lad, who through carelessness had on more than one occasion cooked the 'duff' for dinner badly, was made to take his cinders on deck when it was his time to turn in, and go forward to the fore-rigging, when he had to take one cinder, go up to the cross-tree, and throw it over into the sea, come down the opposite rigging and repeat the act until he had emptied his scuttle. Another who had failed to clean the cabin properly had one night, instead of going to bed, to take a bucketful of sea water and empty it with a teaspoon into another, and so to and fro until morning. On one occasion a poor boy was put under the ballast deck — that is, the cabin floor — and forgotten. He was subsequently found dead, drowned in the bilge water. It was easy to hide the results of cruelty, for being washed overboard was by no means an uncommon way of disappearing from vessels with low freeboards in the shallow waters of the North Sea.

There is so much that is manly about the lives of those who follow the sea, so much less artificiality than in many other callings, and with our fishermen so many fewer of what we call, loosely, 'chances in life,' that to sympathize with them was easy — and sympathy is a long step toward love. Life at sea breaks down conventional barriers, and almost compels

fellowship and an intelligent understanding of the difficulties
and tragedies of the soul of one's neighbour. That rare faculty
of imagination, which is the inspiration of all great lovers of
men, was unnecessary here. The conviction that these men
needed what I had to give, and that it would not be given if
I refused the challenge, was as plain as daylight.

In other words, the field of work offered what I still consider as the most remunerative returns for any man's abilities;
or, to put it in another way, it made me believe that my
special capacities and training could be used to make new men
as well as new bodies. Any idea of sacrifice was balanced by
the fact that I never cared much for the frills of life so long
as the necessities were forthcoming. Science taught me that
'little' and 'big' are relative terms only. The greatest Life
ever lived was no smaller for being staged in a village carpenter's shop among fishermen.

Another movement was just starting at that time which
interested me considerably. It was an organization called the
Public School Camps. An integral part of my summer holidays during these years was spent as medical officer at one of
these camps. For many reasons in England it was wise to run
them on military lines, for besides the added dignity, it
ensured the ability to maintain order and discipline. Some
well-known commandant was chosen, who was a soldier also
in the good fight of faith. Special sites were selected, generally
on the grounds of some big country seat which were lent by
the interested lord of the manor, and every kind of outdoor
attraction was provided which could be secured. Besides
organized competitive games, there was usually a yacht,
good bathing, always a gymkhana, and numerous expeditions
and hikes. All of the work of the camp was done by the
boys, who each served in turn on orderly duty. The officers
were always, if possible, prominent athletes, to whom the
boys could look up as being capable in physical as well as in
spiritual fields. There was a brief address each night before
taps in the big marquee used for mess; and one night there
was always a straight talk on the problems of sex by one of
the medical officers, whom the boys were advised to consult
on their perplexities. These camps are among my happiest
memories. Many men today gratefully acknowledge that

these camps were the turning-point of their whole lives. The secret was unconventionality and absolute naturalness with no shibboleths. The boys were encouraged to be boys in an atmosphere of sincere, if not omniscient fervour. On one occasion, when breaking up camp, a curly-headed young rascal in my tent, being late on the last morning — unknown to anyone — went to the train in his pyjamas, hidden only by his raincoat. At a small wayside station over a hundred miles from London, whither he was bound, leaving his coat in the carriage, he ventured into the refreshment stall of the waiting-room. Unfortunately, however, he came out only to find his train departed and himself in his night-clothes on the platform without a penny, a ticket, or a friend. Eluding the authorities, he reached the huge Liverpool terminus at night to find a faithful friend waiting on the platform for him with a sorely needed overgarment.

Our North Sea work grew apace. Vessel after vessel was added to the fleet. Her Majesty Queen Victoria became interested, and, besides subscribing personally towards the first hospital boat, permitted it to be named in her honour. According to custom the builders had a beautiful little model made which Her Majesty agreed to accept. It was decided that it should be presented to her in Buckingham Palace by the two senior Mission captains.

The journey to them was a far more serious undertaking than a winter voyage on the Dogger Bank. However, arrayed in smart blue suits and new guernseys and polished to the last degree, they set out on the eventful expedition. On their return, everyone was as anxious to know 'how the voyage had turned out' as if they had been exploring new fishing grounds around the North Cape in the White Sea. 'Nothing to complain of, boys, till just as we had her in the wind's eye to shoot the gear,' said the senior skipper. 'A big swell in knee-breeches opened the door and called out our names, when I was brought up all standing, for I saw that the peak halyard was fast on the port side. The blame thing was too small for me to shift her, so I had to leave it. But, believe me, she never said a word about it. That's what I call a lady.'

Our work had now extended to the herring fleets of Manxmen, Irishmen, Scotch, and English off West Ireland. One day we had landed on the Arran Islands, and I was hunting ferns in the rock crevices, for owing to the warmth of the Gulf Current the growth is luxuriant. On the top of the cliffs about three hundred feet high, I fell in with two Irishmen smoking their pipes and sprawling on the edge of the precipice. The water below was very deep and they were fishing. I had the fun of seeing dangling codfish hauled leisurely up all that long distance. If one fell off on the journey up, it was amusing to note the absolute *insouciance* of the fishermen, who assured me that there were plenty more in the sea.

On those wild coasts, calls for help frequently came from the poor settlers as well as from the seafarers. A summons coming in one day from the Fastnet Light, we rowed out in a small boat to that lonely rock in the Atlantic. A heavy sea, however, making landing impossible, we caught hold of a buoy, anchored off from the rock, and then, rowing in almost to the surf, caught a line from the high overhanging crane. A few moments later one was picked out of the tumbling, tossing boat like a winkle from a shell, by a noose at the end of a line from a crane a hundred and fifty feet above, was swung perpendicularly up into the air, and then round and into a trap-door in the side of the lighthouse. On leaving, one was swung out again in the same fashion, and dangled over the tumbling boat until caught and pulled in by the oarsmen.

Another day we rowed out nine miles in an Irish craft to visit the Skerry Islands, famous for the old Beehive Monastery, and the countless nests of gannets and other large sea-birds. The cliffs rise to a great height precipitously, and the ceaseless thunder of the Atlantic swell jealously guards any landing. There being no davit or crane, we just had to fling ourselves into the sea and climb up as best we could, carrying a line to haul up our clothing from the boat and other apparatus after landing, while the oarsmen kept her outside the surf. To hold on to the slippery rock we needed but little clothing, anyhow, for the clinging power of one's bare toes was essential. The innumerable gannets sitting on their nests gave the island the appearance of a snowdrift; and we soon had all the eggs that we needed lowered by a line. But some of the gulls, of whose eggs we wanted specimens also, built so cleverly onto the actual faces of the cliffs,

that we had to adopt the old plan of hanging over the edge
and raising the eggs on the back of one's foot, which is an
exploit not devoid of excitement. The chief difficulty was,
however, with one of our number, who literally stuck on the
top, being unable to descend, at least in a way compatible
with comfort or safety. The upshot was that he had to be
blindfolded and then helped down.

Among the many memories of the Irish coast which gave
me a vision of the land question as it affected the people in
those days, one in particular has always remained with me.
We had made a big catch in a certain bay, a perfectly beautiful inlet. To see if the local fishermen could find a market
within reach of these fishing grounds, with one of the crew,
and the fish packed in boxes, I sailed up the inlet to the
market-town of Bell Mullet. Being Saturday, we found a
market in progress, and buyers, who, encouraged by one of
the new Government light railways, were able to purchase
our fish. That evening, however, when halfway home, a squall
suddenly struck our own lightened boat and capsized her. By
swimming and manœuvring the boat, we made land on some
low, muddy flats. No house was in sight, and it was not until
long after dark that we two shivering masses of wet mud
reached an isolated cabin in the middle of a patch of re
deemed ground right in the centre of a large bog. A miserably
clad woman greeted us with a warm Irish welcome. The
house had only one room, which accommodated the live-
stock as well as the family. A fine cow stood in one corner;
while a donkey tied to the foot of the bed was patiently
looking down into the face of the baby. The father was in
England harvesting. A couple of pigs lay under the bed, and
the floor space was still further encroached upon by a goodly
number of chickens, which, encouraged by the warmth of the
peat fire, not only thought it their duty to accord us a welcome, but — misled by the firelight — kept saluting the still
far-off dawn. The resultant emotions led us on departing to
suggest that out of gratitude we would like to assist with the
erection of a cattle-pen. Our overtures were, however, re-
jected on the ground that 'Shure t'rint would be raised in
the fall' if any such signs of prosperity as farm buildings
greeted the land agent's arrival.

The voyage closed amongst the enormous fleet of Scotch herringers fishing off the Lewis Islands. Millions of herrings are taken. I have seen a mile of nets at a time sunk by the fish, while enough nets were set each night to reach to America and back again. The oil from the fish made the water so glassy that you could sail with a strong breeze and not see a ripple on the surface. The Society as a result established a summer Mission station at Stornaway for these men. A more pious set of men I never met, especially in their rigid keeping of Sunday. We learned to have the profoundest respect and affection for these men.

The introduction of the Mission ship on the seas banished utterly the grog ship. International prohibition of the sale of alcoholic liquors to fishermen on the high seas was obtained, and, the rich being as interested as the poor in maintaining it, it has proved an enormous blessing. But it was not a mere negative law that achieved the end with the great blessings that accompanied it. The grog ship was replaced by the Mission, hardship by friendship and worship. The secret was that a new fleet was built up.

CHAPTER VI

NORTH OF THE ROARING FORTIES

IN 1891, the present Lord Southborough, then a member of our Board, returned from a visit to Canada and Newfoundland. He brought before the Council the opportunities for service among the fishermen of the northwest Atlantic, and I was asked if I would cross the Atlantic in one of our sailing vessels, and look into the problem.

Critical friends have thought that the decision to go was made under strong religious excitement and in response to a deep-seated conviction that material sacrifices or physical discomforts commended one to God. I must disclaim all such lofty motives. I have always believed that the Good Samaritan went across the road to the wounded man just because he wanted to. I do not believe that he felt any sacrifice or fear in the matter. There is everything about such a venture as sailing to Labrador to attract my type of mind, and making preparations for the long voyage was an unmitigated delight.

The good ship Albert, which I selected, was ketch-rigged — much like a yawl, but more comfortable for lying-to in heavy weather, the sail area being more evenly distributed. As her freeboard was only three feet, we replaced her wooden hatches, which were large for lowering patients, by smaller iron ones; and also sheathed her forward along the waterline with greenheart to protect her planking in ice. For running in high seas we put a large squaresail forward, tripping the yard along the foremast, much like a spinnaker boom. Having a screw steering-gear which took two men to handle quickly enough when she yawed and threatened to jibe in a big swell, this proved very useful.

It was not until the spring of 1892 that we were ready to start. We had secured a master with a certificate, for, though I was myself a master mariner and my mate had been in charge of our vessel in the North Sea for many years, we had neither of us been across the Atlantic before.

The skipper was a Cornishman and a martinet on discipline — an entirely new experience to a crew of North Sea fishermen.

Nothing was wanting when at last, in the second week of June, the tugboat let us go, and crowds of friends waved us good-bye from Yarmouth pier-head as we passed out with all our bunting flying. We had not intended to touch land again until it should rise out of the western horizon, but off the south coast of Ireland we met with heavy seas and head winds, so we ran into Crookhaven. Our old patients in that lonely corner were greatly interested in the new venture, and many were the good eggs and 'meals of greens' which were brought down to the ship as parting tokens. Indeed, we shrewdly guessed that our 'dry' principles alone robbed us of more than one 'drop o' potheen,' whose birth the light of the moon had witnessed.

Our ship was just the size of the famous Matthew, and we followed almost the exact footsteps of the great John Cabot, when just four hundred years before he had fared forth on his famous adventure.

Sir Ernest Shackleton in taking the chair for me at a lecture in London stated that the first English vessel which sailed to Newfoundland was called the Grenfell. It would be pleasant to think it was named in honour of my famous old forbear, Sir Richard Grenville, though the business worthy of the steel of gentlemen of his day was chiefly 'splitting weazands.' In one letter upon which he ventured he achieved three different ways of spelling his own name. They left even calligraphy 'to hireling varlets and to shaveling priests.'

As we were not fortunate in encountering fair winds, it was not until the twelfth day that we saw our first iceberg, almost running into it in a heavy fog. The fall in the temperature of the sea surface had warned us that we were in the cold current, and three or four days of dense fog emphasized the fact. Suddenly on the seventeenth day the fog lifted, and a high evergreen-crowned coastline greeted our delighted eyes. A lofty lighthouse on a rocky headland enabled us almost immediately to discover our exact position. We were just a little north of St. John's Harbour, which, being my first landfall across the Atlantic, impressed me as a source for satisfaction. What was our surprise as we approached the high cliffs which guard the entrance to see dense columns of smoke arising, and to feel the offshore wind grow hotter and hotter as the pilot

tug towed us between the headlands. For the third time in its
history the whole city of St. John's was in flames.

The heat was fierce when we at last anchored; and had the
height of the blaze not passed, we should certainly have been
glad to seek again the company of our icy friends outside.
Some ships had even been burned at their anchors. We could
count thirteen raging fires in various parts of the city, which
looked like one vast funeral pyre. Only the brick chimneys of
the houses remained standing blackened and charred. Smoke
and occasional flame would burst out here and there, as the
fickle eddies of wind whirled around as if in sport over the
scene of man's discomfitures. On the hillside stood a solitary
house quite unharmed, seeming to mock the still smoulder-
ing wreck of the beautiful stone cathedral just beside it.
Among the ruins in this valley of desolation little groups of
men darted hither and thither, resembling nothing so much as
tiny black imps revelling in a congenial environment. I hope
never again to see a sight that suggested Gehenna even to a
less active imagination than Dante's.

The cheerfulness of the town was amazing. Scarcely a
'peep' or 'squeal' did we hear, and not a single diatribe
against the authorities. All had suffered together. Nor was it
due to anyone's fault. True, the town water-supply had been
temporarily out of commission, some stranger was said to have
been smoking in the hayloft, Providence had not specially
intervened to save property, and hence this result. It was a
city of hope, not of despair, and to our amazement they were
able to show most kindly interest in problems such as ours,
which seemed so remote at the moment.

I had expected to spend the greater part of our time cruising among the fishing schooners out of sight of land on the
big Banks, as we did in the North Sea, but I was advised
that, chiefly owing to fog, each vessel worked separately and
brought its own catch to market. It would, therefore, be a
much more profitable outlay of time if we were to follow the
large fleet of over a thousand schooners, carrying some thirty
thousand fishermen, women and children, which had just
sailed North for the summer fishery along the Coast of
Labrador. Naturally a good deal of delay occurred owing to
the unusual congestion of business which needed immediate

attention, and the unfortunate temporary lack of facilities; but we got under way at last, and sailing 'down North' for some four hundred miles well outside the land, eventually we ran in on a parallel and made the Labrador Coast on the fourth of August.

Forty years have passed away since that day, and a thousand more important affairs which have occurred in the mean time have faded from my memory; but still its events stand out clear and sharp. Round Hill Island, covered with green verdure, so wonderful a landmark from the sea, its peaks capped with the fleecy mist of early morning, rose in a setting of the purest azure blue. For the first time I saw its ruddy cliffs, their ledges picked out with the homes of a myriad birds. Its feet were bathed in the dark, rich green of the Atlantic waters, edged by the line of white breakers, where the gigantic swell lazily hurled immeasurable mountains of water against its titanic bastions, evoking peals of sound like thunder from its cavernous recesses — a very riot of magnificence. It answers to the description of St. John's Island given by John Cabot as his first sight of the American continent. The great schools of whales, noisily slapping the calm surface of the sea with their huge tails as in an abandon of joy, dived and rose, and at times threw the whole of their mighty carcasses right out of water for a bath in the glorious morning sunshine. The shoals of fish everywhere breaching the water, and the silver streaks which flashed beneath our bows as we lazed along, suggested that the whole vast ocean was too small to hold its riches.

When we realized that practically no man had ever lived there, and few had even seen it, it seemed to overwhelm us, coming as we did from the crowded Island of our birth, where notices not to trespass haunted the dreams of the average man.

A serried rank of range upon range of hills, reaching north and south as far as the eye could see from the masthead, was rising above our horizon behind a very surfeit of islands, bewildering the minds of men accustomed to our English and North Sea coastlines.

At last we came to anchor among many schooners in a wonderful natural harbour called Domino Run, which in

turn would answer to the harbour into which Cabot sailed
and anchored. The distance of three hundred leagues from
Cape Farewell which he had logged corresponds much more
nearly, if we add the drift of the polar current, than does Gull
Island off Newfoundland and the present Cape St. John which
some claim to have been his landfall.

Had we been painted scarlet and flown the Black Jack instead of the Red Ensign, we could not have attracted more
attention. Flags of greeting were run up to all mastheads, and
boats from all sides were soon aboard inquiring what the
strange phenomenon meant. Our object explained, we soon
had calls for a doctor. Indeed, it has been the experience of
almost every visitor to the coast from that day to this that he
is expected to have a knowledge of medicine.

Late in the evening, when the rush of visitors was largely
over, I noticed a miserable bunch of boards, serving as a boat,
with only a dab of tar along its seams, lying motionless a little
way from us. In it, sitting silent, was a half-clad, brown-
haired, brown-faced figure. After long hesitation, during which
time I had been watching him from the rail, he suddenly asked:

'Be you a real doctor?'

'That's what I call myself,' I replied.

'Us hasn't got no money,' he fenced, 'but there's a very
sick man ashore, if so be you'd come and see him.'

He led me to a tiny sod-covered hovel, compared with which
the Irish cabins were palaces. It had one window of odd fragments of glass. The floor was of pebbles from the beach; the
earth walls were damp and chilly. There were half a dozen
rude wooden bunks built in tiers around the single room. A
group of some six neglected children, frightened by our arrival,
were huddled together in one corner. A very sick man was
coughing his soul out in the darkness of a lower bunk, while
a pitiably covered woman gave him cold water to sip out of
a spoon. There was no furniture except a small stove with an
iron pipe leading through a hole in the roof.

My heart sank as I thought of the little I could do for the
sufferer in such surroundings. He had pneumonia, a high
fever, and was probably tubercular. The thought of our attractive little hospital on board at once rose to my mind; but
how could one sail away with this husband and father, prob-

ably never to bring him back? Advice, medicine, a few packages of food were only temporizing. The poor mother could never nurse him and tend the family. Furthermore, their earning season, 'while the fish were in,' was slipping away. To pray for the man, and with the family, was easy, but scarcely satisfying. A hospital with a trained nurse was the only chance for this bread-winner, and neither was available.

I called in, a couple of months later, as we came South before the approach of winter. Snow was already on the ground. The man was dead and buried; there was no provision whatever for the family, who were destitute, except for the hollow mockery of a widow's grant of twenty dollars a year from the Government. This, moreover, had to be taken up in goods at a truck store at their prices, less debts *if* she owed any.

Among the nine hundred patients recorded on that long-ago voyage, some stand out for their peculiar pathos and utter helplessness. In firing a cannon to salute the arrival of the Moravian Mission ship, the gun of a poor Eskimo had exploded prematurely, blowing off both the man's arms below the elbows. He had been lying on his back for a fortnight. The pathetic stumps were covered only with far from sterile rags dipped in cold water. We remained some days, and did all we could for him; but he too joined the great host that is forever 'going west,' for want of what the world fails to give them.

The successful removal of a molar, which has given torture for weeks, in a dentistless country, gains one as much gratitude as the amputation of a limb. One mere boy came to me with necrosis of one side of his entire lower jaw, due to nothing but neglected toothache. It had to be dug out from the new covering of bone which had grown up all around it. The whimsical expression of his lopsided face still haunts me.

Deformities went untreated. The crippled and blind halted through life, victims of what 'the blessed Lord saw best for them.' The torture of an ingrowing toe-nail, which could be relieved in a few minutes, had incapacitated one poor father for years. Tuberculosis and rickets went unchecked. Preventable poverty was the efficient handmaid of these two latter diseases.

There was also endless social work to be done. Education

in every one of its branches — especially public health — was almost non-existent, as were many simple social amenities which might have been so easily accorded.

At one harbour a woman with five children asked me as a magistrate if I could marry her to her husband. They had never been together when a parson happened along, and they were then living in a lonely cove three miles away. This seemed a genuine case of distress; and as it happened that a parson was taking a passage with us, we sent two of our crew over in a boat to round up the groom. Apparently he was not at all anxious; but being a very small man and she a large woman, he discreetly acquiesced. The wedding was held on board our ship, everyone entering into the spirit of the unusual occasion. The main hold was crammed with guests, the ship's bell was rung, and flags flown, guns fired, and at night distress rockets were sent up, and such a meal served as that five had never dreamed of.

Obviously the Coast offered work for us that would not be done unless we did it. Here was real need along any and every line, in a section of our own Empire and where the people embodied all our best sea traditions. They exhibited many of the attractive characteristics, which, even when buried beneath habits and customs the outcome of their environment, always endear men of the sea to the genuine Anglo-Saxon. They were uncomplaining, optimistic, splendidly resourceful, cheerful and generous — and after all, soap and water only make the outside of the platter clean.

We had greatly enjoyed the adventure *qua* adventure. Mysterious fjords which wound out of sight into the fastnesses of unknown mountains, and which were entirely uncharted, fairly shouted an invitation to enter and discover what was round the next corner. Islands by the hundred, hitherto never placed on any map, challenged one's hydrographic skill. Families of strange birds, which came swinging seaward as the season advanced, suggested a virgin field for hunting. Berries and flowering plants, as excellent as they were unfamiliar, appealed for exploration. Great boulders perched on perilous peaks, torn and twisted strata, with here and there raised beaches and great outcrops of black traprock piercing through red granite cliffs in giant vertical seams — all piqued one's curiosity to know the geological story of this unknown land. Some stone arrowheads and knives, brought to me by a fisherman, together with the memories that the Norse Vikings and their competitors on the scroll of discovery who made their first landfall on this the nearest section of the American coast to Europe, excited one's curiosity to know more of these shores. The dense growth of evergreen trees abounding in every river valley and the exquisite streams with trout and salmon and seals attracted one whose familiarity with sport and forests was inseparably connected with notices to trespassers, and flatly contradicted the impression left by the predatory explorers of Columbus's age.

It was a genuine surprise to me one morning to find ice on deck, and a scale of sparkling crystals most beautifully picking out the waterline of our little craft. It was only then that I realized that October had come. We could not stay, even though we felt the urgent call to remain. So 'Heigho for the south'ard,' and a visit to St. John's to try and arouse interest in the new-discovered problems, before we should once more let go our stern-lines and be bowling homeward before the fall nor'westers to dear old England.

Home-going craft had carried our story before us to the capital. The Board of Trade had highly praised our effort. The papers had written of the new phenomenon; the politicians had not refrained from commendation. His Excellency the Governor made our path easy by calling a meeting in Government House and passing a more than appreciative resolution, suggesting our directors be invited to 'repeat the dose.'

The voyage home was uneventful except that I was nearly left behind in mid-Atlantic. While playing cricket on deck, our last ball went over the side, and I after it, shouting to the helmsman to tack back. This he did. But I failed to cut him off the first time, as he got a bit rattled. However, we rescued the ball.

Our report to the Council in London, followed by the resolution sent by the Newfoundland Committee, was followed by a repetition of the venture on a larger scale the following spring, when, with two young doctors and two nurses, we again set out for Labrador. Meanwhile, we had chosen two islands two hundred miles apart for cottage hospitals, one at Battle Harbour, on the north side of the Straits of Belle Isle, and the other at Indian Harbour, out in the Atlantic at the mouth of the great Hamilton Inlet. Both places were the centres of large fisheries, and were the 'bring-ups' for number-less schooners of the Labrador fleet on their way North and South. The first, a building already half-finished, was donated by a local fishery firm of the name of Baine, Johnston and Company. The second building, assembled at St. John's, was shipped by the donors, who were the owners of the Indian Harbour fishery, Job Brothers and Company. Owing to difficulties in landing, this building was not completed and ready for use until the following year, so Dr. Elliot Curwen took charge of the hospital ship Albert, and I cruised as far north as Okkak (lat. 57°) in the Princess May, a midget steam launch, eight feet wide, with a cook and an engineer. As there was no coal obtainable in the North, we used wood, and her fire-box being small the amount of cutting entailed left per-manent impressions on our biceps.

A friend from Ireland had presented this little boat, which I found 'laying-up' on the Chester Race-Course, near our home by the Sands of Dee. My brother repaired her and steamed her through the canal into the Mersey, where, some-what to our humiliation, she had been slung up onto the deck of an Allan liner for her trans-Atlantic passage as if she were nothing but an extra handbag. Nor was our pride restored when on her arrival in St. John's it was found that her funnel was missing among the 'passengers' baggage' in the hold! The close of the voyage proved a fitting corollary. In crossing the Straits of Belle Isle, being the last boat to leave the Labrador for the winter, we ran short of fuel and had to burn our cabin-top to make the Newfoundland Coast, having also lost our compass overboard. Here we delayed repairing and refitting so long that the authorities in St. John's became alarmed and kindly despatched their mail steamer in search of us. I still remember my astonishment, when, on boarding the steamer, the skipper, a very tender-hearted fellow, threw both arms around me with a mighty hug and exclaimed, 'Thank God, we all thought you were gone. A schooner picked up your flagpole at sea.' Poor fellow, only a year or two later he perished with his large steamer, while I still rove this rugged coast forty years later.

That summer we visited the then five stations of the Moravian Brethren, which Society for one hundred and fifty years had been working among the Eskimos of the Labrador. It would be scarcely modest for me to protest that they were any the worse for never having had a doctor among them, but I naturally thought so, especially as I found among the Eskimos a great deal of tuberculosis and much eye trouble.

Around the Moravian Mission stations wooden houses had largely replaced the former 'tubiks' or skin tents, which had been moved as occasion required and so provided for sanitation. These wooden huts were undrained, dark and dirty. No water-supply was provided, and the spaces between the houses were simply indescribable garbage heaps, presided over by innumerable dogs. The average life was very short and infant mortality high. The features of the native life which appealed most to us were the universal optimism, the laughing good-nature and contentment and the Sunday cleanliness of the entire congregation which swarmed into the chapel service, a welcome respite from the perennial dirt of the week-days. Moreover, nearly all had been taught to read and write in Eskimo, though there is no literature in that language to read except the Bible and a hymn-book that have been translated by the Moravian Brethren. At that time a strict policy of teaching no English had been adopted. Words lacking in the language, like 'God,' 'love,' etc., were substituted by German words. Nearly every Eskimo counted, 'ein, zwei, drei.' In one of my lectures, on returning to England, I mentioned that, as the Eskimos had never seen a lamb or a sheep either alive or in a picture, the Moravians, in order to offer them an intelligible and appealing simile, had most wisely substituted the 'kotik,' or white seal, for the phrase 'the Lamb of God.' One old lady in my audience must have felt that the good Brethren were tampering unjustifiably with Holy Writ, for the following summer, from the barrels of clothing sent out to the Labrador, was extracted a dirty, distorted, and much-mangled and wholly sorry-looking woolly toy lamb. Its *raison d'être* was a mystery until we read the legend carefully pinned to one dislocated leg, 'Sent in order that the heathen may know better.'

ESKIMOS AT A MORAVIAN STATION

The Eskimo love for music and ability to do part-playing and singing greatly impressed us, and we spent many evenings enjoying their brass bands and their Easter and Christmas carols. We made some records of these on our Edison phonograph, and they were overpowered with joy when they heard their own voices coming back to them from the machine. The magic lantern also proved exceedingly popular. We were able to show some hastily made lantern slides of themselves, when several tried to feel themselves on the screen. The following season, in giving them some lantern views, we chanced to show a slide of an old Eskimo woman who had died during the winter. The subsequent commotion caused among the little people was unintelligible to us until one of the Moravian Brethren explained that they thought her spirit had taken visible form and returned to her old haunts. The simplicity of mind was again illustrated, when years later one of our survey planes came right down by a group of them. The first question asked, when they recovered speech, was, 'Did you see Christ up there?'

One August evening, I happened to be in the gardens at Nain, when the thermometer stood only a little above freezing. A troop of Eskimo women came out to cover up the potatoes. Every row of potatoes is covered with arched sticks and long strips of canvas along them. A huge roll of sacking is kept near each row and the whole is drawn over and the potatoes are tucked in bed for the night. I could not resist the temptation to lift the bedclothes and shake hands and say good-night to one of the nearest plants, whereat the merry little people went off into convulsions of laughter.

When one reads the story of the Moravian Brethren, however, everyone must be intensely grateful to them for the great amount of good they have accomplished for the Eskimos.

One outstanding feature everywhere impressed an Englishman in Labrador — that is, the absolute necessity for some standard medium of exchange. Till one has seen the truck system at work, its evil effects in enslaving and demoralizing the poor are impossible to realize. All the length and breadth of the coast, the poorer people would show me their 'settling up,' if ever they got one, always showing that they lived and died in debt to their merchant. They never knew the inde-

pendence of a dollar in their pockets and the consequent incentive to and value of thrift. It was incredible to me that
large trading concerns would not pay in cash for valuable
furs, and that so many dealers in the necessities of life should
be still able to hold free men in economic bondage.

This fact was first impressed upon me in an odd way. Early
in the summer a man had come aboard the hospital ship with
a bear skin and a few other furs to sell. We had not only been
delighted with the chance to buy them, but had spread them
all around the cabin and taken a picture of him in the middle.

Later in the season, while showing my photograph album to
a trader, he had suddenly remarked, 'Why, what's B —— doing here?'

'Selling me some beautiful furs,' I replied.

'Oh! was he?' said the man. 'I'll make him sing for selling
the furs for which I supplied him.'

It was no salve to his fretfulness when I assured him that
I had paid in good English gold, and that his 'dealer' would be
as honest with the money as the system had made him. The
trader well knew that the truck system creates slippery,
tricky men; and the fishermen not infrequently retaliate on
the merchant, making the most of his few opportunities to
outwit him.

A few years later a man brought a silver-fox skin aboard my
ship, just such a one as I had been requested by an English
lady to secure for her. As fulfilling such a request would involve me in hostilities (which, however, I do not think were
useless), I asked the man, who was wretchedly poor, if he owed
the skin to the trader.

'I am in debt,' he replied, 'but they will allow me only eight
dollars off my account for this skin, and I want to buy some
food.'

'Very well,' I answered. 'If you will promise to go at once
and pay eight dollars off your debt, I will give you eight gold
sovereigns for this skin.'

To this he agreed, and faithfully carried out the agreement
— while the English lady scored a bargain, and I a very black
mark in the books of my friend the trader, until he saw the
humour of it.

On another occasion my little steamer had temporarily

broken down and to save time I had journeyed on in the jolly-boat, leaving the cook to steer the vessel after me. I wanted to visit a very poor family, one of whose eight children I had taken to hospital for bone tuberculosis the previous year. As the steamer had not come along by night, I had to sleep in the tiny one-roomed shack which served as his home. True, since it stood on the edge of the forest, there was little excuse that it was not larger; but the father, a most excellent, honest, and faithful worker, was obviously discouraged. He had not nearly enough food for his family, clothing was even more at a discount, tools with which to work were almost as lacking as in a cave man's dwelling — the whole family was going to pieces from sheer discouragement. The previous winter on the opposite bank of the same river, called Big River, a neighbour had in desperation sent his wife and eldest boy out of the house, killed his young family, and then shot himself.

When night came, five of the children huddled together for warmth in one bed, and the parents and the rest of the family in the other. I spent the night sleeping on the floor near the door in my sleeping-bag, with my nose glued to the crack to get a breath of God's cold air. The window was nailed down, as not a blanket did the house possess. When I asked, a little hurt, where were a blanket or two which we had sent last year, the mother somewhat indignantly pointed to various trousers and coats, which betrayed their final resting-place, and remarked, 'If you'se had five lads all trying to get under one covering to oncet, you'd soon know what would happen to that blanket.'

Early in the morning I made a boiling of cocoa and took the two elder boys out for a seal hunt while waiting for my little steamer. I was just in time to see one boy carefully upset his mug of cocoa, when he thought I was not looking, and replace it with cold spring water. 'I 'lows I'se not accustomed to no sweetness' was his simple explanation. It was raw and damp as we rowed into the estuary at sunrise in search of the seals. I was chilly even in a well-lined leather coat. But the two shock-headed boys, clad in ancient cotton shirts, and with what had once been cotton overall jackets, were as jolly as crickets, and apparently almost unduly warm. The Labrador has taught me one truth, which as a physician I never forget, which is that coddling is the terrible menace of civilization, and 'to endure hardness' is the best preparation for a 'good soldier.' On leaving, I promised to send to those boys, whose contentment and cheerfulness greatly endeared them to me, a dozen good fox traps in order to give them a chance for the coming winter. Such a gift as those old iron rat traps seemed in their eyes!! When at last they arrived, and were really 'their own' possessions, no prince could have been prouder than they. The next summer as I steamed North we called in at this house. The same famine in the land seemed to prevail, the same lack of apparently everything which I should have wanted. But the old infectious smile was still presented with an almost religious ceremonial, and my friend produced from his box a real silver-fox skin. 'I kep' it for you'se, Doctor,' he said, 'though us hadn't ne'er a bite in t'house. I know'd you'd do better'n we with he.'

I promised to try, and on my way called in at some northern islands where my friend, Captain Bartlett, father of the celebrated 'Captain Bob' of North Pole fame, carried on a summer trade and fishery. He himself was a great seal and cod fisherman, and a man known for his generous sympathy for others.

'Do your best for me, Captain Will,' I said, as I handed over the skin — and on coming South I found a complete winter diet laid out for me to take to that little house. It was a veritable full load for the small carrying capacity of my little craft.

When we arrived at the house on the promontory, however, it was locked up and the family gone. They were off fishing on the outer islands, so all we could do was to break in the door, pile up the things inside, and bar it up again, affixing a notice warning off bears, dogs, and all poachers, and advising Dick that it was the price of his pelt. In the note we also told him to put all the fur he caught the following winter in a barrel and 'sit on it' till we came along, if he wanted a chance to get ahead. This he did almost literally. We ourselves took his barrel to the nearest cash buyer, and ordered for him goods in St. John's for cash to the full amount realized. The fur brought more than his needs, and he was able to help out neighbours by reselling at cash prices. This he did till the day of his death, when he left me, as his executor, a couple of hundred good dollars in cash to divide among his children, and a record of never having again been in want.

It was experiments like this which led me in later years to start the small coöperative distributive stores, in spite of the knowledge of the opposition and criticism it would involve on the Coast. Numerous instances show that as ever these difficulties are never caused by one side only. Many splendid instances of unselfish generosity, as well as some of the reverse, proved that no system alone can cure all ills; it is the personalities behind that count always in the long run.

CHAPTER VII

LABRADOR: THE COUNTRY AND THE PEOPLE

BEFORE A.D. 1000, Norsemen, sailing past a bleak coastline, named the stretches 'Wonderstrands,' because 'they took so long to sail by.' To these early voyagers, as to the explorers who followed in the subsequent centuries, Labrador looked stern and forbidding, and one and all these explorers returned home to report a 'land covered with snow and ice, and unfit for human habitation.' An early Spanish cartographer, when he drew a map of the western world, wrote across a part of it: 'Labrador was discovered by the English. There is nothing in it of any value.'

In the sixteenth century, Basque and Portuguese fishermen were attracted to the shores of Labrador by the wealth of its fisheries and its whales. From that time onward, these industries have been her chief justification for existence. In 1669, a charter was granted 'to the Governor and Company of Adventurers trading from England into Hudson's Bay.'

Later, various trading-posts were established along the Coast, doing business with the Indians who came out from the interior to barter their furs for ammunition and food. It was not until the first half of the nineteenth century that a few permanent fishing villages were allowed to spring up along the Coast so that the hardy Anglo-Saxon inhabitants could pursue their calling during the short months of open water and then move up the long bays for the winter season and the fur-trapping.

Nobody knew who owned Labrador when first we saw it forty years ago, and nobody cared. It had been tossed to and fro between England, America, Canada, Newfoundland, and France. Newfoundland offered its rights to Canada in 1890 for nine million dollars.

When conveyances were made, such maps as existed were not consulted apparently, and no one even cared enough to worry where the boundaries were. One day an impassioned preacher, while praying for Labrador, landed himself in difficulties. He began: 'Thou knowest, O Lord, this great and needy land, bounded on the east by the North Atlantic Ocean, on the south by the mighty St. Lawrence River, on the north by the frigid water of Hudson's Bay, and on the west by —— O Lord, Thou knowest!'

When, later on, light began to be thrown upon Labrador, Newfoundland and Canada spent a couple of million dollars in fighting as to who should own it and as to where was the exact boundary line. The decision of 1927 hung on the original treaty, which was written in the words of the King James Version of the Bible. It was argued that when that describes Christ as walking in 'the coasts of Tyre and Sidon,' it did not mean that He confined Himself to the three-mile limit. Newfoundland, therefore, to her delight and amazement was given, as a strict legal interpretation of the actual words, though nothing of the kind was intended, 'all land drained by the rivers running out on the east coast.' As the Hamilton River runs in at least four hundred miles, cutting through the height of land, this decision involved taking from Canada a serious slice of the hinterland of Quebec. Newfoundland, having thus won far more than she had hoped for, and having formerly offered her rights to Canada for nine million dollars, promptly in 1932 offered them again, for one hundred and ten million dollars.

Newfoundland is an autonomous government, having its own Governor sent out from England, a Prime Minister, and Houses of Parliament in the city of St. John's. Instead of being a Province of Canada, as is often supposed, it stands in the same relationship to England as does the great Dominion herself, with an entire population of less number than one moderate town. Labrador being owned by Newfoundland, legally the Labradormen are Newfoundlanders, though they have no representation in the Newfoundland Government. At Blanc Sablon, on the north coast in the Straits of Belle Isle, the Canadian Labrador begins, so far as the coastline is concerned.

The original natives of the Labrador were Eskimos and bands of roving Indians. The Eskimos, one of the most interesting of primitive races, have still a foothold in the North.

The Montagnais Indians roam the interior. They are a

branch of the ancient Algonquin race who held North America as far west as the Rockies. They are the hereditary foes of the Eskimos, whole settlements of whom they have more than once exterminated. Gradually, with the influx of white settlers from Devon and Dorset, from Scotland and France, the 'Innuits,' as the Eskimos call themselves, were driven farther and farther north. There are less than a thousand on the North Coast of Labrador today. Epidemic diseases and contact with white men have been the cause. The remainder of the inhabitants of the country are white men of our own blood and religion — men of the sea, dear to the Anglo-Saxon heart.

There is a sharp demarcation between southern Newfoundland and the long finger of land jutting northward, which at Cape Bauld splits the polar current so that the shores of the narrow peninsula are continuously bathed in icy waters. That north end of the Island is swept by biting winds, and often for days on end is enveloped in a chilly and dripping blanket of fog. The climate at the tip of the northward-pointing finger is more severe than on the Labrador side of the Straits. A friend of mine, for twenty-seven years factor of the Hudson's Bay Company in Hudson Bay Straits, told us that even in the extreme north of Labrador he never really knew what cold was until he underwent the penetrating experience of a winter at St. Anthony. The Lapp reindeer herders whom we brought over from Lapland, a country lying well north of the Arctic Circle, after spending a winter near St. Anthony, told me that they had never felt anything like that kind of cold. Moreover, the hospital at St. Anthony is farther north and farther east than two of our stations on the Labrador side of the Straits of Belle Isle.

The latitude of Newfoundland and Labrador corresponds to that of England and Scotland. Battle Harbour, Labrador, at the southernmost tip of the country, is almost on a parallel with London, and is the nearest point of North America to the Irish Coast, being almost exactly halfway between New York and England; while the North Cape of Scotland and Cape Chidley are practically in the same parallel of latitude. Thus Labrador and North Newfoundland enjoy the same length of day and night as do England and Scotland. The difference in climate of these two neighbours is accounted for by the fact that, whereas the Gulf Stream bathes the English coast, Labrador perpetually stands with its feet chilled in the icy waters of the polar current.

The dominant industry of the whole colony is its fisheries — the ever-recurrent pursuit of the cod, salmon, herring, halibut, and whale in summer, and the seal fishery in the month of March. It is increasingly difficult to estimate the importance, not merely to the British Empire, but to the entire world, of the invaluable food-supply procured by our hardy fishermen. Its value as a nursery for seamen was considered its chief value in sailing-craft days.

It was among these white fishermen that I came out to work primarily, the floating population which every summer, some twenty thousand strong, visits the coasts of Labrador. It was later that we included the resident settlers of the Labrador and North Newfoundland coasts.

The coast of Labrador is international, in that the British, Canadian, Newfoundland, and American fishermen have equal fishing rights there. This very unusual circumstance is explained by the fact that, previous to the war of the Revolution, the Governor of Boston was Governor of Labrador, and the fishermen among the American colonists pursued their calling all along this coast. Subsequent to the war, the Americans pointed out that as they had not lost the issue they hoped that their privileges might continue unaltered. This was agreed upon, and today they have equal rights in the use of the territorial waters for the hauling of bait and of nets.

The conditions prevailing among some of the people at the north end of Newfoundland and of Labrador itself should not be confused with those of their neighbours to the southward. Chronic poverty is, however, far from being universally prevalent in the northern district. Some of the fishermen lead a comfortable, happy, and prosperous life; but my old diaries, as well as my present observations, furnish all too many instances in which families exist well within the danger-line of poverty, ignorance, and starvation. Hence, our work.

Since those old diaries were written, the inevitable results of the Great War and of the world's political selfishness have nearly brought our whole Colony into the hands of receivers;

while the products of the people's main industries — fish, fur, fish oils and whale oils, and timber have become unmarketable at remunerative prices.   Even the great Hudson's Bay Company and our merchants and banks have suffered terribly, and in the wake of this great depression many of our families are facing nakedness and starvation — though with a courage that with these men of the sea is always best at the times when their backs are to the wall.   In our judgment none of this was necessary. We know perfectly well that the country can carry the people in perfect physical comfort.   It is not God's end that is wrong — it has been ours. Our form of government has failed — wisdom to select capable men has not always been forthcoming. Temptation has proved too great. It was recorded five thousand years ago in the Bible, 'My people love to have it so.'

The privations which the inhabitants of the French or Treaty shore and of Labrador have had to undergo, and their isolation from so many of the benefits of civilization, have had varying effects on the residents of the Coast.   The Labrador fishermen of today find their counterpart in the people of the Southern mountains of the United States. They speak the same Elizabethan English, overlaid, to be sure, with a vernacular of the sea. They were caught behind the Arctic waters of the North, an eddy of civilization, just as the Southern mountaineers were cut off by their hilly fastnesses from the onward march of what we so glibly style 'progress.' They are reactionary in matters of religion and education; and their very 'speech betrays them,' belonging as do so many of their expressions to the days when the Pilgrims went up to Canterbury, or when a certain tinker wrote of another and more distant pilgrimage to the City of Zion.

The people are, naturally, Christians of a devout and simple faith. Their superstitions are of the date and brand when witches and hobgoblins and charms and amulets were generally accepted beliefs. But they are not very different from some which we at times suddenly find that we ourselves do not altogether discredit. Let's touch wood, shall we?

One is surprised, however, to see a fox's or a wolf's head suspended by a cord from the ceiling, and to learn that it

A LONELY SETTLER

A LABRADOR FISHERMAN'S HOME

will always twist the way from which the wind is going to blow. One man had a barometer of this kind hanging from his roof, and explained that the peculiar fact was due to the nature of the animals, which in life 'always went to windward of others'; but if you had a seal's head similarly suspended, it would turn from the wind, owing to the timid character of that creature.

'I never gets sea boils,' one old sea-dog told me the other day.

'How is that?' I asked.

'Oh! I always cuts my nails on a Monday, and then I burns 'em.' The potency of this charm lies in the unusualness of it.

A man came to me once to cure what he firmly believed was a balsam on his baby's nose. The birthmark to him resembled that tree. 'Her shouldn't 'a' gone into t'Bay for that there. Them balsams ain't Labradore trees proper, I says.'

More than once I heard currency, if not credence, given to the statement that the reason why the bull's-eye was so hard to hit in one of our running-deer rifle matches was that we had previously charmed the target. If a woman sees a hare without cutting out and keeping a portion of the dress she is then wearing, her child will be born with a harelip.

When stripping a patient for examination, I noticed that he removed from his neck what appeared to be a very large scapular. I asked him what it could be. It was a haddock's fin-bone — a charm against rheumatism. The peculiarity of the fin consists in the fact that the fish must be taken from the water and the fin cut out before the animal touches anything whatever, especially the boat. Anyone who has seen a trawl hauled knows how difficult a task this would be, with the jumping, squirming fish to cope with, and a host of naked hooks tossing around.

Protestant and Catholic alike often sew up bits of paper, with prayers written on them, in little sacks that are worn around the neck as an amulet; and green worsted tied around the wrist is believed by many to be a never-failing cure for hemorrhage. Friends were at first surprised when I began commending the brass chains worn round the wrist 'against Water Pups,' which are sea boils. The chains keep the dirty oilskin sleeve from touching and poisoning the skin.

We were much surprised one day to notice a family moving their house in the middle of the fishing season, especially when we learned the reason. It was that a spirit had appropriated their dwelling by night, so they moved by day, when the spirit was asleep, to another spot. More than once I have been called in to the case of a baby suffering from ophthalmia, only when blowing sugar in its eyes had failed to cure it. Afterwards one wanted the lovely name 'Ophthalmia' for the next baby.

A colleague of mine was visiting on his winter rounds in a delightful village some forty miles south of St. Anthony Hospital. The 'swiles' (seals) had 'stuck in,' and all hands were out on the ice, eager to capture their share of these valuable animals. But snow-blindness had attacked the men and rendered them utterly unable to profit by their good fortune. The doctor's clinic was long and busy that night. The following morning he was amazed to see many of his erstwhile patients wending their way seawards, each with one eye only treated by his prescription. The other (for safety's sake) was being doctored after the long-accepted methods of the village — tansy poultices and sugar being the favourites. The consensus of opinion obviously was that the risk was too great to venture both eyes at once on the doubtful altar of modern medicine.

On the contrary, I could wish all clergy could enjoy the stimulus of the following: although there have been clergymen of the Church of England and Methodist denominations on the Coast for many years past — devoted and self-sacrificing men who have done most unselfish work — still, their visits must be infrequent. One of them told me in North Newfoundland that, one day as he happened to pass through a little village with his dog-team on his way South, the man of one house ran out and asked him to come in.

'Sorry, I have no time,' he replied.

'Well, just come in at the front door and out at the back, so we can say that a minister has been in the house,' the fisherman answered. Moreover, he meant it.

Every summer some twenty thousand fishermen travel down North in schooners as soon as ever the ice breaks sufficiently to allow them to get along. They are the 'Labrador fishermen,' and they come from South Newfoundland, from Nova Scotia, from Gloucester, and even Boston. Some Newfoundlanders take their families down and leave them in summer tilts on the land near the fishing grounds during the season. When fall comes, they pick them up again and start for their winter homes in the South, leaving only a few hundreds of scattered 'Liveyeres' in possession of the Labrador.

Even today, to the least fastidious, our conditions of travel leave much to be desired. The coastal steamers are packed far beyond their sleeping or sitting capacity. As the little ship noses her way into some picturesque harbour and blows a lusty warning of her approach, small boats are seen putting off from the shore and rowing or sculling toward her with most indecorous rapidity. Lean over the rail for a minute with me, and watch the freight being unloaded into one of these bobbing little craft. The hatch of the steamer is opened, a most unmusical winch commences operations — and a sewing machine emerges *de profundis*. This is swung giddily out over the sea by the crane and dropped on the thwarts of a waiting punt. One shudders to think of the probably fatal shock received by the vertebræ of that machine. One's sympathies, however, are almost immediately enlisted in the interest and fortunes of a young and voiceful pig, which, poised in the blue, unwillingly experiences for the moment the fate of the coffin of the Prophet. Great shouting ensues as a baby is carried down the ship's ladder and deposited in the rocking boat. A bag of beans, of the variety known as haricot, is the next candidate. A small hole has been torn in a corner of the burlap sack out of which trickles a white and ominous stream. The last article to join the galaxy is a tub of butter. By a slight mischance the tub has 'burst abroad,' and the butter, a golden and gleaming mass, with unexpected consideration, having escaped the ministrations of the winch, is passed from one pair of fishy hands to another, till it finds a resting-place by the side of the now quiescent pig.

The cheerful kindliness and capability of the captain, the crew, and the passengers, on whatever boat you may chance to travel, pervades the whole ship, and makes one forget any slight discomfort in a justifiable pride that as an Anglo-Saxon one can claim kinship to these 'Vikings of today.'

For the first vast improvement in these boats, everyone owes a big debt to Messrs. Bowring and family. Their S.S. Prospero was a very real missionary when they first ventured to send her 'Down North.'

The hospitality of the people is unstinted and beautiful. They will turn out of their beds at any time to make a stranger comfortable, and offer him their last crust into the bargain, without ever expecting or asking a penny of recompense. But here, as all the world over, the sublime and the ridiculous go hand in hand. On one of my dog trips the first winter which I spent at St. Anthony, the bench on which I slept was also the top of the box used for hens. This would have made little difference to me, but unfortunately it contained a youthful and vigorous rooster, which, mistaking the arrival of so many visitors for some strange herald of morning, proceeded every half-hour to salute it with a premature and misdirected zeal, utterly incompatible with repose just above his head. It was possible to reach through the bars and suggest better things to him; but owing to the perversity which exists in most things, one invariably captured a drowsy hen, while the more active offender eluded one with ease.

The number of cases of tuberculosis, anæmia, and dyspepsia, of beri-beri and scurvy, all largely attributable to poverty of diet, was in those days very great; and the relative poverty, even compared with that of the countries which I have been privileged to visit, was piteous. The solution of evolutionary problems does not, however, lie in removing a people from their environment, but in trying to adapt the environment and the people to one another.

A visit to one house on the French shore I shall not easily forget. A handsome lad of sixteen years had hip disease, and lay dying. The bed, the house, and everything in it were full of vermin, and the poor boy had not been washed since he took to bed three or four months before. With the help of a clergyman, who was travelling with me at the time, the lad was chloroformed and washed and his wounds dressed. We then burned the bedding. I learned by bitter experience not to trust that to anyone. We provided him with fresh garments and put him into a clean bed. The people's explanation was that he was in too much pain to be touched.

Having seen the gratitude in his face, we left what we could for him and pursued our way. Had he not been so far gone, we should have taken him to the hospital, but he could not possibly have then survived the journey.

Although then a diary often seemed an unnecessary expenditure of effort in an already overcrowded day, one now values the records of these early days of one's life on the Coast. In my notebook for 1895 I find the following:

'The desolation of Labrador at this time is easy to understand. No Newfoundlanders are left north of us; not a vessel in sight anywhere. The ground is all under snow, and everything caught over with ice except the sea. I must describe one house, for it seems a marvel that any man could live in it all winter, much less women and children. It is ten feet by twenty, one storey high, made of mud and boards, with half a partition to divide bedroom from the sitting-room kitchen. If one adds a small porch filled with dirty, half-starved dogs, and refuse of every kind, an ancient and dilapidated stove in the sitting part of the house, two wooden benches against the walls, and two boarded-up beds, one has a fairly accurate description of the furnishings. Inside are fourteen persons, sleeping there, at any rate for a night or two. The ordinary regular family of a man and wife and four girls is to be increased this winter by the man's brother, his wife, and four boys from twelve months to seven years of age. His brother has 'handy enough flour,' but no tea or molasses. The owner is looking after Newfoundland Fishing Rooms, for which he gets flour, tea, molasses, and firewood for the winter. The people assure me that one man, who was aboard the Strathcona last fall just as we were going South, starved to death, and many more were just able to hold out till spring. The man who died, they tell me, ate his only dog as his last resource.'

I sent one day a barrel of flour and some molasses to a poor widow with seven children at Stag Islands. She was starving even in summer. She was just eating fish, which she and her eldest girl, a pathetic half-fed little Anglo-Saxon, caught; and all were drinking water — no flour, no tea, nothing. Two winters before she and her eldest girl sawed up three thousand feet of planking to keep 'the wolf' from the other little ones.

The plucky girl managed the boat and fished in summer, drove the dogs and komatik and did all the shooting for which they could afford powder in winter. To let me better help such cases, I started a Discretionary Fund. They called for immediate help, an S O S no one with a human heart wants to resist. That fund will live as long as I do, and I pray God, long after I am gone on.

To those who claim that Labrador is a land of plenty, I would offer the following incident: At Holton on a certain Sunday morning the leader of the church services came aboard the hospital steamer and asked me for a Bible. Some sacrilegious pigs which had been brought down to fatten on the fish, driven to the verge of starvation by the scarcity of that article, had broken into the church illicitly one night, and had actually torn up and eaten the Bible. In reply to inquiry I gave it as my opinion that it would be no sin to eat the pork of the erring quadrupeds.

Once, when I was cruising on the far North Labrador Coast, I anchored between two desolate islands some distance out in the Atlantic, a locality which in those days was frequented by many fishing craft. My anchors were scarcely down when a boat from a small Welsh brigantine came aboard, and asked me to go at once and see a dying girl. She proved to be the only woman on the whole island among a host of men, and was servant in one of the tiny summer fishing huts, cooking and mending for the men, and helping with the fish when required. I found her in a rude bunk in a dark corner of the shack. She was eighteen, and even by the dim light of my lantern and in contrast with the sordid surroundings, I could see that she was very handsome. A brief examination convinced me that she was dying. The tender-hearted old captain, whose aid had been called in as the only man 'with a doctor's box,' and therefore felt to be better qualified to use it than others, was heart-broken. He had pronounced the case to be typhoid, to be dangerous and contagious, and had wisely ordered the fisherman, who was handling food for human consumption, to leave him to deal with the case alone. He confessed at once that he had limited his attentions to feeding her; and, though helpless for over a fortnight and at times unconscious, the patient had not once been washed or the bed changed. The result, even with my experience, appalled me. But while there is life in a young patient there is always hope, and we at once set to work on our Augean task. By the strangest coincidence it was an inky dark night outside, with a low fog hanging over the water, and the big trap boat, with a crew of some six men, among them the skipper's sons, had been missing since morning. The white-haired skipper had stayed home out of sympathy for his servant girl, and his mind was torn asunder by anxiety for the girl and his fear for his boys.

Finally, the old captain and I were through with the hardest part of our work. We had new bedding on the bed and the patient clean and sleeping quietly. Still the boat and its precious complement did not come. Every few minutes the skipper would go out and listen and stare into the darkness. The girl's heart suddenly failed, and, about midnight, she passed away. The captain and I decided that the best thing to do was to burn everything — and, in order to avoid publicity, to do it at once. So having laboriously carried it all out onto the edge of the cliff, we set a light to the pile, and quite unintentionally began sending out great streams of light into the darkness over the waters away down below us, and actually giving the long-awaited signal to the missing boat. Her crew worked their way through the fog to life and safety by means of the blazing, poor, discarded 'properties' of the soul preceding us to our last port also.

Although our work has lain almost entirely among the white population, still it has been our privilege occasionally to come in contact with the native races and to render them such services, medical or otherwise, as lay within our power. Our doctor at Harrington on the Canadian Labrador is incidentally also Medical Indian Agent of the Canadian Government.

Once, when my own boat was anchored in Davis Inlet, a band of roving Indians had come to the post for barter and supplies. Our steamer was a source of great interest to them. Our steam whistle they would gladly have purchased, after they had mastered their first fears. At night we showed them some distress rockets and some red and blue port flares. The way those Indians fled from the port flares was really amusing, and no one enjoyed it more than they did, for the shouting and laughter, after they had picked themselves out of the scuppers, where they had been rolling on top of one another, wakened the very hills with their echoes. Next morning one lonely-looking brave came on board, and explained to me by signs and grunts that during the entertainment a white counter, or Hudson's Bay dollar, had rolled out of the lining of his hat into our woodpile. An elaborate search failed to reveal its whereabouts, but, as there was no reason to doubt him, I decided to make up the loss to him out of our clothes-bag. You can trust his word absolutely. Fortunately, a gorgeous old purple rowing blazer came readily to hand, and with this and a woolen helmet both of which he put on at once, the poor fellow was more than satisfied. Indeed, on the wharf he was the envy of the whole band.

We had at the time, among the garments on board, three not exactly suited to the white settlers, so I told the agent to let the Indians have a rifle-shooting match for them. They were a fox-huntsman's red broadcloth tail-coat of a cousin of mine with all the glory of gilt buttons, a rather dilapidated red golf blazer, and a cavalryman's white 'Eton coat' with silver buttons and the coat-of-arms on. Words fail me to paint the elation of the winner of the fox-hunting coat; while the wearer of the cavalry mess jacket was not the least bit daunted by the fact that when he got it on he could hardly breathe. I must say that he wore it over a deerskin kossak, which is not the custom of cavalrymen, I am led to believe.

The coastline from Ramah to Cape Chidley is just under one hundred miles, and on it live a few scattered Eskimo hunters. It has been claimed that a larger race of Eskimos called 'Tunits,' to whom the present race were slaves, used to be on this section of the Coast. At Nakvak there are remains of old stone houses suggesting the possibility of truth in this. There have been among the Eskimos, two terrible epidemics of influenza. Like all primitive peoples, they had no immunity to the disease and the suffering and mortality were very high. It was a pathetic sight as the lighter received its load of rude coffins from the wharf, with all the kindly little people gathered to tow them to their last resting-place in the shallow sand at the end of the inlet. The first time they had to bury ten coffins in each grave. It seemed more the sequence of a battle than of a summer sickness in Labrador.

A few million years ago, which is comparatively recently for Labrador, some fresh writhing of Mother Earth's crust forced into the roots of the really ancient coastal mountain range of Labrador with incredible pressure vast quantities of new molten minerals, which thus had to cool down inside it. Since then the covering mountain has been worn off all except the stumps, and the intruder, called Gabbro, everywhere shows. In this odd way, the major part of the earth crust of the country is called Labradorite. When polished, it breaks up the sunlight and flashes back all the colours of the rainbow, especially the bright blues and purples. Recently, a number of guests at the Duke of Westminster's home were being shown a collection of small tables with semi-precious stone tops — such as jade. Each guest picked out the same table as the most beautiful, because it was 'alive.' The pieces, fitted to the centre in wedges, simply danced in the sunlight. The Duke had paid a thousand pounds for it. The table was Labradorite. Unfortunately, it is only in a few places that the marvellous arrangement of its crystals is just right for breaking up the sunlight. Many requests for specimens reached me, and, as it offered to return enough to feed an extra orphan or two, we despatched a crew of Princeton Wops North to procure a few barrels full. They were sent to an island near Nain, which a friend of mine had located, as affording the best and most generous supply.

Apparently the boys went off to the island, which is entirely out of the way of any visitors, without anyone knowing about their departure. They pulled the boat up on the beach, camped, and retired for the night. A big tide was blown up by the heavy wind during the night, and next morning to their horror they found that their boat had been carried away. There was no hope of escape whatever. There is no vegetation on that small island. The water is far too cold to swim to an adjoining island, where even then they would have been no better off. Death literally stared them in the face.

Nothing but a miracle could save them, but the miracle happened! When the boys awoke next morning, the wind had changed. The current had eddied. The boat — filled with water, it is true, but the boat — lay washed up on the shore of the one tiny beach of their island.

The flora and fauna of the country are so varied and exquisite that one wonders why the world of science has so largely passed us by. Not only the ethnologist and botanist, but the archæologist as well, can reap a harvest for his labours here. Many relics of a recent stone age still exist. I have had brought to me stone saucepans, lamps, knives, arrowheads, etc., taken from old graves. It is the Eskimo custom to entomb with the dead man every possession which he might want hereafter, the idea being that the spirit of the implement accompanies the man's spirit.

Years ago in Germany, when the Socialists were wearing beards and moustaches, all respectable people used to shave. Therefore, the Moravians, being Germans, insisted on the Eskimos shaving, as they did themselves. One result was that at one store a stock of razors accumulated, for the Eskimos have practically no hair to shave, and it was inhuman to practise the habit in the Arctic climate of Labrador. Some Eskimos had promised to bring me some stone cooking-pots if I would furnish something to put into the graves in their place. A batch of razors satisfied them to perfection. As I pass by, the thought of a group of old Eskimo warriors sitting on those graves trying to shave makes me wish my eyes might be opened to see them, as were Elisha's of old.

Relics of ancient whaling establishments, possibly early Basque, have been found in plenty at one village, while even today the trapper there needing a runner or shoe for his komatik can always hook up a whale's jaw or rib from the mud of the harbour. Relics of rovers of the sea, who sought shelter on this uncharted coast with its million islands, are still to be found. A friend of mine was one day looking from his boat into the deep, narrow channel in front of his house when he perceived some strange object in the mud. He raised it, and found a long brass cannon, which now stands on the rocks near his house.

It has long been known that Labrador possesses mineral deposits, which in the future may prove of great value, but difficulties of communication, transportation, and mining operations have left these sources of wealth practically untouched, even until today. It is the production of paper from wood pulp, the development of hydro-electric power, wireless, aeroplane communication, electrical prospecting which is bringing to the front this land, so rich in forests and water-power. We now know, both from the reports of exploring parties and from aerial surveys, that the hinterland of Labrador possesses huge preserves of timber, unlimited water-power from her tremendous falls, and, in addition, the potentiality of minerals indicated by the nature of her rock formation, it being the same as the Canadian Shield which only a little farther west has yielded the largest gold and silver, nickel and copper deposits in the world. The mighty Hamilton River pierces the heart of Labrador, and at Grand Falls takes a leap of three hundred and sixteen feet into the canyon below — a jump twice the height of far-famed Niagara. It is narrower than Niagara, but our experienced aeronaut flying over the falls said, 'These falls make Niagara look so shallow from above!'

It was a far cry from Labrador to 'civilization.' All the same, we already are being permitted to see on our northern coast the dawn of a new day; for just as Canada, that once useless 'Lady of the Snows,' has come to her own, just as Alaska, stigmatized but a short while past as 'Seward's Folly,' has claimed her place among the servants of man, so Labrador, a sleeping, chilly giant, is stirring and her forests already ring with the tools of surveyor and engineer.

With this new vision of provision for daily needs, the life of our hardy Anglo-Saxon fishermen of the Northland promises all the physical and material satisfaction which the labour of man's hands and the sweat of man's brow can afford. Meanwhile, the joy of personal achievement is infinitely increased by the challenge flung there to every talent any man possesses — a greater joy far than the manufactured pleasures with which so many vainly seek in civilization to pass away the short day of life.

CHAPTER VIII

THE QUEST OF THE LOAVES AND FISHES

THE end of the second year had come. It was time to return to England. Eagerly we looked forward to it. Money was badly needed for the new hospitals — they had scarcely any equipment. We all hated to go and ask for it. It was infinitely more sacrifice to two young doctors than all low temperatures, high seas, and hard work put together. Yet what difference is there, asking people to lend you a hand, or say, in war-time to lend you a gun, and lending you momentary help? Christ asked complete strangers to die for Him, because He knew what a lot more good there is in men than we believe. Anyhow, it was the more venturesome of the two courses. So my young Australian colleague and I decided to visit Canada and try to raise funds, as our problems were obviously assuming larger proportions than the Society in England felt they could finance. It was to be our own affair, and we had only a limited amount of money for the venture. Also, it was our first visit to Canada, and we knew nothing about it and no one in it. We carried credentials, however, from the Secretary of State and other reputable persons. If we had had experience as commercial travellers, this might have been child's play. But our education had been in an English school and university; and when finally we sat at breakfast at a Halifax hotel we felt exactly like two fish out of water.

Such success as we obtained subsequently I attribute largely to what then seemed to me my colleague's 'consecrated cheek.' He insisted that we should call on the most prominent persons at once, the Prime Minister, the General in charge of the garrison, the Presidents of the Board of Trade and the University, the Governor of the Province, and all the leading clergymen. There have been times when I have hesitated about getting my anchors for sea, when the barometer was falling, the wind in, and a fog-bank on the horizon, but even now, years after, I still recall my reluctance to face that ordeal. But, as it is generally, the obstacles were largely in one's own mind, and the kindness which we received left me entirely overwhelmed. Friends formed a regular committee to keep a couple of cots going in our hospital and to collect supplies; and then passed us on to Montreal with introductions and endorsements.

By the time we reached Montreal, our funds were getting low. But my friend insisted that we must engage first-class accommodations, even though we had learnt to love 'roughing it,' and even if it should prevent our travelling farther west. One result was that reporters insisted on interviewing him as to the purpose of an Australian coming to Montreal; and I was startled to see a long account, which he had jokingly given them, published in the morning papers, stating his purpose was to materialize the All-Red Line and arrange closer relations between Australia and Canada. According to his report my object was to inspect my ranch in Alberta. He woke me up next morning by bubbling with joy over the morning paper.

Our most important interview was with Lord Strathcona. He was President of the Hudson's Bay Company, the Canadian Pacific Railroad, and the Bank of Montreal. As a poor Scotch lad, named Donald Smith, he had lived for thirteen years of his early life in Labrador. There he had found a wife and there his daughter was born. From the very first he was thoroughly interested in our work, and all through the years until his death in 1914 his support was maintained, so that almost the very day he died, my wife and I were actually due to visit him in his country home near London. At his advice we hired the best hall and advertised Sir Donald as our chairman. To save expense my colleague acted in the ticket-box. When Sir Donald came along, not having seen him previously, the doctor insisted on collecting fifty cents from him as from the rest. When Sir Donald strongly protested that he was our chairman, he merely replied that several others had made the same remark. Everyone in the city knew Sir Donald; and when the matter was explained to him in the greenroom, he was thoroughly pleased with our business-like attitude. As we had never seen Canada, he insisted that we must take a holiday and go as far west as British Columbia. All of this he not only arranged freely for us, but even saw to such details as that we should ride on the engine through the Rocky Mountains, and be entertained at his home, called 'Silver Heights,' while in Winnipeg. It was during this trip that I visited 'Grenfell Town,' a queer little place called after Pascoe Grenfell, of the Bank of England. The marvel of the place to me was the thousands and thousands of acres of splendid farmland on which no one lived.

Lord Strathcona later presented the Mission with a fine little steamer, the Sir Donald, purchased and equipped at his expense through the Committee in Montreal.

We went back to England very well satisfied with our work; and I returned the following year and steamed the Sir Donald from Montreal down the St. Lawrence River and the Gulf to Battle Harbour, where our schooner, which had sailed again from England with doctors, nurses, and supplies, was to meet me. We had made a fine voyage, visiting all along the coast as we journeyed, and had turned in from sea through the last 'run,' or passage between islands. We had polished our brasswork, cleaned up our decks, hoisted our flags, all that we might make a triumphant entry on our arrival a few minutes later — when suddenly, Burr — Bur-r — Burr... we rose, staggered, and fell over on a horrible submerged shoal!!! Our side was gored, our propeller and shaft gone, our keel badly splintered, and the ship left high and dry!!! When we realized the dreadful position into which we had put ourselves, we rowed ashore to the nearest island, walked three or four miles over hill and bog, and from there got a fisherman with a boat to put us over to Battle Harbour Island. The good ship Albert lay at anchor in the harbour. Our new colleagues and old friends were all impatiently waiting to see our fine new steamer speed in with all her flags up — when instead, two bedraggled-looking tramps, crestfallen almost to weeping, literally crept in.

A crowd at once went round in boats with a museum of implements. They soon had our boat off, and our plucky schooner took her in tow all the three hundred miles to the nearest drydock at St. John's.

As Sir Thomas Roddick, of Montreal, an old Newfoundlander, had presented us with a splendid twenty-foot jollyboat, rigged with lugsail and centre boom, I cruised North in this to Eskimo Bay, harbouring at nights if possible, getting a local pilot when I could, and once being taken bodily on board, craft and all, by a big friendly fishing schooner. I was so dependent on the settlers and fishermen for food and hospitality that I learned to know them as would otherwise have been impossible. Far the best road to a seaman's heart is to let him do something for you. From the position of a tight corner, needing help and hospitality from entire strangers, one learns how large are the hearts and homes of those who live next to want themselves. I thought I knew the Labrador people before (and among such I include the Hudson Bay traders and the Newfoundland fishermen), that summer made me love them. I could not help feeling how much more sacrifice they gladly and freely made for me than I should have dreamed of doing for them had they come as visitors to my house in London. I have sailed the seas in ocean greyhounds, and in floating palaces, and in steam yachts, but better than any other voyage I love to dwell on the memories of that summer, cruising the Labrador in a twenty-footer.

The gallant little Sir Donald did herself every credit the following year, and we not only visited the Coast as far north as Cape Chidley, but explored the narrow channel which runs through the land into Ungava Bay, and placed Cape Chidley itself on a detached island, and located points of vantage for the sailing vessels on uncharted sections, where the Government later erected marks for their guidance.

There were a great many fishing schooners far north that season, and the keen pleasures of exploring a truly marvellous coast, practically uncharted and unknown, were redeemed from the reproach of selfishness by the numerous opportunities for service to one's fellow men.

In the early part of one summer we were eleven days stuck in an ice-field; and while there the huge mail steamer broke her propeller, and a boat was sent up to us through the ice to ask for our help. The truck on my mastheads was just up to her deck. Nosing our way through the heavy pans of ice gave us a lot of trouble, but we managed to tow the steamer into safety. On board were the superintendent of the Moravian Missions and his wife. Not being seamen, they were specially grateful. The great tub had rolled about so in the Atlantic swell that the big ice-pans nearly came on deck. My dainty little steamer took no notice of anything, and found her way among the pans like Agag 'treading delicately.' We had five hours' hard pulling, however, and kept men out all the time dodging from pan to pan, as they cleared the towline, or carried it round the higher pinnacles of ice on which it kept getting caught.

There is one especially charming feature about a little church at Indian Tickle. It stands in such a position that you can see it as you come from the north, miles away from the harbour entrance, off which lies an unmarked dangerous reef that has brought disaster to many poor vessels. There are no lights to guide sailors on this coast at all, and yet, during September, October, and November, three of the most dangerous months in the year, hundreds of schooners and thousands of men, women, and children were coming into, or passing through, this harbour on their way to the southward. By a nice arrangement the little east window pointed to the north — if that is not Irish — and two large bracket lamps could be turned on a pivot, so that the lamps and their reflectors threw a light out to sea. The good planter, at his own expense, maintained a light there on stormy or dark nights, and steering straight for it brings one to safety. In the Strathcona one fall, we fought out a heavy gale off this very reef; all the others, eleven in number, were lost with all their gear.

That summer, on going aboard a schooner which had signalled us for help, we had found a young man with the globe of one eye ruptured by a gun accident, in great pain, and in danger of losing the other eye sympathetically. Having excised the globe, we allowed him to go back later to his vessel, intensely grateful, but full of apprehension as to 'how his girl would regard him' on his return South. It so happened that we had had a gift of false eyes, and we therefore told him to call in at the hospital on his way home and take his chance on getting a blue one. While walking over the hill near Battle Harbour Hospital, that fall, I ran into a crowd of young fishermen, whose schooner was wind-bound in the harbour, and who had been into the country for an hour's trouting. One asked me to look at his eye, as something was wrong with it. Being in a hurry, I simply remarked, 'Come to hospital, and I'll examine it for you'; whereupon he burst into a merry laugh, 'Why, Doctor, I'm the boy whose eye you removed. This is the glass one you promised. Do you think it will suit her?' I did — and it did.

Later, I was called on board a large schooner off Mugford Tickle, far beyond the visits of any mails. There were two young girls on board doing the cooking and cleaning, as was the wont in Newfoundland vessels. One, alas, was seriously ill, having three days previously given birth to a premature child, and having lain absolutely untouched and helpless, with only a crew of kind but strange men anywhere near. Rolling her up in blankets, we transferred her to the Sir Donald, and steamed for the nearest Moravian station. Here the necessary treatment was possible, and when we left a fortnight later for the South, a Moravian's good wife accompanied us as nurse. The girl, however, had no wish to live. 'I want to die, Doctor; I can never go home again.' Her physical troubles had abated, but her mind was made up to die, and this, in spite of all our care, she did a few days later. The pathos of the scene as we rowed the poor child's body ashore for interment on a rocky and lonely headland, looking out over the great Atlantic, wrapped simply in the flag of her country, will never be forgotten by any of us — the silent, but unanswerable, reproach on man's utter selfishness. Many such thoughts must rise to the memory of the general practitioner. These opportunities of doing more for the patients than simply patching up their poor bodies are opportunities which are a real reward for the art of healing. Some years later, I revisited the grave of this poor girl, marked by the wooden cross which we had then put up, and bearing the simple inscription:

Suzanne

Jesus said, Neither do I condemn thee.

Again our cruise lasted till late into November, without our even realizing the fact that snow was on the ground. Indeed, the ponds were all frozen and we enjoyed drives with dog-teams on the land before we had finished our work on the sea. We had scarcely left Flowers Cove and were just burying our little steamer — loaded to the utmost capacity with wood, cut in return for winter clothing — in the dense fog which so often maintains in the Straits, and were rounding the outer end of the hidden ledges which jut out half a mile from shore, when a huge trans-Atlantic steamer, without a moment's warning, loomed right over our stern. We instantly put down our helm and scuttled out of the way to avoid the wash, and held our breath as the great steamer dashed by at twenty knots an hour, between us and the hidden shoal. She altered her helm as she did so, no doubt catching her first sight of the lighthouse as she emerged from the fog-bank, but, as it was, she must have passed within a few feet of her doom. With our hearts in our mouths, we expected momentarily to see her dash herself to pieces. Then she passed out of sight once more, her light-hearted passengers no doubt unconscious that they had been looking any danger in the face.

Henley, or Château, where the British had erected a fort to defend it against the French, was our last port of call that season. We made an attempt to cross the Straits, but sea and wind caught us halfway and forced us to run back, this time in thick fog. The Straits' current had carried us a few miles in the mean while — which way we did not know — and the land, hard to make out as it was in the fog, was white with snow. However, with the storm increasing and the long dark night ahead, we took a sporting chance and ran direct in on the cliffs. Suddenly we saw a rock on our bow and a sheer precipice ahead, and instantly twisted round on our heel, and shot between the two, for we knew where we were, as that is the only rock like that on a coastline of twenty miles of cliffs. But there really is no room between it and the cliff!!

All along the Coast that year we noticed a change of attitude toward professional medical aid. Confidence in the wise woman, in the seventh son and his 'wonderful' power, in the use of charms, had begun to waver. The world talks still of a blind man made to see nineteen hundred years ago; but even the 'hard-boiled' were beginning to be thrilled by the tales of blind men made to see by 'these yere doctors.' One was one of themselves, a man, who for seventeen years had given up all hope; and two others, old men, parted for years, and whose first occasion of seeing again had revealed to them the fact that they were brothers.

One of my first operations, in spite of the great pain caused by a tumour in the leg, had been refused, as the patient had religious scruples against anæsthetics. But before we sailed, the lady persuaded five good men and true to sit on her while the operation proceeded. It was not a pleasant scene to witness, but it ended well, and all parties were satisfied.

Now, indeed, the conversion of the Coast had proceeded so far that many were pleading for a winter doctor. At first, we did not think it feasible, but my colleague, Dr. Willway, finally volunteered to stay at Battle Harbour. We loaded him up with all our spare assets against the experiment, the hospital being but very ill-equipped for a sub-Arctic winter. When the following summer we approached the Coast, it was with real trepidation that I scanned the land for signs of my derelict friend. We felt that he would be gravely altered at least, possibly having grown hair all over his face. When at length a tanned, athletic figure, neatly tonsured and barbered, at last leaped over our rail, all our sympathy gave way to jealousy.

One detail, however, had gone wrong. We had anchored our beautiful Sir Donald in his care in a harbour off the long bay on the shores of which he was wintering. He had seen her once or twice in her ice prison, but when he came to look for her in the spring, she had mysteriously disappeared. The ice was there still. There was not a vestige of the wreckage. She must have sunk and the hole frozen up. Yet an extended period of 'creeping' the bottom with drags and grapples had revealed nothing, and, anyhow, the water not being deep, her masts should have been easily visible. It was not till some time later that we heard that our trusty craft had been picked up some three hundred miles to the southward and westward, well out in a heavy ice-pack, and right in among a big patch of seals, away off in the Atlantic Ocean. The whole of the bay ice had evidently gone out together, taking the ship with it; and the bay had then neatly frozen over again. The seal hunters from the S.S. Ranger laughingly assured me that they found a patch of old 'swiles' having tea in the cabin. They passed her a friendly rope, and she at length felt the life of the rolling wave beneath her once more, and soon lay safely ensconced in the harbour at St. John's. Here she was sold by auction, and part of the proceeds divided as her ransom to her plucky salvors.

CHAPTER IX

WHITE THUNDER

IN NEWFOUNDLAND the great sealing captains are the aristo-
crats of the fishermen, and unquestionably are an unusually
fine set of men. The work calls for peculiar training in the
hardest of schools, for great self-reliance and resourcefulness,
besides skill in handling ships and men. A generation ago, the
doyen of the fleet was Captain Samuel Blandford. Today it is
a Captain Abraham Kane. 'Captain Sam' fired me with tales
of the hardships to be encountered and the opportunities and
need for a doctor among three hundred men hundreds of
miles from anywhere for a full two months. The result was a
decision to return early one year from my lecture tour and go
out with the seal hunters.

At twelve o'clock of March 10, 1896, the good ship Neptune
hauled out into the stream at St. John's Harbour, Newfoundland, preparatory to weighing anchor for the seal fishery.
The law allows no vessels to sail before 2 P.M. on that day,
under a penalty of four thousand dollars' fine — nor may any
seals be killed from the steamers until March 14, and at no
time on Sundays. The whole city of St. John's seemed to be
engrossed in the one absorbing topic of the seal fishery. It
meant if successful some fifty thousand pounds sterling at
least to the Colony; it meant bread for thousands of people, it
meant for days and even weeks past that men from far-away
outports had been slowly collecting at the capital, till the
main street was peopled all day with anxious-looking crowds,
and all the wharves, where there was any chance of a 'berth'
to the ice, were fairly in a state of siege.

First let us go down to the dock and visit the ship before she
starts. She is a large barque-rigged vessel, with auxiliary
steam, or rather one should say a steamer with auxiliary sails.
The first point that strikes one is her massive build, her veritable bulldog look as she sits in the water. Her sides are some
eighteen inches thick, and sheathed and resheathed with
'greenheart' to help her in battering the ice. Inside she is

ceiled with English oak and beech, so that her portholes look like the arrow-slits of the windows of an old feudal castle. Her bow is double-stemmed — shot with a broad band of iron — and the space of some seventeen feet between the two stems solid with the choicest hardwoods. Below decks every corner is adapted to some use. There are bags of flour, hard bread, and food for the crew of three hundred and twenty men; five hundred tons of coal are in her bunkers for the hungry engine in her battle with the ice-floe. The vessel carries only about eighteen hundred gallons of water and the men use five hundred in a day. This, however, is of little consequence, for a party each day brings back plenty of ice, which is excellent drinking after being boiled. This ice is of very different qualities. Now it is 'slob' mixed with snow born on the Newfoundland coast. This is called 'dirty ice' by the sealers. Even it at times packs very thick and is hard to get through. Then there is the clearer, heavy Arctic ice with here and there huge icebergs frozen in; and again one encounters the smoother, whiter variety known as 'whelping ice' — that is, the Arctic shore ice, born probably in Labrador, on which the seals give birth to their pups.

The masters of watches are also called 'scunners' — they go up night and day in the forebarrel to 'scun' the ship — that is, to find the way, or leads, through the ice. This word comes from 'con' of the conning-tower on a man-of-war.

Fortunately, this year a southwest wind had blown the ice a mile or so offshore. Now all the men are on board. The vessels are in the stream. The flags are up; the whistles are blowing. The hour of two approaches at last, and a loud cheering, renewed again and again, intimates that the first vessel is off, and the S.S. Aurora comes up the harbour. Cheers from the ships, the wharves, and the town answer her whistle, and, closely followed by the S.S. Neptune and S.S. Windsor, she gallantly goes out, the leader of the sealing fleet for the year.

There have been two or three great disasters at the seal fishery, where numbers of men, astray from their vessels in heavy snow blizzards on the ice, have perished miserably. Sixteen fishermen were once out hunting for seals on the frozen ice of Trinity Bay when the wind changed and drove the ice offshore. When night came on, they realized their terrible position and that, with a gale of wind blowing, they could not hope to reach land in their small boats. Nothing but an awful death stared them in the face, for in order to hunt over the ice men must be lightly clad, so as to run and jump from piece to piece. Without fire, without food, without sufficient clothing, exposed to the pitiless storm on the frozen sea, they endured thirty-six hours without losing a life. Finally, they dragged their boats ten miles over the ice to the land, where they arrived at last more dead than alive.

It is the physical excitement of travelling over broken ice, tossing on the bosom of the mighty ocean, with the skill and athletic qualities which the work demands, that makes one love the voyage. Jumping from the side of the ship as she goes along, skurrying and leaping from ice-pan to ice-pan, and then having killed, 'sculped,' and pelted the seal, the exciting return to the vessel! But it has its tragic side.

On this particular voyage we were lucky enough to come early into the seals. From the conner's barrel, in which I spent a great deal of time, we saw one morning black dots spread away in thousands all over the ice-floes through which we were butting, ramming, and fighting our way. All hands were over the side at once, and very soon patients began needing a doctor. Here a cut, there a wrench or sprain, and later came thirty or forty at a time with snow-blindness or conjunctivitis — very painful and disabling, though not fatal to sight.

One morning we had been kept late relieving these various slight ailments, and the men being mostly out on the ice made me think that they were among the seals, so I started out alone as soon as I could slip over the side to join them. This, however, I failed to do till late in the afternoon, when the strong wind, which had kept the loose ice packed together, dropped, and in less than no time it was all 'running abroad.' The result of this is that one cannot get along except by floating on one piece to another, and that is a slow process without oars. It came on dark and a dozen of us who had got together decided to make for a large pan not far distant; but were obliged to give it up and wait for the ship which had long gone out of sight. To keep warm we played leap-frog, caps, and hop, skip, and jump — at which some were very proficient. We ate our sugar and oatmeal, mixed with some nice clear snow; and then, shaving our wooden seal bat-handles and dipping them into the fat of the animals which we had killed, we made a big blaze periodically to attract the attention of the ship.

It was well into the night before we were picked up; and no sooner had we climbed over the rail than the skipper came and gave us the best or worst 'blowing-up' I ever received since my father spanked me. He told me afterwards that he was really so relieved by our safe return that he was scarcely conscious of what he said. Indeed, any words which might have been considered as 'unparliamentary,' he asked me to construe as gratitude to God.

Our captain was a passenger on, and prospective captain of, the S.S. Tigris when she picked up those members of the ill-fated Polaris expedition who had been five months on the ice-pans. He had gone below from his watch and daylight was just breaking when the next watch came and reported a boat and some people on a large pan, with the American flag flying. A kayak came off, and Hans, an Eskimo, came alongside and said, 'Ship lost. Captain gone.' Boats were immediately lowered, and nineteen persons, including two women, and one baby — born on the ice-pan — came aboard amidst cheers renewed again and again. They had to be washed and fed, cleaned and clothed. The two officers were invited to live aft and the remainder of the rescued party, being pestered to death by the sealing crew in the forecastle, it was decided to abandon the sealing trip, and the brave explorers were carried to St. John's, the American people eventually indemnifying the owners of the Tigris.

In hunting my patients, I started round with a book and pencil accompanied by the steward carrying a candle and matches. The invalids were distributed in the four holds — the after, the main, the forecastle, and foretopgallant forecastle. I never went round without a bottle of cocaine solution in my pocket for the snow-blind men, who suffered the most excruciating pain, often rolling about and moaning as if in a kind of frenzy. To them the cocaine gave wonderful relief. Very often I found that I must miss one or even both holds on my first rounds, for the ladders were gone and seals and coals were exchanging places in them during the first part of the day. Once down, however, one shouts out, 'Is there anyone here?' No answer. Louder still, 'Is there anyone here?' Perhaps a distant cough answers from some dark recess, and the steward and I begin a search. Then we go round systematically, climbing over on the barrels, searching under sacks, and poking into recesses, and after all occasionally missing one or two in our search. It seems a peculiarity about the men, that though they will 'lie up,' they will not always say anything about it. The holds were very damp and dirty, but the men seemed to improve in health and fattened like the young seals. It must have been the pork, doughs, and excellent fresh meat of the seal. We had boiled or fried seal quite often with onions, and I must say that it was excellent eating — far more palatable than the dried codfish, which, when one has any ice-work, creates an intolerable thirst.

The rats were making a huge noise one night, and a barrel man gave it as his opinion that we should have a gale before long; but a glorious sunshine came streaming down upon us next morning, and we had to decide that rats were really no wiser than men.

On Sunday, when it is illegal to kill the seals, I had a good chance to watch them. They came up, simply stared at the ship, now from sheer fat rolling on their backs, and lying for a few seconds helpless, with tail and flippers beating the air. These baby seals resemble nothing so much as the South Sea parrot fish — that is, a complete round head, with somewhere in the sphere two huge black dots for eyes and a similar one for a nose. These three form the corners of a small triangle, and as for the rest, except for the tail, one could not easily tell which was the back and which the belly of a young white-coat — especially in stormy weather. For it is a well-ascertained fact that Nature makes the marvellous provision that in storm and snow they grow fattest and fastest. I have marvelled greatly how it is possible for any hot-blooded creature to enjoy so immensely this terribly cold water as do these old seals. They paddle about, throw themselves on their backs, float and puff out their breasts, flapping their flippers like fans over their chests.

The heaving of the great pans, like battering-rams against the sides of the Neptune, made a woesome noise below decks.

We were often glad of the thirty-six inches of hardwood covering. Every now and then she steamed ahead a little and
pressed into the ice to prevent this. I tried to climb on one
of the many icebergs, but the heavy swell made it dangerous.
At every swell it rolled over and back some eight feet, and as I
watched it I understood how an iceberg goes to wind. For it
acted exactly like a steam plough, crashing down onto one
large pan as it rolled, and then, as it rolled back, lifting up
another and smashing it from beneath. A regular battle
seemed to be going on, with weird sounds of blows and groan-
ings of the large masses of ice. Sometimes, as pieces fell off, the
water would rush up high on the side of the berg. For some
reason or other this berg had red-and-white streaks, and
looked much like an ornamental pudding.

On Sundays we 'laid up' and rested. I had taken a host of
cheap hymn-books with me, knowing the seamen's love for
music, and many fine songs we had sitting out on the decks on
fine Sundays.

One Sunday morning some men came aboard and reported
a wreck on the ice. She got round the island, a wind offshore
having cleared the ice from the land. Three other vessels were
behind her. Hardly, however, had she got round when the
northerly wind brought the ice back. The doomed ship now
lay between the main or fixed, frozen, shore ice and the immense floe which was impelled by the north wind acting on its
whole irregular surface. The force was irresistible. The ship
backed and butted and got twenty yards into a nook on the
main ice, and lay there helpless as an infant. On swept the
floe, crashed into the fixed ice, shattered its edge, rose up out
of water over it (which is called 'rafting'), forced itself on the
unfortunate ship, rose over her bulwarks, crushed in her sides,
and only by nipping her tightly avoided sinking her immediately. Seeing that all was lost, her captain got the men and
boats onto the pans and took all they could save of food and
clothes; but before he had saved his own clothing, the ice
parted enough to let her through and she sank like a stone,
her masts catching and breaking in pieces as she went. A sor-
rowful march for the shore now began over the ice, as the three
hundred men started for home, carrying as much as they could
on their backs. Many would have to face empty cupboards

and hard times; all would have days of walking and rowing and camping before they could get home. One hundred miles would be the least they must travel, or two and even three hundred for some, before they could reach their own villages. Some of these poor fellows had walked nearly two hundred miles to get a chance of going on the lost ship, impelled by hunger and necessity.

Of our Labrador harvests of the sea, after the cod, far the greatest is this hair-seal fishery. One is more than ever convinced today that the existence of this important source of wealth to Labrador is being seriously depleted: the newer vessels are so powerful, the more recent methods of discovering the whereabouts of the helpless baby seals by regular aeroplane services and by the addition of wireless equipment which enable vessels to direct one another to the 'patches of seals' — that is, their nurseries, the skill of the captains and crews, and finally the impossibility of enforcing laws calculated to prevent losses of those seals killed and not hauled direct to the ship, but left on the ice in great heaps — all these factors can in our opinion have but one end. We who love the North can ill-afford to fail to lodge our protest about a course of action which means to our families another serious loss of a chance to keep hunger from their doors. On this particular voyage we brought home only twenty-three thousand seals, but we must have killed nearly double that number.

The Government of the Colony, on the other hand, feels that it cannot interfere to protect the young seals, since it considers the present revenue derived from the seal fishery, the hoary antiquity of the custom, and the interest vested in the industry are all too powerful to be tampered with. Another turn of the wheel of fate may mean that the increasing shortage in numbers and the lessened value of the seals in this depression will automatically provide the only possible remedy.

In the spring of 1897, I was asked by the Council to sail to Iceland with a view to opening work there, in response to a petition sent in to the Board by the many long-liners and trawlers, who were just beginning their vast fishery in those waters, especially from Hull and Grimsby. I shall not soon forget our first view of the cliffs of the southern coast of Iceland. We had called at Thorshaven in the Faroë group to see what we could learn of the boats fishing near Rockall; but none were there at the time. As we had no chronometers on our own boat, we were quite unable to tell our longitude — a very much needed bit of information, for we had had fog for some days, and anyhow, none of us knew anything about the coast. So seeing one day a Grimsby boat fishing, I threw out my kayak and went aboard. 'Where's Iceland, skipper?' I asked. 'Way there,' said he, pointing with his thumb. 'Can you show me on your chart?' 'What chart? I hasn't got no chart, and couldn't read it if I had, and I've been coming this way for forty years now!'

Our cruise carried us all around the island — the larger part of our time being spent off the Vestmann Islands and the mouth of Brede Bugt, the large bay in which Reikyavik lies. It was off these islands that Eric the Red threw his flaming sticks into the sea. The first brand which alighted on the land directed him where to locate his new headquarters. Reikyavik means 'smoking village,' so-called from the vapours of the hot streams which come out of the ground near-by.

They were a simple, kindly, helpful people, living in a barren and frigid country, with no trees except in one extreme corner. The cows were literally fed on salt codfish and the tails of whales, while the goats grazed on the roofs of the houses, where existed the only available grass. There are dry, hard, and almost larval deposits over the whole surface of the land which is not occupied by perpetual snow and ice. The hot springs which abound in some regions only suggest a forlorn effort on the part of Nature at the last moment to save the situation. The one asset of the country is its fisheries, and of these the whale and seal fisheries were practically handed over to the Norwegians; while large French and English boats fell like wolves on the fish, which the poor natives had no adequate means of securing for themselves.

It was now thought wise that I should take a holiday, and through the kindness of my former chief, Sir Frederick Treves, then surgeon to the King, whose life he had just been the means of saving, I found myself for a time as his guest on the Scilly Islands. There we could divert our minds from our various occupations, conjuring up visions of heroes like Sir Cloudesley Shovel, who lost his life here, or of other scenes of

daring and of death that these beautiful isles out in the Atlantic have witnessed. Nor did we need Charles Kingsley to
paint for us again the visit of Amyas Lee and Salvation Yoe,
for Sir Frederick, as his book, 'The Cradle of the Deep,'
shows, was a past-master in buccaneer lore. Besides that, we
had with us his nephew, the famous novel-writer, A. E. W.
Mason.

Treves, with his insatiable energy, had organized a grand
regatta to be held at St. Mary's, at which the Governor of the
Island, the Duke of Wellington, and a host of visiting big-
wigs were to be present. One event advertised as a special
attraction was a life-saving exhibition to be given by local
experts from the judges' stage opposite the grandstand on the
pier. This, Mason and I, being little more than ornaments in
the other events, decided to try and improve upon. Dressed
as a somewhat antiquated lady, just at the psychological moment Mason fell off the lofty pier-head with a loud scream —
whereupon, disguised as an aged clergyman, wildly gesticulat-
ing and cramming my large beaver hat hard down on my
head, I dived in to rescue him. A real scene ensued. We were
dragged out with such energy that the lady lost her skirt, and
on reaching the pier fled for the boat-house clad only in a
bonnet and bodice over a bathing-suit. Although the local
press wrote up the affair as genuine, the secret somehow
leaked out, and we had to make our bow at the prize distribution the following evening.

On leaving England for one of these North Sea trips, I was
delayed and missed the hospital ship, so that later I was obliged to transfer to her on the high seas from the little cutter
which had kindly carried me out to the fishing grounds.
Friends had been good enough to give me several little delica-
cies on my departure, and I had, moreover, some especially
cherished personal possessions which I desired to have with
me on the voyage. These choice treasures consisted of some
eggs, a kayak, a kodak, a chronometer, and a leg of mutton!
After I was safely aboard the Mission hospital ship, I found to
my chagrin that, in my anxiety to transfer the eggs, the kayak,
the kodak, the chronometer, and especially the leg of mutton
to the Albert, I had forgotten my personal clothing. I appreciated the fact that a soaking meant a serious matter, as I had

to stay in my bunk until my things, which were drenched during my passage in the small boat, were dry again.

While the skipper was at work in the tobacco locker one morning, he heard a fisherman say that he had taken poison.

'Where did you get it?'

'I got it from the Albert.'

'Who gave it to you?'

'Skipper ——,' mentioning the skipper's name.

At this the skipper came out trembling, wondering what he had done wrong now.

'Well, you see, it was this way. Our skipper had a bad leg, so, as I was going aboard for some corf mixture, he just arst me to get him a drop of something to rub in. Well, the skipper here gives me a bottle of red liniment for our skipper's leg, and a big bottle of corf mixture for me, but by mistake I drinks the liniment and gave the corf mixture to our skipper to rub in his leg. I only found out that there yesterday, so I knew I were poisoned, and I've been lying up ever since.'

'How long ago did you get the medicine?'

'About a fortnight.'

This man had got it into his head that he was poisoned, and nothing on earth would persuade him to the contrary, so he was put to bed in the hospital. For three meals he had nothing but water and a dose of castor oil. By the next time dinner came round, the patient really began to think he was on the mend, and remarked that 'he began to feel real hungry-like.' It was just marvellous how much better he was before tea. He went home to his old smack, cured, and greatly impressed with the capacity of the medical profession.

The North Sea Mission fleet now numbered thirteen boats, had several shore institutes around England, Scotland, and Ireland, and almost an indefinite number of activities. Holland and France had followed our lead, and the Œuvres de Mer of Paris had hospital schooners with both the Iceland and Grand Bank fisheries. The banishment of the grog vessel had been followed by greatly improved conditions in our English fishermen's quarters, and I published one summer a list of over one hundred drinking-saloons, along the quayside at Great Yarmouth, that had been closed up since we began, just for want of custom. Fishermen are clannish folk, and even in public worship like to keep together. Little chapels for worship sprang up specially for fishermen in many places, and a real revolution, fully appreciated by owners, as well as by wives and children, had begun, and has continued since.

CHAPTER X

SAINT ANTHONY

In June, 1899, the hospital steamer Strathcona was launched at Dartmouth, England, the chief donor again being Lord Strathcona. She was eighty feet long, small for Atlantic work, but larger than the vessel in which Drake sailed round the world, or Dampier raided the Spanish Main, or than the Speedy, which Earl Dundonald made the terror of the French and Spanish.

In the fall I steamed her, an empty shell, round the South of England, to fit her up at our Yarmouth wharf. Then, in company with a young Oxford friend, I left for Labrador, crossing to Tilt Cove, Newfoundland, direct from Swansea in an empty copper-ore tanker. On this I was rated as purser at a salary of twenty-five cents for the trip. Most tramps can roll, but an empty tanker going west against prevailing winds in the 'roaring forties' can certainly give points to most of them. Her slippery iron decks and my involuntary sideways excursions into the scuppers still spring into my mind when a certain Psalm comes round in the Church calendar, with its 'that thy footsteps slip not.'

At the end of that voyage, I wrote to my mother: 'We have just steamed into Battle Harbour, and guns and flags gave us a welcome after our three years' absence. The hospital was full and looked splendid. What a change from the day, now seven years ago, when we first landed! What an oasis for patients from the bleak rocks outside! I never thought to remain long enough in this country to see it.'

There is always a romantic charm about cruising in the fall of the year on the Labrador. The long nights and the occasional heavy gales add zest to the shelter of the islands and the sense of safety in the harbours and fjords. The tang of the air, the young ice that 'makes' every night, and the fantastic midnight dances of the November auroras in the wintry sky, all make one forget any worries or troubles.

Before leaving England, we had received letters from the

North Coast of Newfoundland, begging us again to include their shores in our visits, and especially to establish a winter station at St. Anthony. The people claimed, quite rightly, to be terribly poor. One man with a large family whom I knew well, as he had acted as guide for me on hunting expeditions, wrote, 'Come and start a hospital here if you can. My family and I are starving.' This man was a keen hunter, and, with his rickety old single-barrel, muzzle-loading gun, used to wander along far out over the frozen sea, with an empty stomach as well, trying to get a seal or a bird for his family. At last he shot a square flipper seal and dragged it home over the ice. The rumour of his having killed it preceded his arrival and even while skinning it a crowd of hungry men were waiting for a share of the fur. Not that any was due them, but here there is a delightful semi-community of goods.

I had once spent a fortnight at St. Anthony, having taken refuge there in the Princess May when I was supposed to be lost by those who were cut off from communication with us. I had also looked in there each summer to see a few patients. My original idea was to get a winter place for our Indian Harbour Staff, and I proposed opening up medical work at St. Anthony each October when Indian Harbour closed, and closing in June when navigation was reopened. So we hired a room in a trader's cottage, used a glorified cupboard for a surgery, and engaged our old guide to drive our dogs and pilot us.

North and south of the little village where we had settled were similar other villages, around which we hoped to make many trips. This became impossible, as patients collected in near-by houses, some of them operative cases whom we felt we could not leave. So we selected a motherly woman, whom we had learned that we could trust to obey orders, and trained her as best we could with some of these sick people.

To me that first winter was one long delight. The dog-driving, the intimate relationships with the people on whom one was so often absolutely dependent, the opportunity to use for the real help of good folk in distress the thousand and one small things which we had learned — all these made the knowledge that we were shut off from the outside world nothing but a pleasure.

LABRADOR IN SUMMER

Our dogs have a wonderful instinct for finding their way under insurmountable difficulties, and they have often been the means of saving the lives of their masters. Once I was driving a distance of seventy miles across country. The path was untravelled for the winter, and was only a direction, not being cut or blazed. The leading dog had once been across the previous year with the doctor. The 'going' had then been very bad; with snow and fog the journey had taken three days. A large part of the way lay across wide, frozen lakes, and then through woods. As I had never been that way before, I had to leave it to the dog. Without a single fault, as far as we knew, she took us across, and we accomplished the whole journey in twelve hours, including one and a half hours for rest and lunch.

The real Labrador dog is a very slightly modified wolf. A good specimen stands two feet four inches at the shoulder, measures over six feet six inches from the tip of the tail, and will scale a hundred pounds. The hair is thick and straight; the ears are pointed and stand directly up. The large, bushy tail curves completely over onto the back, and is always carried erect. The colour is generally tawny, like that of the grey wolf, with no distinctive markings. The general resemblance to wolves is so great that at Davis Inlet, where wolves come out frequently in winter, the factor has seen his team mixed with a pack of wolves on the beach in front of the door, and yet could not shoot, being unable to distinguish one from the other. The Eskimo dog never barks, but howls exactly like a wolf, in a sitting posture with the head upturned. The Labrador wolf has never been known to kill a man, but during the years that I have spent in the country I have known the dogs to kill two children and one man, and to eat the body of another. Our dogs have little or no fear, and, unlike the wolves, will unhesitatingly attack even the largest polar bear.

No amount of dry cold can affect the dogs. At fifty degrees below zero, a dog will lie out on the ice and sleep without danger of frostbite. He may climb out of the sea with ice forming all over his fur, but he seems not to mind one iota. Often his breath freezes over his face so that he has to rub the coating off his eyes with his paws to enable him to see the track.

The distance travelled and the average speed attained depends largely on other factors than the dog power. We have covered seventy-five miles in a day with comfort; we have done five with difficulty. Ordinary speed would be six miles an hour, but once I did twenty-one miles in two hours and a quarter over level ice. Sails can sometimes be used with advantage on the komatik as an adjunct.

Weight on your komatik is a vital question, and, not knowing for what you may be called upon, makes the outfitting an art. The sledge should be eleven feet long. Its runners should be constructed of black spruce grown in the Far North, where wood grows slowly and consequently is very tough and yet quite light. The runners should be an inch thick, eleven inches high, and about twenty-six inches apart, the bottoms rising at the back half an inch, as well as at the front toward the horns. The laths are fastened on with alternate diagonal fastenings, are two inches wide, and close together. Such a komatik will 'work' like a snake, adapting itself to the inequalities of the ground, and will not spread or 'buckle.' The dogs' traces should be of skin and fastened with toggles or buttons to the bow-line. Dog-food must be distributed along the komatik trail in summer, though the people will make great sacrifices to feed 'the Doctor's team.'

A light rifle should always be lashed on the komatik, as a rabbit, seal, a partridge, or a deer gives often a light to the eyes with the fresh proteids which they afford, like Jonathan's wild honey. In these temperatures, with the muscular exercise required, my strictest vegetarian friends should permit us to bow in the House of Rimmon.

When crossing wide stretches of country, we are often obliged to camp if it comes on dark. It is quite impossible to navigate rough country when one cannot see stumps, windfalls, or snags; and I have more than once been obliged to walk ahead with a light, while caught in the forest looking for our tilt, or even to search the snow for tracks with the help of matches when my torch has carelessly been left at home.

A gun, however, is a temptation even to a doctor, and nearly cost one of my colleagues his life. He was crossing a big divide, or neck of land, between bays, and was twenty miles from anywhere, when his dogs took the trail of some deer, which were evidently not far off. Being short of fresh food, he hitched up his team and also his pilot's team, leaving only his boy driver in charge, while the men pursued the caribou. He warned the boy very strictly not to move on any account or they might be lost. By an odd freak, a sudden snowstorm swept out of a clear sky just after they left. They missed their way, and two days later, starving and tired out, they found their first refuge, a small house many miles from the spot where they had left the sledges. When, however, they sent a relief team to find the komatiks, they discovered the boy still 'standing by' his charge.

You must always carry an axe, not only for firewood, but for getting water — unless you wish to boil snow, which is a slow process and apt to burn your kettle. Also, when you have either lost the trail or there is none, you must have an axe to clear a track as you march ahead of your dogs. Then there is, of course, the question of food. Buns baked with chopped pork in them give one fine energy-producing material and do not freeze. A sweet, dry, hard biscuit is made on the Coast which is excellent in one's pocket. Cocoa, cooked pork fat, stick chocolate, are all good to have. Our sealers carry dry oatmeal and sugar in their 'nonny bags,' which, mixed with snow, assuage their thirst and hunger as well. Pork and beans in tins are good, but they freeze badly. I have boiled a tin in our kettle for fifteen minutes, and then found a lump of ice in the middle of the substance when it was turned out into the dish.

A friend, returning from an island, was jogging quietly along on the bay ice when his team suddenly went wild. A polar bear had crossed close ahead, and, before he could unlash his rifle, the komatik had dashed right onto the animal. The team were all around him, rapidly snarling themselves in their traces. The bear, instead of running, stood up and showed fight. The man had just time to draw his hunting-knife across the traces and so save the dogs, caring much more for them than he did for the prey. Whilst his dogs held the attention of the bear, he was able, though only a few feet away, to unlash his rifle — and very soon ended the conflict.

Winter travelling of a doctor on the Coast sometimes involves considerable hardship. Once our doctor lost the track, and he and his men had to spend several nights in the woods.

They were so reduced by hunger that they were obliged to chew pieces of green sealskin which they cut from their boots and to boil their skin gloves over a fire which they had kindled.

I am often asked, 'Do you wear furs in the house in winter?'

'No, nor outside either.'

'Then how do you keep warm?'

'By using common sense, and by doing a little work on the problem.'

The factors are, first, keeping your body fit and eating the right foods. Secondly, when you have generated heat, all you have to do is to keep it in. Use light, loose, impervious clothing with no leaks, and do not forget to make it as bright and beautiful as you can. You must not perspire or you will freeze later. You will not find a marble statue any warmer because you put a fur coat on it, or a room get warm because there is a stove in it, if all the windows and doors are left open to the icy blast of an Arctic winter.

The first thing in clothing is the material — impervious to wind and water, light in weight, inexpensive, tough, smooth on the outside so as to shed snow, and beautiful. Just such a material can be ordered through our offices in any color, and the English firm which invented it calls it 'Grenfell Cloth.' Admiral Byrd used it at the South Pole, MacMillan at the North. We all use it. The only leak in the top garment might occur around the face, but a trimming of fur inside and outside the edges stops that when the string is pulled tight. The hood, of course, is sewed fast to the tunic. An inset with a rubber band closes the sleeves, and a long glove, with only the 'gun finger' and thumb separate, comes up to the elbow with a separate strap at the wrist. The trousers, in one piece, come up to the armpits under the 'kossak' or 'dickey,' while they fit close to the sides with zippers.

Light sealskin boots are the best for all weathers, but in cold, dry seasons, deerskin dressed very soft is better still and warmer. The skin-boot should be sewed with sinew, which swells in water and thus keeps the stitches water-tight. These skin-boots are made by the Northern Eskimo women, who chew the edges of the skin to make them soft before sewing them with deer sinew. The art of chewing, as they are brought up from childhood to help their mothers in this way, is a highly developed one among the little Eskimo girls of North Labrador. The women wear out their teeth in this way at an early age.

One great joy which comes with a work such as ours is the sympathy one gets with the really poor. One learns how simple needs and simple lives preserve simple virtues, which get lost in the crush of advancing civilization. One bitter winter night, a blizzard of snow caught me and my dogs after dark in a strange district. After midnight the dogs brought me to a tiny cottage. There were no lights. The goodman, a stranger to me, was in bed asleep. When I hammered on the door, a cheery voice answered, and in a minute or two the door opened and I was blown inside by the storm. Yet cheerfully the stranger slipped on some clothes and straight from his bed went out, carrying an old hurricane lantern, to feed my dogs; while his wife, after she had lit a fire in the freezing cold room, busied herself making me some cocoa. Milk and sugar were provided, and not till long afterwards did I know it was a special little hoard kept for visitors. Later I was sent to bed — quite unaware that it was the only one, and that the good folk had spent the first part of the night in it themselves. While I slept warm and snug, the last half of the night they spent on the adjoining floor. Nor would they accept one cent in return for their hospitality. ''Tis the way of the Coast,' the good fellow assured me.

Another time, my host for the night had gone when I rose for breakfast. I found that he had taken the road which I intended to travel to the next village, some fourteen miles distant, just to break and mark a trail for us, as we did not know the way; and secondly, to carry some milk and sugar to 'save the face' of my prospective host for the next night, who had 'made a bad voyage' that year. Still another time no less than forty men from Conche marched ahead on a twenty-mile track to make it possible for our team to travel quickly to a neighbouring settlement. The man who walked to the village fourteen miles distant was a Roman Catholic, and the neighbour to whom he carried the milk and sugar was a Methodist.

One day that winter a father of eight children sent in from a near-by island for immediate help. His gun had gone off while his hand was on the muzzle and practically blown it to pieces. To treat him ten miles away was out of the question, so we brought him in for operation. To stop the bleeding he had plunged his hand into a barrel of flour, and then tied it up in a bag, and as a result the wounded arm was poisoned way up to the elbow. He preferred death to losing his right arm. Day and night for weeks our nurse tended him, as he hovered between life and death with general blood poisoning. Slowly his fine constitution brought him through, and at last a secondary operation for repair became possible. We took chances on bone-grafting to form a hand; and he was left with a flipper like a seal's, able, however, to oppose one long index finger and 'nip a line' when he fished. But there was no skin for it. So my colleague and I shared the honours of supplying some. Pat — for that was his name — has been a veritable apostle of the hospital ever since, and has undoubtedly been the means of enabling others to risk the danger of our suspected proselytizing. For though he had English Episcopal skin on the palm of his hand and Scotch Presbyterian skin on the back, the rest of him still remained a devout Roman Catholic.

Another somewhat parallel case occurred the following year, when a dear old Catholic lady was hauled fifty miles over the snow by her two stalwart sons, to have her leg removed for tubercular disease of the ankle. She did exceedingly well, and the only puzzle which we could not solve was where to raise the necessary hundred dollars for a new leg — for her disposition, even more than her necessity, compelled her to move about. While lecturing the following winter in America, I asked friends to donate to me any of their old legs which they no longer needed. Soon I found myself the happy possessor of two good wooden limbs, one of which exactly fitted my requirements. A departed Methodist had left it behind him, and his wife, a Baptist, donated it to me through a Congregational clergyman, and I, an Episcopalian, had the joy of seeing it a real blessing to as good a Roman Catholic as I know. As the priest now says, there is now at least one Protestant leg in his parish.

Called one day to a distant village, we came to a cottage where the father of five children had a great, swollen knee, which he was unable to put to the ground. It had loose, hard, cartilage bodies in it. We do not like opening a working-man's knee-joint and fishing around inside it, especially when the operation must be done in a fisherman's tiny cottage. But this time there was no alternative. I remembered the old days when surgeons did all their operations under clouds of carbolic spray. So we filled all available buckets with perchloride of mercury, and helpers kept pouring it over the whole scene of action while I worked — and we thus got a perfect result.

On another occasion we reached a house at midnight, found a boy with a broken thigh, and had to begin work by thawing out a frozen board in order to plane it for splints; then pad and fix it; and finally give chloroform on the kitchen table in the early hours in order to set the limb. Once we even had to knock down a partition in a tiny house, make a full-length wooden bath, pitching the seams to make it water-tight, in order to treat a spreading cellulitis. Now it would be a maternity case, now a dental one, now a gunshot wound, or an axe cut with severed tendons to adjust, now pneumonia. Often in solitary and 'unlearned' homes, we would ourselves do the nursing and especially the cooking, as that art for the sick is entirely uncultivated on the Coast. In this way our winter passed speedily.

In the spring the new hospital steamer was brought out by my old crew, and closing St. Anthony, we once more began the work among the fishing fleets off the Labrador Coast for which I originally came out.

The northern end of Labrador is extremely interesting to cruise. The great mountain ranges run out here right to the waterline, and form a marvellous sea-front of embattled cliffs from two to three thousand feet in height. The narrow passages which here and there run far into the mountains and represent old valleys scooped out by ice action are dominated all along their length by frowning peaks, whose pointed summits betray the fact that they overtopped the ice-stream in the glacial age.

Once before in the Sir Donald we had tried to navigate the narrow run which cuts off the island on which Cape Chidley stands from the mainland of Labrador, but had missed the way among the many openings, and only noted from a hilltop, like Moses, the course we should have taken. Below us was a boiling current, whose vicious whirlpools, like miniature maelstroms, poured a foaming torrent from Ungava Bay into the Atlantic. We had with us a Moravian Brother, delegated to select a site for a new station to carry on work from the extreme North among hitherto unreached Eskimos.

It was, however, with our hearts somewhere near our mouths that we made the attempt to get through this year, for we knew nothing of the depths except that the Eskimos had told us that large icebergs at times drove through the run. We could steam nine knots, and we essayed to cover the tide, which we found against us as we neared the narrowest part — which is scarcely a hundred yards wide. The current carried us bodily astern, however, and glad enough we were to drive stern foremost into a cove on one side and find bottom in thirteen fathoms of water, to hold on to till the tide should turn. When at last it did turn and we got under way, it fairly took us in its teeth, and we shot through, an impotent plaything on the heaving bosom of the resistless waters. Later we returned safely, with a site selected and a fair chart of the 'tickle,' since named 'Grenfell Tickle' by His Excellency the Governor, Sir William MacGregor, who visited it in 1908.

When winter again closed in, I arranged for an old friend, a clerk of the Hudson's Bay Company, to stay with me at St. Anthony, and once more we settled down in rooms hired in a cottage. This time we had an arrangement with a paternal Government to help out by making an allowance of twenty-five cents each for medicine for such patients as could not themselves pay that amount — which, in those days, was quite a large number. So many pathetic cases were impossible to treat as I would wish to be treated that in spring I had to tell the people that without a hospital I could not again face the work at St. Anthony. An expedition into the woods was at once arranged, with a hundred men and thrice as many dogs. We camped among the trees, and at the end of a fortnight came home, hauling behind us the material for a thirty-six by thirty-six-foot hospital.

In the forest, our kitchen was dug down in thick woods through six feet of snow, and our main food reliance was on boiled 'doughboys' — the 'sinkers' which, with a slice of fat pork and a basin of bird soup, were as popular as lobster *à la*

Newburg at Delmonico's or Sherry's. Incidentally, I learned what hunger meant. Not being an expert axeman, or particularly good with a pit-saw, I undertook to supply the food. Calculating on the quantity needed by a hundred convicts at hard labour in England, we hauled in on sledges the amount for two weeks. Our hungry hundred men ate it in one day!

This hospital was opened six months later, and, with enlargements, functioned until 1927, when it was replaced by a large fireproof building, with every modern fitting.

The next summer we had trouble with a form of selfishness which I have always heartily hated — the liquor traffic. Suppose we do admit that a man has a right, for physical pleasure, to damage his body by swallowing a toxin, he certainly has no more moral right to lure others to their destruction in order to gain money from them than a filibuster has a right to spend his money in gunpowder and shoot his fellow countrymen. To our great chagrin we found that an important neighbour near one of our hospitals was selling intoxicants to the people — girls and men. One girl, found drunk on the hillside, brought home to me the cost of this man's 'right to do as he liked,' reminding me of the old days at 'The London' amidst the crime and misery caused by the sale of alcohol in the purlieus of the East End.

This man and I had had several disagreements, and he had warned me not to land on his premises on pain of being 'chucked into the sea.' But when I tested the matter by landing quite alone from a rowboat, though a large crowd of men gathered round while we discussed matters, his Coast-born hospitality overcame him, and as his bell sounded the dinner call, he promptly invited me to dine with him. I knew that he would not poison the food, and soon we were glowering at one another over his own table.

That summer, we were steaming to our Northern hospital from the deep bay which runs in a hundred and fifty miles. About twenty miles from the mouth, a boat hailed us out of the darkness, and we stopped and took aboard a wrecked crew of three men. They had struck our friend's well-insured old steam launch on a shoal, and she had sunk under them. We took them aboard, boat and all, wrote down carefully their tale of woe, and then put the steamer about, pushed as near the wreck as we dared, and anchored. Her skipper came forward and asked me what I intended doing, and I told him that as Lloyd's agent I was going to survey the wreck. A little later, he again came to ask permission to go aboard the wreck and look for something he had forgotten. I told him 'Certainly not.' Just before sunrise the watch called me and said that the wrecked crew had launched their boat, and were rowing towards the steam launch. 'Put our boat out at once, and drive them back,' was an order which our boys obeyed with alacrity and zest. It was a very uneasy-looking three men who faced me when they returned, though they were full of bluff at what they would do for having their liberties thus interfered with.

We discovered that the water only entered the wreck at low tide, and then only forward; so by buoying her with casks, tearing up her ballast deck, and using our own pumps as well as buckets — at which all hands of my crew worked with a will — we at last found the hole. It was round. There were no splinters on the inside. We made a huge bung from a tree-trunk, plugged the opening, finished pumping her out, and before dark had her floating alongside us. Late that night we were once more anchored, this time opposite the dwelling-house of my friend the owner. We immediately went ashore and woke him up. There is a great deal in doing things at the psychological moment; and by midnight I had a deed duly drawn up, signed and sealed, selling me the little steamer for fifty cents. I see still the look in his eye as he gave me fifty cents change from a dollar. He was a self-made man, had acquired considerable money, and was keen as a ferret at business. The deed was to me a confession that he was in the plot for barratry, to murder the boat for her insurance.

On our trip South we picked up the small steamer again, and towing her to a Hudson's Bay Company post we put her 'on the hard,' photographed the hole, with all the splintering on the outside, and had a proper survey of the hull made by the Company's shipwright. The unanimous verdict was 'wilful murder.' In the fall, as her own best witness, I tried to tow her to St. John's, but in a heavy breeze of wind and thick snow I lost her at sea — and with her our own case as well. The law decided that there was no evidence, and my friend, claiming that he had lost both the boat and the insurance, threatened to sue me for the value.

The sequel of the story came a year or so later. I had just returned from the North. It used to be said always that our boat 'brought up the keel of the Labrador'; but this year our friend had remained until everyone else had gone. Just as we were about to leave for England, the papers in St. John's published the news of the loss of a large, foreign-going vessel, laden with fish for the Mediterranean, near the very spot where our friend lived. On a visit to the shipping office I found the event described in graphic language by the skipper and mate. Our friend the consignee had himself been on board at the time the 'accident' had happened. After prodigies of valour they had been forced to leave the ship, condemn her, and put her up for sale. Our friend, the only buyer at the time on the Coast, had bought her in for eighty dollars.

It was the end of November, and already a great deal of ice had made. The place was six hundred miles north. The expense of trying to save the ship would be great. But was she really lost? The heroics sounded too good to be true. All life is a venture. Why not take one in the cause of righteousness? That night in a chartered steam trawler, with a trusty diver, I steamed out of the harbour, steering north. My skipper this time was known everywhere as a very devil-may-care sea-dog, and among the most famous of the seal hunters.

The way he drove our little craft, with ice inches thick formed by the driving spray all over her bridge and blocking the chart-room windows, made one glad to realize that the good sea genius of the English was still so well preserved.

When our distance was run down and we hauled in for the land, we had to heave to (with the ship sugared like a Christmas cake) and wait until we were able to recognize our position in the drifting snow. At length we located the islands; and never shall I forget, as we drew near, hearing the watch call out, 'A ship's topmasts over the land!' It was the wreck for which we were looking.

It took some hours to cut through the ice in which she lay before we could get aboard; and even the old skipper showed excitement when at last we stood on her deck. Needless to say, she was not upside down, nor was she hurt in any way, though she was completely stripped of all running-gear. The diver reported no damage to her bottom, while the mate told us that the fish in her hold were dry, and her hatches still tightly clewed, never having been stirred.

With much hearty good-will our crew jettisoned fish enough into our own vessel to float the craft. Fearing that so late in the year we might fail to tow her safely for such a distance, and remembering the outcome of our losing the launch, we opened the stores on the island belonging to our friend, and found both blocks and sails, neatly labelled and stowed away. We soon had our prize not only refitted for sea, but also stocked with food, water, chart, and compass, and all essentials for a voyage across the Atlantic, if she were to break loose and we to lose her. The last orders were to our mate, who was put aboard the prize with a crew, 'If not St. John's, then Liverpool.'

Though we had sixty fathoms of anchor chain on each of our wire cables to the ship, we broke one in a seaway the first night out, and had to haul under the lee of some cliffs and repair damages. Often for hours together the vessel by day, and her lights by night, would disappear, and our hearts would jump into our mouths for fear that we might again fail. But at last, with all our bunting flying and both ships dressed as if for a holiday, we proudly entered the Narrows of St. John's Harbour, the cynosure of all eyes. The skipper of the barrated vessel and our friend had meanwhile gone to England, so the Government had them extradited. The captain, who was ill with a fatal disease, made a full confession, and both men were sent to prison.

That is how we 'went dry' in that section of the Labrador.

CHAPTER XI

BUNKERS

AN APOLOGIST for the old days of slavery in the Southern States of America may still believe that a primitive and uneducated people is better off under the régime of paternalism, peonage, and slavery. Possibly they are. After all it is a question of standard; but for my part I would rather starve than submit to it. As we view life, it seems a practice belonging to the Dark Ages.

One day I was talking to one of the most charming of our Labrador settlers. As I looked around the poor little cottage, I wondered if the old man's proverbial generosity was the sole reason why he and his wife had come to poverty in their old age. He had been one of the best of the local trappers. He told me that, whenever his hunt had procured him everything that he could need or want for the ensuing winter, one of the clerks always took him around the store again, in order that he might show his loyalty to the Company by taking up a little more than he could pay for, and so keep his name as a debtor on their books. They were sure of him thus. It was the custom of trade on the Labrador in those days.

It is never easy for a man in a primitive country to keep a credit balance. But we believed that it could be done; and it was for that reason that we started our little coöperative stores among the poorer fishermen in scattered villages. As fighting propositions, and considering the open hostility which the move engendered, they have certainly lent more thrills to a 'missionary life' than has the Arctic Ocean.

Government relief failed to cope with the evils of the 'truck' system of trade. Indeed, in the opinion of thinking men, it only made matters worse.

In my early days on the Coast a poor man came to me as a magistrate to settle a case for him against his trader. The autumn previous he had given the trader a hundred dollars in cash with which to buy him a new net. The trader had been unable to secure the twine for this; but when the man came in the spring to get his usual advance for supplies, the trader deducted the hundred dollars cash from the amount of the fisherman's bill. Yet that fisherman actually appealed to me as a Justice of the Peace to have the trader punished. Custom compelled the actual cash to be returned.

On another occasion one of my fishermen friends and I were sitting on a gunning point, shooting ducks as they flew by on their fall migration. I suddenly noticed that he did not even attempt to fire at a wonderful flock of eiders which passed directly over our heads. 'Whatever is the matter, Jim?' I asked. 'I settled with my merchant today,' he replied, 'and he won't advance me nothing for winter. A duck or two won't matter. 'Tis the children I'm minding.' The fishery had been poor, and not having enough to meet his advances at the trader's, he had sold a few quintals of fish outside for cash, in order to get things like tinned milk which his merchant would never have allowed him on winter credit. He had been caught and the trader had retaliated. We went to the trader to find out how much the poor fellow was in debt. His debit account on the books read over three thousand dollars, carrying over a period of many years.

We were lying at anchor in an open roadstead when a trader came aboard and took out a summons against a native, who had obtained an advance of supplies from him and was not returning any fish. An inspection of the cottage revealed no assets, and, as it is not legal to seize a fisherman's house or boat for debt, there was nothing to offer the plaintiff except the blessing of the Court. However, his boat had hardly rounded the headland out of sight when the defendant, stripping off his coat and waistcoat, produced a fine white fox skin, which he offered to sell to the Judge! This spirit was the child of the system.

Summer frosts on the coasts of Labrador made the growing of vegetables precarious, except by the few families who remain at the heads of the long bays all the year around, far removed from the polar current. None of our very abundant native berries are naturally sweet, so in order to preserve them for winter consumption we must import all our 'sweetness.' We must also import cotton, wool, and many other vital necessities of life, though the Coast provides firewood, lumber, fish and game, and skins for boots or clothing. On the other hand, we export our codfish, salmon, seals, trout, oil, whales, and fur. A medium of exchange is as imperative for us as for other parts of the civilized world.

From every point of view, therefore, we were encouraged to start coöperative stores, a plan which has proved eminently successful in England. All attempts to meddle with the economic methods of the *status quo* met with unfriendly criticism in the Colony generally, and these small coöperative, distributive stores were no exception. Some of the criticism, however, came from our best merchant friends, who warned us that to teach coöperation would mean burning our fingers. Though there proved to be some truth in that contention, I still believe that the people are honest, and that the laziness and indolence which some display is in most cases due either to despair or to the inability to work properly on an utterly insufficient diet.

Matters went from bad to worse as years went by, and finally culminated in a village called Red Bay, on the north side of the Straits of Belle Isle. One autumn as we made our last call, there we found the fishermen with their Lares and Penates packed, waiting for us on their fish stages. They begged us to give them a passage South, as they could no longer keep body and soul together on that section of the Coast. That night, at a conference called to consider the problem, it was decided that the people must be their own merchants, sharing the risks and dividing whatever profits might accrue. We pointed out to them that the life of the fisherman and the trapper is at best a gamble, and that the reason they like credit advances is that it makes the other man carry the risks.

At the time of the formation of this coöperative store, we thought it a significant fact that not one shareholder wished to have his name registered, and one and all they were opposed to having the little building labelled as a store — so ingrained in them was their fear of their suppliers. A year's savings of all the seventeen families of the place aggregated only eighty-five dollars, so we had to lend them enough to enable them to purchase their first cargo. That loan has been repaid years ago. Today not a barrow-load of fish leaves that harbour except through the coöperative store. Due solely to that little effort, the people of the village have been able to tide over a series of bad fisheries and every family is free from debt. Though the Red Bay Coöperative Store celebrated its thirty-eighth birthday with only a modest five per cent dividend, that was a creditable record in a year when so many failures and bankruptcies were occurring, not only in Newfoundland, but in other more favoured parts of the world. Moreover, the effort has helped materially in making the social life of the village more of that coöperative type which is the one and only basis in the world on which a kingdom of peace and righteousness can exist. Even in the terrible winter of 1932, when the Government had to feed fifty thousand fishermen and their wives and families, since it was impossible to sell their fish, Red Bay folk did not go hungry.

During my first winter at St. Anthony, the young minister of a local church often stopped on his rounds at the same houses as we did on ours, and the problem of coöperation was frequently discussed. Before taking Orders he had been trading, and had so disliked the methods that he had retired. He promised to help us organize a coöperative store on the Newfoundland side of the Straits.

When the day arrived for the initial meeting, the chosen rendezvous was a village some fourteen miles to the north of us. The evening before, the minister sent word that he could not be present, as he had to go to another hamlet in his mission, twenty miles to the westward, in order to hold a service. As we knew how much weight his opinion carried with the fishermen, this was a heavy blow, especially as the traders had notified me that they would be present in a body to block our project if they possibly could. Fortunately, we remembered that the clergyman did not know the way; so it was possible to persuade his dog-driver to work around gradually and end up at our meeting. Our friend was, therefore, present willy-nilly, but he proved a broken reed, for in the face of the traders he went back on coöperation.

It so happened that our komatik broke through the ice as we were taking a short cut across a bay to reach the meeting, and we arrived just in time to hear the traders joking the minister for having been tricked. It was a dark, crisp, cold night, and the howling of the hundreds of dogs which had hauled people to the scene from all over the countryside made a dismal chorus outside the windows of the little house. Fear of the old régime lay heavy on the gathering. No one but the traders dared speak, and they talked all the time. Only one courageous old fisherman raised his voice, but his maiden speech evoked hearty applause. 'Doctor — I means Mr. Chairman — if this 'ere copper store buys a bar'l of flour in St. John's for five dollars, be it going to sell it to we for ten? That's what us wants to know.'

For a long time no one was found who dared to take the management of the venture, but at length the best-loved fisherman on the shore stepped into the breach. What he lacked in 'learning' he made up in optimism, pluck, and unselfishness. It is an age-honoured custom on the Coast to give free meals to all travellers, be they men or dogs or both, and lodging to boot. Customers of the new store came from so far away that they had often to stay overnight, and it was always to Harry's house that they went. Profits on their small purchases were slight in any case, and non-existent by the time the customers had been fed and lodged. So we printed, mounted, framed, and despatched to our friend the motto, 'No more free meals. Each meal will cost ten cents in advance.' His grateful reply informed us that he had hung the card up in the 'best room.' The next time we 'blew in' to Harry's house, we found the legend hanging with its face to the wall. Later this little store was absorbed by the larger new one at St. Anthony, as being so close by.

Our third outpost of coöperation was located at a village seventy-five miles to the westward called Flowers Cove. Here the parson came in with a will. Being a Church of England man, he was a more permanent resident. He said, 'I am a poor man, but I'd sell my extra boots in order to be able to put one more share in the store.' He kept his word, and what was more important, he put in his brains. Everyone in the vicinity who had felt the burden of the old system joined the store. One poor Irishman walked seventy miles along the Straits shore to catch me on my next visit, and secretly gave me five dollars to invest for him in the store. ''Tis all I have in the world, Sir, saving a bunch of children.' For years afterwards, every time I visited that part of the Coast, Paddy came for a private interview to enquire after the health of the 'copper store,' until the day when he triumphantly produced another five dollars for a second share, 'out of me profits.'

The War proved fatal to this, our largest and practically our oldest effort. Success was its undoing. It had paid dividends as high as thirty per cent, owing to careful buying, rapid rises in prices, and general prosperity. Their trade increased so largely that the coöperators purchased vessels to do their own transportation, cornered herring — which in that section of the Coast had risen to ten dollars a barrel — and allowed their successful manager to refuse large sums for their fish in the local market and to export it direct to Europe instead. The Committee admitted subsequently that they had not exercised even the minimum of control which they should have done. Their two largest cargoes were both lost at sea under circumstances which admitted of their claiming no insurance. The upshot of the whole matter was that a year or so later that store had to be sold for debt. It was bought in by a family of local fishermen, and now under their control is running successfully as a private venture. Even so, being under the direction of people who live and spend their profits in the neighbourhood, such ownership is a great advance over the absentee trader. Everyone in America is familiar with the serious attempt which is made by endless advertising to persuade purchasers to deal with their neighbourhood shopkeepers. The many advantages to the community of such a course are even more obvious on the fringes of civilization.

Spurred by the benefits of the Red Bay Store, the people of a little hamlet some forty miles away determined to coöperate also. The result was a fine little shop near our hospital at Battle Harbour. The fact that the first year this venture did six thousand dollars' worth of business put a match to the wrath of those whose opposition had hitherto been that of rats behind the wainscot. They succeeded in having a Commission appointed by the Government and sent down to enquire into the work of the Grenfell Association as being 'a menace to honest trade.' The Commission and even the lawyers all told me that they had been bitterly prejudiced against the whole Mission by misrepresentations and the gossip of hearsay, even before they began their exhaustive enquiries on the spot. Their findings were a complete refutation of all the accusations, however, and proved the best possible advertisement for us. As in many other similar instances, the effort to discredit proved a boomerang; for certainly in no other way could we have secured the approval of the Government for our work. Twenty thousand copies of the Commission's Report were printed and distributed. Thus in large measure an end was put to really hurtful rumours, some of which could not help finding credence among simple-minded people.

St. Anthony coöperative store — the Spot Cash Coöperative Company, Limited — has shown a steady, healthy growth, and is today a vital part in the life of the place. The chequered days of its first bitter experience, due entirely to the negligence of the outside manager, still have their unfortunate aftermath of distrust in the minds of some of the people. In spite of all, however, it is doing far and away the biggest business in the neighbourhood. It buys goods wholesale in the United States and Canada as well as in St. John's, and since its reorganization, now many years ago, on a sound basis, it has not once missed paying a dividend. In 1931 its trade amounted to over fifty thousand dollars. It has supplied orders from many of the outlying villages, and even from the extreme north of Labrador. Incidentally, it has made St. Anthony the cheapest place in which to buy necessities anywhere in the North, while its renewed and enlarged premises in the centre of the community give a sense of solidarity. Its successful management has been made possible in large measure by a series of local young men and women who have returned from Business Colleges in the United States, their training having been made possible for them by Lady Grenfell through her educational work.

We are particularly grateful for one aspect of the whole coöperative movement on the Coast. Politics have not been permitted to intrude, and stress has been laid on forbearance, brotherliness, and self-reliance. The endeavour has been to inculcate everywhere that only thus can they enjoy the balance of profit which makes the difference between plenty and poverty on this isolated Coast. Only photographs of conditions as they were in the old days will induce the present generation to admit that want and squalor in their villages had ever reached the depths which we recall only too vividly. Those who enjoy the new day are unable and unwilling to believe what their parents went through.

Even politicians are admitting today that it is not essential that Labrador should grow flour or sugar to be happy and content and independent. Stephen King-Hall's little play, called 'B.J. One,' with its gospel that coöperation, not competition, must in future be the axis around which the economic world revolves, was heralded over the British Broadcasting Corporation, and even the most 'stand-pat' Bombastes Furioso sees that nothing is to be gained by attacking a world which confers a knighthood on Norman Angell, for showing how war injures everybody.

It seems only just in this connection to say that the summer of 1910 brought me a fine crop of personal worries, and probably deservedly so, for no one should leave his business affairs to another without guarantees, occasionally renewed, that all is well. Business is not to my liking. Moreover, I have an over-readiness to accept as helpers men whose qualifications are sometimes of their own rating. My troubles came through the coöperative stores.

None of the stores at the beginning of the venture were incorporated and the liability on them was therefore unlimited. Though I had always felt it best not to accept a penny of interest on the money I had put into them, their agent in St. John's had allowed them great latitude in credits. But it was a bolt from the blue when I learned that the merchants in St. John's were owed twenty-five thousand dollars by the stores, and that I was being held responsible for every penny of it. One can have little heart in his work if he feels that everyone looking at him thinks he is a defaulter. So I had to find some way out. The merchants were told the facts and asked to meet me at the office of one of them, to go over accounts, and try to find some plan to settle.

The next discovery was that the manager of the little store at St. Anthony, who was an exceedingly pious man — whose great zeal for cottage meetings and that form of religious work had led me to think too highly of him — had neglected his books and his work, and given credit to everyone who came along. The St. John's agent claimed that he had made a loss of twelve thousand dollars in a year.

I cashed every available personal asset which I could. The beautiful Emma E. White, also a personal possession, arrived in St. John's while we were there, with a full load of lumber, but it and she sailed straight into the melting-pot. The merchants, with one exception, were all as good about the matter as men can be. They were perfectly satisfied when they saw that one meant to face the debt squarely. One was nasty about it, saying that he would not wait. Whether he gained by it or not is hard to say. He was paid first, anyhow. The standard of what is really remunerative in life is graded differently. With the sale of a few investments and some other available property, and the help of a friend, the liability was so far reduced that, with what the stores paid, only one merchant was not fully indemnified, and he generously told me not to worry about the balance.

The incident was not the fault of the people of the Coast. Often I had been warned by the merchants that the coöperative stores would fail and that the people would rob me. There were badly kept books, and a number of fishermen disclaimed their debts charged against them. I am sure, however, that they did not go back on me willingly. It was the management, not the people or the system, which was at fault. Several of the stores are still running splendidly, and pay regular dividends to their fishermen shareholders.

Our experiments in coöperation, though carried out on so restricted a scale, convinced us that, if our profits could be kept on the Coast, the next-to-nature life had enough to offer in character as well as in comforts to attract a permanent population.

Along the French Shore in Northern Newfoundland the people were more densely settled than on the Labrador proper; the hinterland was small and the opportunities for supplementing the income earned by fishing correspondingly fewer. Moreover, the polar current, split by the most northerly cape of Newfoundland, as it enters the Straits of Belle Isle, renders that section of land most liable to summer frosts, with a far worse climate than in the Labrador bays. Gardening there is consequently less remunerative.

For years we puzzled our brains to discover some way to add to the earning capacity of the people in that section. It must be an enterprise which would be both coöperative and distributive. I had been told that there was plenty of timber to justify running a mill in one of the big bays, but that no sawmill paid in Newfoundland. All the same we were spurred by the poverty which we had seen in Canada Bay, about sixty miles south of St. Anthony. Also we knew that in our district labour would be cheaper than in the southern part of the Island — for our labour in winter usually went begging.

The Government wisely gave us a special grant, as our enterprise if successful would relieve them of the necessity of giving the inevitable poor relief in that locality. The whole expense of the undertaking fell on me personally for the Board of the Mission of those days felt it was outside their sphere. Moreover, we had already built St. Anthony Hospital, in spite of the fact that they had discouraged it from the first.

The people had no money to put into the sawmill venture, and the peculiar circumstances prevented my asking for help from friends outside. So it was with foreboding that we ordered a mill as if it were a pound of chocolates, and arranged with two young Englishmen to come out to help, for their expenses only. Three hundred dollars also had to be paid for the necessary survey and line cutting, and houses must be erected and furnished. At that time I had never seen a mill and doubtless my very ignorance supplied me with the courage to go ahead. I admit that, when I heard that one piece of the machinery included a boiler and weighed three tons, my misgivings were not lessened.

Snow was already lying on the ground when at last our summer's medical cruise was over and we could visit the scene of the new venture. A tiny cottage had been erected among the trees. It was small and damp. In the morning its walls inside were white with frost until the fire had been going for some time. However, the huge boiler, that 'bugaboo' of my dreams, lay safely on the bank. 'How did you get it there?' was my first query. 'We warped the vessel as near to the land as we could, then hove her close ashore and put skids from the rocks off to her. Over these we slid the boiler onto the bank, everyone hauling it up with their tackles.' The survey, though carried out by the Minister of Agriculture's own son and accepted by the Government, was poorly marked, and indeed has given us untold trouble ever since — for we have never been able to determine exactly where our boundaries lie.

Christmas and New Year's had come and gone before the demands of the hospital abated sufficiently for us to turn our thoughts once more to the new enterprise. The only difficulty of making the fifty-mile journey by dogs lay in the fact that there were no trails, and most of the way led through virgin forest, where windfalls and stumps and dense undergrowth made the ordinary obstacle race a marathon in comparison. We knew what we were in for, since, in our eagerness to begin dog-driving when the first snow fell, we had wandered over the tops of small trees hidden by snow, fallen through, and literally floundered about under the crust, unable to climb onto the surface again. Not so very long before, a man bringing his komatik down a steep hill at Conche missed his footing on the hard snow path and fell headlong into the great drift beside the trail. The heavy, loaded sledge ran over him and pressed him still deeper into the bank. Struggling only made him sink farther; and an hour later the poor fellow was discovered, smothered to death.

No one knew the way from St. Anthony to the mill, and we could not hear of a single man who had ever gone across the country in winter. We hoped to do that fifty miles in two days. To steer by compass sounded easy, but that perverse instrument persisted in pointing to the precipitous cliffs and impenetrable thickets. At length we struck a river, and argued that if we followed it we should come out at the head of the bay, thereby having only three miles of salt-water ice to cross. Our hopes came to nothing, however, for the stream proved a veritable torrent, leaping over rapids and falls through great ice canyons. Instead of gliding over a glassy surface as we had pictured, we found ourselves treading, like Agag, between heavy ice blocks.

Today there is a good trail cut and blazed, so that even carrying patients over that long haul is little more than a 'joy ride'; though there is always enough challenge left in the journey to lend it tang.

I recall another occasion when we were trying to cross Hare Bay and one of my dogs fell through the ice. It was ten below zero with a biting wind. When just a mile from the opposite shore, I jumped from the komatik to try the ice edge, it gave way suddenly and in I fell. The best advice on that day was to 'keep cool.' Even with a mile of the fastest sprinting I could manage, my clothing soon became like the armour of an ancient knight and, though in those days I was accustomed to break the ice in the morning to bathe, running in a coat of mail was a novel experience.

On the fourth day we reached the mill, to find that logging had progressed satisfactorily, and the future looked rosy for this latest attempt to give work and food and money and self-respect instead of a dole. The boxes of machinery for cutting timber were being unpacked — the weird iron parts having to us all the piquancy of a Chinese puzzle, with the added zest of knowing what potential they stood for, when rightly arranged.

One accident alone marred the record of that first year. A party of children had been crossing the ice in the harbour on their way to school, when it gave way, dropping a number of them into the treacherous rapids of that bit of water. One of the English volunteers was a first-class athlete and saved five lives, but two of the children had been drowned. The young fellow himself was so badly chilled that it had taken the hot body of the father of one of the rescued children, wrapped up in bed with him in lieu of a hot-water bottle, to restore his circulation.

That first year only one trouble at the mill proved insurmountable. The log-hauler would not deliver the goods to the rotary saw. When subsequently we discovered that the whole apparatus was upside down, it did not seem so surprising, after all! The second year, however, was our hardest time. For the bills for the lumber which we had sold were not paid in time for us to buy the absolutely essential stock of food for the people for the winter. Like King Midas of old, it was food, not cash, which they needed in their mouths; and without the food, the men could not go logging. When finally we could see our way to purchase those supplies for the loggers, the whole bay was frozen over, and the cargo had to be landed by the mail steamer, nine miles away from the mill. Somehow, the little hospital steamer Strathcona must carry it up the bay. So it was decided that, as we could not possibly butt through the ice, we must butt over it.

Every movable thing, including chains and anchors, was shifted to the after end of the ship and piled up there with the barrels of pork, molasses, flour, and sugar, all the ship's boats and heavy weights, so as to bring her forefoot above the water-level. Then we banged into the ice, running up onto it and crashing through, but doing no damage whatever to the steamer's hull. It was very hard work to back her astern for another drive, so every available man stood on the rail on one side, each carrying a weight, and then at the signal rushed to the other side, and so backward and forward, giving the boat a good roll. Slow as it was, we got there, and that in true Biblical fashion, literally 'reeling to and fro like drunken men.'

Labrador has many other things to offer besides her wonderful fisheries as a claim for admission into the hegemony of worth-while nations. Her valuable furs are no mean contribution to both the comfort and the beauty of the civilized world. Under the old régime, trappers were not allowed to buy traps, or even salmon nets. They hired all such gear 'on halves,' which meant that half the catch went to the owner of the outfit, while the other half was also retained by the owners, the trapper taking out such goods at their store as he required, but at whatever price the merchant cared to charge against his account.

In my early days fur on the Labrador was very cheap. Even a silver fox seldom fetched a hundred dollars, while lynx, wolverine, beaver, mink, bear, and other skins were priced in proportion. In spite of this, some men made a good living out of furring. We came to the conclusion that to breed animals in captivity would not only improve conditions along this line, but would also save poor settlers from having on their hands pelts which were often useless. Sometimes a big storm would prevent a trapper getting around his fur path, and meanwhile mice or another fox might come along and partially eat a fine fur caught in a trap. Again, a poor man might find an animal out-of-season which had slept on wet snow or ice and frozen his fur to it, so that in order to get up he had had to pull out his own King (long) hairs. Of course that renders the pelt practically valueless, but the temptation to get even fifty cents was often too great, and the man would kill the animal.

Thus it came about that we decided to start a fox farm at St. Anthony. We chose a location close to the hospital; and we rejoice today to know that the idea was correct, though at the moment we had neither experience nor time to teach us how to manage the animals.

The Labrador red fox is quite common, and, like the white, breeds in holes and sand-dunes. A litter of foxes may include black, red, silver and patches, but never white. The white fox is a smaller animal and a distinct species. Foxes feed largely on mice, and on a small creature much like a grey mole, called a lemming. These in turn feed on the roots of plants. When the lemmings are plentiful, so are our common foxes, and *vice versa*.

In our little experimental farm we soon had a dozen couples — red, white, patch, and one pair of silvers. Some of the young pups were very tame, but we did not have success in breeding them. Either they died or their parents ate them. A Harvard professor who happened to be cruising with me that summer records that I was carrying 'fifteen little foxes on board the Strathcona to St. Anthony for starting the fox farm. Some of the little animals had been brought aboard in blubber casks and their coats were very sticky. After a few days they became very tame and played with the dogs, were all over the deck, fell down the companionway, were always having their tails and feet stepped on and yelping with pain, when not yelling for food. The long-suffering seaman who took care of them said to me, "I been cleaned out that fox box. It do be shockin'. I been in a courageous turmoil my time, but dis be the head smell ever I witnessed."'

The reds and patch foxes in my farm became very tame, and always ran out to greet us. One of the reds loved nothing better than to be caught and hugged, and squealed with delight when you took notice of it. The whites, and still more the silvers, were always very shy. Every schooner's crew entering the harbour was interested in the fox farm, and a deeply cut pathway up the hill was soon worn by the feet of fishermen going up to see the animals.

As we had had no success with raising the young fox pups, when Prince Edward Island began its work in fox-breeding we decided to discontinue our experiment, as we had neither time nor money to carry on the work properly. Most unfortunately, too, the foxes in our farm developed a kind of sickness which resembled strychnine poisoning. This killed three of the animals which were our especial pets.

In the summer of 1907, a schooner's crew offered me four live young silvers for two hundred dollars, but at that moment we had enough of the animals and refused to buy them. In 1914, one of our distant neighbours who had caught a live slut in pup sold her and her little brood for ten thousand dollars.

Since those days a number of fox farms have sprung up both in Newfoundland and Labrador, and have met with more or less success. The Hudson's Bay Company has a very large fox farm at Romaine; and there is also a successful one running at Piastre Bay. Though fox-breeding is an interesting hobby, it requires almost as much patience as running an orphanage. On the other hand, are not sheep, angora goats, oxen, and other domestic animals merely results of similar efforts? If fox-farming should one day entirely supersede the use of the present sharp-toothed leg trap, no small gain in humane treatment of dumb creatures would be effected. Though the fur trapper as a rule is a gentle creature, the 'quality of mercy is not strained' in furring any more than it is in the seal fishery.

Outwitting foxes is not so easy as those who talk slightingly of 'the lower animals' seem to suppose. One winter two men from North Newfoundland, who had a plan to get rich by securing rare fox skins, stayed in the North when the fishing fleets were driven South by the close of open water. It came out later that they had obtained from a friend a lot of poison, with which they intended to make their fortunes, though they knew perfectly well that the use of poison in catching fur-bearing animals is strictly forbidden by law.

It so happened that a large whale had been driven ashore that fall; and near the carcass they made their camp, knowing that foxes would be sure to be attracted by the feast. Just before Christmas a violent storm broke up the standing ice and washed the whale clean away. It took a lot of discussion before they decided to give up the herrings which they had designed for their own Christmas dinner, to be used as bait; but, as one of the men argued, 'a good fox is worth more than a meal.' So they filled up the herrings with the poison, found a trail on the snow where a fox had been passing to and fro, placed the poisoned bait on it, and hid away to watch results. A fine silver fox soon scented the herring, and, snapping it up, swallowed it in a gulp. They could easily have shot the foy, but decided not to for fear of injuring the pelt with bullet holes. So they watched Reynard make for the woods, and then followed close behind, waiting for him to drop in his tracks. They were not skilled trappers and soon lost their way. On looking around, they were surprised to see the fox following them. They casually dropped another herring and went on without stopping. Sure enough, Brother Fox gobbled the second herring with as much gusto as he had the first. A third time they repeated the attempt, but again Master Reynard was left licking his chops. By this time he was a bit wary and would not come within gunshot. The day ended with the last herring dropped and the fox farther than ever behind, with a knowing grin on his face. Evidently he was a bit puzzled at finding so many fat herrings on that pathway of his. The men swore that he had some internal antidote for their poison. They never laid eyes on him again; but we trust that on Christmas morning he was laughing loudly in his den at the two would-be hunters, thinking of their lost herrings, their lost fox and their lost self-respect.

Mink-breeding is now proving remunerative, and is doing well on the Coast, as it is in America and Canada. Animal genetics is practically a new science. It undoubtedly has a great future and much to give the world. Special leave of absence was granted to Professor Darling, of Edinburgh, to do a preliminary survey of Labrador in 1932, but so far we have been unable to get the thousand dollars required to meet the necessary expenses — the state of finances in America

and Europe alike being so unfortunate. Amongst the endless
fears and doubts, many men of good heart are no longer able
to help 'divers good causes,' even one like this which is of
world-wide interest.

CHAPTER XII

RESIDUARY LEGATEE

In my boyhood I used to collect postage stamps, butterflies, and birds' eggs. When we sailed to Labrador, however, a new chance presented itself, and I started to collect children. The truth is I chanced upon a couple, a little boy and girl, who had no parents. They lived in a very poor hamlet by the sea and they did not have one single possession — not even the clothes they stood up in were their own. The other poor folk of the village had kept them alive; but so great was the want in that place and so deeply in debt were the fishermen that when the winter came on, the merchants who come North each summer packed up all their goods. As there was no chance whatever of the people paying for any of the food, they started South, leaving the miserable little settlement to sink or swim as best it could.

When those fishermen came aboard our hospital schooner late that fall, little did they know what was going to happen to any of them, particularly those two 'nobody's children.' Our schooner was under a hundred feet long and much smaller than the Santa Maria or the Mayflower, but to those two waifs she must have looked like a veritable Leviathan. We took those two little Labrador orphans to England with us; and today, forty years later, they can look back on a happy and useful life.

Everyone crowded to see the Eskimo Encampment at the World's Fair in Chicago, held just forty years ago. The most popular side-show was a little boy, the son of a Northern Chieftain called Kaiachououk; and many a coin was flung into the ring that Prince Pomuik might show his skill with the thirty-foot lash of his dog-whip. One man, of all those who stared with idle curiosity at the little people from the Labrador, took an interest in the child. It was the Reverend C. C. Carpenter, who had spent some years of his early life as a clergyman on our Coast.

When the Exhibition closed, all the Eskimos were sent back

to the North. Mr. Carpenter, however, did not forget his little friend, and continued to write to him, though he never received any answers to his letters.

One dark, foggy night in August, 1895, we sailed into the entrance of that marvellous gorge called Nakvak. We had determined to push as far north as the most northerly white family on the Labrador. As we nosed our way cautiously some twenty miles from the entrance, our watch suddenly sang out, 'Light on the starboard bow!' Immediately our steamer's whistle echoed and reëchoed between those towering cliffs. Three rifle shots answered our signal, and soon a boat bumped against our side, and a hearty Englishman sprang over the rail. It was George Ford, the factor of the Hudson's Bay Company's post. He told us of a band of Eskimos who had gone still farther up the fjord, carrying with them a dying little boy. Next day we found Pomuik, naked and haggard, suffering from an insidious hip disease, lying on the rocks beside a tiny tubik.

We steamed South again, taking the sick lad with us, for the Eskimos had been only too happy to be rid of him. Pomuik brought with him his only treasure, a letter from a clergyman in Andover, Massachusetts, this same Mr. Carpenter. It contained a photograph, and, when I showed it to the boy, he said, 'Me even love him.' All this I posted back to Mr. Carpenter to let him know his boy was being cared for.

Some weeks later, the answer to our letter came back. It read, 'Keep him. I write for "The Congregationalist," a magazine here in the States, and the children in "The Corner" will be his guardians. He must never be cold or lonely again.' So the 'Corner Cot' came into existence in Battle Harbour Hospital, and the little Eskimo boy occupied it for the brief remainder of his life.

On my return from England the following summer, the first to greet me was Pomuik. 'Me Gabriel Pomuik now,' he explained. A good Moravian Brother had come along during the winter and christened the child by the name of the Angel of Comfort.

In a sheltered corner of a little graveyard on the Labrador rests the body of this 'happy Prince.' The doctor in charge of that hospital wrote me that when he died the wards seemed

desolate without his smiling face. The night he was buried
the mysterious aurora lit up the sky. The Eskimos always
call the Northern Lights 'the spirits of the dead at play.'
To us it seemed a shining symbol of the joy in the City of the
King that another young soldier had won his way home.

As vividly as if it were yesterday there flashed across my
memory a visit to the isolated cottage of a lonely Scotch
settler. The watch had sighted the S O S signal on the shore,
and we hove our little steamer to in the wind. A dead woman
lay on the floor of the lonely little log house when I entered,
and a dying man was on the board settle. It was our first
experience of influenza. When day broke, we dug a grave
and buried both parents. After we had filled in the hole,
there were five little children sitting disconsolately facing us
on the mound of sand. Then and there the Labrador collection of derelict children began.

We had anchored among a group of islands to give the
people a chance of coming aboard the hospital ship. Suddenly
a boat bumped our side, and a woman climbed over the rail
with a bundle under each arm. On my chartroom table she
laid the two bundles and proceeded to untie them.

'There is something wrong with them, Sir,' she explained.
Examination showed that, although their eyes looked right,
both children were as blind as kittens with congenital pos-
terior polar cataracts.

'Have you any other children?' I asked the mother.

'Yes, four.'

'Where is your husband?'

'Killed by a gun accident three months ago.'

'Then how do you manage to keep food for the babies?'

'Indeed, I can't.'

'Whatever are you going to do with them?'

'I'm going to give them to you, Doctor.'

When we got under way, it was rough and the babies made
such a noise that the helmsman stuck his head into the chart-
room, which was directly behind the wheelhouse, to see what
could be the matter.

'What are you going to do with those, Sir?'

'Shh. They're blind and quite useless. When we get outside, we'll drop them over the rail.'

He stared at me for a second before he turned back to his wheel. A few minutes later in popped his head again.

'Excuse my being so bold, but don't throw them over the side. We've got eight of our own, but I guess my wife'll find a place for those two.'

I did not throw them overboard; neither did I send them to the home of that modern saint. I simply added them to my collection. When they were old enough, we sent them to the School for the Blind in Halifax. On their return to us, Dr. Andrews operated and gave partial sight to both of them. For some years they were industrial teachers at one of our little centres on the Coast. They can see colour, read very large print, distinguish faces, and run about the rocks by themselves — pleasures which were denied them until they were twenty years old.

Two years ago one of those twins married a fine young fisherman, and last summer as soon as we had anchored in her harbour she climbed over the rail of the Strathcona. Proudly she showed me her baby — a fine, healthy little boy. As I complimented her she said, 'He don't seem to take much notice.' A cold chill went over me as I asked her to let me have a look at the child. It was as I had feared. He had been born blind in both eyes.

In various ways my adopted family grew at an alarming rate, once it became known that we were acting the rôle of unofficial residuary legatee for derelict children. A little while ago we were sailing across a large bay with a crew of half a dozen college boys who had come 'down North' for the summer at their own cost and charges, because they had discovered that it is more fun pulling a lame dog out of a hole than 'putting' a small white ball into one. When we landed, we started to wander around the deserted headland. Just outside the poverty-stricken little village, we passed the doorless and windowless frame of a log cabin perched up against the face of the sheer cliff. Curiosity led us to peep inside, though there were no signs of life. Suddenly one of the boys, looking up at a hole in the low ceiling, exclaimed, 'Why, there's someone looking down at us through that chink.' In a trice he was up on the lofting. 'There are four naked kiddies up here,' he called down.

An hour later our sentry, who had been left to watch the cabin, reported that a woman with a baby in her arms had gone in at the door. She told us that her husband had gone North three months before and nothing had been heard of him since. When we found the log cabin, she had been out looking for berries on the hillside to feed the nestlings.

'What can we do to help?' we asked as she brought the children down from the rafters and out into the sunshine.

'For God's sake, take them and feed them. I can do no more.'

Vermin, the inevitable accompaniment of poverty and squalor, had not been avoided even though the children had no rags to cover them. How could we take them back in our jolly-boat, over seven miles of open sea, without clothing. In a second every boy with me had his coat off, and a well-clad child in his arms. What a credential of modern youth that act was! When we left, the poor mother brought up the rear of our procession carrying the baby. Today that little family is fed, clothed, going to school, and started on the road to a useful life.

So the tale has grown. Some children came to us because they were orphans, some because they were not. One of our boys came from Cape Chidley itself; others came from as far south and west as Bay of Islands in Southern Newfoundland. I am constantly asked, 'But why do you have a Children's Home in Newfoundland? Can't the Newfoundlanders look out for their own dependent children?' Northern and Southern Newfoundland should be differentiated from the point of view of climate, education, and opportunity. We built our Children's Home at the north end of the northern peninsula of Newfoundland for reasons of efficiency and economy, but the children who make up the family are largely drawn from the Labrador side of the Straits of Belle Isle. Often also, the destitution of a family of Newfoundlanders makes it impossible for us to leave children in such poverty. We have now a second collection in Labrador, the headquarters being the Lockwood School at Cartwright.

During the passing years the building expanded with the increasing family. At one vital point in its career its capacity was doubled by the generosity of one of our volunteers,

Mr. Francis Sayre, son-in-law of the late President Wilson. But the building was made of green wood, it contracted with our very necessary central heating, the roof leaked, the windows rattled, the snow blew in around the doors and windows and seemed to filter between the very clapboards themselves. Our bills for heating were enormous. So was the drain on strength and patience of the good lady volunteers for whom the problem of caring for fifty-odd children was acute enough anyway without the additional worry of frozen pipes, no proper day nursery for the little children, no isolation room for the sick, no attic storage, rats and mice, no storeroom for food. How sorely and how long we needed a concrete building properly planned, large enough to accommodate the numbers whom we had to turn away for lack of space, easily kept warm, with separate wings for boys and girls, and a crêche for the babies! And this is how we finally got it.

We worked for it. We calculated that the cheapest way to build a fire-proof, wind and-damp-proof building would be to build it of concrete blocks. So we estimated the number of blocks needed as nearly as possible, and, rating the cost of each at twenty-five cents, we set out and collected 'Bricks.' William Adams Delano, of New York, one of our directors, president of the Architects' Institute, drew the plans freely. Some friends gave special fittings, some gave memorial beds, and one or two gave memorial rooms. Everyone locally gave work, and as soon as the universities finished commencement a number of students from Princeton, with Professor William Gillespie, professor of higher mathematics, came North and volunteered to excavate and install the foundation, while all the mechanical engineering was looked after by one of our own boys from North Labrador. It took two years to finish it — our seasons for building are short — but it surely has come to stay, and hundreds of children have already had 'the gospel preached to them' by the loving care of ladies who are living in the North, not for what they can get out of it, but what they can bring to it. If my reader doubts what such a home means to the helpless and hopeless, do come and see. We have arranged now for four special steamers to come on a round trip all the way from Quebec to see the wonders of the Coast and to visit at least four of our many stations each summer. You can stay over a boat — you can enjoy salmon and trout fishing, and other things besides!

One of our worst difficulties has been the half-orphan — a child with the father or mother living; more often the helpless mother having to be left behind. I still look back with sorrow on the day when we took three little children whom we found starving, as their father had died. I had to leave the eldest boy behind, as otherwise the mother would have had no one to 'fend for her.' The three children grew to be fine, healthy young people. One now lives close by us, has a charming home and lovely children of her own. But the lad left behind was never able to provide food enough, and he gradually failed and finally died of tuberculosis. Whether he starved himself to give his mother food, I do not know.

Only last year one of my colleagues visited by chance on one of his komatik rounds a poor family with seven children. He found the father stretched on the floor by the stove, unable to speak. My friend rushed off to get the food which the family had been too proud to ask for, but the father died four days later. His wife insisted that he had gone without food himself for the sake of the children.

To Labrador's way of thinking, God is the Giver of all children. Man's responsibility is merely to find food and clothing for them as best he can, once they are in the world. If these 'gifts of God' suffer, or are a burden to other people besides the parents, that is a trick of fate. It is the philosophy of the ignorant and the thoughtless — almost the animal, and it makes the lives of the women of the Coast terribly hard.

For years, owing to the lack of any boarding-schools in the country and owing to our very scattered population, we were sometimes obliged to accept bright children from isolated homes and give them a chance at 'learning,' even though they had both parents living, and so had not the claim of being orphans, half or whole. Whether the parents in these cases have been able to pay anything or not, the children are always worth the expenditure. Indeed, the children in our orphanages do most of the work themselves; and thanks to the invaluable help of the Needlework Guild of America, through its Labrador Branch, the clothing problem has been taken care of.

ORPHANS SAWING THEIR WINTER WOOD

ORPHANS IN WINTER DRESS

Today, after forty years, we have orphanage-boarding-schools at four widely separated centres, where any child can be brought. From this flotsam and jetsam of a barren Coast, with 'nothing worthy to offer mankind,' have come some of our most efficient and loyal helpers. The students of Yale University are responsible for one of these centres, Princeton for another, and friends in Chicago for a third, while St. Anthony Orphanage is a truly international effort.

We rejoice to reflect that the problem of underprivileged children in Labrador can be solved as long as our schools and orphanages carry on. The one test for efficient surgery in these practical days is its 'end results.' Surely that is God's test for our lives. Certainly it is not only the gauge of the value of the outlay in child life, but its justification and in nine cases out of ten its more than satisfying reward.

CHAPTER XIII

OPEN SESAME

THE only real joy of possession is the power which it confers for a larger life of service. When politics and finance, international as well as national, are actuated by that conviction, permanent peace will become possible. The solution of the problem of inducing the millennium is most likely to be furthered by wise and persevering work among the children. The children of Labrador are the hope of the future of this country as they are that of every land. Their true education — the leading them out of themselves — to fit them for wise citizenship has been cruelly neglected during the few generations of Labrador's history.

It is a truism that the illiteracy, backwardness, ignorance, and superstition of large numbers of the inherently fine Anglo-Saxon stock who make up the population of Labrador and North Newfoundland are their greatest handicap in a life already made difficult enough by its physical environment.

The denominational spirit fostered by compulsory sectarian schools is terribly emphasized in Newfoundland and Labrador. All monies granted by the Government for education are handed to the separate denominations for sectarian schools. Such a course is almost writing ourselves down as still living in the Middle Ages, when the clergy had a monopoly of polite learning. In our sparsely populated country it means that one often found a Roman Catholic, a Church of England, a Methodist, and a Salvation Army school, all in one village — and no school whatever in an adjoining hamlet. I recall that in St. Anthony, where there was already a Church of England school, a Methodist school, and a Salvation Army school, at one time we were menaced with the threat of a fourth — like a new Egyptian plague, but entailing more dangerous and more permanent results.

We were sure that the young lives entrusted to us were having as good medical care for their bodies as we could provide. We determined to have that paralleled for their

minds if we could manage it, regardless of what the parents
of the village children did. Is not true religion a thing of the
intellect as well as of the heart? Fancy trying to inculcate
it by 'two periods a week of forty minutes each devoted to
sectarian teaching'! My picture of myself at the age of seven
sitting on a bench for forty minutes twice a week learning to
be religious made me sympathize with Scrooge when the
Ghost of the Past was paying him a visit.

Despite the fact that there is nothing so reactionary as a
religious prejudice well embedded, and although our efforts to
have the local schools combine had signally failed, we determined to start a school of our own. Unfortunately, the only
building available was not so good as the accommodation
which we had provided for our pigs — for fat pork is rightly
considered a *sine qua non* down North.

One of the great lacks in child development on the Coast,
particularly deplorable to an Anglo-Saxon, was the absence of
games and toys. One of the first things we noticed on the
Labrador was the absence of dolls; and though our second
season we brought out and distributed a trunkful, we found
that the dolls were nail-high on the walls as ornaments, and
well out of reach of the children.

The generous help of trained volunteers, especially a
trained kindergartner, enabled us to introduce organized play
for the first time. It caught like wildfire among the children,
and it was refreshing to see them in groups by the roadside
memorizing 'All on the Train for Boston.'

Our fishermen have definite, though often singular, ideas
of what Almighty God does and does not allow; and among
those pursuits unquestionably on the local 'Index,' dancing
holds the first place. The laxity of foreigners on this article
of the Credo is proverbial. Immediately one realized that the
local Solons judged our kindergarten to be introducing the
thin edge of the wedge of wickedness, and that our venture
would come to grief unless such rumours could be nipped in
the bud, I sought out the two local clergy. Together we
knocked at the door of the kindergarten. The first game was
irreproachable — every child was sitting on the floor. The
next, however, aroused the suspicion of the vigilance committee, for the children were choosing partners. Even so no

wright School, in large measure the gift of a lady in Texas, has already forty students; while our latest educational effort at St. Mary's River, the special charge of students of Princeton University, opened recently with twenty-eight boys and girls. We long for the day when we shall see a boarding-school at Red Bay. It would not only be an educational blessing to that scattered community and section of the Coast, but would serve as a stimulus to the little weaving and industrial training school which we have been running there for some years. At each of these centres, some proportion of the scholars are permanent, the rest returning in summer to their isolated homes, to learn there the daily duties of their own environment.

The Moravian Missions among the Eskimos have for many years run an excellent boarding-school for some thirty-five children at Makkovik; and Commander MacMillan has recently started a school for the Eskimos at the more northerly Moravian station at Nain.

One day I met a very small boy walking unconcernedly down the gangplank of the mail steamer, lugging over his back a heavy kitbag.

'Who are you?' I asked.

'I'm Percy.'

'Where do you come from?'

'North Labrador, Sir.'

'What have you come to St. Anthony for?'

'To get learning.'

He was a small orphan from a remote village of our northern Coast. He had come along with all he owned, because he had heard that children would be given a chance at the Grenfell School. Today he is married and doing well as a trapper and fisherman, having had his 'schooling' and returned to his own village in the Far North. Only this last summer (1931) he entertained us for tea there in his cosy little cottage at Hebron.

Many years ago we were running South from our long northern trip before a fine leading wind. Suddenly we noticed a small boat with an improvised flag standing right out across our bows. Thinking that at least it was some serious surgical case, we ordered 'Down sail and heave her

ST. ANTHONY SCHOOL

ONE BUILDING OF THE LOCKWOOD SCHOOL AT CARTWRIGHT

to,' annoying though we felt it to have the delay. A solitary white-haired old man climbed with difficulty over our rail. 'Good-day. What's the trouble? We're in a hurry.' The old man most courteously doffed his cap and stood holding it in his hands. 'I wanted to ask you, Doctor,' he said slowly, 'if you had any books you could lend me. We can't get anything to read here.' A feeling of humiliation almost immediately replaced the angry reply which had sprung to my lips. Which is really charity, skilfully to remove his injured leg if he had had one, or to afford him the pleasure and profit of a good book?

'Haven't you got any books?'

'Yes, Sir, I've got two, but I've read them through and through long ago.'

'What are they?'

'One is the "Works" of Josephus,' he answered, 'and the other is Plutarch's "Lives."'

He was soon bounding away over the seas in his little craft, the happy possessor of one of our moving libraries.

The Carnegie libraries have emphasized a fact that is to education and the colleges what social work is to medicine and the hospitals. Our faculties, like our jaws, atrophy if we do not use them to bite with. Thanks to the generosity of Mr. Carnegie and others, we now have about seventy-five of these library boxes, containing a selection of some fifty books each. The hospital steamer each summer moves these peripatetic libraries one more stage along the Coast. The coöperation of teachers and librarians who come and give us splendid voluntary service more than doubles the usefulness of the libraries as it does that of the workers themselves in their special spheres. The world's workers have everything to gain by coöperation, whatever their field, and whether it is a question of nationalism or internationalism. When men pull together, efficiency increases in geometrical progression.

For years we were not able through shortage of funds to attack the problem of the education of the small groups of children in our most isolated little settlements, many of which are never touched by the Government mail steamers. As Mahomet could not possibly come to the mountain, it had to go to him. A lady and a Doctor of Philosophy, whose life had been spent in teaching, and who therefore might have been excused from discontinuing that function during her long vacations, came down at her own expense to one of these tiny villages to teach for the summer. With loyal devotion she has continued and enlarged that work during all the intervening twenty years. She built up a band of volunteer teachers, who come each summer to these remote hamlets, live with the fisher people in their cottages, and gather their pupils daily wherever they can find a vacant room.

It has always helped us 'down North' to remember the stand which Archbishop Ireland took for public schools. He knew full well that it requires the fabulous Jack to overcome the hoary giants of prejudice and ingrained custom. A Church of England clergyman whom we were influential in bringing out to the Coast started an undenominational boarding-school in his district, assuming this care in addition to his many other burdens connected with his far-flung parish. When, after years of splendid service on the Labrador, he was obliged to return to England owing to ill-health, the Grenfell Association took over the school. Today I am more than ever persuaded that a chain of undenominational boarding-schools should be started which would react for the great benefit of the country.

Who would ever think of giving an Episcopal pill or a Methodist plaster? My convictions on the subject of education in the North are no less firm today than they were twenty-two years ago when I wrote to my wife: 'Ignorance is the worst cause of suffering on our North Coast, and our "religion" is fostering it. True, it has denominational schools, but these are used to bolster up special ecclesiastical bodies, and are not half so good as Government schools would be. The "goods delivered" in the schools are not educational in the best sense, and are all too often inefficiently offered. Instead of making the children ambitious to go on learning through life, they make them tired. There is no effort to stimulate the play side, and in our north end of the Colony there are no trades taught, no new ideas, no manual training — it is all so-called "arts" and Creeds.'

Once we had assumed schools and orphanages as an interpretation of the maxim, 'Let the little ones come unto me,' it became imperative to find industrial outlets for the more promising students, to enable them to make their lives useful to their country and satisfactory to themselves. This special branch of supplementary education has been under the entire charge of Lady Grenfell from its very inception. It has been no small responsibility, not only to raise the funds for sending some twenty boys and girls out each year to the United States or Canada, but to arrange for their scholarships, their transportation, their clothing problems, their eyes and their teeth, their adjustments to a new *milieu* — in fact, all the vagaries and vicissitudes of so large and so complex and so scattered a 'family.' Moreover, she assumed this in addition to the cares of our own family, the constant help she gives me personally in every branch of the work, and the practical interest she has always taken in so important a problem as the Industrial Department.

This Supplementary Educational Department has always kept in mind the elimination of imported workers, remote eventuality though that may be. The aim has been to train the young people along technical lines as far as ever possible, and not to give a so-called classical education. Moreover, it has always been made clear to each student going out to England, Canada, or the United States that he is being offered this opportunity, not for his own sake, but that he may return and be a channel for helping his own people more efficiently because of what he has been able to become. Considering the lure of the easier life which civilization holds before the minds of these young people, we consider that the proportion of the students who have maintained their idealism and their love for their own country so strongly as to make them return is very creditable to their fine Anglo-Saxon heritage. Of the hundred students whom Lady Grenfell and her colleagues have sent out, over eighty have returned to their own land. They are now serving the Coast, some as mechanical engineers, electricians, plumbers, shoemakers, teachers, dressmakers, cabinet-makers, trained nurses, dietitians, stenographers, managers of little coöperative stores, industrial teachers; while we can boast at least one tanner, one tinsmith, and two clergymen in the number. Both boys and girls have always been required to work during their term of education, to earn as much as possible towards their expenses. Before being sent out, moreover, each one is always required to promise that, in consideration of the chance he is getting, he will return to Labrador or North Newfoundland and give at least two years' service — of course they must be paid for this — to their country and people. Once they have remained for two years and seen how much they can offer for the amelioration of their own environment, the ones with the high ideal of service — and they are in the majority — remain for life.

Of course we have had failures. Human nature is the same regardless of degrees of latitude. Some of the colleges and technical schools to which we sent these students, generous as those schools have invariably been in giving us scholarships and every possible help, gave them everything which may count as education except this very inspiration to use what they had received for the benefit of those who had not had their advantages. It was of no interest to us whether Jack should wear a black tail coat and a top hat, or an oilskin and a sou'wester; and we certainly did not wish Janie to add to her troubles by getting the habit of wearing shoes with silly heels two inches high, or using lipstick, or any other artificial adornment to her healthy and bonnie face.

If you were to visit the Coast today and question any one of the students who has returned, you would not find one who would admit that he had lost anything, even so far as the material things of life are concerned. Rather they would tell you that, having been 'led out of themselves,' they had found through that education those opportunities for service to their fellow men, which have altered their lives, and for which they can never be sufficiently grateful to the kind friends, whom they do not know personally in most instances, but whose vision and whose generosity have made the new life possible for them.

A boy came to me one day on my ship when my surgical clinic was over. No, he did not want to trouble me for medicine or surgery. What he wanted, like Percy, was 'learning.' He was sixteen years old and a bit of a carpenter. He could read a little, as his Scotch mother had taught him. When I asked him if he could pay for his education, he said, 'No, Doctor, but I'll work ten hours a day as a carpenter if you will give me one hour a day teaching.'

He was our first 'outside' student. The Pratt Institute in Brooklyn gave us a scholarship for him. That was thirty years ago. In 1927, when we built our first reinforced concrete, fireproof hospital, with electric light, central heating, and modern plumbing, we did not send to New York or any other outside place to secure a master mason, mechanic, electrician, plumber, or one 'educated' man. This boy, having become our chief mechanic, took entire charge of the construction of the building. The special technical workers under him were also local boys, trained in the States or Canada. The Governor came down for the opening of the building. There was not one leak in the plumbing, not one crack in the plaster, not one short circuit in the lighting. Entirely self-taught, this man plays the organ in church. He is also Government surveyor, supervises our machine shop, a repair dock, a furniture-making department. As his hobbies, he runs the short-wave wireless and a Marconi of six-hundred-metre wave-length by rule of thumb, and acts as one of the chief directors of the fishermen's local coöperative store.

All three of his sons have been given supplementary, outside education through the Grenfell Association, and two of them, grown to manhood in their turn, have returned to the Coast, to find their life-work and opportunity there.

CHAPTER XIV

WHO HATH DESIRED THE SEA?

OUR fishermen never pray for ships to be wrecked. There is some little doubt amongst those of us who own boats as to whether such a prayer might not prove a boomerang. However, I have known sincerely religious men pray that, if there was going to be a shipwreck, at least it might be in their neighbourhood!

On one occasion, when our cattle were so short of food that it looked as if they must starve that winter, a large steamer loaded with five thousand tons of barley ran on the rocks a few hundred yards from our barn. We did not suggest to the skipper that it was an answer to prayer, even if we thought that it was; especially as there have been so many wrecks on our Coast that we might have obtained a bad name as wreckers.

The people were genuinely surprised when I added to my other responsibilities that of surveyor of shipping for Lloyd's, north of latitude fifty-two, as well as commissioner for wrecks. The Graveyard of the Atlantic was at that time said to be Cape Race in Southern Newfoundland, many hundreds of miles to the south of us. I remember five steamers being piled up on the top of one another at one time there. New inventions, such as the wireless, direction signals, and the fathometer, have altered all that. Now the direct route through the Straits of Belle Isle and the Gulf of St. Lawrence is no longer nearly as exciting as of old.

The S. S. Mexico, with a cargo of general food supplies, was our first experience of wrecks. She ran full speed into an almost perpendicular cliff on the west end of Belle Isle in a dense fog and immediately sank. Till winter set in, barrels of flour, uninjured except for a half-inch layer of dough coating the outside, were picked up floating to and fro along the Coast. For weeks fishermen with improvised corkscrews mounted on long poles were using her hold as a magnified bran pie, and hooking up hams, cheeses, kegs of butter, and whatever came within reach of their tentacles!

The next large wreck was the Mariposa, a beautiful boat with many passengers aboard, bound from Montreal to England. She ran on the western ledge of Forteau Point, and was picked clean by the local fishermen before the close of open water. Incidentally, our own nautical outfits profited, as gear useful to us but valueless to small boats was brought to our neighbouring hospital in lieu of fees. Many other wrecks have followed as the years have gone by. The S. S. Greetlands, laden with cattle food, and two large Norwegian vessels with cargoes of apples in barrels, and flour. Then, just as one winter came on, the S. S. Nordfelt, with five thousand tons of coal in her hold, stranded and stuck on a flat reef a mile offshore. She is there still, now many years later. Hundreds of tons of coal have we purchased for our hospitals and steamers, the people's dog-teams hauling it over the ice to the shore.

Next came the great Scotsman, wrecked on the east end of Belle Isle, one bitter day before Christmas. Nine lives were lost trying to land on the Island. Our fishermen, venturing out in all kinds of small craft, saved many valuable bales of plush, cretonnes, assorted silks, and other Christmas goods which were bound out from England to Montreal. All winter long, the local churches were brightened by a plethora of plush whenever the congregation gathered for worship.

The S. S. Baucis was another 'opening of the windows of heaven,' according to Labrador's, but not Lloyd's, version of the incident. One winter, just when all the fishermen were wondering what they would do for flour, this great French steamer, with five thousand tons of whole wheat in bulk, ran high and dry on a flat reef just east of Blanc Sablon. All that was necessary was to put your ship alongside her hull and bore a hole in it with an acetylene torch to have a stream of wheat pouring into any receptacle you provided. The Strathcona was filled twice over, bunks and all, and many of our poor benefited enormously. The gain was double-barrelled, since they had to devise methods of grinding the whole wheat, generally with stones, and so were forced to use whole wheat bread, which they consider dirty and unfit for human consumption. Usually not only will they refuse to purchase it, but the Newfoundland Government dare not give it out in their 'able-bodied poor relief supplies,' for fear of losing face with their constituents.

The Erling, the Rose of Torridge, the Walrus, the Windsor Lake, the Viking, and many more flash across my memory, their ghosts always rising to remind us of them as I steam past their last resting-places on stormy nights. One of the most important was the wreck of His Majesty's first-class cruiser Raleigh, a boat worth five million dollars. She ran ashore almost on the bones of another of His Majesty's ships which had unwillingly accepted the hospitality of the same reef thirty years previously. The Raleigh became a total loss. Thirteen of her crew were drowned trying to land. The hereditary zeal of our people for salving was considerably cooled by the captain, who immediately forbade the shore people to touch anything. Uncle Silas was telling the astonished crowd, when I went ashore next morning, that he was only picking up an armchair which had washed ashore when a bullet from the ship whizzed into the mud under his nose and almost hit his fingers. For years, one of the sights of the voyage across the Atlantic by this route was the wreck of this great battleship still standing right side up just as she went on the rocks, and looking as if she were steaming into the bay. After eight years the Navy blew her up, but even today the people are making useful money by collecting brass and copper which have been blown off her hull.

By far the most dramatic wreck, however, was that of the large, new, Hudson's Bay Company steamer, the Bay Rupert, loaded with every variety of supplies for all the northern posts of that great Company. She and her cargo were valued, all told, at approximately two million dollars. She ran on an uncharted shoal in the open Atlantic, fourteen miles directly out from one of our northern capes, called Cape Harrigan. The conical rock poked its sharp nose through her engine-room floor, but she rested otherwise on a flat shelf, her bow hanging over one end in eighteen fathoms of water and her stern over the other in twenty fathoms. The passengers were at once conveyed in her beautiful power lifeboats to the nearest desert island, some nine miles distant, where with the lumber which they were carrying, and with cattle and supplies, they were made comfortable till help came. Oddly enough, that barren island had always been known as the 'Farmyards,' but never a cockerel had crowed there until the arrival of this ship-wrecked crowd, bringing with them several crates of chickens. When the sea was rough, a heavy breaker in eight feet of water at low tide sent huge volumes of water right over the doomed ship. It was one of the most wonderful sights imaginable.

Wireless messages were sent to me as Lloyd's Agent. Alas, we were hundreds of miles away at St. Anthony, just awaiting the arrival of the Governor, a beloved friend, to open the new hospital. By wiring to St. John's, the Government's large and fast mail steamer, the S.S. Kyle, was soon on the scene of the wreck and collected safely all the stranded people.

As we were steaming north three weeks later, we suddenly sighted a strange steamer on the horizon, apparently broken down. It proved to be the same S.S. Bay Rupert, still trans-fixed like St. Simon Stylites on his pole. We paid many visits to the abandoned ship, and my crew of 'wops' thoroughly en-joyed the dangerous adventures of those days. We salved a great many supplies of much value to the Coast. Every variety of goods, from hardwood sledges to barrels of gun-powder, and from new guns and rifles to cases of chewing-gum, were included. Above all, we got the most wonderful series of moving pictures from every point of vantage, including from her own masthead, Varick Frissell climbing up the mast and balancing on the truck while he took them. To help some of the Eskimos of that northern section of the Coast, we mothered a number of their small boats out to the wreck, and I was re-warded the first day by catching a warrior incontinently beating open a box of T N T with the back of his axe, 'to look what was in it.'

None of us will ever forget the high living of those days when Strathcona lunches included Kraft's cheese, mango chutney, nuts, oranges, and unlimited hams and tongues.

As it was my task from the bridge to keep an eye on the weather and on the deserted Strathcona anchored on the shoulder of the same shoal, I had been able to collect much valuable hardwood, plate-glass windows, and also a good deal of mahogany from the main staircase and lounge, though later some of this had to be thrown overboard and towed to the Strathcona when our rowboat was already carrying a full load.

From my eyrie I could also watch the men working in the main hold, a necessary precaution, as in reality the movements of our Eskimo visitors had become almost as much of a source of anxiety to me as the weather.

Observing a large case which they had opened and promptly thrown aside, I went down to examine it. One of the tins which it contained had been opened with an axe. Out of it was oozing our delectable Kraft's cheese! The inconsequential methods of the Eskimos in salving were amusing, when they were not pitiable. Though they were fifteen miles out in the Atlantic in small, open motor boats, they continually wasted time by sitting around smoking, and filled the very limited carrying space in their boats with anything from funnels to twisted iron rails. I asked the honourable opener of the case why he had cast it aside. 'Me no like,' he replied. The Eskimo told me afterwards that he thought it was a kind of soap gone bad.

On the bridge I discovered a beautiful bath in the captain's bedroom, and yielding to temptation decided to try and salve it. After getting it loose with great difficulty, I found that it would not pass through either of the two doors leading out on the deck. However, by taking off its legs and chopping a large hole through the sitting-room wall, then removing the door and its hardwood lintel and uprights, we dragged the prize out at last. The ship was at a considerable angle, and we and the tub literally glissaded together down to the lee rails. Forty feet below us lay the little boat. By that time it was too late to risk trying to lower our latest booty into her, so I lashed it to the rail and left it, hoping to reclaim it the next time we came aboard the wreck. However, when we returned to look for it, it was gone — to the bottom of the deep blue sea as we surmised.

A month later, long after the wreck had sunk, we happened to spy that bath high up on a beach, near the spot where we had anchored. A Labrador settler friend told us he had found it lashed to the rails and had thought it was abandoned.

'But it was mine,' I argued. 'I can prove it. Here are the four legs I unscrewed from it. Anyhow, what good can it possibly be to you?'

'Oh!' said he, 'I thought perhaps my wife might like to have a bath some day.'

His home happens to be on the komatik trail, and the pathos of the bathless North overwhelmed us.

'It is yours, brother. Here are its legs. May it dispense its blessing to many a weary traveller from your hospitable home!'

No one approached in enthusiasm Tommy, our small cabin-boy, whom we turned loose into the holds each morning. His particular *métier* proved to be that of a ferret in a rabbit hole. One day, just as we started for the wreck, we had struck so hard on a half-sunken case that it nearly proved fatal to the thin planks of our little boat. Hauling the case alongside, it proved to be full of chocolate plaques done up in silver paper. When we sampled it, we had to let the case go, for the salt water had dissolved out all the sugar — as had happened to all the cases both of the hard candies and the sugar itself. We were grateful enough to have escaped this new danger from chocolate, but its effect on Tommy was only to make him register a vow. A little later he came to my eyrie and reported the discovery of a large new section into which he had crawled. To prove his assertion that the articles in it had not yet been damped by the sea, he deposited before me half a dozen cardboard boxes containing new woolen sweaters and ladies' knitted caps. The entrance to his burrow was only just above the water-line. It was pitch-dark inside, and the opening too small to induce me to try to enter. I provided him with some matches, and he disappeared again down the hole, exactly like a second Alice in Wonderland. He returned after a few minutes with some chewing-gum, which was a new delicacy to him, and therefore untouched; but from the state of his face it was evident that the same had not held true of some dry chocolate.

There might have been 'a better 'ole' and had there been time we might have 'gone to it,' but under the circumstances Tommy had no trouble in finding disciples. Soon a goodly stream of dry new clothing, interspersed with bars of chocolate, came filtering through the passageway and was quickly removed to the deck to keep dry. At that moment the crew of a passing fishing schooner came aboard and asked permission to share in the salvage. This was more than gladly accorded; but when it came to permission to go down the private rabbit hole, Tommy insisted on his proprietary rights and maintained them in the face of all comers, even though I had to return to my vantage-point that I might endeavour to forestall our all being salved into Davy Jones's locker in one glorious *débâcle*.

At length a heavy gale broke suddenly upon us late one afternoon. We were on board the wreck at the time with not one soul left on the Strathcona, which was anchored a few hundred yards away on the top of the peak which formed the reef. She had broken loose and drifted off twice before, and we had been exceedingly fortunate to overtake her. So great was the opportunity to salve necessities that once again we had failed to take warning. Many Eskimos were with us at the time, and we at once ordered all of them to make for the land, which was fully fourteen miles away. Our dory was loaded when the storm hit us and we sent her back to the Strathcona, which she eventually reached after a furious battle with the rising gale and sea.

Our only other boat, a small lifeboat belonging to the wreck, was alongside. We were lowering an enormous four-sheave iron block into her by means of old ropes which we had cut from the rigging. The boat was directly below us, looking a mere speck, so far was she from the upper deck from which we were working. Suddenly there was a cry of horror — the ropes had broken!!! This meant that our only possible hope of escape was gone. Our dory had no chance whatever of getting back to us, and the Strathcona was already drifting off the ledge where we had anchored her. But as suddenly as the rope had parted, the tiny boat shot up apparently from the ship's side, and we saw the mass of iron disappear into the angry waves, sinking between the lifeboat and the big iron wall of the Bay Rupert's side. It ripped away and carried with it to the bottom only a foot or two of the boat's gunwale. To climb down a dangling rope into a small boat and get away safely from a steamer's perpendicular side in a rough sea is a task which has to be experienced to be realized. Our boat was made fast by the double rope of one of the ship's falls to supplement her painter, for, if she were to break away leaving us hopelessly marooned, we would pass out of the vale of tears and no one ever be the wiser. Indeed, in this fight Old Neptune had one more good try — a great onrushing wave lifted the boat halfway up to the deck where we stood, drove her bow through the loop above the block, and then precipitately fell away, leaving our last hope dangling high in the air, literally clinging on by her eyelids. We had no illusions that the loop could hold her long. If she fell out of it, she must certainly capsize and sink. But the miracle happened. Almost immediately a heavy rebound swell swept back along the whole length of the iron wall of the Bay Rupert's sides, and our little boat lay in the water again right side up, actually laughing up at us.

Even after getting away, our troubles were far from over, for picking up the Strathcona with a loaded boat and only two old oars proved a dangerous game. In order to save the lifeboat, we had to tow her all the way to land, full of water, which was possible only because she had two air-tanks. Then there was our promise to shepherd home the Eskimo boats. We felt that we must do this, as the storm was growing more violent each minute, and the darkness denser. The drag of the submerged lifeboat behind our little steamer now proved a not unmitigated evil, for as it was we overtook the last two motor boats still some miles out from land, and had to slow down and shoo them in, like chickens into a coop.

As the entrance to the tiny harbour of which we had made a special survey lay right along the big cape, it offered us not only the best anchorage, but some miles less to go, so all the boats headed for it. The opening is literally little wider than the ship and the depth of the water only seven fathoms, while the channel itself is not straight. We were well aware that there was yet one more thrill which there was no escaping. The uncharted shoals which we had to pass on the way were now breaking furiously, so we managed to see them in good time. When at length we got our anchors down and our beloved little ship was safely at rest, our troubles were past. There we lay for five days, and, when the storm was over, we climbed to the top of the cliffs and gazed out to sea with our telescopes. The staunch old wreck was no longer visible. Her buffetings were over. She had fought a good fight, though as usual Father Neptune won in the end.

Early one summer we had a very close squeak of losing the Strathcona. While we were trying one morning to get out of a harbour, a sudden breeze of wind came down upon us, drove in an enormous ice-floe and pinned us tight, so that we could not move an inch. The pressure of the ice became more severe moment by moment, and meanwhile the ice between us and the shore seemed to be imperceptibly melting away. We tried every expedient we could think of to keep enough ice between us and the shore rocks, to save the vessel being swept right over the rocky headland, towards which the strong tidal current was steadily forcing us. To make matters worse, we struck our propeller against a pan of ice and broke off one of the flanges close to the shaft. It became breathlessly exciting as the ship drew nearer and nearer to the rocks. The apex of the cape was at last only a few yards ahead. There was only one ice-pan between us and the cliffs and the pressure was terrible. We had hastily put our boat out on the ice and some food and blankets in case our steamer sank. Twisting around helplessly as if in the arms of a giant, we were swept past the dangerous promontory, and to our infinite joy carried out into the open Atlantic where there is plenty of sea room. We only had to abandon our boat.

For years not a single island, harbour, reef, or cape had any lighthouse to mark it, and many boats were unnecessarily lost as a result. Most of our schooners are small. Many are old and poorly found in running-gear. Their decks are crowded with boats, barrels, wood, and other impedimenta, so that to reef or handle sails on a dark night is next to impossible. Below they are often crowded with women and children going North with their men for the summer fishery on the Labrador Shore. I have often had to crawl on my knees to get at a patient, after climbing down through the main hatch. These craft are quite unfitted for a rough night at sea, especially as there are always icebergs or big ice-pans about. So in the spring the craft all creep North along the land, darting into harbours before darkness falls, and leaving before dawn if the night proves 'civil.'

We had frequently written to the Government about this neglect of lights for the Coast. But Labrador has no representative in the Newfoundland Parliament, and legislators who never visited Labrador had unimaginative minds. Year after year went by and nothing was done. So I spoke to outside friends of the dire need for a light near Battle Harbour Hospital. I have seen a hundred vessels come and anchor near-by in a single evening. When the money for the light was

donated, our architect designed the little building, and a friend
promised to endow the effort, so that the modest salary of the
lighthouse keeper might be permanent. The material was
already cut and sent North when we were politely told that
the Government could not permit private ownership of lights
— a very proper decision, too. At the same time they told us
that the first Labrador lighthouse would be erected near Battle Harbour. This was done, and the Double Island Light has
been a veritable Godsend to thousands of fishermen since that
day.

One hundred miles north, at Indian Tickle, a place also
directly in the run of all the fishing schooners, a light was much
needed. On a certain voyage coming South with the fleet in
the fall of the year, we had all tried to make the harbour, but
it shut down suddenly before nightfall with a blanket of fog
which you could almost cut with a knife. Being inside many
reefs and unable to make the open, we were all forced to
anchor. Where we were, none of us knew, for we had all
pushed on for the harbour as much as we dared. There were
eleven riding lights visible around us when a rift came in the
fog. We hoped against hope that we had made the harbour.
A fierce northeaster gathered strength as night fell, and a
mighty sea began to heave in. Soon we strained at our anchors
in the big seas and heavy water swept down our decks from
stem to stern. Our patients were dressed and our boats made
ready. Gradually we missed first one and then another of the
riding-lights; and it was not difficult to guess what had happened.

When daylight broke, only one boat was left — a large vessel called the Yosemite — and she was drifting right down
towards us. Suddenly she touched a reef, turned on her side,
and we saw the seas carry her over the breakers, the crew
hanging on to the channel plates on her bilge. Steaming to our
anchors saved us, but all the vessels went ashore and became
matchwood.

In the morning we made out the land, but before we could
get our anchors or slip them, our main steam pipe gave out and
we had to blow down our boilers. It became now a race between the engineers trying to repair the damage and the
shortening hours of daylight. On the result depended quite

possibly the lives of us all. I cannot remember one sweeter sound than the raucous voice of the engineer calling out, just in the nick of time, 'Right for'ard,' and then the signal of the engine-room bell in our little wheel-house. The Government has since put a fine little light on White Point, the very point off which we lay on that disastrous night.

Farther north, close by our hospital at Indian Harbour, is a narrow tickle known as the White Cockade. Through this most of the fishing fleet must pass going both North and South. Here also we had planned for a lighthouse. When we were forbidden to put out material at Battle Harbour, we suggested moving it to this almost equally important point. It fell under the same category of *verboten*, however, and soon the Government put a good light there also. The fishermen, therefore, suggested that we should offer our peripatetic, would-be lighthouse to the Government for some new place each year.

In 1908 occurred the second real hurricane which I have ever seen. It began on Saturday, July 28, with flat calm and sunshine alternating with small, fierce squalls. Though we had a falling barometer, this deceived us, and we anchored that evening in a shallow and unsafe open roadstead about twenty miles from Indian Harbour Hospital. Fortunately, our suspicions induced us to keep an anchor watch, whose warning made us get up steam at midnight, and we brought up at daylight in the excellent narrow harbour in which the hospital stands. The holding ground there is deep mud in four fathoms of water, the best possible for us.

The fury of the breeze grew worse as the day went on. Every one of the fishing boats in the harbour filled and sank with the driving water. With the increase of violence of the weather, we got up steam and steamed to our anchors to ease if possible the strain on our two chains and shore lines — a web which we had been able to weave before it was too late. By Sunday night the gale had blown itself away, and Monday morning broke flat calm, with lovely sunshine, and only an enormous sullen ground sea.

Knowing that there must be many comrades in trouble, we were early under way, and, dancing like a bubble, we ran north, keeping as close inshore as we could, and watching the coastline with our glasses. The coast was littered with remains. Forty-one vessels had been lost; in one uninhabited roadstead alone, some forty miles away from Indian Harbour, lay sixteen wrecks. The shore here was lined with rude shelters made from the wreckage of spars and sails, and in these the women were busy cooking meals and 'tidying up' the shacks as if they had lived there always.

One vessel, a large hardwood, well-fastened hull, we determined to save. Her name was Pendragon. The owner was aboard — a young man with no experience who had never previously owned a vessel. He was so appalled at the disaster that he decided to have her sold piecemeal and broken up. We attended the auction on the beach and bought each piece as it came to the hammer. Getting her off was the trouble. We adopted tactics of our own invention. Mousing together the two mastheads with a bight of rope, we put on it a large hoop traveller, and to that fastened our stoutest and longest line. Then, first backing down to her on the very top of high water, we went full speed ahead. Over she fell on her side and bumped along on the mud and shingle for a few yards. By repeated jerks she was eventually ours, but leaking so like a basket that we feared we should yet lose her. Pumps inside fortunately kept her free till we passed her topsail under her, and, after dropping in sods and peat, we let the pressure from the outside keep them in place. When night fell, I was played out, and told the crew they must let her sink. My two volunteer helpers, Albert Gould and Paul Matteson, however, volunteered to pump all night.

While hunting for a crew to take her South, we came upon the wreck of a brand-new boat, launched only two months previously. She had been the pride of the skipper's life. We felt so sorry for him that we handed the Pendragon over for him to work out at the cost which we had paid for the pieces.

With fifty-odd people aboard, and towing a long tail of nineteen fishing boats, we eventually got back to Indian Harbour, where everyone joined in helping our friends in misfortune till the steamer came and took them South. They waved us farewell, and, quite undismayed, wished for better luck for themselves another season. Proper charts of the Labrador were then non-existent, like lighthouses, and we were eager to have an adequate survey made.

Just after the big gale, His Excellency Sir William Mac-Gregor, then Governor, was good enough to come and spend a short time surveying on our North Coast. He was an expert in this line, as well as being a gold-medallist in medicine. I acted as pilot among other capacities on that journey, and was unlucky enough to run the steamer full tilt onto one of the only sandbanks on the coast in a narrow passage between some islands and the mainland! The little Strathcona, following behind, was in time to haul us off again, but the incident made the captain naturally distrust my ability, and as a result he would not approach the shore near enough for us to get the observations which we needed. Although we went round Cape Chidley into Ungava Bay, I could not regain his confidence sufficiently to go through the straits which I had myself sounded and surveyed. So we accomplished it in a small boat, getting good observations. Our best work, however, was done when His Excellency was content to be our guest. The hospital on board was used for the necessary instruments — four chronometers, two theodolites, guns, telescopes, camp furniture, and piles of books and printed forms.

Many a time in the middle of a meal, some desired but to us unlucky star would cross the prime vertical, and all hands had to go up on deck and shiver while rows of figures were accumulated. Sir William told us that he would 'rather shoot a star any time than all the game ever hunted.' One night my secretary, Albert Gould, after sitting on a rock at a movable table from five o'clock till midnight, came in, his joints almost creaking with cold, and loaded with a brass pile of figures which he assured us would crush the life out of a monkey. My mate that year was a stout and very short, plethoric person. When he stated that he preferred surveying to fishing, as it was going to benefit others so much, and that he was familiar with the joys of service, he was taken promptly at his word. It was a hot summer. The theodolite was a nine-inch one and weighed many pounds. We had climbed the face of a very steep mountain called Cape Mugford, some three thousand feet high, every inch of which distance we had to mount from dead sealevel. When at last Israel arrived on the summit, he looked worried. He said that he had always thought surveying meant letting things drop down over the ship's side and not carrying ballast up precipices. He distinctly failed to grasp where the joy of this kind of service came in — and noting his condition, as he lay on the ground and panted, I decided to let it go at that.

The Governor was a MacGregor and a Presbyterian, and was therefore a believer in keeping Sunday as a day of rest. But after morning prayers on the first fine day, after nearly a week of fog, he decided that he had had physical rest enough, and to get good observations would bring him the recreation of spirit which he most needed. So he packed up for work, and happened to light on the unhappy Israel to row him a mile or so to the land. Iz was 'taken all aback.' He believed that you should not strain yourself ever — least of all on Sundays. So from religious scruples he asked to be excused, though he offered to row anyone ashore if he was only going to idle the hours away. Israel subsequently cultivated the habit of remaining in bed on Sundays — thereby escaping being led into temptation, as even Governors would not be likely to go and tempt him in his bunk.

I have had others refuse to help in really necessary work on Sunday. One skipper would not get the Strathcona under way in answer to a wireless appeal to come to a woman in danger of dying from hemorrhage forty miles distant. When we prepared to start without him, he told me that he would go, but that it would be at the price of his soul and we would have to be responsible. We went all the same. Yet keeping Sunday for a day of rest I firmly believe to be a characteristic of infinite value to our people.

Our charts, such as they were, were subsequently accepted by the Royal Geographical Society, who generously invited me to lecture before them. Later, in 1911, they were good enough to award me the Murchison Prize. Much of the work was really due to Sir William, and as much of it as I could put on him to the Sabbatarian Iz.

CHAPTER XV

NOW IT CAN BE TOLD

On an Italian wall recently I saw posted one of Mussolini's epigrams. It read, 'We must not be proud of our country for its history only, but because of what *we* are making it today.' We all know that the irreducible minimum for the ideal country is that it should enable everyone to have a home, however humble, to dwell in safety, and to be able to earn a sufficiency. Under such circumstances any people could live contentedly.

On our Coast, statistics of only a few years ago showed that one out of every three deaths among the people was due to tuberculosis, while approximately one out of every three *native* babies dies before reaching one year old. There were then no milk-producing animals in the country except a couple of cows and a handful of goats, while the system of barter trade and chronic poverty put artificial milk quite out of reach of the fishermen. We had seen undernourished mothers keeping wizened infants alive by chewing dry bread and so predigesting it, and then feeding it to the baby from a spoon. They had discovered that then the baby might survive until it was able to digest it itself. Those mothers were all unconscious of the chemistry of their procedure, since an infant of less than six months old has not the glands necessary to enable it to convert the useless starch into assimilable sugar.

Here in a land with not one endemic disease such as malaria or yellow fever, with pure, bracing air and plenty of sunshine, free from crowding and human exhalations, our records each year showed true scurvy, hardly known now elsewhere, untreated infantile paralysis, blindness from eye ulcers, marasmic children, rickets, and almost every form of deficiency disease. The tocsin MILK! MILK! MILK! echoed in our ears far more insistently and frequently than the church or the school-bell.

As there was not one single road in the country, every family had to keep half a dozen big dogs for hauling firewood and for travelling in winter. These were as hard to provide for as the rest of the family. They had, however, developed the faculty of providing for themselves by night. If I had to select an animal which has unquestionably evolved a capacity since the last ice age, I should choose one of these dogs. They are as resourceful as Al Capone and require a Sherlock Holmes to bring them to justice.

A soft-hearted naturalist friend once sent me the most beautiful, white, Husky dog from America. Admiral Peary had given it to him as a puppy, but apparently it had not, as a grown dog, fitted into its environment. A photograph showed it basking in the sun by a lovely brook in New England. My friend was writing a story of the dog for children. He wished it to end its days nobly serving humanity in a medical mission in its homeland.

The morning after its arrival, one of my big dogs was found dead in the dog-pen. The next day another followed suit. This time suspicion fell on the white, angelic vision which had been presented to us. He was given a private apartment, and no more casualties occurred.

Later it was found that he had escaped one night, and, though in the morning he presented the countenance of a white lamb, he also presented a very suspicious shape. Better precautions were taken, and for the nonce things in the village were peaceful. Then once more the angel disappeared. This time he never came back — in the body. He had been shot gorging on a neighbour's bull, which he had killed in the night on the other side of the harbour. I never read his biography; but I am told that in the last chapter he disappeared into the far frozen North in the service of his fellow countrymen. I only hope that wherever he is he has not been accorded powers of aerial progression.

These dogs occasionally go hunting in packs exactly like wolves. I have known them kill a large polar bear. One of our own team, a thoroughbred Husky, literally 'heard the call of the wild' and answered it. He vanished and was given up for lost. One day a man from a near-by village came to complain to me, as a magistrate, that on two separate occasions a sheep had disappeared from his village, and that a wolf's tracks had been seen on the snow. No wolves have been in that neighbourhood since we came on the Coast. A baited trap was set and a couple of armed sentries were hidden to keep watch. In due time a huge, stealthy black shape stole out of the woods, attracted by the bait. Our men are excellent snipers. We had to admit that the jet-black culprit was our long-lost Nigger! We would have preferred to have expended the compensation on producing milk.

A cow eats two tons of hay on ration diet during one winter. We had not then cleared land to grow hay, and it cost forty dollars a ton landed. For our hospitals and orphanages we used dried milks. But a dole even in the form of milk was intolerable to an independent people if it could be avoided.

That 'milk providence 'of Alaska, the late Reverend Sheldon Jackson, came to our aid in this dilemma with advice to repeat on our side his own eminently successful experiment with reindeer. His Excellency the Governor travelled the Coast with us yet another summer to 'obsairve' and help us decide on the wisdom of our making such a venture. The famous Kew Garden authorities identified our mosses and lichens, and other summer and winter growths which we collected and sent them, as 'exactly right' for reindeer food.

North Newfoundland and Labrador have been the home of the woodland and barren-land caribou for centuries. These animals are closely enough allied to domestic reindeer to mate with them successfully. They do not know the difference themselves. The Newfoundland woodland caribou is a little larger than a reindeer, probably due to access to better food.

These animals (*Rangifer tarandus*) are very readily domesticated. They mix with cattle, develop more affection than a horse, and infinitely more than a cow. We tried it out with a faun which we caught swimming in a fjord, keeping it on the hospital ship with us. It became so friendly that when I rowed ashore, it would jump overboard and swim after me; and when I returned, swim back to the ship. When I walked around its paddock ashore, it would follow close at my heels, and if I were outside the wooden fence, would stand on its hind legs, and more than once hurt its ankles trying to climb over after me.

These apparently gentle, timid animals have an amazing vitality. The fact that they have contrived to exist in Newfoundland so long, with very little practical protection against endless numbers of enemies, especially the Bots-fly, and men armed with huge guns loaded with buckshot, proves this. They have survived cold, scanty food, deep snow. During the last thirty years the railways have brought innumerable sports-men armed with repeating rifles within a few miles of their victims. I have seen huge piles of these wild caribou lying frozen in heaps on the platforms of the Newfoundland way-side stations. So great has been the slaughter that of late years all shooting of caribou has had to be forbidden, in order to try to preserve the stock before it is too late.

On the other hand, from a hillside I once watched one of our driving-stags, which was tethered on the snow below and feed-ing. Suddenly I noticed the largest of our Husky dogs stealing towards him. Fortunately, the stag did also and got ready in time. The big dog leaped for the deer, which stood up on his hind legs and hit his adversary such a straight blow from the shoulder as to send him flying head over heels, so hurt and surprised that he did not take any further chances.

Reindeer are the most economical animals on earth to keep. There is no need ever to build any shelter for them — they sleep comfortably in the open all the year round. One does not have to feed them, as they can obtain what they want far more easily than you can give it to them. They cannot live on hay, anyhow; but in a few minutes, with their large, splay feet, with the always sharp chitinous shell of their hoofs, they can cut down through even hard frozen snow far more readily than I could dig with a steel shovel. Once, when driving a deer all day, I took a spade, thinking to help out my tired steed at night with his supper. However, he not only dug down more quickly than I could, but he always 'struck oil' and I did not. What was more, he preferred to dig his own fresh moss, for often we carried bags of moss on the sledge, as we thought we could not allow him to spend the night digging, and expect him to haul the express all the next day.

Every part of a reindeer is valuable. Alive, he is good for transport. The milk is rich and excellent for either butter or cheese. Incidentally in our case, their trekking made pathways and cut ditches which helped to drain the surface of the land, and they aided by their manure in improving the pastures for our cattle. Also they formed a great source of interest to visitors, who are an asset to any country. Dead, their skins afford the best insulating covering known. The most northern Eskimos prize them for clothing above all else. For sleeping in the woods in winter on the snow, everyone who can possibly procure them uses reindeer skins. The people can make chamois leather (of deerskin) for moccasins or clothing, which is windproof, light in weight, and when embroidered and tasselled as they use it, possesses a beauty complement of very real value in an Arctic winter.

The meat is excellent for food. The stretched bowel makes a translucent window-covering, or bags for preserving and carrying minced meat, like sausages. The sinew of the back makes the most efficient thread obtainable, and costs nothing when dried in the sun and stripped as wanted for sewing purposes. When a water-tight seam is needed, such as the covering of a canoe or a wading-boot, sinew swells as the tiny holes made by sewing swell in water, so that not a weep of moisture will run through and give one that fatal experience in cold — wet feet. The tendons neither rot nor tear the skins.

As breeders, reindeer compare more than favourably with cattle for regularity. Every spring from the second, and occasionally from the first, year they will have one, and sometimes two fauns. Being polygamous, a very few stags are necessary to serve a large herd; so that there are plenty of superfluous stags for meat or work. The increase is very rapid. The famous George Kennan told me that in Siberia he often purchased full-grown deer for fifty cents each, and even as low as twenty-five cents, for dog food. The two thousand deer being driven from Alaska to the Mackenzie River increased so largely in the long two-year journey that over a thousand had to be sent back, and even then more were delivered than had been contracted for.

The fecundity of deer may be a positive nuisance. The wild herds in lands which man has stigmatized as 'barren lands' have reached millions. The huge herds have taken a week to pass a given spot. The pictures taken by J. B. Tyrrel and others show endless ranks of heavily horned stags blotting out the horizon, like ancient hordes of spearmen — suggesting the remark of the man who, after looking with open mouth for some minutes at a giraffe, exclaimed, 'There ain't no such beast.'

TRAVELLING WITH REINDEER

REINDEER AT REST

During the years we were running our herd we had no epidemic troubles with the deer, except once when we lost a few in summer from a kind of pneumonia which ceased directly we moved the herd to a new feeding ground.

Lastly, there is in the North unlimited pasture land with endless fodder — all now being wasted. The indigenous caribou have been so seriously depleted in our country that many natives have never even seen one; but today these natives sometimes starve for lack of so attractive and easily handled an animal, which can convert unused potential into the direct service of mankind. The new science of animal genetics can greatly multiply the value, size, and number of such animals by its scientific methods.

We raised the money to purchase our herd of reindeer largely by the help of the *Boston Transcript* and a grant from the Agricultural Department in Canada. That the Canadian Government has taken up the problem again in the West and purchased a very large herd for the Mackenzie River district shows their attitude to this effort at adaptation as a wise and economic measure. On the advice of experts we bought our deer in Lapland.

Our difficulties were, first of all, that the deer had to wait in Lapland to haul to the landwash enough moss to last the three hundred of them across the Atlantic. Snow was late in the fall of 1908, and without the snow they could not haul. The steamer did not arrive, therefore, on our side until the sea was frozen over and the deer, instead of being landed in Labrador as we had intended, had to be put ashore on the frozen sea off North Newfoundland. Three Lapp families whom we had hired to teach our people how to herd the deer came across with them. Though many of the animals in landing on the ice off Crémaillière fell through into the sea, they proved hardy and resourceful enough to reach the land, where they gathered around the tinkling bells of the old deer without a single loss from land to land.

One of our workers at St. Anthony that winter wrote that 'the most exciting moment was when the Lapp woman was lowered in her own sledge over the steamer's side onto the ice, drawn to the shore, and transferred to one of our hospital komatiks, as she had hurt her leg during the voyage. The sight of all the strange men about her frightened her, but she was finally reassured, threw aside her coverings, and clutched her frying-pan which she had hidden under a sheepskin. When she had it safely in her arms, she allowed the men to lift her and put her on the komatik.' When the doctor at the hospital advised that her leg would be best treated by operation, her husband said, 'She is a pretty old woman and doesn't need a good leg much longer.' She was thirty-five!

The herd throve splendidly and multiplied regularly. By 1913 the original three hundred brought out in 1908 had increased to fifteen hundred, in spite of difficulties utterly unexpected, in spite of having sent fifty to Canada and two lots of twelve to clubs, and some winters of having killed one stag each fortnight for the hospital. The management of the herd locally was in the capable hands of an Irish Major, a friend of mine who had had experience ranching in Mexico. He came over especially and paid all his own expenses. We owe him much, for even in winter he lived and camped with the herd.

Unfortunately, the Lapps did not like the country. They complained that North Newfoundland was too cold. A rise in salary kept three of the men, but when the third season they demanded even higher pay we decided, wrongly, I fear, to let them go. The old herder warned me, 'No Lapps, no deer'; but I trusted too much to the ability of locally trained men, and was particularly worried at that time over Mission finances. The love of the Lapps for the deer is like a fisherman's for his vessel — a ruling passion. The Lapps always contended that the work was too hard, since they had always to be away from camp, there being no wolves in the country to keep the herd together and make them obey the warning summons of the bells of the old does. They warned me again and again that we must have a big fence or all the deer would go off into the country.

We had applied to the Newfoundland Government for protection and a grant towards the expense of the reindeer experiment, since it was being carried out solely and only for the welfare of their people, and the far-sighted Canadian Government had subscribed already — but we could not awaken interest at headquarters.

No sooner had the deer arrived than difficulties with the

people began. They are accustomed always to carry a gun for shooting birds or rabbits for food. I had known only one deer killed on that great promontory of North Newfoundland since I arrived on the Coast fifteen years previously; but very soon we heard that 'Uncle Joe' had shot a caribou. A visitor had offered to buy a good pair of antlers. Shortly a fisherman brought in a fine head. He claimed that he had not even noticed that it had one of our numbered tags through the cartilage of the ear.

We at once renewed our application to the Government for protection and also asked for more herders, as we felt that if they had even a small share in ownership they would be more interested. To our amazement the Government contributed only the salary of one herder, but refused the only protection which was of the least value. We had applied to run a fence from the bottom of Pistolet Bay across ten miles to the bottom of Hare Bay — a natural neck of land — and for a law prohibiting the killing of any deer at all inside the enclosure. All that they would sanction was that 'no *reindeer* may be killed north of the line stated.' This only made matters ten times worse, for if the deer either strayed or were driven purposely just across the line (which they would not permit us to fence), the killing of them was thus legalized.

The people knew that the deer had cost us fifty-one dollars each and were as private property as our cows, which incidentally we had bought for an even smaller sum. A petition, signed by a number of the 'voters' of the district, went to St. John's to protest against the deer being given protection. They petitioned to have the deer done away with, as 'they led so many into sin'; and some wiseacre added the clause, 'and are a danger to our lives, for when our dog-teams get a scent of them they run away with us.' This priceless document was returned to me by the Government with a comment on the fact that it was the wish of the free voters not to give us protection. Votes loom very large in the eyes of the politicians in a free and sovereign state with a total population not a quarter the size of a single large modern city. As argument was useless, we at once started a counter-petition in the district. This in turn was signed by every one of the independent lawmakers who had signed the *first* document. However, as we were in bad odour at court because of our having started cash coöperative stores to help the poor people, we were left to fend as best we could.

Statistics show that we did not do badly. For our sins we had in summer to cope with numbers of schoonermen, who constituted one of our most difficult problems. Fauns were running with the does when the sea-ice opened, and at the same moment these men from South Newfoundland came sailing along the coast in hundreds, anchoring for the night in our harbour, and going on north next morning. If I had been a youth on such short rations as many of them were, and if, as they always did, I had had the family blunderbuss on my shoulder in the hope of a sea-gull or a duck, and suddenly saw a fat reindeer in a lonely corner looking me guilelessly in the face, perhaps, as Paddy said, I should have found that the one thing which I, too, could not resist was temptation.

Our only asset was that I was a magistrate. But when a man, too ignorant to read, is brought before you and tells you that he never heard of a reindeer and knew that the Government said it was lawful to kill caribou there, or that he was bound North and might never be near us again, what advantage was it to us to bother to entertain him all summer free in our jail, quite possibly at our expense? Moreover, we found that every time we put a local poacher in that miserable hut called by courtesy a jail, his friends always made it harder and harder for our herders if ever the roaming herd happened to leave them stranded some dirty night in the vicinity of any of their homes. It was the old story of the servant when he reigneth.

On one occasion there were five poachers together in our jail, and 'only standing-room left.' When I hired a man to march around outside with a loaded rifle, he found that he had enemies to guard against both inside and out, and the task became obviously futile. All through the struggle the Grenfell Association was spending a great deal of badly needed money locally and giving endless relief in the neighbourhood. I had to be owner, complainant, judge, and jailer all rolled into one.

One day the herders reported that the herding dogs, digging down through the snow, had discovered the body of a freshly killed reindeer. The animal had been shot by bullets from a twenty-two bore rifle, but there were no other clues to the crime. Fortunately, that small bore is seldom found on our Coast, most of our hunters still using a round bullet in their old muzzle-loading shotguns. So we at once dispatched our policeman to search every house in every village near, and to bring back every twenty-two bore rifle he found. Shortly he returned with three. A very expert Hudson's Bay Company factor was with me at the time, a man who had been in their service in the wilds all his life. He carefully examined the bullets, compared them with those of his own 'twenty-two' which he used for shooting grouse, and assured me he could tell one bullet from another. So we chopped off a good round of beef from the frozen bullock in the storehouse, took a few witnesses and the local policeman, and had bullets fired from all the rifles in succession into it. The bullets were then extracted and kept separate. Suspicion rested so strongly on one of the owners of the rifles that the guilty party could scarcely have been any of the others. We therefore felt justified in arresting him.

When the case came up, we called our Hudson's Bay Company friend and in open court handed him the various bullets, all mixed up, we having previously kept a control. Without any difficulty or hesitation whatever he separated them again by the different marks which the rifling in the barrels had made in the lead. On that evidence we convicted our man and fined him the minimum, namely, two hundred dollars. To our surprise, almost immediately, a cheque for the two hundred dollars came to us from the well-paid keeper of the new Government lighthouse about thirty miles distant, who happened to be the culprit's brother-in-law. The grim humour was this time that the Government got the two hundred dollars, the prisoner got his freedom, while we lost a deer and got nothing whatever except the hard feeling of a number more of our neighbours.

As an offset to this unhappy memory there comes to my mind the memory of another legal case. A policeman from the South one day brought into my office a weird machine that had been manufactured for a still, and trailing behind it a genial Irishman, who had a wife and eight children and no other assets except a debt to myself and others. It was the depth of winter. Paddy cheerfully owned up to moonshining.

'You have no food and no firewood home?'

'None, Your Honour.'

'If you go to jail your family will freeze as well as starve?'

'Yes, Your Honour.'

'Then don't plead guilty. When I say in court, "Paddy, are you guilty?" you say, "Not guilty."'

He said it over several times. He went out of the room and came back in and said it again. We thought matters were 'all set.'

There were few diversions in those days and the courthouse was crowded. Paddy was the cynosure of all eyes and in the seventh heaven. To bring him to earth, I explained that I was not a doctor, but a magistrate, and to be very careful what he said, and to address me as a magistrate. Then we began, the policeman jogging Paddy to stand at attention.

'Paddy, are you guilty or not guilty?'

'Guilty, Your Majesty!' and he looked around the court with supreme self-satisfaction.

'Oh! You are, are you? Then the law says that for a first offence you must pay to His Majesty the King one hundred dollars. You can have until Saturday to get it, or else go to jail.'

On Saturday at noon, Paddy came over with a bag containing forty-eight dollars.

'The King cannot take it,' I told him. 'He has to have a hundred, or you have to go to jail. You can have one more hour to get it.'

Paddy lived in a Catholic village eight miles away. Our village was at that time more than half Methodist, and the sects were only just beginning to improve on the Jews and the Samaritans. With a very heavy heart, I wended my way to the little courthouse. To my amazement, when the court opened, in the face of the excited audience Paddy handed across the table the bag, this time with one hundred dollars in it.

I discovered later that he had fallen in with a very soft-hearted young fisherman who had been unable to resist the eight children, and had literally emptied every penny he had into Paddy's bag. No one could allow that, so, as on other occasions, I had to have a share in this religious exercise. As I thought of it afterwards, Paddy got the fun and the whiskey and we got the experience; but after all, as I went to bed, it seemed to me that it was a more economic policy than having to assume eight naked and hungry children in the middle of winter — for our orphanage was 'chock-a-block.'

In 1914 the War began. Our reindeer herders preferred real war to petty squabbles, utter lack of coöperation and ignorance on the part of the very people the reindeer effort was designed to benefit. The two leading herders had already gone with a herd of fifty deer, ironically enough, to the Peace River district in Canada. The next year, having committed the herd to the tender mercies of those 'who stayed by the stuff,' I joined the Harvard Surgical Unit and went to France.

Two years later, when I visited that section of the Coast, only two hundred and thirty of our fifteen hundred deer could be found. As a result, we at once asked the Canadian Government to allow us to remove them into their territory in order to try to save the sorry remnant. Most generously they arranged to care for them. With our large schooner, a number of volunteers, and the crew of my hospital steamer, we set out to catch the deer.

None of us had ever used a lariat, but we built a large corral hidden by woods and drove the deer into it. We somehow lassoed and carried lashed on barrows to the beach about one hundred and forty deer. By that time the excitement in the herd became so great that some of the larger stags rushed headlong into the corral wall, and two broke their necks. A breach was made in the stockade, however, and altogether forty deer escaped. Thereupon we had to build a new corral, for nothing on earth would bring the deer near the old one again. The new enclosure was on a promontory. Success was just within our grasp when somehow the leading stag scented danger and rushed down into the sea, all the other deer following, exactly like the Gadarene swine. But far from breaking their necks or being drowned, they swam gaily direct to another headland a mile away; and long before we could get a boat and follow them, they had landed 'safe on the other shore.' But, all told, we managed to get one hundred and fifty.

We landed these at Rocky Bay in Canada, where the Canadian herders took charge, subsequently removing them to Anticosti Island. There Mr. Menier, who had purchased the island, let them run wild. Anticosti is as large an area as Wales. Mr. Menier had literally turned out everyone living on the island, paying their way to British Columbia and arranging with the Canadian Government to give them a start there. The whole island was a vast game preserve, centring around his palatial 'Halle de Chasse.'

It was agreed that if ever we were able to restart reindeer herding in Labrador, we were to have up to a thousand deer returned to us. The island of Anticosti has since been resold and some lumbering operation permitted there. The deer apparently did so well that they became too numerous for the available food-supply. Many were reported to have perished on that account, as did the elks in western Canada.

Just as we were removing our deer, we received too late promises of protection for them from the Newfoundland Government if we would continue the experiment. But we had proved our point — that the country could support tens of thousands of deer on the spare and otherwise useless spaces, and that the cost would be minimal, the land improved and the return sure.

Of the forty deer which escaped onto the headland, we later saw but one — and he was dead, with our lead tag in his ear. The rest had all been poached before we returned the following season — and the interior of North Newfoundland is once more a profitless waste.

CHAPTER XVI

ADRIFT ON A PAN OF ICE

ON EASTER SUNDAY, the 21st of April, 1908, it was still winter with us in northern Newfoundland. Everything was covered with snow and ice. I was returning to the hospital after morning service, when a boy came running over with the news that a large team of dogs had come from sixty miles to the southward to get a doctor to come at once on an urgent case. A fortnight before we had operated on a young man for acute bone disease of the thigh, but when he was sent home the people had allowed the wound to close, and poisoned matter had accumulated. As it seemed probable that we should have to remove the leg, there was no time to be lost, and I therefore started immediately, the messengers following me with their team.

My dogs were especially good ones and had pulled me out of many a previous scrape by their sagacity and endurance. Moody, Watch, Spy, Doc, Brin, Jerry, Sue, and Jack were as beautiful beasts as ever hauled a komatik over our Northern barrens. The messengers had been anxious that their team should travel back with mine, for their animals were slow at best, and moreover were now tired from their long journey. My dogs, however, were so powerful that it was impossible to hold them back, and though I twice managed to wait for the following sledge, I had reached a village twenty miles to the south and had already fed my team when the others caught up.

That night the wind came in from sea, bringing with it both fog and rain, softening the snow and making the travelling very difficult. Besides this a heavy sea began heaving into the bay on the shores of which lay the little hamlet where I spent my first night. Our journey the next day would be over forty miles, the first ten lying on an arm of the sea.

In order not to be separated too long from my friends I sent them ahead of me by two hours, appointing as a rendezvous the log tilt on the other side of the bay. As I started the first rain of the year began to fall, and I was obliged to keep on what we call the 'ballicaters,' or ice barricades, for a much longer distance up the bay than I had anticipated. The sea, rolling in during the previous night, had smashed the ponderous layer of surface ice right up to the landwash. Between the huge ice-pans were gaping chasms, while half a mile out all was clear water

Three miles from the shore is a small island situated in the middle of the bay. This had preserved an ice bridge, so that by crossing a few cracks I managed to get to it safely. From that point it was only four miles to the opposite shore, a saving of several miles if one could make it, instead of following the landwash round the bay. Although the ice looked rough, it seemed good, though one could see that it had been smashed up by the incoming sea and packed in tight again by the easterly wind. Therefore, without giving the matter a second thought, I flung myself on the komatik and the dogs started for the rocky promontory some four miles distant.

All went well till we were within about a quarter of a mile of our objective point. Then the wind dropped suddenly, and I noticed simultaneously that we were travelling over 'sish' ice. By stabbing down with my whiphandle I could drive it through the thin coating of young ice which had formed on the surface. 'Sish' ice is made up of tiny bits formed by the pounding together of the large pans by the heavy seas. So quickly had the wind veered and come offshore, and so rapidly did the packed slob, relieved of the inward pressure of the easterly breeze, 'run abroad,' that already I could not see any pan larger than ten feet square. The whole field of ice was loosening so rapidly that no retreat was possible.

There was not a moment to lose. I dragged off my oilskins and threw myself on my hands and knees beside the komatik so as to give a larger base to hold, shouting at the same time to my team to make a dash for the shore. We had not gone twenty yards when the dogs scented danger and hesitated, and the komatik sank instantly into the soft slob. Thus the dogs had to pull much harder, causing them to sink also.

It flashed across my mind that earlier in the year a man had been drowned in this same way by his team tangling their traces around him in the slob. I loosened my sheath-knife, scrambled forward and cut the traces, retaining the leader's trace wound securely round my wrist.

As I was in the water I could not discern anything that would bear us up, but I noticed that my leading dog was wallowing about near a piece of snow, packed and frozen together like a huge snowball, some twenty-five yards away. Upon this he had managed to scramble. He shook the ice and water from his shaggy coat and turned around to look for me. Perched up there out of the frigid water he seemed to think the situation the most natural in the world, and the weird black marking of his face made him appear to be grinning with satisfaction. The rest of us were bogged like flies in treacle.

Gradually I succeeded in hauling myself along by the line which was still attached to my wrist, and was nearly up to the snow-raft, when the leader turned adroitly round, slipped out of his harness, and once more leered at me with his grinning face.

There seemed nothing to be done, and I was beginning to feel drowsy with the cold, when I noticed the trace of another dog near by. He had fallen through close to the pan, and was now unable to force his way out. Along his line I hauled myself, using him as a kind of bow anchor — and I soon lay, with my dogs around me, on the little island of slob ice.

The piece of frozen snow on which we lay was so small that it was evident we must all be drowned if we were forced to remain on it as it was driven seaward into open water. Twenty yards away was a larger and firmer pan floating in the sish, and if we could reach it I felt that we might postpone for a time the death which seemed inescapable. To my great satisfaction I now found that my hunting knife was still tied on to the back of one of the dogs, where I had attached it when we first fell through. Soon the sealskin traces hanging on the dogs' harnesses were cut and spliced together to form one long line. I divided this and fastened the ends to the backs of my two leaders, attaching the two other ends to my own wrists. My long sealskin boots, reaching to my hips, were full of ice and water, and I took them off and tied them separately on the dogs' backs. I had already lost my coat, cap, gloves, and overalls.

Nothing seemed to be able to induce the dogs to move,

even though I kept throwing them off the ice into the water. Perhaps it was only natural that they should struggle back, for once in the water they could see no other pan to which to swim. It flashed into my mind that my small black spaniel which was with me was as light as a feather and could get across with no difficulty. I showed him the direction and then flung a bit of ice toward the desired goal. Without a second's hesitation he made a dash and reached the pan safely, as the tough layer of sea ice easily carried his weight. As he lay on the white surface looking like a round black fuss ball, my leaders could plainly see him. They now understood what I wanted and fought their way bravely toward the little retriever, carrying with them the line that gave me yet another chance for my life. The other dogs followed them, and all but one succeeded in getting out on the new haven of refuge.

Taking all the run that the length of my little pan would afford, I made a dive, slithering along the surface as far as possible before I once again fell through. This time I had taken the precaution to tie the harnesses under the dogs' bellies so that they could not slip them off, and after a long fight I was able to drag myself onto the new pan.

Though we had been working all the while toward the shore, the offshore wind had driven us a hundred yards farther seaward. On closer examination I found that the pan on which we were resting was not ice at all, but snow-covered slob, frozen into a mass which would certainly eventually break up in the heavy sea, which was momentarily increasing as the ice drove offshore before the wind. The westerly wind kept on rising — a bitter blast with us in winter, coming as it does over the Gulf ice.

Some yards away I could still see my komatik with my thermos bottle and warm clothing on it, as well as matches and wood. In the memory of the oldest inhabitant no one had ever been adrift on the ice in this bay, and unless the team which had gone ahead should happen to come back to look for me, there was not one chance in a thousand of my being seen.

To protect myself from freezing I now cut down my long boots as far as the feet, and made a kind of jacket, which shielded my back from the rising wind.

By midday I had passed the island to which I had crossed on

the ice bridge. The bridge was gone, so that if I did succeed in reaching that island I should only be marooned there and die of starvation. Five miles away to the north side of the bay the immense pans of Arctic ice were surging to and fro in the ground seas and thundering against the cliffs. No boat could have lived through such surf, even if I had been seen from that quarter. Though it was hardly safe to move about on my little pan, I saw that I must have the skins of some of my dogs, if I were to live the night out without freezing. With some difficulty I now succeeded in killing three of my dogs — and I envied those dead beasts whose troubles were over so quickly. I questioned if, once I passed into the open sea, it would not be better to use my trusty knife on myself than to die by inches.

But the necessity for work saved me from undue philosophizing; and night found me ten miles on my seaward voyage, with the three dogs skinned and their fur wrapped around me as a coat. I also frayed a small piece of rope into oakum and mixed it with the fat from the intestines of my dogs. But, alas, I found that the matches in my box, which was always chained to me, were soaked to a pulp and quite useless. Had I been able to make a fire out there at sea, it would have looked so uncanny that I felt sure that the fishermen friends, whose tiny light I could just discern twinkling away in the bay, would see it. The carcasses of my dogs I piled up to make a windbreak, and at intervals I took off my clothes, wrung them out, swung them in the wind, and put on first one and then the other inside, hoping that the heat of my body would thus dry them. My feet gave me the most trouble, as the moccasins were so easily soaked through in the snow. But I remembered the way in which the Lapps who tended our reindeer carried grass with them, to use in their boots in place of dry socks. As soon as I could sit down I began to unravel the ropes from the dogs' harnesses, and although by this time my fingers were more or less frozen, I managed to stuff the oakum into my shoes.

Shortly before I had opened a box containing some old football clothes which I had not seen for twenty years. I was wearing this costume at the time; and though my cap, coat, and gloves were gone, as I stood there in a pair of my old Oxford

University running shorts, and red, yellow, and black Richmond football stockings, and a flannel shirt, I remembered involuntarily the little dying girl who asked to be dressed in her Sunday frock so that she might arrive in heaven properly attired.

Forcing my biggest dog to lie down, I cuddled up close to him, drew the improvised dogskin rug over me, and proceeded to go to sleep. One hand being against the dog was warm, but the other was frozen, and about midnight I woke up shivering enough, so I thought, to shatter my frail pan to atoms. The moon was just rising, and the wind was steadily driving me toward the open sea. Suddenly what seemed a miracle happened, for the wind veered, then dropped away entirely, leaving it flat calm. I turned over and fell asleep again. I was next awakened by the sudden and persistent thought that I must have a flag, and accordingly set to work to disarticulate the frozen legs of my dead dogs. Cold as it was I determined to sacrifice my shirt to top this rude flagpole as soon as the daylight came. When the legs were at last tied together with bits of old harness rope, they made the crookedest flagstaff that it has ever been my lot to see. Though with the rising of the sun the frost came out of the dogs' legs to some extent, and the friction of waving it made the odd pole almost tie itself in knots, I could raise it three or four feet above my head, which was very important.

Once or twice I thought that I could distinguish men against the distant cliffs — for I had drifted out of the bay into the sea — but the objects turned out to be trees. Once also I thought that I saw a boat appearing and disappearing on the surface of the water, but it proved to be only a small piece of ice bobbing up and down. The rocking of my cradle on the waves had helped me to sleep, and I felt as well as I ever did in my life. I was confident that I could last another twenty-four hours if my boat would only hold out and not rot under the sun's rays. I could not help laughing at my position, standing hour after hour waving my shirt at those barren and lonely cliffs; but I can honestly say that from first to last not a single sensation of fear crossed my mind.

My own faith in the mystery of immortality is so untroubled that it now seemed almost natural to be passing to the portal of death from an ice-pan. Quite unbidden, the words of the old hymn kept running through my head:

'My God, my Father, while I stray
Far from my home on life's rough way,
Oh, help me from my heart to say,
    Thy will be done.'

I had laid my wooden matches out to dry and was searching about on the pan for a piece of transparent ice which I could use as a burning-glass. I thought that I could make smoke enough to be seen from the land if only I could get some sort of a light. All at once I seemed to see the glitter of an oar, but I gave up the idea because I remembered that it was not water which lay between me and the land, but slob ice, and even if people had seen me, I did not imagine that they could force a boat through. The next time that I went back to my flag-waving, however, the glitter was very distinct, but my snow-glasses having been lost, I was partially snow-blind and distrusted my vision. But at last, besides the glide of an oar I made out the black streak of a boat's hull, and knew that if the pan held out for another hour I should be all right. The boat drew nearer and nearer, and I could make out my rescuers frantically waving. When they got close by they shouted, 'Don't get excited. Keep on the pan where you are.' They were far more excited than I, and had they only known as I did the sensations of a bath in the icy water, without the chance of drying one's self afterwards, they would not have expected me to wish to follow the example of the Apostle Peter.

As the first man leaped on my pan and grasped my hand not a word was spoken, but I could see the emotions which he was trying to force back. A swallow of the hot tea which had been thoughtfully sent out in a bottle, the dogs hoisted on board, and we started for home, now forging along in open water, now pushing the pans apart with the oars, and now jumping out on the ice and hauling the boat over the pans.

It seems that the night before four men had been out on the headland cutting up some seals which they had killed in the fall. As they were leaving for home, my ice-raft must have drifted clear of Hare Island, and one of them, with his keen fisherman's eyes, had detected something unusual on the ice. They at once returned to their village, saying that something living was adrift on the floe. The one man on that section of coast who owned a good spy-glass jumped up from his supper on hearing the news and hurried over to the lookout on the cliffs. Dusk though it was, he saw that a man was out on the ice, and noticed him every now and again waving his hands at the shore. He immediately surmised who it must be; so little as I thought it, when night was closing in the men at the village were trying to launch a boat. Miles of ice lay between them and me, and the angry sea was hurling great blocks against the land. While I had considered myself a laughing-stock, bowing with my flag at those unresponsive cliffs, many eyes were watching me.

By daybreak a fine volunteer crew had been organized, and the boat, with such a force behind it, would, I believe, have gone through anything. After seeing the heavy breakers through which we were guided, as at last we ran in at the harbour mouth, I knew well what the wives of that crew had been thinking when they saw their loved ones depart on such an errand.

Every soul in the village was waiting to shake hands as I landed; and even with the grip that one after another gave me, I did not find out that my hands were badly frostburnt — a fact which I have realized since, however. I must have looked a weird object as I stepped ashore, tied up in rags, stuffed out with oakum, and wrapped in the bloody dogskins.

The news had gone over to the hospital that I was lost, so I at once started north for St. Anthony, though I must confess that I did not greatly enjoy the trip, as I had to be hauled like a log, my feet being so frozen that I could not walk. For a few days subsequently I had painful reminders of the adventure in my frozen hands and feet, which forced me to keep to my bed — an unwelcome and unusual interlude in my way of life.

In our hallway stands a bronze tablet:

> To the Memory of
> Three Noble Dogs
> Moody
> Watch
> Spy
> Whose lives were given
> For mine on the ice
> April 21st, 1908.

The boy whose life I was intent on saving was brought to the hospital a day or so later in a boat, the ice having cleared off the coast temporarily; and he was soon on the highroad to recovery.

We all love life, and I was glad to have a new lease of it before me. As I went to sleep that night there still rang through my ears the same verse of the old hymn which had been my companion on the ice-pan:

'Oh, help me from my heart to say,
        Thy will be done.'

CHAPTER XVII

IN DOUBLE HARNESS

In June, 1909, I had finished another long lecture tour in England trying to raise funds, while my colleagues had the hospitals and dog-driving on the Coast. The time had come to sail westward again, and I was dreading the ordeal of saying good-bye to my aged mother, perhaps for the last time. I had begged her not to come again to Liverpool to see me off, that I might avoid the long, slow parting as the ship left the dock, and the loved form got ever smaller and less distinct till it disappeared.

New ideas are rare, but suddenly a brilliant one flashed across my mind, in answer to my despondency. Why not take my mother with me to America? True, she was seventy-eight years of age, had been born in India, and had lived a very active and exacting life. I was to receive an M.A. from Harvard, and an LL.D. from Williams College. It would make the occasions ten times as enjoyable to myself to have her share them. She would be far more thrilled than if she received degrees herself — and if — well, she could sleep just as peacefully on one side of the Atlantic as on the other; while I knew that the generous Americans would love to see her and welcome one of the real saints of earth.

My earliest and most devoted volunteer worker was Miss Emma White, of Boston. Today, twenty-five years later, I can recall seeing her, straight from her desk in the office of the Congregationalist Library, entering St. Anthony, sitting on the bow of a schooner which we had built in our mill, while written below was the legend of her own name, in whose honour the ship was dedicated. Miss White is still at her seat in the Library, but her soul is still in Labrador.

Her advice was sought and taken on the question of my mother's visit; with the result that we sailed together on the Mauretania for New York. The Cunard Company gave my mother a lovely suite of rooms, with a great four-poster brass bed, which, little though I knew it at the time, was to serve me well in the most monumental adventure of my whole life.

The Mauretania took four and a half days to reach New York. On the second day out, a delightful Scotchman, with a burr as characteristic as a bagpipe, introduced himself to me with his family. He had been born in Stirling, and his name was Stir-r-ling, and he lived in Chicago. He valued life, exactly as I did, for its glorious opportunities, and he played shuffle-board (deck tennis not being invented), took afternoon tea, and when we talked said worth-while things, having travelled much and been 'educated' and not merely informed. One girl was a graduate of Bryn Mawr University under the famous Miss M. Carey Thomas as President, the best-known women's university in America. Her sister was as charming as herself, and we hobnobbed naturally, for both were full of gaiety and humour.

My own activities in life had engrossed my whole being so completely that the idea of marriage had never entered my head. Now I am uncertain as to whether we should or should not take a course in the philosophy of it. My own experience says very decidedly 'No'; but after twenty-odd years of married life I am not sure either whether this decision should be made public by the husband or the wife. Anyhow, marriage came to me 'out of the blue' — the true blue itself — and a new, happier, and more useful life began. A surgeon considers it justifiable to record end results long before over twenty years have elapsed. Why not a layman? Anyhow, the above is the most sober opinion of a mere husband and of one who knows that no celibate has any right to speak on this subject.

These intervening years have been characterized in civilization by an almost miraculous advance in human knowledge — also in divorces, failures to enforce laws or commandments, and in the apotheosis of self-expression. The relationship of one to the other of these or their causes I must leave to my readers, asking them to remember that, from my viewpoint, human knowledge, except that based on experience, can never be a correct criterion of wisdom.

I am aware that there is no special virtue in keeping the Ninth Commandment, not to envy your neighbours their happiness or their goods, when one is fully occupied otherwise. As for special providences, personally I never pray for a fair wind for my hospital steamer which might mean a head wind for the schooners. Beyond asking for God's good hand upon my unworthy self in everything, the marriage problem in particular had never been a petition of mine for any special providence. I still think, however, that it came more graciously as it did.

By the third day out, a fact that previously had never caused me any worry got on my mind. I was on the 'greyhound of the Atlantic,' and those interested in the pool on the day's run had been completely fooled, for the Mauretania had set a new day's record of over six hundred miles. The universal hustle of our American cousins had often amused me. Yet here I was, becoming acutely conscious that I stood in sore need of it myself. 'Ships that pass in the night,' with courses presumably as different as the girl's and mine, might never meet again; while the captain assured me in triumph at dinner that we should land in two more days!

As for 'the girl in black,' I knew neither whence she came nor whither she was going, nor why she was in black. Indeed, all I did know was that she was down on the passenger list, and also with the dining-saloon steward, as 'Mr. Stirling and family.' An old school friend on board at that time, manager of Lord Northcliffe's great pulp interests on our Coast (Sir Mayson Beeton), jokingly quizzed me when I was late for an appointment one night, as to how I came to be walking round with 'the girl in black,' the handsomest girl on the ship, and what her name was. I wondered why he asked me. But as a matter of fact both of these were questions, which, according to Hoyle, are considered taboo at certain times. So we let the name go as 'the girl in black.'

As to her name, had I had any doubt, although I am not considered to be lacking in courage usually, I am certain that at that particular time I should not have dared to ask Mrs. Stirling. Necessity has no respect even for a coward heart, and I realized that twenty-six knots an hour demanded action. To take the more venturesome of two paths has always been an axiom with me, and I remembered what that splendid old patriot, Nehemiah, put on record. When the Persian tyrant noticed that his mind was low, and asked him if he wanted anything, he knew that to make a petition displeasing to the

LADY GRENFELL
1927

King involved immediate death. He records, 'I prayed to
God, and I said to the King, may it please...', all in the same
breath. Well, I did the same thing, and in return received the
real shock of my life. 'But you do not even know my name!'
The name of a Labrador reef does not matter. You have only
to avoid it, anyhow, and it probably has a dozen, for conferring
names is a favourite pastime of explorers. But now on that
account I seemed to be in real danger of shipwreck. Even a
perversion of truth could not help me, convenient as that may
be in time of trouble, for I knew I could not stand catechizing.
Labrador seafaring habits, however, came to my rescue, for
they had accustomed me, on the spur of the moment, to act
first and think after. 'That is not the issue,' I answered. 'The
only thing that interests me is what it is going to be.'

Years later, 'the girl in black' told me that once at Bryn
Mawr she was invited to come and hear a medical missionary
talk about Labrador, and that she had refused in no un-
measured terms. I thought at the time there at least was possibly another reason for my faith in providence in small things.

I have known even Britons who are not at their best on the
rolling wave, but such genius as our family has displayed has,
so history assures us, shone best on a quarter-deck, and on this
occasion it pleased God to add another naval victory to our
annals. Perhaps no previous suitor had tried to carry her by
assault. Perhaps Nelson's greatest victory was when he put
his telescope to his blind eye, ignored all suggestions to the
contrary, and just went for the enemy, as at Copenhagen.
That has been the family way, anyhow.

The generosity of my friends, considering the mental abnormality that characterizes this not uncommon experience of
life, will condone in me a wicked satisfaction that my lack of
appreciation of the blessing of a rapid voyage was paralleled
by the joy that my mother preferred that blessed brass four-
post bed to even a chair on the promenade deck. When, just
before landing, I told her that I had asked a fellow passenger
to become my wife, I am certain, had the opportunity offered
at the moment, she would have tumbled down the Mauretania's grand staircase again as she had once done when bid-
ding me good-bye at the pier in Liverpool. But that invaluable
four-poster proved a stabilizer, and, though her equanimity

was plainly upset, it only showed itself in an unaccustomed tear rolling down her cheek — one of the tears I cost her that at least brings me no regrets.

When the girl's way and mine parted in that last word in material mêlées, the customs-house shed in Manhattan after the arrival of a big liner, I realized that in reality an armistice only rather than a permanent settlement had been achieved. True, there was no stern father in the case, but there was a mother and a home, both in Chicago and at Lake Forest. These loomed up as formidable strongholds for a homeless wanderer to assault, especially as I had no alternative to keeping a whole series of appointments essential to my work among the fishermen and just postponing the 'campaign on the western front' until later. Moreover, the fact that there was neither brother nor sister, niece or nephew, to fill the void, if I carried off 'the girl in black' to the other end of the continent, was a very serious consideration. But the inexorable schedule that kept me in the East, and the generous hospitality of friends that meant so much to my mother, afforded the blessing that work always carries with it — an occupied mind, though the greatest of all ventures loomed up as more and more momentous as the fateful day drew near for me to turn my face westwards.

This visit to my wife's beautiful country home among the trees on the bluff of Lake Michigan in Lake Forest was one long dream. My mother and I were now made acquainted with the family and friends of my fiancée. Her father, Colonel MacClanahan, a man of six feet five inches in height, had been Judge Advocate General on the staff of Braxton Bragg, and had fought under General Robert E. Lee. He was a Southerner of Scotch extraction, having been born at Nashville and brought up there in Tennessee. A lawyer by training, after the war, when everything that belonged to him was destroyed in the Reconstruction Period, and being still a very young man, he had gone North to Chicago and begun life again at his profession and eventually become head of the bar. There he had met and married, in 1884, Miss Rosamond Hill, daughter of Judge Frederick Torrence Hill, of Burlington, Vermont, but who, since childhood and the death of her parents, had lived with her married sister, Mrs. Charles Durand, of Chicago.

The MacClanahans had two children — the boy, Kinloch, dying at an early age from tuberculosis of the hip joint. Colonel MacClanahan himself died a few months later, leaving a widow and one child, Anne Elizabeth Caldwell MacClanahan. She and her mother lived the greater part of the time with her sister, but she, alas, had also passed away a year before.

The friends with whom my fiancée had been travelling were next-door neighbours in Lake Forest. They made my short stay doubly happy by countless kindnesses; and all through the years, Mr. Stirling gave me not only a friendship which meant more to me than I can express, but he also came to Labrador to study our problems and gave his loving and invaluable aid and counsel in our work, as well as endless help, until he too crossed the divide in 1918.

At Lake Forest, in spite of my many years of sailor life, I found that I was expected to acquit myself in many activities I had left long ago to landlubbers, among other things, to ride a horse, my fiancée being devoted to that means of progression. The days when I had ridden to hounds in England as a boy in Cheshire stood me in some little stead, for, like swimming, tennis, and other pastimes calling for coördination, riding is never quite forgotten. But remembering Mr. Winkle's experiences, it was not without some misgivings that I found a shellback like myself galloping behind my lady's charger.

My last essay at horseback riding had been just eleven years previously in Iceland. Having to wait a few days at Reikyavik, I had hired a whole bevy of ponies with a guide to take myself and the young skipper of our vessel for a three days' ride to see the geysers. He had never been on the back of any animal before, but was not surprised or daunted at falling off frequently, though an interlude of being dragged along with one foot in the stirrup over lava beds made no little impression upon him. Fodder of all kinds is very scarce in the volcanic tufa of which all that land consists, and any moment that one stopped was always devoted by our ponies to grubbing for blades of grass in the holes. On our return to the ship, the crew could not help noticing that the skipper for many days ceased to patronize the lockers or any other seat, and soon they were rejoicing that for some reason he was unable to sit down at all. He explained it by saying that his ponies ate so much lava that it stuck out under their skins; and I myself recall feeling inclined to agree with him.

The experiences of those days in Lake Forest live in that part of one's mind that surely does not have to be replaced every seven years. Something somewhere in the human make-up does not get destroyed this side of the grave, whether memory is a window through which spirit communicates with body, or whether it is a library, proof against every kind of oxidizing process, slow like that always going on, or fast like that by fire, I do not know.

Achievement or failure, not doles or accidents, have always loomed up in my experience as the dominant events in my life. I thank God for this terrestrial achievement. A ring had sealed the fact of success. But 'the girl in black' has just looked over my shoulder and says, 'No, I can't let you put that down to your land accomplishments. Let's call it another Grenfell naval engagement.'

Our wedding had been scheduled for November, and for the first time I had found a Labrador summer long. In the late fall I left for Chicago on a mission that had no flavour of the North Pole about it. We were married in Grace Episcopal Church, Chicago, on November 18, 1909. Our wedding was followed by a visit to the Hot Springs of Virginia; and then, heighho, and a flight for the North. We sailed from St. John's, Newfoundland, in January. I had assured my wife, who is an excellent sailor, that she would scarcely notice the motion of the ship on the coastal trip of three hundred miles. Instead of five days, it took nine; and we steamed straight out of the Narrows at St. John's into a head gale and a blizzard of snow. The driving spray froze onto everything, till the ship was appropriately sugared like a vast Christmas cake — another providence. It made the home which we had built at St. Anthony appear perfectly delightful. My wife had had her furniture sent North during the summer, so that now the 'Lares and Penates' with which she had been familiar from childhood seemed to extend a mute but hearty welcome to us from their new setting.

We have three children, all born at St. Anthony. Our elder son, Wilfred Thomason, was born in the fall of 1910; Kinloch Pascoe in the fall of 1912, two years almost to a day behind his brother; and lastly a daughter, Rosamond Loveday, who followed her brothers in 1917. In the case of the two latter children the honours of the name were divided between both sides of the family, Kinloch and Rosamond being old family names on my wife's side, while, on the other hand, there have been Pascoe and Loveday Grenfells from time immemorial.

Only an insane man could expect one personality to possess all the talents valuable for perfect work. Nor can two possess them. Our experience, however, is rather Einsteinian than Newtonian. Twice one has been more than two in personality. Looking back on twenty-three years, marriage has been a geometric rather than an arithmetic factory in my records.

'The girl in black' was a born organizer. Her Scotch ancestry and her college career together certified that. Organization needs, besides patience and expenditure of energy, a peculiar vision, not specially granted to the seafaring mind. Order has a new quartering on our shield.

In old days my best friends often felt like holding back help because they feared the work could not 'carry on' without the founder. There is little doubt of that now. Each department — and how many new ones there are! — runs by itself. 'What every woman knows' is literally true in every normal Scotch married life. More than once, I've heard 'the girl in black' called 'Maggie.' Nothing in these days of depression has helped us more than the orderliness of the ramifications of this work and its many scattered little offices, and the fact that so many important posts are held by volunteers. I used to feel that all my responsibility to the public for their help was ended if we did the work to the best of our power and as economically as we could. I had to learn that was far from enough, and 'the girl in black' has shielded me by her highly trained business capacities from many troubles. An autobiography is a book of confessions. Our work would not have been where it is today, without 'the girl in black.'

By bringing into coöperation the personal service of so many of her highly trained friends, the Child Welfare Department and the Educational Fund, the management of which has been one of her special interests, came into being. It was good to educate the children who had no others to guide or provide for them. It was an imperfect service not to equip them with the mechanical training that would fit them to avail themselves of the opportunities of their country and enable us to expand our work.

Every autumn 'the girl in black,' besides her own family, mothered a batch of boys and girls from Labrador to institutions from Truro Agricultural College, Nova Scotia, to Berea in Kentucky, including Pratt Institute, New York, Wentworth Institute, Boston, Rochester Athenæum, Upper Canada College, Toronto, and to business and technical schools wherever she could personally secure the necessary opportunity. Everything from an outfit, a route, a ticket, and a personal guide had to be arranged. I have a photograph of her on a truck with sixteen students who had just reached Sydney, in Cape Breton, 'for distribution.'

Her determination to keep open house on the Coast, and how through the years she has been able to add that to her contributions, I must leave to 'wops' and workers and visitors and people. I counted fifty-eight at the *al-fresco* supper after the usual Sunday evening 'Sing' on one occasion, and twenty fishermen to a sit-down dinner in the sun porch at another, and I thanked God.

In the keeping in touch with friends and helpers, in her courage and vision in discovering new ways of earning instead of begging help for different activities in turn has lain, however, her most unique contribution; for even in a thankless task like raising money to keep our work going, she prefers any honest labour to the dole, and has shown that many love to give work who could not possibly give money. I venture to suggest that not a few of the most successful of her efforts have been new features in the missionary world.

Everyone uses a calendar. Millions are sold. Why should not a Mission make a better one than anyone else? The conception and the venture on twenty thousand, so as to cut the production cost to a minimum, were due to 'the girl in black.' The artist of King George's Christmas card did the original painting. Raphael Tuck, internationally famous for art reproduction, did the technical work. But the vision, the venture, the hardest work of marketing and the amazing result of eight thousand dollars to the funds were due entirely to 'the girl in black.' Thirty-five hundred unsold copies remained. The covers were removed, framed, and sold as souvenirs both on the Coast and at home. The fifty-two photographs of Labrador were divided between souvenir picture albums and covers for charming boxes of candies, and the publicity and profit from these are still being returned to Labrador.

A congestion of industrial goods made some new method of marketing them imperative. We knew they were what the public wanted, and that they were worth the cost. A new idea came to the rescue. Why not secure a truck, get volunteers to drive it, and arrange summer sales at holiday resorts in the foyers of hotels? It all sounds so easy now. But there were a thousand difficulties at first, and the amount of writing and personal interviewing, and the preliminary outlay, which was large, all needed hard work, business acumen, and vision, and the peculiar courage of naturalness. Perfectly splendid girl volunteers rallied round, sales were organized from Florida to Maine. New power was given to the workers in Labrador to give out more labour and to many more children and poor women the gospel of the love of God was preached in actual loaves and fishes. But the *fons et origo* was once more 'the girl in black.'

Again hers was the launching of Dog-Team Tavern, twenty miles south of Burlington, on a Vermont highway, to be furnished free, to be run by volunteers, who cleared its unavoidable overhead expenses by selling teas to tourists and washing up dirty crockery for the love of God, in order to help market products of industrial work made by far-off fishermen. This venture shows the same faith exactly that brought the same results, and in the same ways, that Paul speaks of in the Epistle to the Hebrews, and that many a Christian never believes could be accomplished outside the Bible. Such things are not looked for today. Yet this whole effort also has materialized exactly as it was dreamed in the heart and mind of 'the girl in black,' who has mothered it like many another from the first. Those who have so nobly served in it longest are the first to realize this, that the fact that many visitors have come all the way from New York, Boston, Philadelphia, and from farther to visit it, suggests its success, and raises hopes of a similar work in winter in cities, and perhaps on other highways, and in the service of other good causes as well as ours, in the days to come. The Dog-Team Tavern is advertised by pointers over one hundred miles of road. Volunteers produced them and put them up. Think of Jonathan Edwards considering a volunteer Scotch girl, and another from Texas, and another from Bryn Mawr, driving an old borrowed car around New England and nailing up pictures of dog-teams on posts, as being 'preachers of the Gospel.' Anyway, we do.

Our telephone this afternoon announced: 'Your head worker is in the hospital here. Her car skidded and turned over twice.' Lady Grenfell telephoned three hours later: 'L—— is back at the Dog-Team Tavern again. She crawled out of the window after the car made two somersaults, got forty men to turn the car right side up, and she has limped back to the Tavern in it, with only a cut and a bruise or two.'

Even as this book goes to press, there are two new ventures on the tapis to help us carry on in these days, difficult for all the world, but especially so for a population like ours, small, isolated, and even before the depression, living often close to the hunger-line. This time it is puzzles, made specially for us by Raphael Tuck, of London, and 'containing two hundred pieces of the polar regions, to help build up the work in Labrador,' and a bazaar, undertaken at the suggestion of Miss Phillips, of the Animal Rescue League. With her help and that of other generous friends, this fair is to be held in Boston in November. Both these efforts call for courage and for untold work, but knowing 'the girl in black,' I have faith to believe that she and her colleagues will put them through.

What do I think of marriage? What do I think of my digestion? I consider it a pathological symptom to think of either. The title of this chapter best describes my experience. I once watched a large camel and a tiny cow harnessed together in Egypt, and doing excellent work with a plough. I feel like the smaller partner, grateful for redoubled capacity. In every way marriage is as natural as any other condition of life on earth. Like Labrador, the 'early explorers' said, 'It is of no use to man.' We think, however, that it was they who were no use.

No thinker can believe for a moment that the worth-while-ness of life is what we get out of it. No one who enters life, or school, or club, or country, or marriage, possessed of that spirit, will find any human institution a success. Mere physical beauty certainly does not ensure permanency of love. It cannot. It does not last. Yet marriage has made it last. Look at Darby and Joan — hand in hand at the eventide of life, facing together the last experience of us all with the same smile with which they faced the first. Is that a failure? An inevitable cause of failure of all human ideals is selfishness. Call it sin if you wish: I am no stickler for labels. Whatever you style it, 'self first' is the negation of the *raison d'être* of our being on earth at all. It and lasting happiness, married or unmarried, are as incompatible as alkalis and acids, or perhaps better, as fire and gunpowder.

Like business, sport, ventures of all and every kind, marriage to be a success must be entered with a will to succeed, as must faith in man and even in God. The incidents of a day must be looked at in due perspective, not as to their little reaction of myself, whether it is *my* ease, *my* stomach, or *my* dignity, but the effect on the other half — the team. Only one selfish player in the best team on earth can lose the game if he 'hogs the ball' when he should pass it to give another player the glory of the touchdown.

We two, anyhow, are signing this chapter together. When we began, we believed marriage to be a part of God's plan for men's and women's happiness on earth, enabling them to help the world just so much more, since union means more strength and wisdom and courage. Now that we are on the last lap and the final goal seems not so far away, we are holding hands closer than ever, confident that the final experience of life also will be easier to face thus, and indeed become only another joyous venture, when these worn-out bodily machines of ours shall be discarded, and on the other side we shall work again, in new fields, together.

CHAPTER XVIII

THE SIGHT OF SALT WATER UNBOUNDED

IN APRIL, 1912, a large meeting was held in New York to reorganize the management of our work. The English Royal National Mission to Deep Sea Fishermen was no longer able or willing to finance, much less to direct, affairs which had gone beyond their control, and we felt it imperative to arrange an organization of an international character to which all the affairs of the enterprise could be turned over. The International Grenfell Association was incorporated at that time. It consists today of a Board of Directors representing the Grenfell Association of America, the Grenfell Association of Great Britain and Ireland, the New England Grenfell Association, the Grenfell-Labrador Medical Mission, and the Grenfell Association of Newfoundland. Each one of these component societies has two members on the central Council. These directors have ever since been giving most generously of their time, their money, and their interest to the wise and efficient administration of our work. To these unselfish men and women Labrador and North Newfoundland, as well as I, owe a greater debt than can ever be repaid.

That winter had been a most busy time for us. The New Year found us in Florida and thence we journeyed to Colorado and the Pacific Coast, where at Santa Barbara a special meeting had been arranged by our good friend Dr. Andrews, who every summer for eighteen years travelled all the way from his home there to St. Anthony at his own expense to afford our fishermen the inestimable benefits of his skill as an eye specialist. Many years ago, the following note came to me from an eager-would-be patient: 'Dear Dokker Gransfield. When be the eye spider coming to St. Anthony? I needs to see him bad.' Six weeks of lecturing nearly every night in a new town in Canada on our way East gave me a real vision of Canadian life and an admiration for its people, who are making a nation of which the world is proud.

It would appear that I possessed an insatiable love of lecturing. Nothing is farther from the truth. But the brevity of life is an insistent fact of our existence, and the inability to do good work on the Labrador for the lack of that help which is gladly given if only one will take the trouble to show the reasonableness of the expenditure, makes one feel guilty if an evening is spent quietly. Lecturing is without question the most uncongenial and least romantic task I have been called upon to do; but in a work like ours, which we are thankful to feel has shown a steady growth through these past forty years, and which is not under any special church, funds must be raised largely through voluntary subscriptions.

For the first seven years of my work I never spent the winters in the country — nor was it my intention ever to do so. Besides the general direction of all the branches of our activities, my special task as superintendent has been, and must doubtless remain, the raising of the budget, just as my particular charge on the Coast itself is the hospital steamer Strathcona. Owing to our frozen sea, it is only possible to operate the ship in summer — and only necessary then, as the fishing fleets are only on the Labrador during the months of open water. The actual work and the life in the North is an indescribable rest to both my wife and myself after the nervous and physical drain of a lecture tour. One used to wonder at the lack of imagination in those who would greet us, after long, wearisome hours on the train or in a crowded lecture hall, with 'What a lovely holiday you are having!' We have learned to regard this oft-repeated comment only with amusement.

A lecture tour does include some of the pleasantest experiences of life, bringing one into contact with many people whom it is a privilege to know. But eternal vigilance is the price of avoiding a breakdown. One's memory is taxed far beyond its capacity. To forget some things and some people and some kindnesses are unforgivable sins. A new host every night, a new home, a new city, a new audience, lead one into lamentable lapses. A man in the train once asked me how I liked Toledo. I replied that I had never been there. 'Strange,' he murmured, 'because you spent two days in my house!' On another occasion at a crowded reception I was talking to a lady on one side and a gentleman on the other. I had caught neither name. They did not address each other, and I felt I must remedy matters by making them acquainted, and mumbled, 'Please let me present you to Mrs. M-m-m.' 'Oh! don't trouble,' he responded. 'We've been married for thirty years.'

We had just completed a lecture tour in behalf of Labrador in Scotland. My train was already blowing off steam in the station, and I had heard the guard shout 'All aboard' and the sound of snapping doors. I could see my wife frantically waving to me from a carriage far down the platform, and was putting my best foot forward to make a 'getaway,' when some obstructionist at the wicket-gate held his hand out across my pathway. Shaking hands had become epidemic with me. I grasped it hastily, shook it heartily, and continued my flight. A strong feeling that I must have been recognized flashed over me, for I had become an unusual centre of attraction. Even my ardent friend from the gate was pursuing me, apparently with a determination of pressing even more parting attentions upon me. I was not mistaken. He was the ticket collector!

It is my invariable custom in the North to carry a water-tight box with matches and a compass chained to my belt.

One night I had turned into bed in a very large, strange room without noting the bearings of the doors or electric switches. My faithful belt had been abandoned for pyjama strings. It so happened that to catch a train I had to rise before daylight and all my possessions were in the dressing-room. I soon gave up hunting for the electric light. It was somewhere in the air, I knew, but beating the air in the dark with the windows wide open in winter is no better fun in your night-clothes in New York than in Labrador. A tour of inspection revealed no less than five doors, none of which I felt entitled to enter in the dark in *déshabille*.

An independent life has left me with a dislike of asking strangers the way to any place I am seeking. The aversion is more or less justified by the fact that outside the police force only very exceptional persons can direct you, especially if they know the way themselves. On my first visit to New York I could see how easy a city it was to navigate, and returned to my host's house on Washington Square in good time to dress for dinner after a long side trip near Columbia University and Bellevue Hospital. 'How did you find your way?' my friend asked. 'Why, there was just enough sky visible to let me see the North Star,' I answered. I felt almost hurt when he laughed. It is natural for a polar bear not to have to inquire the way home.

Perhaps the greatest danger of a lecture tour is the reporter, especially the emotional one, who has not attended your lecture. I owe such debts to the Press that this statement seems the blackest of ingratitude. My controversy with this class of reporters is that they are too generous, and put into one's mouth statements which on final analysis may be cold facts, but which, remembering that one is lecturing on a work among people whom one loves and respects, it would never occur to me to slur at a public meeting. No one who tries to alter conditions which exist can expect to escape making enemies. I have seen reports of what I have said at advertised meetings which were cancelled subsequently. I have followed up rumours and editors have expressed sorrow that they have accepted them from men who had been too busy to be present. But *qui s'excuse, s'accuse*, and my conclusion is that the lecturer is practically helpless.

For many years after our marriage my wife most generously acted as my secretary, having especially learned typing and shorthand in order to free me from that burden, and for the last twenty-four years, the span of our married life so far, has helped me enormously on this line. But lecture tours are the despair of us both. One cannot keep abreast of one's correspondence.

It was just after the first of June, 1912, when again we found ourselves heading North for St. Anthony, only once more to be caught in the jaws of winter. For heavy Arctic ice blockaded the whole of the eastern French Shore, and we had to be content to be held up in small ice-bound harbours till strong westerly, offshore winds cleared the way. Having looked into matters at St. Anthony, we immediately turned our faces southward again to inspect the new venture of the Institute.

For a long time we had felt the need of some place in St. John's where work for fishermen could be carried on, and which could be also utilized as a place of safety for girls coming to that city from other parts of the Island. My attention was called one day to the fact that liquor was being sent to people in the outports C. O. D. by a barrel of flour which was being lowered over the side of the mail steamer rather too quickly onto the ice. As the hard bump came, the flour in the barrel jingled loudly and rum leaked profusely from the compound fracture.

The Strathcona was at work one day in a harbour in the Straits of Belle Isle, and around us were a number of large Banking vessels from the New England coast, each with a crew of twenty to twenty-five men. When I returned home, I found the skipper of one of them awaiting me on deck. He was considerably excited. It seemed that on the way North, the crew had taken his vessel into St. Pierre for stores, and then, taking French leave, had loaded the vessel up with intoxicants. At the moment they were all out in their dories, and so he urged me to search the vessel at once. His reason was that the crew were so dangerous when drunk, and he was unable to do anything, since they were so violent and outnumbered him twenty to one. We rowed aboard a little later, and found things exactly as he had said, and seizing the opportunity cleaned the whole lot out, loaded it onto the Strathcona, and steamed away to our next port of call. Not till two years later did I meet that skipper again, and he laughingly reminded me of the trick he had played on his crew.

'I hope it helped you out and enabled you to get a good voyage,' I said, thinking of the men's families.

'Yes, Sir. It helped me out all right. When the men got back, they were furious. They picked up the dories and the anchor, and sailed all the way back to St. Pierre and got another load. Moreover, they almost helped me out of a job when they told the owners.'

On a previous occasion I had dumped a seizure of liquor over the side, and had been warned that such an action laid even a Mission steamer under suspicion. The smell of it led more than one reformer to suspect our ship before we got rid of it in St. John's, and the twinkle in the eye of the officer into whose boat we delivered it made us fear that King George never saw any of it after all our trouble.

On two previous occasions, before the Government had asked me to act as unpaid Justice of the Peace, serious cases arose, which we had to deal with for lack of any other authority present. The first was when we found the dead bodies of three young women lying side by side on the floor of an empty hut. Suspicion was somewhat disarmed, by one man, left to watch, seeing an Eskimo half-breed come rowing to the house with some lumber he had been away in the forest to saw for their coffins. He could only say that they died after drinking tea, made from the leaves of a plant near-by, for lack of the genuine article. The plant was hemlock. The women died with the identical symptoms described by Socrates. This man was sent for trial to St. John's. He returned years later, complaining that he had been turned out of a comfortable lodging, where he was fed and clad, and even given tobacco, and that with no work to do.

The second was a worse case, because the criminal admitted the guilt when there was no way to escape, and accepted a purely amateur sentence. This, as we both regarded it years afterwards, was unquestionably a very severe one. It had, however, atoned in part to the victim in the only way possible.

In St. John's there was no 'Foyer des Pêcheurs,' and no one wanted fishermen straight from a fishing schooner either in his home or beside him in church. As one man said, 'It is easy for the parson to tell us to be good, but it is hard on a wet, cold night to be good in the open street.' It is harder still 'to be good' if you have to find shelter in a brightly lighted room of a saloon, where music is being played. The boarding-houses for the fishermen, where thousands of our young men flocked in the spring to try for a berth in the seal fishery, were nothing short of calamitous. Finally, unsophisticated girls coming from the outports to the city ran terrible risks, having no friends to direct and assist them. The Institute which we had in mind was to include a department for girls as well. No provision was made in the city for the accommodation of wrecked crews.

My personal attitude toward alcohol is known to my friends — and to my enemies. A man does not need alcohol and is far better without it. A man who sees two lights when there is only one is not wanted at the wheel of my vessel or of my motor car. It is true that in many countries the rich can flaunt the laws which they do not like, until, as with the prohibition law in America, they can force the people to believe that they cannot carry out any law which the wealthy choose to pay to break.

There is a far more serious element in the loss of confidence that is even now shaking America than those who are keeping boot-leggers admit. More than once I have been at dinners where nearly everyone at the table boasted that he regularly broke the law. I recall one cocktail episode in particular. A lady had chaffed me for not drinking intoxicants even in a prohibition country, in reply to my query as to why she herself indulged in them. From her general contour, no urgent reason for her doing so presented itself to my medical eye. She replied, 'Because I like them.' Noticing a triple string of priceless pearls around her neck, I was surprised into the retort. 'I would greatly like the pearls which you are wearing, Madam, but fortunately for you I have a conscience. It would not be easy if I took them.'

The English and Scotch papers are ridiculing the 'awful failure' of this law of the land, and lamenting at the same time that their liquor-making men are out of work. To the unprejudiced reader this sounds a trifle incongruous. They add that the 'wet plank' has, however, caused immense quantities of hard liquor to be hoarded in warehouses, ready to ship across at the first moment. Shares, even in distilleries, have gone up. For these philanthropists hope that the terrible results of prohibition will need immediate solace, by being drowned in whiskey.

But to return to the problem of a Seamen's Institute. As vested interests would be arrayed against us as prohibitionists, it was obviously futile to put up a second-rate affair in a back street. I had almost forgotten to mention that the capital boasted already an old Seamen's Home, but it had gradually become a roost for boozers, so when we, as trustees, made an inspection of it, we decided on immediate closure. After a few years of collecting funds for our Institute, our friends, some of them, developed 'cold feet,' and, moreover, reports were circulated by ill-wishers that the whole thing was a piece of personal vanity and not in the least needed. So the matter was submitted to the Governor for advice.

He realized fully that a big need required a big remedy, and heartily endorsed the plan for the building. My own view, which time has fully justified, was that only so large a building as one costing two hundred thousand dollars could ever hope to meet the problem. The merchants in St. John's came to our aid with their accustomed really noble generosity, and with the help of friends outside the Colony, in the year 1911, with approximately a hundred and seventy-five thousand dollars in hand, we came to the time of laying the foundation stone. But the hostility of enemies was not over.

We obtained the promise of King George V that if we connected the foundation stone with Buckingham Palace by wire, he would, directly after the ceremony of his Coronation in Westminster Abbey, press a button at three o'clock in the afternoon and so lay the stone across the Atlantic. The services of our good friends in the Anglo-American Telegraph Company did the rest.

On the great day His Excellency the Governor made an appropriate speech. Owing to the difference in time of about three hours and twenty minutes, it was shortly before twelve o'clock with us. The noonday gun was fired from the Narrows during the Governor's address. Then followed a prayer by His Lordship the Bishop of Newfoundland and Bermuda — and then, dead silence. Everyone was waiting for our newly crowned King to put that stone into place. A second had passed, the Governor had just said, 'We will wait for the King,' when 'Bang, bang,' went the gong to notify us that His Majesty was at the other end of the wire. Slowly the great stone began to move. A storm of cheering greeted the successful effort; and all our enemies could say was, 'It was a fake.' Nor might they have been so far off the mark as they supposed, for we had a man with a knife under the platform ready to make that stone come down if anything happened to the wire so that the device did not work. You cannot go back on your King. Fortunately, our subterfuge was unnecessary.

If the summer of 1910 had brought me a large crop of personal worries in connection with our coöperative stores, it was a little later that same year that one of the most forward steps for the Mission was made. The late Mr. George B. Cluett, of Troy, New York, built specially for our work a beautiful three-masted schooner. She was constructed of three-inch plank and sheathed with hardwood for use in our ice-fields. Mr. Cluett had asked me if I would like any words from the Bible on her plate, and I had suggested, 'The sea is His, and He made it.' We were somewhat surprised, however, when we discovered that the fine bronze tablet in her bore the inscription, 'This vessel with full equipment was presented by George B. Cluett to Wilfred T. Grenfell. The sea is His, and He made it.'

Mr. Cluett's idea was that, as we had heavy expenses in carrying endless freight so far North, and as it was often broken or damaged or lost in transit, the schooner could not only obviate this trouble by carrying our own freight, but in winter, when our sea is frozen, could earn enough to dead-head our own freight charges.

During the early years of the War we found freights easy to obtain, when the George B. Cluett was not in our direct service. Later, an inexperienced captain, running her too far before the trade winds during a voyage to Brazil, found himself too close to a lee shore to beat off and was forced to anchor. A passing Brazilian gunboat towed her ten miles out to sea for safety; but when she reached port at last, she found an injunction placed on her for ten thousand dollars. It was an iniquitous charge, but we were forced to pay it before our vessel could put to sea again. This delayed her so long in harbour that she was riddled with boring worms which are so numerous in those warm waters, and she sank on the voyage home in the roadstead of the Bahamas. A suit was at once instituted against the Brazilian Government by one of our directors, a well-known marine lawyer in Boston, and was won in three courts after appeals had been made, the salvage being reduced to eight hundred dollars from ten thousand. A further appeal was made, however, and year after year the final trial has been delayed, so we have never been able to get back one cent, though fifteen years have elapsed since the first judgment was given in our favour. Nor does it look in the least probable that justice is procurable in Brazil, which

I write in the hope that some honest Brazilian may take the matter up for his country's honour. Our lawyer brought to my notice an ancient case in England, where a marine lawsuit was not finally settled for over one hundred years, during which time every single soul interested on both sides had died.

Our lost schooner has been replaced by a new one, once more made possible by the Cluett family, than whom this work has no truer friends. The beautiful new vessel is fitted with powerful new heavy oil engines, is run chiefly by a volunteer crew, with a free engineer supplied each summer by another old friend in Boston. Her first voyage was begun from T Wharf in Boston, and in her hangs a fine photograph of Mr. and Mrs. Henry Ford, who came to a farewell meal on board just before we sailed. This send-off we kept absolutely secret, but in some way it leaked out so that the civic authorities had to send a special posse of police to the old wharf to make it possible for our distinguished guests to get to and from the ship.

Another event of that day stands out vividly in my memory. Mayor Curley of Boston invited me to lunch at the City Hall and to accept a loving-cup on behalf of the Corporation, at the very hour that Mr. and Mrs. Ford were to be our guests on board. Most graciously, we were allowed to adapt the times so that I could attend both functions. It was a great encouragement to realize how times have changed for the better when a Roman Catholic chief magistrate of Boston hands to the Protestant leader of an international mission on a ship lying at the head of the fateful T Wharf such a delightful bouquet as a large silver cup, which is now a highly prized ornament in my Sanctum.

In 1921 the beautiful little S.S. Strathcona was badly rusted out. She had had, besides several strandings, to lie in winter in the heavy ice of our harbour, since at that time we had no haul-up slip. She had twice filled with water when sucked down by the pressure of the ice. Twice we had had to saw and dynamite her out of the grim grip of Jack Frost. When examined by Lloyd's surveyor, owing chiefly to the unavoidable 'sweating' in winter her steel ribs were found to be literally almost thin enough to shave with, her deck-beams were letting down the deck, and the bolts which held the deck-house were so reduced to skeletons that we still preserve specimens among our curios, as an example of what moth and rust can do in the way of corruption in the North.

Lady Strathcona came to our aid and most generously reconditioned the steamer for us. In 1923, however, late in the fall in a gale of wind, she sank in a hundred and fifty fathoms of water, conquered at last, after a quarter of a century's plucky service, by Father Neptune, whom she had so long defied. Though some things precious to myself went down with her, no lives were lost, the crew being picked up in their dory by a fishing schooner that 'chanced their way.' I have only the satisfaction of knowing that somewhere, all those fathoms down, the legend on her brass wheel is preaching to the fishes, which our patron saint, St. Anthony, is said to have done also when no one else would listen to him. It reads, 'Follow Me, and I will make you fishers of men.'

On our arrival at Southampton, a former civil engineer, who lives near-by, chanced to speak to me of a fine little steam yacht lying on the hard for sale at a bargain price. Friends blamed me for buying it. It was, as they said truly, 'too big to send across on the deck of a transport,' and, being only eighty-four feet long, 'too small to steam across.' They were certain 'we could never hire anyone to risk his life crossing the western ocean on a steamer only able to carry thirteen tons of coal.' It was 'foolish to think of it, and criminal to allow it,' on my part.

I could only reply that I had not the slightest intention of hiring anyone to take her across, but I was going to ask friends to take her over voluntarily as a service to the Labrador. This may have looked like 'passing the buck,' but it was a job I would have loved myself had I been free from other work; and it wasn't a week before we had applicants aplenty for the opportunity.

When leaving Southampton in June, the little ship, which we had rechristened Strathcona II, was anchored just under the S.S. Berengaria, giant of the seas. My whimsical friend the captain could not resist the temptation, as a fellow trans-Atlantic steamer commander, of calling on the captain of the Berengaria and offering to carry messages across the sea for him. When the captain of the Berengaria had gazed away

ABE, MATE OF THE HOSPITAL BOAT

A LABRADOR PRODUCT!

down over his rail at the 'mosquito' below, he countered by requesting the privilege of taking Strathcona II in davits for his westward voyage and dropping her off on the other side.

Our tiny little craft went by way of Vigo and the Azores and arrived in St. John's, Newfoundland, with five tons of coal to spare. They lost nothing coming over but their one sheep which had been destined for a festive dinner when the halfway mark was reached. That sheep, however, seemed to prefer drowning to roasting. When the captain and engineer handed over the boat to us, they certainly did not express any regrets that their splendid services were not even partially cancelled by dollars.

But we have been getting ahead of our story, and must retrace our steps once more to 1913.

CHAPTER XIX

LIGHT AND SHADE

AT THE close of 1913, after a heavy lecture tour in America, my wife and I found ourselves at my old home in England, enjoying a few days' rest prior to taking a month's holiday, which would direct our minds into other channels than Labrador and enable us subsequently to return to our various problems with fresh enthusiasm and strength. Boxing Day, therefore, found us bound for Rome.

For a time one is glad to forget the future and its uncertainties and live in the past and its accomplishments. Sitting in the Coliseum in the moonlight, we conjured up the picture of gladiators fighting to amuse the 'civilized' men of their day, and gentle women and innocent men dying horrible deaths for truths which are still today by far our most priceless heritage.

It must be confessed that so-called religious buildings, religious pictures, and religious conventions of all sorts soon pall on my temperament. Doubtless it is a defect in my make-up, like my inability to appreciate classical music. It is still quoted against me in the family circle that I asked an important Doctor of Music of London, visiting our Coast and offering generously to give a concert in the school hall, but finding this impossible owing to the demise of one of the keys on the venerable piano, 'But is it an important note?'

In almost every English home Brindisi is a household word, especially in one like ours with literally dozens of relatives who have served India either in the Army or in the Civil Service. So I was glad to sail for Athens from that port. Patras also woke an answering note in my mind as it has long been a distributing centre for our Labrador fish. Indeed, we saw three forlorn-looking Newfoundland schooners lying at anchor in the harbour.

Both in Greece and Rome, one almost resented the fact that a place civilized thousands of years ago, and which had loomed so large in one's youthful imagination as the home of Socrates, of Plato, of Homer, of Achilles, of Spartan warriors and immortal poets, should be so small and so barren. In Athens one saw so many interesting relics within a few hundred yards that one had the sensation of having eaten a meal too rapidly. When one sat in Xerxes' Seat and conjured up that old picture, and saw the meaning to the world of the great deed for which men so gladly gave their lives to defeat a tyrant seeking for world power, it made one love the old Greeks.

On Mars Hill we stood on the spot where one of the very greatest figures in history pleaded with his fellows to accept love as the only permanent source of power and happiness. But as in our modern civilizations, every monument, every bas-relief, every tombstone showed that physical fighters were their ideal.

Though the Turks had been carrying off the precious historic marbles of Ephesus to burn in their kilns as lime for their fields, still the preservation of the city surprised us. Here again we stood on the very rostrum where Saint Paul had stood when he had trouble with a certain coppersmith. At the time of our visit, the only living inhabitant of the once great city was a moth-eaten ass which we saw tethered in a dressing-room beneath the stage of this famous auditorium.

The anachronism of buzzing along a Roman road, which had not been repaired since the days of the Cæsars, on our way to Pergamos, in the only Ford car in the country at that time was punctuated by our having to get out and shove whenever we came to a cross-drain. The night at Soma, which is the terminus of the branch railroad in the direction of Pergamos, we spent in the 'best hotel.' Only half of this structure, however, was intended for humans. A detachment of unfortunate Turkish soldiers was billeted below in the quarters designed for the other animals. Snow lay deep on the ground, and it was bitterly cold. The wretched soldiers were sleeping literally on the stones of the floor. We were cold, and we felt so sorry for them that, after we had enjoyed a hot breakfast, in a fit of generosity we sent them a couple of baskets of Turkish specialties. Later in the day we noticed that wherever we went a Turkish soldier with a rifle followed us. As guide to speak the many dialects for us we had a Greek graduate of the International College at Smyrna, a delightful and intelligent young fellow, proud of a newly acquired American citizenship. At last we stopped and bribed the soldier to tell us what the trouble was. 'Our officers thought you must be spies since you sent gifts to Turkish soldiers,' he admitted finally.

At Pergamos a Greek Christian invited us to be his guests on the Greek Christmas Eve. It was the occasion of a large family gathering of fine young men and handsome, dark-eyed girls. The house had all the accessories of a delightful Christian home. When the outer gates had been locked, the inner doors bolted, and the blinds carefully drawn, and when all possible corners had been examined for spies, the usual festivities were observed. These families of the conquered race have lived in bondage for some four hundred years, but their patriotism has no more dimmed than did that of ancient Israel under her oppressors. They danced for us the famous Souliet Dance — memorial of the brave Greek girls who, driven to their last stand on a rocky hilltop, jumped one by one over the precipice as in the dance each in turn reached the edge, rather than submit to shame and slavery.

At Constantinople, the kindness of Mr. Morgenthau, the American Ambassador, and the optimism bred by Robert College and Girls' School, left delightful memories of even the few days in winter we were able to spend there. The museum alone is worth a long journey to see — it was like a leap back into history. It seemed but a step beyond it to the Neanderthal skull and our Troglodyte forbears.

Owing to the necessity of reaching England quickly for our lecture tour, we returned by train through Bulgaria and Serbia, with brief stops at Budapest and Vienna. The month's holiday had done for us just what we hoped — started us on our lecturing with a feeling that after all Labrador was a worth-while spot for one's life-work. It helped also to lessen the fatigue of the lectures by travelling in a motor car of my brother's, in which we lived, moved, and had our being — and our meals by the roadside — all the way from an old Border castle on the line of the old Roman Wall almost to Land's End. Then once more the Mauretania carried us to America, whence we wended our way northward to Labrador as soon as the winter's ice broke up on the Coast.

Early in July, the Duke of Connaught, the Governor-General of Canada, paid us a long-promised visit. It was highly appreciated by the fishermen, who would possibly have given him more undivided attention if he had not been thoughtful enough to send his band ashore, knowing that the people had never heard one before. The uniform of the band-master was so resplendent that he was instantly mistaken for the Duke, who was clad in simple mufti — about which the people experienced much the same feeling as did a little boy at one of my lectures, years afterwards. On seeing Lady Grenfell in the lobby, he looked up at her and remarked tearfully, 'I have shaken hands with a real knight, but he left his armour at home.'

In the autumn of 1915, I was urged by the Harvard Surgical Unit to make one of their number for their proposed term of service in a base hospital in France. Having discussed the matter with my directors, we decided that it was justifiable to postpone the lecture tour which had been arranged for me, in view of this new opportunity.

It was Christmas and snow was on the ground when I arrived in France. There was much talk of trench feet, and cold. Our life in the North had afforded us some experiences more like those at the front than most people's. We were forced to try and obtain warmth and mobility combined with economy especially in food and clothing. I, therefore, ventured to send to the *British Medical Journal* a summary of deductions from our Labrador experiences. Clothes only keep heat in and damp out. Thickness — not even fur — will never warm a statue; and our ideal has been to obtain light, wind- and water-proof material and a pattern which prevents leakage of the body's heat from the neck, wrists, knees, and ankles. Our skin boots, by being water-tight and roomy, remove the cause of trench feet, and the defects, either in wet and cold or in hot weather, of woollen cloth are obvious.

One of the soldiers who came under my care had a bullet wound through the palm of his hand. I happened to ask him where his hand had been when hit. He said: 'On my hip. We were mending a break in our barbed wire at night, and a fixed rifle got me, exactly where it got my chum just afterwards, but it went through him.'

'Where did your bullet go?'

'I didn't know,' he answered.

An examination of his trousers showed the bullet in his pocket. It was embedded in three pennies and three francs which he happened to be carrying there, and which his wounded hand had prevented his feeling for afterwards.

Pathos and humour, like genius and madness, are close akin. One of the boys told me of his chum who was very 'churchy' and always carried an Episcopal Prayer Book in his pocket — for which he was not a little chaffed. For a joke one day he was presented with a second that a messmate had received, but for which he had no use. His scruples about 'wasting it' made him put it in his pocket with the other. Soon after this, in an advance, he was shot in the chest. The bullet passed right through the first Prayer Book and lodged in the second, where it was found on his arrival in hospital for another slight wound. He at least will long continue to swear by the Book of Common Prayer.

One day, walking with other officers in the country, we stumbled across a tiny isolated farm. As usual, the voice of the inevitable Tommy could be heard from within. They were tending cavalry horses, which filled every available nook and corner behind the lines at a period when cavalry was considered useless in action. Having learned that one of these men had been bodyservant to a cousin of mine, who was a V.C. at the time of his death, I asked him for the details. The Germans had broken through on the left of his command, and it was instantly imperative to hold the morale while help from the right was summoned. Jumping on the parapet, my cousin had walked to and fro there encouraging the line amid volleys of bullets. Suddenly a bullet passed through his body and he fell forward into the trench. Protesting that he was all right, he despatched his orderly to tell the Colonel that he could hold out until he should come back; but on his return he found that my cousin was dead. But help came, the line held, and the German attack was a costly failure. His servant had collected and turned in all his little personal possessions of any value which he found on the body.

'I think you should have got a Military Cross,' I said.

'I did get an M.C.,' he answered.

'I congratulate you,' I replied.

'It was confinement to barracks. A bullet had smashed to

pieces a little wrist watch which the Captain always carried.
It was quite valueless, and I kept the remnants as a memento
of a man whom everyone loved. But a comrade got back at me
by reporting it to headquarters, and they had to punish me,
they said.'

When at the close of the period for which I had volunteered,
I had to decide whether to sign on again, my inclination was
to stay for at least another term; but as my commandant informed me that he and a number of the busier men felt that
duty called them home, and that there were plenty of volunteers then to take our places, my judgment convinced me
that I was more needed in Labrador.

Since the original chapter on my brief experience at the
War was written, the whole world has been forced to accept
new and revolutionary ideas of values. Long ago, the despised
John the Baptist was beheaded for telling his generation that
the material was after all ephemeral. Christ was put to death,
as many a pacifist has been, because the pride of the practical
man and the current scientist precluded their understanding
that any 'mere emotion' could be of greater value for achievement than steel and high explosives.

Internationalism is already beginning to be the slogan of
thinkers. They are even approving the contention that patriotism and nationalism, after all, are not synonymous terms.
If a perfect world could be run by robots on the basis of
mathematics, logic, and force, the world would immediately
act on that conclusion and would become a federation of
nations, with free trade and free intercourse. The fact is, however, that fear has driven convinced free-traders to hide behind walls they call tariffs, hoping possibly to prove once for
all the terribly inevitable results.

The most ardent Bombastes Furioso now admits in his
sober moments that men are less likely to fight if they have
nothing to fight with; and that disarmament may after all be
a rational measure. Is it the emotion called fear, and not logic,
which prevents disarmament between the nations?

It seems unthinkable that all the supposed rulers, governors,
wise men, and sages could possibly have all alike been fooled
by the will-o'-the-wisp, and based their lives and policies on
illusion. All the great warriors and founders of empires, all

the conquering heroes of the ages, could they all have been so radically wrong in their mentality as to have been following a phantom; and all their untold expenditures of men, money, and material been used for destruction and not for the real upbuilding of anything durable and abiding?

Is it possible that we, even we, have ears that hear not, eyes that see not, and hearts that do not understand? If we have, what is the emotion which keeps us from admitting it?

CHAPTER XX

THEY THAT DO BUSINESS IN GREAT WATERS

IN THE past, transportation has been our greatest difficulty. Communication during the winter months was only possible by relays of dog-teams coming all the way from Quebec. Volumes of adventure could be written about the experiences of our mail-men. Two winters we arranged to side-track the mail across the Straits of Belle Isle, since we get a weekly mail by dogs at our Newfoundland stations. It was for this reason that we were forced forty years ago to make our winter headquarters at St. Anthony. To us, who have to raise the budget for our work, communication spells existence.

Of all the many mail-men, Ernest Doane, who undertook this attempt to carry the mail across the Straits, took the greatest risks. He is still the only man in the world's history who ever crossed that terribly dangerous running ice in winter. The narrowest place is nine miles wide, and occasionally violent storms from the east drive with irresistible force millions of tons of heavy floe into the V-shaped Straits from the Atlantic. The turmoil of the enormous masses grinding and smashing and turning over under the irresistible pressure, or 'rafting' or being forced over or under other huge pans, is one of the wildest sights in nature to watch. It is a veritable struggle of those most terrible giants, wind, frost, sea, and heavy tides. Not presence of mind, but absence of body, is then man's best hope.

In order to attempt the crossing, Doane constructed a very light canvas flatboat, and also a small, light, tough sledge, put together with neither screws nor nails, but only skin lashings. Either the boat or the sledge could be carried in the other, according to whether it was open water or ice he must cross. In these he stowed food and such light accessories as his long training as a skilful trapper had taught him would be of most service: a compass, a water-tight matchbox, a knife, an axe, a sleeping-bag being *sine qua non*. It took a life's experience to choose wisely a point of departure that would allow for the drift of both wind and current. Research has shown how subject the tides themselves are in this section to wind; that sometimes an entire tide will miss out; that both rising and falling tide flow in the same direction, to say nothing of the fact that the flow direction differs as one crosses from one side the Straits to the other — all facts that have cost many a mariner dear in the old days.

It is not to be wondered at that Doane twice nearly lost the mails and his life by drifting beyond Anchor Point into the open Gulf of St. Lawrence. Since crossing in one day was impossible, he had to sleep on a floor which might capsize at any moment and throw him into eternity by way of an icy sea in the thick darkness. His reward was only fifty dollars for each venture. After four crossings he resigned office — and no successor has been found.

Today, wireless telegraphy and the radio have partially solved this problem of communication. Volunteers have erected amateur wireless plants at three of our hospitals, though, as there is a Marconi wireless station in Sandwich Bay, the plant erected there has not yet received a license. Thanks to friends, we own ten radio sets which meet all the receiving needs of their several localities. Formerly, Labrador was able to get news from the outside world only once in the winter. Now we can hear Big Ben striking in Westminster, listen to preachers in New York, switch on public news and concerts from Schenectady or Chicago, hear the words of lectures from Montreal sooner than the people sitting in the backs of the halls where they are delivered, talk to fellow beings in Berlin, or even send messages to cousins in New Zealand, which by calendar are received hours before we start them off. With the advent of television, Labrador can be an ideal summer resort, as well as a sportsman's winter paradise, where you can shut out the noise of civilization when you wish.

A great source of loss to our poor fishermen comes from damage to vessels by storm or ice or rocks. Every wooden vessel, for its own welfare, should really go on dock for repair and cleaning once a year. For generations the only docks in the whole Colony were in the extreme South, and every fishing craft northbound was sure to waste invaluable time going out of the way to reach it in a season of open water already made too short by ice conditions. Fish are often to be caught long before the schooners can get down North, and they cannot by any means remain long. These facts suggested to us that such an assistance to a people living by fishery in the North was an elemental necessity. When that violent cyclone drove forty-one vessels onto the rocks of Labrador, I could pull off only one or two with any advantage, though many of the rest could easily have been repaired on a drydock had one been at hand. However, for them to attempt to go far to the South, through six hundred miles of open Atlantic in their badly crippled condition, was quite impracticable. Fishermen are poor economists, anyhow, and it was not easy for them to understand, when insurance was being paid for the loss of their ship, that it was really they who were standing the loss, since, almost without exception, they were all in mutual insurance companies or clubs.

The need was further forced upon us when nine vessels drove ashore in one harbour in the Straits of Belle Isle. The larger number of these could easily have been saved had there been a haul-up slip within reasonable reach. As it was, all were lost, and hundreds of people went hungry as a result. Often heroic attempts were made to save these craft. One resourceful skipper, at low tide, battened down canvas on the inside over the gaping hole in the ship's bilge, filled up as much space as he could with hard ship's biscuit, then nailed down stout boards again on the top of the mass of biscuits, and over that strengthened the ballast deck. With the pumps going, he worked his way South, the swelling-up of the biscuits caulking the hole sufficiently to enable him to keep her afloat.

To save another which I had myself hauled off the rocks, we keel-hauled a heavy topsail under the leaky bottom, then flung in peat between the canvas and the ship, and with the pumps were able to free the craft of water, while we partially patched her on the inside. In that condition her skipper sailed her five hundred miles to a drydock.

So we decided that in these days it was an interpretation of the Gospel (provided no one else would attempt it) to consider the saving of vessels as on a par with the service rendered in sending home wrecked crews after they had lost everything, including all chance of getting even food for the long winter. To us it seemed on a par with the value of hospitals for saving men suffering from food deficiencies which had been caused by their having lost their vessels.

So we let our great need for a haul-up slip in the North be known. Years later, our director and friend of years, Mr. Hollis French, told us that, if a dock were needed so badly, we might send him an estimate of the cost, and an anonymous donor would consider giving it to us. The result was that in 1930 we opened in St. Anthony a beautiful dock, onto which we could haul vessels up to one hundred and fifty feet on the keel which needed repairs. It is a veritable hospital for injured craft.

The only outside skill we commandeered to erect it was that of a diver with his outfit. All the rest was done by our local boys, and before it was finished one of the Labrador boys was an accomplished diver, and our friend from outside returned home without his diving-suit and gear. The cost of the dock was thirty-seven thousand dollars, and, had we had to import labour, would have been double that. Not one of us to this day has any idea who paid the bills. It must have been hard for even so Christian a donor to keep his left hand from knowing the cheques his right hand signed.

Our good friends the critics (for we do owe them debts for helping to make us toe the mark) dubbed it another 'Grenfell's folly,' and it was not without trepidation that even so confirmed an optimist as myself awaited results. Excitement ran high when in the autumn, returning to St. Anthony I met the Labrador orphan, now our electrical engineer and in charge of the new dock, and asked him how much loss my 'new folly' would mean to our budget. Even that first year it proved much less than I had feared; and in 1931 the dock has shown a balance of profit even after allowing for depreciation. Better than that, each year it has saved several schooners.

In 1931 we ourselves towed in one schooner with her rudder gone, and another, a large Banker, for a distance of over one hundred and fifty miles. She had been on the rocks, and when we took her in tow for forty-eight hours the crew had been working day and night at the pumps at the rate of seven thousand strokes an hour. Over fifty schooners docked there this summer, and one or two steamers. Even one with a broken shaft was repaired and proceeded on her fishing voyage.

In all our work, each of us is but one small factor. Government, merchants, friends, and fishermen have all helped and encouraged the efforts so untiringly that to write the story as if it were the biography of one man's work would be enough to destroy any value the record carried. One man is only a tiny cog in the economy of God, and without these generous helpers one man could accomplish practically nothing.

A politician, no doubt, would have proclaimed as the most important advance in these past years the fact that the boundaries of Labrador in 1927 were finally settled by the greatest lawyers in England and the highest of all tribunals, His Majesty's Most Privy Council. So long as in our crude civilization natural boundaries must exist, this *is* of importance. Certainly it cost more than any other activity for Labrador has ever cost. We hope it may bring much return in labour, which is, after all, the real blessing of earth. It did give us the benefit of a good chart of Hamilton Inlet, a chart paid for by Canada, which, as it lost many times the territory which Newfoundland ever expected to get, is obliged to be contented with the joy of service, and the knowledge that its work will help greatly to develop the coming tourist traffic, in bringing prospectors to the Coast, and by opening a field for investment in mines, power, and timber. Timber we know to be there, and almost unequalled water-power owing to the Grand Falls, the Yale Falls, both among the world's finest of panoramas. It was the discovery of so much mineral wealth in exactly the same geological formation farther west which has helped to make Canada the richest precious-metal-producing country in the world.

Only a few years ago, so prosaic, and one might almost say scientific, an enterprise as a survey of a country just because it was scientific would hardly have been considered any part of the 'preaching of the Gospel.' Religion apostrophizes much more the merits of the anchorite and the 'withdrawal from all practical business activities.' This mundane occupation of making safer the lives of the men who 'go down to the sea' and of opening up the country to the world outside asserted itself to me with ever-increasing insistence, not only by day, but often in visions of the night, as being better Christianity than waiting to play the Good Samaritan to the surviving families of those fishermen who had been drowned because no reliable chart existed.

The best way to get rid of an enemy is to make him your friend, so we gathered up all the available charts of the entire Coast, from the picturesque products of the famous Captain Cook to those which we had ourselves painfully made and suffered from in years gone by, and decided to devote every bit of time and energy possible to the problem of making a reliable chart.

The British Admiralty wished to help, but had no boat to spare. They promised to send a steamer as soon as one was free. The Canadian Government needed a harbour of refuge in the North Labrador for their grain boats going to England by the new Hudson Bay route and so they wanted to help also, but were not allowed to land surveying parties. The cost of a proper chart would probably run into a very large sum of money. Our directors in those anxious times had no funds to spare for the purpose. I had none myself. There must be as much money as ever on the globe's surface if we are really to believe modern science that there is no waste. A ridiculous quatrain got running through my head:

'There was a young lady said, Why
Can't I see down my ear with my eye?
If I put my mind to it, I surely can do it,
You never can tell till you try!'

So we tried; and a great deal of it was already accomplished in 1931. It happened in this way:

A member of my own profession, the Professor of Physiology of Harvard University, by name Alexander Forbes, a lifelong friend, had developed air-mindedness and had even permitted an ancient shellback like myself to ride with him over New England to Boston, in his Waco plane. This all-round scientist also owned a fine power schooner which he navigated himself. The other essential element, international coöperation, was also his. The whole labour, practically all the expense as well as the planning, he nobly assumed. Without Dr. Alexander Forbes none of it would have been possible.

Rumour has it that Oxford and Harvard always do co-operate. Moreover, this coöperative spirit is always infectious. Messrs. McColl of Quebec donated ten thousand gallons of their excellent gasoline. Lord Wakefield gave one thousand gallons of lubricating oil. The Furness-Withy Line gave free passages to and fro to five workers coming from England. The Newfoundland Government gave us freight on their steamers and free customs entry and licenses. A number of able specialists gave us voluntary service. The Geographical Society of New York undertook to reduce the observations and to prepare the chart, which we estimate will cost them many thousands of dollars. The Royal Geographical Society in London were only so far in a financial position to give their blessing and their endorsement. Our boats carried reserve supplies for the survey party, and the Strathcona joined in the work and gave any possible help she could, consonant with her other obligations. Dr. Forbes found insurance too expensive, and pilotage impossible, so he sailed his own vessel without any loss over the whole Coast. Occasionally he went ahead in his Waco plane, which from ten thousand feet up in clear weather enabled him to outline a course for his vessel free of the shoals which showed up in the photographs taken from that height.

From a mile up in the air I have looked down on Labrador's shores. Even from that height the distances and tasks that have seemed so great through the centuries appeared as easy to overcome as ten thousand tasks that have been accomplished with far less promising outlook. In the bottom of the aeroplane was a round hole, through which protruded a camera. The Englishman who was handling it told me that he had been in the air doing this work, in various parts of the world, without a single month's break, for sixteen years, both in the tropics and in the cold, without one accident. To be 'up in the air' seems to him just as ordinary an occupation as walking down a sidewalk, and though he covered with his pictures six hundred square miles in an hour, it was no more romantic to him than taking photographs in a studio in a city. This able veteran of the air took some nine hundred nine-by-twelve-inch oblique pictures. From these another helper, by his own new method, can work out all the data required for

our purposes, except the soundings. He did an extensive trian-
gulation to locate the pictures exactly.

Dr. Forbes also secured Mr. Noel Odell, the famous climber
of Mount Everest, and once a Professor of Geology at Harvard, now at Cambridge University, England. He ascended
many of our most important mountains, and, though results
are not yet released, he declared that Labrador mountains
afford climbers all the thrill of the Alps, though of all the
highest peaks that rise near the Coast, nothing much over
five thousand feet was measured. Inland from Hopedale,
however, mountains over sixty-two hundred feet have been
reported. Three planes flew from tidal water to the Grand
Falls, the Yale Falls, and back to the Coast in under five
hours. As all our trappers take six weeks going in and out by
canoe up the rivers, and as dangers are very great, especially
when there is much ice in the turbulent rivers in the spring
and only very few supplies can be carried, our aerial service,
which could be easily supplied, would be of great value.

In 1932, I received a preliminary notice that the British
Admiralty had purchased and fitted out an especially sheathed
sixteen hundred ton steamer, and were sending her out in the
spring for an unlimited period to complete the survey of the
Coast of Labrador. For many days I was walking on air, in
a state of what my friends called 'a psychic uplift,' for the
new survey is to include hydrographic soundings and reliable
charts.

For forty years I have been cruising this coast-line among
fishermen, and have climbed some of its peaks near the
shore-line. It is of great interest to science to know the
heights, for it is supposed by some that this is the highest part
of the whole of the eastern side of the American continent.
Another point is the fact that, as one gets towards the northern
end, the peaks are of the Matterhorn type, with apparently
unglaciated tops. Scientists are greatly interested in finding
out whether the old ice-cap of this continent ever completely
overwhelmed the whole of the eastern range. The discovery
of pre-glacial flora here suggests that they have remained
without having been ever totally displaced by the ice.

The expedition gave no new names to the endless unnamed
islands, capes, rivers, bays, mountains, or harbours; but some

fishermen, to whom I was explaining that we hoped to give a complete map in a year or two for their safety, immediately replied, 'We are praying God you will not leave the old Eskimo names and places, for none of us can pronounce them, and most of them are alike, anyhow.'

This survey will help to open up Labrador in the only way at present possible. With the dark clouds now hanging over all financial enterprises, it will afford North America, at much less cost and much closer home, fjords, waterfalls, salmon rivers, icebergs, Eskimos, Indians, auroras, as well as the Greenland glaciers and the Midnight Sun (of which Norway holds no monopoly), all included in a short, inexpensive, and exhilarating holiday trip.

Much water has gone under the bridge since the early days on the Labrador. Our airplanes have shown that it was not the limitations of the Labrador, but of the early observers that was the trouble. A solitary Viking, a Genoese of the fifteenth century, a lonely Breton seaman, even a Major in the English Army may be excused for pessimism. There is some bad in all of us. Even today a financier escaping from the troubles of the monetary system of civilization might hae his doots alone on a Labrador beach; but the rankest materialist with no hopes beyond the accident called death could not be a sceptic about the value of Labrador if he had sailed with us through the air over that great country.

CHAPTER XXI

NEW VENTURES

THE synonym, of my best-on-earth friends, for the members of our Council is deliberate, and is their minimal due. For years they have gathered at their own cost from hundreds of miles distant, at an expense of time far more important to them than even the not inconsiderable dollars, just to shoulder responsibilities for others. Before the quite unusual plan of this International Grenfell Association was formed, the very idea was scouted by more critics than I care to think of as being 'impossible.' 'You cannot get an international group of business men to voluntarily give the time and expense to attend meetings for any Society — at any rate, not for long enough to understand its business.' Fortunately, I could not believe that, for the most orthodox faith is but as sounding brass unless it takes the form of personal sacrifice. Pessimism and Christianity are the acids and alkalis of philosophy. It is enough to record that our directors have, to a man, died in their boots.

The one and only parson on the Board, while a student at Amherst, had enlisted as a Labrador 'wop.' I had allocated him to a group of totally isolated islands, and had thrown in also the conundrum of how to get there, as no regular boat service of any kind touched that part. He had already graduated in my estimation when he arrived at his post in an open fishing boat. The record of his services as doctor, lawyer, parson, teacher, and general Pooh-Bah, during his long vacation there entirely at his own expense, entitled him to junior and senior graduation in one bound. The experiences of the summer and the strong strain of shrewd common sense that permeated his theology led us to urge him to join our Council. In spite of a family and the endless calls of a large parish, he has ever since served on it. It was he who not only suggested the raising of an endowment, but put his broad shoulder to the wheel and started it rolling.

The view of those who are willing to foist all the least at-

tractive challenges of life on the Almighty and call that
'faith in God,' to me is a negation of our responsibility for
bringing God's Kingdom on this earth. It is so much pleas-
anter to spend funds than collect them; even as it would be
easier to practise medicine in London, if I could rely on the
Almighty to heal the blind and make the lame walk in Labrador by simply reminding Him that He had forgotten them.
A pessimistic parson is an anomaly, an impractical parson is
a menace in proportion to the increase in intelligence of the
man-in-the-street.

Raising money has become a recognized profession. That
fact is sealed by a college diploma. The evidence that its
efficiency in placing the concrete problems at issue before a
much larger public in an intelligible way than is otherwise
possible is endorsed by the enormous number of people who
give their share through that professional channel. Sloppiness is never excusable — in work for God's Kingdom it is
criminal.

Our Council were unanimous in the decision to try to raise
a partial endowment, and a professional man was secured!
I can see some of my readers shiver. In the inexperience of
my youth, I resented the idea that God Himself is a supplicant
even for our help. It was easy to say that raising money to
help others spells lack of faith. Professional mendicancy was
the ugly synonym which, when I was young, made me resent
advocating anything, for fear of what others might think.

Our professional's first proposition was to spend his next
long holiday, at his own expense, in Labrador; and to bring
his family and study the problem at first hand. He was young.
He was modest. But he could ill spare the money. Now in
retrospect I can think of no one effort of ours which has accomplished more of permanent value to Labrador, or been
more in line with God's will, than the Endowment Fund.
This is no place for details. It was a poor time to beg. The
War had made money very 'tight,' and promises, like pie-
crust, are proverbially poor material to rely upon.

Lady Grenfell and I accompanied the mobile unit, and associated with us was a most orthodox Princetonian, beloved
of wops, who has been more familiar to us stripped to the waist
and picking rocks and blue clay from foundations in Labra-

dor than in the conventional accoutrements of an amateur Shylock. How often I have seen him toilfully conveying after midnight large bags in a hotel elevator to a bedroom far from the haunts of gangdom, though in those palmy days the Heroes of Chicago had not yet developed their wholesale businesses.

Accustomed to a four-hour watch below during the season of open water, I had learned to sleep through anything except such special impulses as a dragging anchor, a rising sea, or an actual collision; but even after a wearisome evening's lecture, it took a long apprenticeship to allow me to sleep while Lady Grenfell and Bill kept up the clink! clink! clink! of the 'Aberdonian's friend,' as it was counted out from one bag into another; or calling the names, addresses, promises, gifts, and cataloguing and getting all receipts ready, well into the 'wee sma' hours,' so as to start the next day with a clean sheet.

Dr. Charles X, an unusually healthy-looking young surgeon, and a most valued and long-time colleague on the Coast, was suggesting to a stranger a reason for helping Labrador. The lady turned on him with 'You ought to be ashamed of yourself — a strong young man like you. If I were like you, I'd go up and help those people myself.' Though taken utterly by surprise, he did not 'behave himself unseemly,' but suggested regret at being where he was. 'Well, never mind, I meant to give something,' and she pulled out and handed him a cheque for a hundred dollars. Evidently the amazed expression which, at this new development, succeeded the cloud over his not unattractive features, struck some new chord, for hastily snatching back the cheque she tore it into fragments and, throwing it on the floor, wrote another one and sealed it in an envelope. He thought it wise to be moving on, as he already felt himself to be the cynosure of more eyes than he was accustomed to. He is still puzzled why that lady made the second cheque for five hundred dollars. Certainly, not because of 'much speaking' on his part.

The endowment campaign proved a complete success. We did not acquire any overwhelming amount before we all had to hurry back to what we considered 'our work.' But after two years a nucleus had been acquired that relieves both workers and directors of many anxious hours. The importance of this hard piece of work was emphasized by the fact that death comes unexpectedly even to middle age.

My beloved surgical expert colleague, John Mason Little, of Harvard, suddenly passed on from his home in Boston. It had been his own wish even after death to be associated with the place 'where the happiest days of his life had been spent.' His loved ones regard our changing bodies as we always do, just the temporary medium which enables one's personality to function. All of it that can persist are its ashes. In the simplest of urns we took his back to the Coast, and in the face of the rocky cliff above the hospital he had served so well, we laid them, sealed, with a small marble slab bearing the legend: 'John Mason Little. Our True Friend.'

Every summer from far and near people of all shades of thought gather on a Sunday afternoon on the hilltop, to praise God for speaking audibly sometimes, so that even our ears hear; and just to ask Him we, too, may so live that men may be glad also some day that we had been on earth.

I have been anxious ever since to put up a memorial to his service in the form of a clock-tower with a four-faced clock that has been given us, glassed-in so as to keep the snow off its faces. It was an old timepiece which for years marked the flight of time in a village church near Kingsley's haunts at Clovelly. It has been put in order and sent out freely to await the time when we can put it up in some suitable tower, near the spot where we worked together.

New churches have been built by the people the past few years, at North-West River and at St. Anthony. The latter has been named 'The Little Church of Saint Andrew the Fisherman.' A perfectly beautiful, very simple, stained-glass window has been made and donated for the chancel by the skilled and loving hand of a lady in Brooklyn. It depicts that prototype of so many of our people, landing on the beach of the old Sea of Galilee, with the painter of his boat in one hand and an oar in the other. This is the first painted window of its kind ever in our North Country, and as an object of beauty has a never-ending uplifting power.

Moreover, for the first time in history we own a parsonage.

A centre for the special work of the Church on earth has great value, if organized religion is to be helpful to what Christ called 'my Father's business.' Through the kindness of our friends, the parsonage was launched on its venture of faith, just as were the greenhouses, hospitals, clothing store, and so on.

Kerosene is both expensive and dangerous in wooden buildings with children around, as we found when the orphanage in Sandwich Bay was destroyed by fire. We have long realized that not only our light bills, but our heat and power bills will be permanently lowered when we can afford to harness some of our water supplies. The new water and power supply at Cartwright, for which a lady in Rochester, New York, is responsible, is nearly finished; the magnificently unselfish work of two summer crews of wops on the construction of this has been one of the best apologies for Christianity I have ever seen.

In St. Anthony we were unable to raise the money to carry out the design of our beloved consulting engineer in Boston for a hydro-electric plant. His survey showed it could be done, especially now that the control of the power-house can be at headquarters without necessitating an extra man at the dam. So our own men have installed a concrete block powerhouse. We regretted greatly not being able to avail ourselves of all the free water-power going to waste, but more immediate challenges to help faced us.

Last season, our northernmost waters were so full of fish that we saw large schooners loaded in a fortnight, one alone having a cargo of three thousand quintals. However, it cost the owner more to catch it than he could get for it in the market, and he would have been the gainer had he stayed at home. So plentiful was fish that summer that, when taking soundings in shallow water as we approached a strange shore for an anchorage and were using the light fishing jigger instead of the heavy lead, we had to give it up; for every time the lead came up, it brought with it a codfish instead of a mathematical record!

Yet, when we had fish we did not want, and our next-door neighbours had flour they could not sell, there was no way to adjust matters. During the winter our little Colony was in great financial straits and had to try to feed up to sixty thousand fishing folk. In the spring, after an utterly insufficient diet at six cents a day, they had to face a fishery half-fed, half-outfitted, half-clad, or else stay at home idle. I tried in every way that I could to get grain put in sacks and sent down North in our supply steamer, which could have carried many tons quite free of cost, as she was going direct from New York to Labrador in any case. Many influential friends tried to help me, but though a Senator went himself to the Red Cross in Washington, the only answer I could get was that Congress had forbidden any of the wheat to be given away outside the country. We had to buy, therefore, and sent down what little we could afford and friends gave us some hand-stone grinders, as the great need of the whole-wheat had been painfully demonstrated by the numerous cases of beri-beri, neuritis, and paralysis on the Coast. We also sent North a few hundreds of sacks of beans that I had bought in early spring at a bargain. The breakdown of supply and demand is a periodic one through the centuries, and will be so until the world accepts the fact that its present interpretation of nationalism is as foolish as it is disastrous and that high tariff walls are no real solution.

The new instantaneous freezing process has been a real advance. Years ago, we were trying to help our poorer trappers to get more out of their calling, and incidentally attempting to introduce a new way of providing furs for ladies at home without the need of catching animals in steel traps, by having farms in which to rear fur-bearing animals, like any other domesticated wild animal. Having no experience, and very little time to devote to the animals, our actual breeding met no success, as has been related.

Mr. John Hays Hammond fostered the experiment in Labrador by building a fur-farm near Cartwright and by sending down a young biologist from Washington as his manager. The story goes that in winter, when Mr. Birdseye was catching rock cod through the ice to feed his animals, he noticed one very bitter day, with temperature away below zero and with the wind sweeping the ice, that the instantly frozen fish, when thawed out in the kitchen, jumped about again; while on warmer days they did not do so. A long and most courageous expenditure of time and money enabled him to discover the secret. But for his brave wife, and subsequently other friends, he would have had to abandon his quest. The secret is a very simple one, after all, but of vital, even revolutionary importance, to any number of food products, such as New Zealand and Australian mutton, fruit of all kinds, including even fresh things such as raspberries and citrus fruits. The process enables mankind to put on the table all the year round, in exactly the same condition as the day it was killed or picked, any article of food which would otherwise be perishable and seasonal.

When a food cell containing water is frozen slowly, the water forms a crystal of ice, which grows large in proportion to the time it takes to form. Eventually, it is larger than the original amount of water and it bursts the envelope of the cell, as indeed it will that of a solid cannon ball if shut up within it. On the other hand, if the freezing is instantaneous, no such thing can happen. When instantly frozen and then thawed out, the cells do not leak, no mushy quality results, and neither the taste nor the composition is altered. The muscle cells were able to contract again — and so cause the fish to jump about. The indirect results of this effort of Mr. Birdseye's have been of great commercial benefit to the Coast; and so indirectly, if in no other way, the fox-farm idea is bearing fruit. Moreover, the Hudson's Bay Company are still running the original foxfarm.

By far the most enterprising knight of commerce in the North is the 'Honourable Company of Merchant Adventurers,' known as the 'Hudson's Bay Company.' They immediately and at very great expense applied the Birdseye discovery to one of our best products, the fat, cold-water, North Atlantic salmon. Recently, a company consisting mostly of fishmongers of London were entertained at dinner, and different varieties of salmon were served. When the guests were asked to select the most palatable fresh salmon, sixteen out of the twenty are said to have selected Labrador salmon which had been frozen by this method, thawed out again, cooked and served. Queen Mary purchased at an Exhibition some Labrador frozen salmon. A short while after, we were accorded an interview at Buckingham Palace, when, after reminding her that our first little Labrador hospital steamer had been by her wish christened the Princess May (her name in those days), I ventured to ask what Her Majesty had thought of the salmon. It is only because her reply was so complimentary that I have recorded the incident.

The difficulties of prejudice and vested interests make it as hard to introduce a new product into a European market as it is to forbid the sale of an old product in America. As always, money was lost in experimenting, and more salmon was put on the market than it could bear at first. At the moment, depression was playing havoc with every commercial company; and the easy way would have been to give up the attempt. The chivalry of the genuine adventurer in commerce is just as real as that of the pulpit or forum. So far this particular discovery has been a vital message of love to many, for it has meant just the difference between hunger and sufficiency to the families of our salmon fishers. For thus, they are able to sell their catch straight from the net, without cutting the bones out, without salt which many now could not afford, and without having to put it in barrels; and that at an even better price than before. Because of its low price, it certainly will mean in time access to a delicious and valuable food for many in our big cities, such as my old friends in the East End of London, who never otherwise would be able to afford such a delicacy. In addition, our fat codfish, similarly preserved, are on trial, and will one day unquestionably supplant the present salt product and so command new markets as a far more palatable product. 'The Company' have also been testing our halibut by having a ship of their own to catch it on the newly discovered Halibut Banks, and treat it also by the new process, while its liver contains, it is said, five times the vitamines of cod-liver oil.

The Hudson's Bay Company have been real pioneers also in developing other native products, and have spent huge sums in finding industrial remunerative work for the Eskimos and Indians, who form the larger part of their clientèle in the North. Their embroidery on deerskin and sealskin, their bead and silk work, and their recent efforts to market our berries and all local assets deserve the heartiest gratitude of all who love Labrador. On one occasion many years ago, I had felt it

my duty to hold up the chief trader of their head post on a
question of cash payments. Our industrial and coöperative
efforts had brought us much hostility from the old order of
traders. I was alone, with only a small fishermen crew, and I
suppose I looked discouraged and disheartened as I walked
back down the Company's wharf to my boat. I felt I should
be misunderstood and probably misrepresented in England,
and that I had lost friends when I most needed them. That
night a young clerk came alongside our boat. He gave me an
envelope, saying, 'I wanted you to know you had one friend
here, anyhow.' There was ten dollars in the envelope. Ten-
dollar bills were very scarce in those days in Labrador, but
something invisible besides the bill made it worth many tens
to me. I do not wonder that that boy, as he was then, has
made his mark in the world, and is a trusted and honoured
man today. Would anyone suggest that the ten dollars was
the only important factor that has prevented that incident
from slipping from my memory all these years later? Something like that was said of a woman that once merely wiped a
Carpenter's feet with her hair, and bathed them with her tears.

Whaling made great strides for a few years when a Norwegian company brought to Gready Islands, Labrador, huge
portable buildings and a big 'mother' steamer. These men
were of no little assistance, for they were genuinely interested
in our work, and helped liberally with coal, whale meat,
hospitality, and especially by locating a number of uncharted
rocks which even we of the inner circle of the wrecked had
never discovered. They were bitterly attacked, however, and
subjected to much hostility by moribund vested interests, and
their activities so restricted that they were forced to abandon
the enterprise. Now as we pass Gready, we sadly lament the
lost circulation of money and labour, for, as usual, nothing
else whatever was substituted by the destructive critics. The
irony of the dénouement, however, lies in the fact that the
prices of whale oil, bone, fertilizer, and other products have
all fallen steadily to so low a figure that the only other and
much older local factory on the Coast has also been forced to
close down, and that after suffering serious losses during these
past lean years. At least the Norwegian company was saved
such an aftermath.

In the fall of 1930, fishermen were settling up for their voyage and for winter at Battle Harbour. The office of the old company, Baine, Johnston and Company, was in their large storehouse. As usual at noon, the doors were locked while all hands adjourned for lunch. An hour later, the whole place was in a blaze. A strong wind was blowing. Everyone worked to save the village, but so fierce was the conflagration that even the Marconi pole on the top of the hill was burned. Our first hospital and its auxiliary buildings all went. After thirty-eight years, we felt the loss bitterly, for the triumphs and defeats of all our early work seemed to cluster around that, our original building. A cigarette end thrown onto a floor on which lay a good deal of excelsior, fresh from the unpacking of the winter supplies, caused the fire. The real things of life cannot be burned, however, and already a new school, small hospital, and out-buildings are functioning under Dr. Moret and his wife at St. Mary's River, the basin that forms the mouth of a beautiful salmon stream. It is a much better situation. It is free to go its own way, for it owns its own lands, has its own water-supply laid on the house, is only seven miles away from Battle Harbour, and is on the mainland and consequently much more accessible in winter.

Meanwhile, Cartwright has begun to be developed as the coming capital of the Labrador. Already the boarding-school is going full swing, and a letter this week by airplane from the lady in charge gives an encouraging account of progress, especially of the way the people of the bay and district are benefiting and rallying around it.

That very letter was left by mail plane at St. Anthony. The pilot very kindly took up our dental officer there for a few minutes in the air, while the mail was being sorted. Fog shut in suddenly, and the plane and its occupants were never seen again. A plane kindly lent by a director, with a volunteer crew, at once flew North and searched the Coast, and so did one sent by the Government — alas, without any success.

From the lady head of our Cartwright station, the letter brought me this — 'My time of service is up, but I literally cannot tear myself away. Will you accept me for another term of three years?'

At North-West River, Dr. Paddon has been given the use of

the power yacht Maraval, a donation by a lady in New York, and with it he is able really to get around his district with Indian Harbour Hospital as his outside base in summer.

Harrington Hospital Station and Mutton Bay Nursing Station on the Canadian Labrador have made much progress. Dr. Hodd is now Justice of the Peace, Agent for the Indians, has a new boat of his own, and has been accorded a new stone wharf by the Canadian Government. A fine X-ray apparatus and electric light have been added to his equipment and the efficiency and range of his work have been materially increased.

Forteau also has leaped ahead under the able service of the nurse in charge and a Scotch volunteer with a burr, and all that it signifies. In spite of the terrible experiences of unsold voyages of fish, a new courage has possessed this village. Judging by the quantities of potatoes produced, even from clearings-away among the tangled tuckamore, stunted trees and roots that run for miles, one would expect at least one worker there to be a Bridget rather than a Lebe; but both are Scotch workers. If only one of the village oracles could write as they talk, we could publish a book that would make even 'Alice in Wonderland' tremble for its laurels. No big buildings, no great outlay of money, just real religion expressed in the humblest and most ordinary activities, and lo! joy and peace reign, that money cannot buy. If the dreams of these two modern apostles, sent out as were those of old to preach the Gospel and heal the sick, come true, we all may yet want to end our days in Forteau.

Flowers Cove has also expanded. A stable, a pony, a new industrial house, an experimental garden, all suggest progress. Perhaps the best advance there is the election of twelve selectmen to prevent graft in the use of public money, as well as more wisely to use the allocations secured from the Government. Nowhere else in the whole of Newfoundland has that experiment been attempted, and it has received the Government's warm sanction.

The new dispensary and service rooms at Batteau mean more efficient work, while the little houses for summer workers at George's Cove and Boulter's Rock and Seal Islands are indeed small, but so are mosquitoes and streptococci. Love is

NORTH-WEST RIVER HOSPITAL

BATTLE HARBOUR

invisible as well as blind, and those little centres are unanswerable sermons.

Of greenhouses, agriculture, industrial additions, education, volunteers, and orphanages I have already written, and yet there are many more 'sermons in stones' and 'gospels in running brooks' to record.

The sermons of this Mission, preached in trying by a thousand ways to put a picture of the work and its needs before the public, are perhaps less conventional than others, but not one whit less factors in achieving the end desired, carrying the convincing message of real love to our neighbours and to God because delivered in New York or London and not in the romantic setting of the Labrador. These are the work of 'the man behind,' and of the woman behind him.

Making and selling things for charities is recognized as religious. Why not enable those who cannot crochet or knit or sew, or even carve or paint, to help in the way they can? Some folk make music and sell it. King David made a joyful noise as his contribution many times. Why not hire the Metropolitan Opera, and throw in Chaliapin and his great company as well? Would he like to help? Why not? Everyone else did. Dramatists have souls and hearts as well as doctors and parsons. Madame Schumann-Heink, Madame Louise Homer, and many another, are amongst those as well known for their helpfulness as Clara Barton or Florence Nightingale. What would one performance cost? Ten thousand dollars!!!! Far too much to risk on one meeting, I thought. Yet it was entirely undertaken by volunteers. They are the real heroes of faith. Eight thousand dollars for Labrador was realized as the result of their united work. I confess again I was amongst the timorous at first, but our 'most venturesome' motto, and my confidence in 'What Every Woman Knows' (the teaching of Barrie's famous play), persuaded me. The opera has been an annual affair ever since. The making of a film like that of the Viking demanded time, risk, financial outlay, all kinds of special business knowledge and methods, and it actually cost two lives. The film has meant more already to others, especially to Labrador, than many lives ever give for the true purpose of life.

The inestimable help rendered by the clothing store to the

Coast has already been referred to. Till we brought in sheep, all wool was imported. Naturally it was very expensive, and only too frequently unprocurable at all by the poor. All our workers love the winter months better than the summer. But *we* do not have to face it without 'woollies.' Warm garments are an essential link in the chain of life in the North, and while 'further down' folk rely entirely on fur and feathers, we cannot do so. Our clothing problem has been one of the most difficult to solve rationally.

Our present system is an infinite advance on that of thirteen years ago. The new clothing store has become a regular department. As the Government allows this charity in free of taxation, none may be, or ever is, sold for cash. It must be given out, for work preferably, freely if necessary. The head of this department is now on the regular staff, and in summer has to have at least two volunteers to help. Orders on the clothing store are given out through regular channels and exchanged on certain days at the store. Half the cost of living, which must of necessity be very cheap on our Coast, is clothing. The ability to carry on this clothing-supply work means development along many lines. All kinds of public needs for which not one cent is available can be in time met in this way. On the other hand, the unemployed are thus protected from doles, and at the same time fitted out for work when it comes along, and through it all their self-respect is preserved.

A fishing voyage to Labrador not only involves wet and calls for changes of clothing, but only in warm clothing can the work be done at all, since it must be done in the atmosphere of the polar current. It may not be a conventional way of loving your neighbour, but even if money were available, which it is not, it may yet be regarded as desirable as payment on a gold standard.

The change in the fisheries since the War, and the falling markets, together with the removal of much of the fishery outfitting from St. John's to Catalina, the headquarters of the Fishermen's Union, diminished greatly the number of outport fishermen frequenting St. John's, with the result that the patronage of the Seamen's Institute fell increasingly into the hands of the oversea men, longshoremen, and seal fishermen, while the women's quarters became almost exclusively for girls from the outports who came to find work in the city. Increasing pressure on the Girl's Department, which has always been self-supporting, induced the directors to give them more of the space, while the rest of the building, still reserving the rights of the fishermen to use its privileges, was taken over by the Y.M.C.A. to afford a home for its splendid activities in the capital. Admirable work has been carried on.

The town rallied around the Institute, and for some time it did not cost the budget of the Association anything, even the repairs and taxes all being carried by the Y.M.C.A. and the Y.W.C.A. Only these last two years, when the total collapse of all our markets not only hit the fishermen, but nearly also swamped the merchants, and even the Government of the Colony found it hard to escape bankruptcy, have we been asked for any financial help.

An active committee at St. John's is carried on still, there never having been any time when just this very uplift which the Institute affords has been so sorely needed. Alas, there is need now to renew the heating system, which in the lapse of years has become uneconomic. Moreover, increase of expenses has allowed a modest debt to accumulate, as so many members have been unable to meet their dues. So our directors have once again decided partially to accept the responsibility for the budget; but if ever there was a *quid pro quo* for money invested in Y.M.C.A. enterprises, it surely is in St. John's at the Institute.

Charles Kingsley was bitterly attacked for saying it was better Christianity to clear out your neighbour's back yard than to pray to God to heal him when he is dying from typhoid. Well, that is what our Y.M.C.A. is teaching. The glory and the challenge of Christ to youth vanish when creeds and conventions supplant a real cross of some kind.

The old adage about the merciful man being merciful to his beast applies in Labrador just as surely as it did in Palestine. So much of the joy and the usefulness of life on the Coast depends on our 'motor power,' that forward steps for men's welfare there should go pace by pace with forward steps for the comfort of these his ever-faithful friends.

The fishermen, being often too poor to feed and house themselves properly, have not treated their dogs as they ought.

These fine animals have been regarded too often as having no feelings. They have suffered from bad housing, bad feeding, and general lack of care and affection — which a dog craves every whit as much as a man does. We have tried to do something to teach kindness to these noble animals. Our dog-races have become the Blue Ribbon of all our games, and everyone longs to have the best team. All the many teams entering the competition are inspected. The owners do not like to be thought to neglect their dogs; but better still it has been found invariably that those who win the races are the teams whose masters never use a whip.

Recently through the insight and kindness of a lover of dogs, a great advance has been made. This member of the Board of the Animal Rescue League has built for us a most marvellous and up-to-date kennel, which not only gives our dogs a comfortable, clean, and 'modern' home, but serves as an example to the whole Shore of the way dogs should be treated. At each tide the sea rises into the bottom of the runways and washes out the kennel. Moreover, on hot summer days the dogs can get into the water if they wish.

'These Eskimo dogs are vicious brutes,' says one writer. 'When driven by hunger they will eat the unwary driver.' Today I have just read in the last number of the magazine of the quite unvicious Royal Geographical Society, 'Today we had to kill one of our faithful dogs for food. We had only three left when we got home.'

The newly arrived Christian Viking on the Labrador tells us that he found nine natives sleeping under boats. He pulled them out, and, finding that they could not speak his language, he killed them. The Christian world has ever since calmly classed the Eskimos as ferocious savages, because when the next comer arrived, a Christian missionary, speaking German, the poor creatures returned the compliment.

If you are anxious to do for your neighbour what you know he would do for you, what blame attaches to you if you do it first? Thus, on one occasion, arriving after a long, hard day at a patient's lonely house, I found him too ill to come out, and discovered that he had made no provision for feeding my dogs, who are never fed till night. After fifty miles hauling a heavy sledge, at twenty below zero, with no breakfast, concessions must be extended even to the Christian stomach. My host begged me if I had any 'vicious' dogs to shut them up in an outhouse, as he owned a sheep. I had a perfect gem of a dog called Kite, purchased near Cape Chidley. He weighed eighty pounds, and later he helped to save my life. He was not more vicious than I was, but I thought it would be well to shut him up — his appetite was so robust. It was sunny in the morning. My host felt better and came out to see me off. He saw me going to the outhouse to release my friend.

'Don't open that door!' he cried. 'My sheep is in there!' I had to go in, however, but I could not find the sheep. Kite lay smiling on a wisp of hay. I had to leave him behind. He could not walk. He weighed over a hundred pounds. He had 'taken that stranger in.' He was not a bit vicious!

It would be immodest for me to claim that possibly the most far-reaching of all our new ventures in usefulness has been my Discretionary Fund. Anyway, here is its *apologia pro vita*:

'Cold as charity this morning!' said the house surgeon one day, snapping his fingers.

'There's the thermometer, exactly ten degrees warmer than yesterday. It is only just zero,' I answered.

'Feels colder, anyhow,' he replied. 'I guess we shall be colder at Christmas.'

'No one here is ever cold now at Christmas, thank God.'

'Then why does everybody say, "cold as charity" and mean it?' he asked.

'Why, when a great country like America has most of the gold in the world, can it be facing a financial crisis?' I retorted. 'How can its assets be frozen? Was not Scrooge and Marley's world frozen until the touch of Tiny Tim thawed it?

'Charity run by mathematics or by logic will always be a dole and little more. What is love, anyhow, without personality? The very daily papers now show that finance, politics, and current science are learning slowly a little about the rigid limitations of mere facts and figures. Here again in life is an unaccounted for "H factor" of the quantum theory. That is why all advanced minds today admit that the materialism of the last century failed. Even those who do not yet admit it, in any and every field of real work are bound to work as if they did, if they want to get anywhere. So it is that the working of this invaluable fund has encouraged all our efforts by the visible results.

'Here is an excellent example right under our noses. We met Dick Field first by chance. The Strathcona had broken down, and I was cruising along ahead alone in the jolly-boat, and sought shelter at night at a little house of which I saw the smoke on the end of the promontory south of Sandy Bay. There were Dick and his wife and six youngsters in the shack, and that was practically all except a trifle of dry flour, the bones of a sea-gull, and at night not one blanket or one bit of bedcovering among the lot. I slept on the floor in my bag, with nose to the crack under the door for air. The family had to give up ventilation to keep warm.

'Instead of giving a dole and passing on, even in so dire a plight I made Dick give me the pelt of a silver fox he had, and traded it for him farther down the Coast. That skin actually afforded that family an entire winter's diet. Beyond a few garments, we gave nothing, except absolute orders to put every pelt he got into a barrel and sit on it if anyone came to buy them. He followed that plan to the end of his life. During those last years, he built a cottage in Adlavik Islands for the summer fishing, became independent, and, when he joined his ancestors, left me three hundred dollars in cash to use for the benefit of his family. But it was the Discretionary Fund which made this possible, a fund, the point of which is, that the sanity of any venture upon which it was spent was left to an individual.'

'Go on,' said the house surgeon. 'Let's have another.'

'You know John Doe? Fine fellow, isn't he? Absolutely honest, and you know the work the whole family, including the girls, put in to meet their account when first they lost their boat in that bad storm, and this year again when their fish is of no value. Mrs. Doe gave me eighty-three as fine grass baskets as ever were made. When you remember that she had to gather the grass herself and to manage for that family, including making the clothing from rags almost like patchwork quilts, and keep the house warm with her husband away on the fur path, and cook so as to eke out the supplies, besides protect the larder, you cannot help taking off your hat to her. The fact is, you cannot help that same unknown "H factor" inside your scientific soul enjoying the personal challenge to help out.

'It was at the Holy Islands I first met them. They were sharing a tilt with George Topler and his four. A more woe-be-gone problem I never faced. I still have the list of "assets" — adults four, children nine. No home, no boat, no money, two ancient muzzle-loading guns, equally dangerous at either end. Wardrobe, nil. One kitchen stove — an ancient wreck left by the last occupant of the shack they were sheltering in. No fishing-stage. No need for trunks — such clothing as they owned was every stitch in service, even in summer. Fox-traps, about half a dozen, remnants. Fish, seized for debt. Gunpowder and shot, nil. Government charity — a small supply of flour, tea, and molasses, but not enough to keep body and soul together, much less to fit for hard work. Prospects, nil, except almost certainly beri-beri in spring — a painful paralysis disease due to food deficiency. These two families had just migrated North in search of better hunting grounds.

'A week later, fortune threw me right into the arms of the very man who had owned the old house, stage, and stove, into which these wanderers had walked. He was a genial Irishman. His family had all departed and left him alone in the world. His small schooner had conveniently sunk at the wharf and had been insured fully. No one quite knew the exact cause of her demise, except as he himself suggested, "It was about time she went, after me paying insurance on her for all them years, Sir, and me giving up the fishery too. Yes, the water's very deep there."

'"You did not use any unlawful means to save her, I hope, Paddy — because, you see, I'm a magistrate?"

'"'Deed I didn't" — and I thought I detected a twinkle in his eye as he said it. "The little darling's gone, though — God bless her," he added with almost a real sigh of regret. What would an Irishman be without the "H factor," and a large one at that?

'Anyhow, he let me buy out all his interests for a paltry thirty dollars, and gave me a quittance with his blessing. That began it. What a pleasure it has been to watch those families pull themselves up!

'Everyone likes rearing rabbits or white rats. These human beings could never have accomplished what they did on charity. They felt some person cared for them as individuals, and it made all the difference in the world.

'Each year as I pass the Islands I think of that old "schedule of assets" and wonder whether any charity need really be cold, even in Labrador.'

In 1930 a winter gale lost them their only fishing boat. This fund once more brought hope to them by an advance for a new boat.

In very few works like ours have I known a Discretionary Fund lodged in the hands of the workers on the spot; though in reality, far greater responsibilities are allotted them. It would seem that our real faith, even in our representatives, does not often go quite so far as trusting them with money to give away. In endless cases, this personal 'vitamin' is as lacking in organized charity as is a life-giving vitamin from the best white loaf. Boards of directors never quite like Discretionary Funds. It certainly increases their worries. Yet that is exactly what God supplies each of us with — infinite responsibility — and we regard that as the best thing in life. The trouble with the dole is that it lacks that very vitamin, and sooner or later it leads to paralysis.

I would close this with one more example of how a Discretionary Fund works. A friend, reading in our magazine the story of Uncle George, left a small sum in her will to be used for his benefit. Until his death, it was most carefully handled. He never wanted for anything wherewith to enable him to live. When he lost his big boat, we advanced him another. When he lacked anything, we saw that he got it. He passed away recently, unspoilt and independent. He left no money for his family, but he had still the same superb confidence that God would stand by them also as He had by himself. We know, of course, that this help will be conveyed through human hands. All such things are. The gift is doubly blest, however, for it is a great encouragement to us to be able, now both these friends are gone, still to carry out exactly what I cannot help feeling the donor somehow watches with pleasure, if, as seems possible, those ahead of us can look back. A special treasurer in Boston receives, nurses, and disburses the actual cash. The man-in-the-field directs the tactics.

CHAPTER XXII

'THE GOOD EARTH'

A CAREFUL review of efforts to make the land yield us its increase revealed how purely predatory our Labrador people still were. They had treated Labrador as if it were a South Sea island, where man is able to live by grabbing breadfruit and yams supplied ready-made by Mother Nature. Labrador was just a drain, like the lake on the hill-top at Harrington, from which the hospital drew its supply and never troubled to see that any more water ran into it. For centuries, since predatory explorers first visited America, native races and Nature's gifts have been increasingly exploited and depleted.

A review of our natural assets showed how many more we possessed than some countries which for centuries have supported populations infinitely larger than ours in reasonable comfort. Even in the sunny Riviera, if it were not for the terraced cliff-sides made with endless labour, where would be Italy's grapes, and olives, and fruits? Where would Holland be without its man-built, closely guarded dykes, and its never-ceasing pumps? Even there man must now reclaim the sunken Zuyder Zee to supply from its bottom the needs of their people. Why do the Chinese still die by millions in famines? Because they have used their trees for fuel and never reforested, and because of the terrible floods of their uncontrolled rivers. The control by man of great rivers like the Ohio has ended the same woes in America, and the British Raj alone has averted the old periodic famines in India.

Convention regards hospitals as religious propaganda; but so are cemeteries and crematories! Surely provision for food should be considered as more essential than either. Our Labrador work entered on a new era when, with expert help and some hard work, we began to speed production by starting farming in the North. Moreover, fifty years ago, who would have conceived that the part of Labrador which we were willing to forget as being 'north of Scotland' could be an invaluable way-station on the route of travel from Europe to America; yet all thoughtful people are today regarding the

Greenland-Labrador airway as the coming route for rapid and safe transport. Alas, for the pettiness of our little minds!

In Labrador in the past we had always worked on the axiom that 'back to the land' simply meant 'face to the sea.' Looking over this book to see what was our former attitude toward farming to my dismay I found the matter disposed of in the laconic heading of the professional who made the index. The very first entry read, 'agriculture in Labrador unsuccessful.'

Now we know that it was we who were unsuccessful, just as were the Cabots and the Cartiers and the Cortereals who stood looking at the country and declared it was 'all of no use,' which should read 'nothing ready for us to grab.' For years we had been satisfied to say, 'The season for growing is too short.' It took desperation to engender enough faith to reply, 'Very well, then, we will make it longer.' If the ground is frozen until July, seeds placed in it then naturally will not germinate until too late for the vegetables to mature. Friends in Greenwich, Connecticut, presented us with a greenhouse. By July of the year following we had plantlets fully three months old, ready to go into the ground. That autumn, when the fishermen saw cabbages weighing even up to eighteen pounds in our gardens, they wanted them, and the next year we sold fifteen thousand plantlets to local families along one section of the Coast. Now we sell every little plant which we can spare of those we raise in our available space. We have added a second and a third larger greenhouse given us by the Garden Clubs of America. Today all around that North Shore our fame is bruited, or, as the people say, 'fruited,' in increasing thousands of young plants.

Other discouragements have been fought one by one. The cabbage and turnip seed which were purchased at considerable cost, though tended with truly motherly care, frequently failed. The young plants often withered in the garden plots soon after the first leaves broke the ground. Endless white lice destroyed the Petrowski turnips, which had come all the way from Alaska; and every variety of plant, even the homely potatoes, were found to have enemies 'lying in wait to devour them.'

Our chief problem was to know how to destroy the pests.

This time we found our salvation at the Massachusetts State College of Agriculture at Amherst, when one of their professors has come at his own expense and taught us the effective remedies, and year by year inspects our agricultural efforts and suggests progressive steps. In order to make the carrying-out of such expert help permanent, we have had three of our Northern boys educated in agricultural colleges.

Another greenhouse has been erected at North-West River, where 'our professor' assures us that far the widest range of possibilities awaits our experiments. In just this locality, three quarters of a century ago, our good friend the late Lord Strathcona grew all the vegetables needed for his station. The result was that he never had much sympathy for Labrador sufferers from diseases due to vegetable deficiency.

The unanimity of opinion of my medical colleagues on this branch of our work, and at St. Anthony the real genius of James Tucker, the student whom we sent to Truro, leave one deeply regretful that we did not years ago divert even some of our hospital resources for the development of the agricultural department. Its progress today is showing us clearly that such efforts of previous settlers were like much faith in God, destroyed by the burden of endless little discouragements rather than by being blown up or frozen. One year, when there was practically no income from the fisheries, and when the families must have starved or lived on doles — when they could be obtained — our chief pæan of joy was that the gardens under cultivation had increased thirty per cent. As a result, many of our people, instead of standing idle all day long like the breadlines of other countries, are employed in clearing and preparing ground for the coming years. Reliable seed must be put within their reach. Loans of farming tools are still necessary, as are means to destroy pests. Glass for frames is urgently required in each settlement.

The value of trees to hold snow and to afford shelter from wind, moreover, is being learned through agricultural efforts, whereas harbour laws, jail sentences, and even sermons, all of which we tried, failed to inculcate it. As a result, the uplifting value of beauty around the homes and villages may yet be restored. Unintelligent vandalism has done us incalculable harm.

We had made repeated efforts to develop the use of our local peat. We cut it and dried it and burned it in our own home. We bought up every booklet on the subject which we could find. We even preached about it. Everybody said it was splendid, but nobody burned it. We are told in Holy Writ that no man can give another spiritual faith; but we failed to secure adherents even to material peat. One and all, including our Irish neighbours, scouted it. One step forward in this effort began when we were driving through Bavaria, and noticed a long line of what appeared to be soldiers marching in single file across the horizon. When we came up to them, they proved to be strong, thin poles, each of which had been speared through a dozen briquettes of peat and then stuck into the ground, thus enabling it to dry quickly in the wind and sun, and to some extent to shed the rain. A second step was taken when a number of men, who were paying fees in labour, together with a gang of wops, some of whom were waiting to proceed to one of our other stations, put a fine road right through to a big peat bog at St. Anthony. We made a third step when we discovered that peat, mixed with the heads and bones and offal of codfish, with kelp and seaweed, made an invaluable compost for gardens; and that land from which peat was removed became pasture land.

Today we are thrilled with the news of a yet greater future. Among the poor but home-loving Scotsmen who go out apparently to supply a steady demand for presidents of banks and other business corporations in the United States and Canada, one has given expression to that love by erecting at his old home a fine agricultural institute. As peat is the largest unused potential immediately accessible in the neighbourhood, much experimentation has been done with it. The irony of the new discoveries is the suggestion that now peat bogs can be made so remunerative, owing to their agricultural capacities and at such reasonable expense, that the Highlanders will no longer have to leave their glens, and there may be a depression in the export of Scotch presidents of banks!

Every cent which we can spare is now being devoted to extend the agricultural department at each of our centres. For though our own schooner, the George B. Cluett, brought potatoes and vegetables from Prince Edward Island this autumn at half the price of most years, what use is that if the fishermen cannot sell their fish, if their fur no longer pays to catch it, and if their pulpwood is too cheap to pay to cut it?

This year we offered some small advances in the spring to purchase seed and tools, and some to fishermen who would otherwise have been unable to get sea-boots or even hooks and lines, much less canvas for sails and fuel or paint for motor boats. The tiny agricultural loans were all repaid, but, as the fishermen could pay nothing in cash, they worked out the loans on the new gardens of the nearest nursing station, under the direction of the nurse. One man, who had had no chance to fit out for the fishery, was spending all summer on his gardens. In the autumn, this man had sixty barrels of potatoes and more than a sufficiency of turnips and cabbages. Such practical advice and simple remedies for the cutworm and cabbage caterpillar as Professor Sears was able to give not only turned the scale in many gardens and provided food where otherwise none would have been this winter, but he was thus able to arouse from discouragement those who had abandoned hope. What better holiday could any professor of agriculture hope for? It is not time yet to judge what potential we have, but we have grown fine alfalfa (Grims), made a good start with white artichokes which are perennial, and have even ripened pumpkins at St. Anthony.

Animal husbandry has made steady progress, chiefly because the dog problem has been solved, *vi et armis*. Dogs must now be shut up in summer, and, if found loose, may be destroyed. This is certainly hard on our dogs, but there is no alternative. We have had to help some poorer neighbours out with wire and even nails for proper dog-pens, for the dogs are otherwise kept in far too small kennels. To try and set an example of what we owe to dogs, and to encourage kindness to all animals, a friend from Maine offered us his help in the form of beautiful new headquarters kennels at St. Anthony. These give shelter to the dogs always in winter at night if they desire it, and in summer allows the sea to rise and fall in half their runways so that the dogs can keep themselves just as clean as ever they like. Example does what no precept will, and we could devise no surer method of improving the accommodations for and care of dogs along the Coast. We have tried to cross our Huskies several times with milder-tempered dogs, such as wolf hounds, Chesapeakes, and old English sheep-dogs, so as to lessen the danger to cattle, but so far we have never had good results. In Greenland, the dogs are smaller than ours. They are also subject to a tapeworm disease, dangerous to man, from which ours are free. We therefore destroyed some kindly brought to us by Dr. Cook.

Cows have increased considerably, and our thoroughbreds have spread their strain all around our North Coast. At Flowers Cove this year Parson Richards, to save the valuable and much-needed cream, on the day his calf was born removed it from the cow, separated all the cream from the milk, substituted two tablespoons of cod-liver oil at each feeding, and in the autumn had far the finest calf in the village.

Our Duroc Jersey pigs have been eminently successful, both in clearing land and producing pork. The black-faced sheep imported from Scotland have shown their ability to eat almost any of the ordinary wild plants which cover our terrain before it is cultivated. They were sent us because they are one of the very few sheep which can be fattened on heather.

We are now raising large rabbits, while the Hudson's Bay Company is breeding both foxes and mink in Sandwich Bay. Young foxes cannot thrive on an entirely fish diet, and we are hoping the young rabbits may step into the breach. In old days, it was found necessary to pass a law that servants and apprentices might not be fed salmon more than four times a week.

We have also made an attempt to introduce bees. Several lots came by mail, hatching out just after arrival. Our people never having seen any except wild bumble-bees, which are very rare, were much disturbed at first as to 'who was going to bring the food to the bees every day.' At first, the bees did well, and stored a good many pounds of honey. Unfortunately, however, no one understood them, and we failed to notice they were eating their store before winter came, only finding that out when the bees perished. They were seen collecting honey over the hill-tops in a harbour as far as three miles away (evidently being short of the flowers they needed). We are delighted that a bee expert has offered to come down for his summer holidays and give such protagonists of labour

LABRADOR SHEEP

CABBAGES — A TRIUMPH

another chance. It seems plain, however, that, with honey at less than six cents a pound by the barrel, it will not pay to feed bees through our winter, and that their devotion can only be rewarded by death in the autumn; and new bees brought by post each spring. *Sic transit gloria mundi.*

Another very promising experiment was also tried out recently with great success. An expert on food preservation came North for the summer, dividing her time between St. Anthony and Cartwright. The fishermen's wives were invited to bring salmon, fresh from their husbands' nets, to classes held in our schoolrooms, and were then taught the whole process of canning fish and local berries. Our steam cooker allowed only six students to 'cook their cans' at once. At first, conservatism held the women back, but very soon there was the keenest competition when it was discovered that including the container a pound can of fat fresh salmon could be preserved for winter at three cents per tin and the can could be used three times over. The season ended with many good pounds of salmon and fine berries stored away in many homes, where the high fat and proteid content will be exceedingly valuable this winter. Another outcome was that one of our own local girls was sent to Massachusetts State College, in order to learn the valuable art of food preservation. We hope this will result in the beginning of a really large movement. For this year all we could get for these magnificent salmon was two cents per pound when they were fit for instantaneous freezing, and much less than that on an average when the fishermen have to cure, salt, and barrel them.

One of our most beloved girl volunteers was responsible for yet another effort in animal husbandry. Miss Marion Moseley, of Chicago, undertook to start regular child welfare work. To accomplish that, fresh milk was essential. Her slogans were, 'Goats in every village!' — 'Goats, the only machine to turn Labrador rocks into milk!' — 'Goats, the greatest mothers in the world!' The spring following, news reached us from Chicago of the gift of eight goats, the most highly bred milk-producers in the goat world, worth something like five hundred dollars apiece. Simultaneously came the news that the goats would be freighted down to us by rail and ship. We had had little experience with goats, but a good deal with local freights, and we at once entered our protest. Thrilled with gratitude for these noble gifts, we dreaded the criticism which would surely follow if any 'fell by the wayside.' We broadcast an SOS to say that, if strangers had made such sacrifices for Labrador's sake, would not some one risk perhaps even more in the same spirit, and personally conduct these baby missionaries to their fields of operation? The answer is still recorded in pictorial form in my *sanctum sanctorum.* It is a large rotogravure from the *New York Times* Sunday illustrated edition. Underneath is the legend, 'The Labrador Goat Brigade Leaves for the North.' It portrays eight beautiful girls, each accompanied by a beautiful goat, and all seated on the deck of a steamer. Incidentally, it was a timely compliment to the 'spirit of Illinois,' for just then the records of gangster operations in their largest city were earning it a very different reputation. These Toggenburgs and Anglo-Nubians thrived well, but gave us much trouble with local gardens which are never too well fenced in. One local sage 'reckoned them goats was too high bred anyhow.' So at our own stations cows have replaced goats, but 'in spots' goats are still apostles of Miss Moseley's unassailable gospel of milk, and are preaching love to their neighbours perhaps as eloquently as would homilies or erudite sermons. We are convinced that if one hundredth part of the money expended in relief to able-bodied men were expended, not only in the North, but everywhere, in animal and vege-table adaptation and development, every country in the world would be better off.

Amongst the many much-neglected assets of Labrador has been its regular immense crop of various kinds of wild berries. The Hudson's Bay Company has exported large quantities of blueberries to America. Experiments have shown that through cultivation these blueberries can be enlarged to the size of small grapes. There are five varieties of blueberries in New-foundland. One especially, the 'Pennsylvanicus,' is very sweet and grows on a large stem, so that the berries are easily picked. As blueberries thrive only on acid soils and stand almost any amount of cold, our country is ideal for their culture. Probably the same is true of our endless cranberries, yellow bake-apples, and red currants. Farther to the southward in Newfoundland, wild raspberries are extraordinarily numerous. Everywhere in the woods the tiny but deliciously flavoured little white capillair berries abound. Experience has left no doubt whatever in our minds that experiment, work, and venture can make our grossly misrepresented land products as valuable as our rich sea harvests will one day again become.

Meanwhile, higher and higher barriers are raised in the name of nationalism against even the importation of those very things for lack of which hunger and poverty are being suffered. Duties against these very berries, just as against the highly valuable fish, prevent them from reaching their natural markets even in their own continent. Barriers between man and man can never benefit the world or any section of it. Meanwhile, those responsible do not realize that they are their own victims. Instead, they consider such policies patriotism. Bolshevism, because 'international' and modified, does not become Christian. It is still born of fear and folly.

As for the harvest of the air, that too needs only the same rational treatment. Our ducks, geese, and wild birds, and even their eggs properly taken care of, can be made to go a very long way toward affording an ample living to many thousands of people.

On a lecture tour a few months ago, as we drove through the black country in England, through the environs of Glasgow, and later through South Wales, one of the saddest sights on earth greeted us — English, Scotch, and Welshmen with nothing to do! There was no drunkenness, no rioting, even good-humour and courtesy, all of which made only more terrible the hopeless idleness. Today's papers, the first day of a new year, report that twelve million are out of work in America, and one hundred and fifty thousand children are being fed on charity in Philadelphia. Yet America has three quarters of the gold on earth, and the Western States are not irrigating new lands. The fault seems to lie in the faulty and restricted distribution of the food which the world needs rather than in overproduction. Bananas are being burned by the hundreds of tons. Endless sacks of coffee are being dumped. Even wheat is being burned. Cotton, copper, rubber, beef, fish, and numberless other necessities are entirely lacking in one place and in useless abundance in others. The final word of wisdom cannot be to raise more tariff walls which will only still further impede circulation. When we left Labrador last autumn, fish was lying unsold in countless tons and the people were without flour. A week later in New York, tens of thousands of men were in bread-lines and needed fish, while wheat was rotting in the near-by granaries and legislatures were increasing 'Protection' as a cure-all for the trouble.

CHAPTER XXIII

ÆSCULAPIUS

IF A clam stirs in the mud, it is probable that some other clam is affected, objects, and criticizes. Criticism is a sign of activity. It is the presumptive evidence of life. The very words 'Medical Missionary' today irritate some people as connoting to them a claim to motives superior to those of the practitioner who must live by his fees.

In Labrador it has become the custom for all our medical officers to meet once a year to discuss progress. On one occasion, amongst other criticisms of the year which we discussed was a report of the first annual meeting of Newfoundland doctors held in St. John's, which none of us had been able to attend. The Chairman had stated there were no hospitals outside the capital. This we considered scarcely fair. Our records showed many patients who had paid their fare North from St. John's itself, in order to come to St. Anthony for treatment. Moreover, we knew that our hospitals at Battle Harbour, Indian Harbour, and North-West River at least deserved recognition. We therefore decided to ask the College of Surgeons of America to send a representative from their committee for standardizing hospitals, to inspect St. Anthony and Twillingate, hardly daring to hope that they would do so. We made Twillingate Hospital possible by raising most of the money; but far more important, we had the whole staff appointed from our own workers.

Although history shows that the mere multiplication of medical and surgical machinery has not necessarily marked the most efficient eras for the protection of public health, nevertheless modern medical science, so far as art can aid nature to heal, has every right to assume that the great centres of civilization have an advantage over the outposts, and that the certificate of the value of a body which represents a nation's leaders in a particular science is of real importance.

It was a great encouragement when both St. Anthony and Twillingate hospitals received their grades as A 1 institutions for healing, if only because it meant that we were giving our neighbours the kind of treatment which would spell a message of real love if given to us. There was also enough of the old Adam left in us to make us smile when we learned that we were the only hospitals in the Colony that had been granted the coveted honour.

One central hospital would have been the least expensive way to carry on our work on the Coast, but utterly inefficient under our present conditions of transportation. We had now decided that the five hospitals, located on an average of one hundred and fifty miles apart, were as close together as we could provide medical and surgical help at a cost within our means, even though there were still no roads in our end of the country and aeroplanes were not yet considered practical. However, we could provide for maternity cases and emergencies by placing nursing units between each two hospitals. Forteau Station had proved an undeniable success. It had saved many lives, and many anxious times for us doctors. Once at Flowers Cove, when I was passing through on snow-shoes late in May, when the rivers were open and dog-teams no longer available, a young man was brought to me with his leg shot to pieces by his gun which had gone off in the boat. I had controlled the bleeding with needle and thread from his mother's sewing-box and amputated the limb with my pocket knife, as I had with me only what I stood up in. After three days, it seemed that the lad had a fair chance for recovery. As it was imperative for me to proceed on my journey at once, a picked crew ventured through the running ice, which was still blocking the Straits of Belle Isle, and carried my patient comfortably across in a fishing boat to the door of the nursing station at Forteau, where unquestionably his life was saved by our nurse.

The case of a man who had shot his arm off in midwinter, that of a six-year-old boy who had drunk boiling water from a kettle on the stove, several maternity cases, all of whom owe their lives to Forteau, cannot be forgotten; but far beyond that is the routine but splendid constant prophylactic service which a nursing station affords. So when the chance came, a nursing centre was built at Flowers Cove, on the Newfoundland side of the Straits, to take care of the western north

A LABRADOR NURSE AND HER CHARGES

FLOWERS COVE NURSING STATION

coast. This station, with its nurse and industrial worker, has now a very large range of work. Labour in return for help given in emergencies has enabled the nurse there to begin an experimental garden and pasture, while we shall soon see these devoted workers with at least one pony. A ten-mile walk for that nurse to a case is by no means rare, and many rounds have to be done in stages. One day this autumn we called at this station. The ladies did not return until late at night, each having covered on foot some twenty miles already that day.

Later, another nursing unit was built at Mutton Bay, in order to divide the distance between Harrington and Forteau, which is impassable in winter. As years went by, a small winter centre for the Battle Hospital staff was built at Hatter's Cove, in St. Louis Bay; and a nurse was placed at Conche, between Twillingate and St. Anthony. Her services were made possible to the fishermen by the generosity of one of our volunteer workers who had herself seen conditions in winter, and by the poor people themselves who guaranteed her board, lodging, and transportation. A permanent nurse is now stationed at Cartwright and one at Batteau each summer. In summer also, nursing aides are placed in other small centres.

This is no place for a panegyric on nurses. I wish I had the pen of a Tennyson to portray efficiently all we owe them. Even then one could not do them justice. The best testimonial I have to offer has been my recurrent appeals to them to come and help. It requires poetry, it seems to me, adequately to describe that spiritual element in healing and in bringing comfort which these highly trained nurses, with a vision of the Christ, carry with them. God knows men have carried sacrificial love almost to the limit, but how crude their hands have seemed in comparison, how rough and inadequate their best efforts, how material and hard the presentation! There have often been occasions when, watching our nurses at work on this resentful Coast, we felt that the very devils themselves must cry out as they did in His days on earth when they saw the Master at work. We try never to leave them alone at their posts, and the admirable combination of a trained industrial teacher and social worker living with them has seemed to us the duplication in these prosaic days of the sending out of the Apostles two by two, to be also achieving similar ends.

Go and stay in one of these nursing stations at Christmas time if you have any doubts on this matter. You may not find central heating or running water or modern plumbing, and few indeed of the physical frills of life which our civilization has made necessities for us. But you will find a quality which the materialism of today may still call negligible, but which goes on 'turning water into wine, and the wooden cup to gold.'

Ironically enough, the very destructibility of the material which we have had to use for building during these years has been a great source of trouble. The Emily Beaver Chamberlain Hospital at North-West River was destroyed by fire. The Gordon School and Orphanage at Muddy Bay were burned, and the parsonage at Cartwright. Later, our first hospital and buildings at Battle Harbour, which for over thirty-eight years had served the Coast so well, followed suit. Through the generosity of friends, each of these has been replaced. At North-West River, a far more efficient hospital now carries on the work, the Gordon School and Children's Home has been replaced by the larger Lockwood Boarding-School, the centre of the new settlement growing up at Cartwright; while Battle Harbour settlement has been moved up St. Louis Bay to the mouth of St. Mary's River, where also a boarding-school, nursing station, and summer hospital now are at work. We decided to abandon Hatter's Cove nursing station, as all the people had moved away.

The work at Harrington has increased also. A new boat has been built there for the use of that station, and electric light and an X-ray plant installed. The Government has given a new stone pier and a water-supply. The doctor in charge has been made a Justice of the Peace and Government Agent for the Indians.

The new station at Cartwright is already functioning. The doctor in charge divides his time between Cartwright, the new 'Battle Harbour at St. Mary's River,' and the coast villages between. At Spotted Islands and Batteau he has small summer dispensaries run by volunteers; and industrial centres at Boulter's Rock, Seal Islands, and George's Cove. The station also boasts a new boat.

To our farthest-flung northern centre a new and very efficient motor ship has been added — the Maraval, the gift of a friend in New York. The Maraval is a beautiful and powerful motor-driven vessel, with considerable carrying capacity. She is excellent in a seaway. She has helped greatly to solve the problems of that district, now that the fall in fish values has so crippled the large fleet of fishing schooners, for whose benefit the hospital at Indian Harbour was originally built. Like the Strathcona, she is ever filled with anything from school children to agricultural supplies, if not too busy with patients. She broke down, however, this summer, was towed fifty miles to cross our pathway by the mail steamer, when we in the Strathcona had the fun of pulling her by the nose for many miles to our own new drydock at St. Anthony. Dr. Harry Paddon and his wife are the motive powers behind this station at North-West River. I am often told that this station and its work are the most beautiful and appealing of all. The whole *entourage* is utterly unlike the outside coast.

To extend the chain of hospitals farther northward, the Hudson's Bay Company, at their own expense, has erected a beautiful little nursing station at Nain, thus endorsing our views that, in the conditions of life existing on the Labrador, no other satisfactory policy is possible.

One of the most important achievements has been Twillingate Hospital. For years the only general hospital in Newfoundland for the benefit of the whole country and its widely scattered poor people was the Government hospital at St. John's, in the extreme South of the Island. Transportation alone formed an insuperable barrier to its efficiency. Lives were unnecessarily lost and endless suffering caused even in reaching our St. Anthony Hospital from the great Notre Dame Bay, only a hundred miles to the southward of us. In winter, sufferers in that district could not reach St. Anthony to the North or St. John's to the South. We had learned only too painfully that no doctor could give the service he knew was required unless he had some centre to which to bring his patients. Moreover, skilled nurses and more or less expensive equipment were imperative.

Year after year, I had visited Twillingate, the main centre of the fishery in that district, in the hope of somehow helping them to obtain a modern medical centre in their time of need. The local doctor, the leading merchants, and especially the fishermen, were all eager about it. For years no progress was possible. The central Government would not listen to the plea for a hospital grant. No wonder we felt aggrieved that, while one hundred and fifty thousand dollars was spent on one road 'de luxe' at the capital, Notre Dame Bay could get no allocation for even a cottage hospital.

Again I had secured volunteer help for that district. Dr. Hugh Greeley, now Professor of Medicine at the University of Wisconsin, and Dr. Harrison Webster, marshal of his class at Harvard, and subsequently killed in the Great War, came North. Largely with their own hands they adapted the old staff house of a disused copper mine at Pilley's Island and started a hospital there. A Government grant of two thousand dollars a year, even with what patients could afford, left so large an annual deficit that it was essential to have volunteer nurses. For years this little hospital filled a great need, but it was utterly inadequate really to meet the demands of so large and so scattered a clientèle.

One day, as the fortnightly mail steamer was landing its quota of patients at St. Anthony, my attention was especially called to one of the number. He was an elderly, white-haired seaman, with a strikingly beautiful and resigned face, but evidently suffering great agony. He told us he had waited patiently and long for the first steamer to push North through the ice in spring, and he had evidently been tenderly cared for. The voyage, however, had been greatly protracted by ice-fields packed against the cliffs by the onshore wind, and there had been no skilled help available on board. I went ahead to the hospital to make sure there should not be a moment's delay, but before the hand-borne stretcher reached the door the grim struggle had been lost — and won. I decided then and there that Notre Dame Bay should have a hospital if it could be done.

Shortly afterwards, I received in New York a gift of twenty-five thousand dollars towards 'hospital work on our Coast.' It was decided at once to allocate it for Twillingate. Our directors decided that they could not assume the upkeep of another large hospital. With this sum behind them, however, the local committee were able to secure a promise from the Government of ten thousand dollars per year for maintenance. At that time, Dr. Charles Parsons, who off and on for several years had been on our staff, and who was a Gold Medallist in surgery and senior graduate of the famous Johns Hopkins Hospital, volunteered to assume full responsibility for this new venture. From that day to this, he has made steady progress. The pressure from increasing numbers of patients became so great that a further grant of fifty thousand dollars was made by our good friend in New York. This enabled a new large wing to be opened. Though it has been necessary to treble the original annual grant of the Government, Dr. Parsons's outstanding abilities as a man of common sense and business acumen have enabled small committees in every neighbouring hamlet and cove from which patients come to supplement from their small means enough to keep that hospital out of debt.

I saw the face of my patient who died on our wharf for only a minute, but I am certain he is content now, even with the price he had to pay for being a link in this chain.

The training of many local nurses in the Twillingate district has been an infinite boon to many lives, while the indirect value of the hospital to the financial conditions of the people of the Bay is beyond conception. Thanks to the leadership of Dr. Parsons, this work has been carried on without cost or responsibility to the International Grenfell Association.

There is always a risk in human affairs that the real objective of an enterprise will get lost in the details; as when a most devoted clergyman refused to proceed with a wedding service until two tiny bridesmaids had been removed from the church because they had no hats on.

It might, therefore, be well, at the risk of redundancy, to say that, while as a doctor we know that men are born neither free nor equal, the aim of this effort is to interpret the Christian Gospel by helping in His name less privileged neighbours to become both, in the truest sense.

While I frankly accept that by no other way than by loving your neighbour as yourself can this be done, and freely admit that that is the most difficult thing on earth to do wisely, a doctor of medicine expresses his love for his neighbour by crossing the road to attend to his physical wounds rather than by hurrying to Jerusalem to say prayers for his benefit.

In this chapter one has tried to touch on some of the signs of continuing life in that department of the services by which we think we are still seeing new men being made out of old, as we undoubtedly are seeing children with better physical bodies growing up around us. The blind are made to see, the physically lame to walk, the materially naked clothed, and the materially hungry fed, and that, either entirely freely or else, better still, at a cost within a reasonable reach of the 'wounded neighbour.'

We have always tried to secure eminent specialists in particular branches of medicine. Doubtless it was completely illogical to suppose that these hard-worked men, who could earn large fees by staying home, should come to Labrador for any 'silly' emotional reasons, and pay all their own expenses just to help a few fishermen.

We asked them, however, and they came — from California, from Boston, from Philadelphia, from Cincinnati, from England, and from Canada. Eye specialists, lung specialists, orthopædic specialists, nose and throat specialists, dental surgeons — an array of knights whose lives and weapons are consecrated to a modern vision of the Grail. They have inaugurated a new era of hope for the sick and the needy of Labrador.

A gentleman at whose house I was a guest told me that when still a youth he had fought in the Civil War, been invalided home, and advised to take a sea voyage for his health. He therefore took passage with a Gloucester fisherman and set sail for the Labrador. The crew proved to be Southern sympathizers, and one day, while my friend was ashore taking a walk, the skipper slipped out and left him marooned. He had with him neither money, spare clothing, nor anything else; and as British sympathies were also with the South, he had many doubts as to how the settlers would receive a penniless stranger and Northerner. Seeing his schooner bound in an easterly direction, he started literally to run along the shore, hoping that he might find where she went and catch

her again. Mile after mile he went, tearing through the tuckamore, or dense undergrowth of gnarled trees, climbing over
high cliffs, swimming or wading the innumerable rivers,
skirting bays, and now and again finding a short beach along
which he could hurry. At night, wet, dirty, tired, hungry,
penniless, he came to a fisherman's cottage and asked shelter
and food. He explained that he was an American gentleman
taking a holiday, but had not a penny of money. It spoke
well for the people that they accepted his story. He told me
that they both fed and clothed him, and one kind-hearted
man actually the next day gave him some oilskin clothing and
a sou'wester hat — costly articles 'on Labrador' in those
days. At last arriving at Red Bay, he found his schooner
calmly at anchor. He went aboard at once as if nothing had
happened, and stayed there (having enjoyed enough pedes-
trian exercise for the time being) and no one ever referred
to his having been left behind. He was now, however, forty
years later, anxious to do something for the people of that
section of the Shore, and he gave me a thousand dollars
toward building a small cottage for a district nurse. Forteau
was the village chosen, and Dennison Cottage was erected
as a nursing station and dispensary. It forms an admirable
halfway house between Battle and Harrington hospitals,
each being about a hundred miles distant. A local trader
once wrote me: 'Sister Bailey is doing fine work. The nursing
station is a blessing to the people of this part of the Shore.'
Who would think that, by a little act of kindness done forty-
odd years ago to an old soldier, we should now be reaping the
benefit? Do the ripples of unselfish deeds really last forever?
It is little deeds of kindness which will bring peace and righteousness to earth. Then life is a field of honour, after all,
and what we give to it is the measure of what we get out of it.

CHAPTER XXIV

WORK AS MEDICINE

THE difficulties encountered in work along the North New-foundland and Labrador Coast are due for the most part to ignorance and poverty and not to lack of character in the local fishermen. There are drawbacks like the polar current, and what some would regard as a plethora of ice and snow for a somewhat undue portion of the year. There are the difficulties of a population scattered in little villages strung along a stormy coast-line, with infrequent communication by mail steamer in summer, and with the isolation intensified in winter by the frozen sea and a land without roads or rail-roads or motor cars or airplanes. All one can count on as a highway is the vast blanket of snow and ice; the only means of transport being the team of faithful dogs, which at present is the sole harbinger of Mr. Henry Ford's contribution to the comfort and happiness of people in similar remote settlements elsewhere in the world.

The great need and the great desire of our fishermen for themselves was and is, not charity, but work — remunerative labour, the fruits of which will enable them to buy the food and clothing which spell the difference between resistance or non-resistance to nutritional diseases such as beri-beri, scurvy, rickets, and tuberculosis, which are the bane of the Coast. Secondly, they need — although they do not always recognize the need — interesting work which will enable them to use and develop their native resources and the natural handiness which is the heritage of seafaring folk all over the world. Lastly, they need the type of work which will offer them the durable satisfaction of producing something which not only pleases them, but makes a sufficient appeal to outsiders to be purchased on its merits, and not out of charity.

It was this challenge to find such work for them, an appeal which, like that of the medical, surgical, social, and educational work, is all the stronger because its potentiality is greater than its actuality, which led to the beginning of our

Industrial Department. A generation ago, the lives of the women of our Northern coasts were particularly drab. Though conditions are better today, to them still fall the prosaic tasks of rearing large families, which household duties made almost impossibly difficult because of meagre supplies and no conveniences, and of gardening where the bones of Mother Earth are unduly numerous and exposed. Their lives must be spent largely indoors at monotonous and heavy duties; while the men, whose summer days are spent on the sea and whose winter days are passed in the forest trapping or cutting wood, have greater mental and physical variety and so more possibilities for healthful living.

To create a nation of paupers would have been a disaster; so from the beginning the rule was laid down and strictly adhered to that food and clothing must be earned by work of some kind, and not doled out except in cases of extreme poverty and pressing need.

Is it worth while to pay for hospitals to do patchwork on already damaged human machines? Is it remunerative to spend time and money on crippled humanity when there is so much constructive work which could be done for those who are not and need never become crippled? Is the Greek or the Roman philosophy of ridding the world of the defective, after all, true wisdom? Is the attitude of the ages which we call 'Dark,' which regarded the cripple as a source of humour, and even purposely deformed children in order to exact high prices for them as jesters at kings' courts, or else regarded them as cursed of God and linked with the Devil and so tortured them and killed them as witches, a wiser course of action than modern humanitarianism? We consider our Industrial Department as perhaps the most important answer which we can make to the solution of these questions.

There existed on the Coast the native industry of rug-hooking, to which the women were accustomed from earliest childhood. The Devonshire and Cornish and Scotch ancestors of our fisherfolk must have brought out this industry with them from Old England at the same time that it migrated to New England. Rug-making was an ideal industry with which to begin. It did not have to be taught; it was essentially a 'spare-time' occupation; little or much could be done at one time without any risk of injury to the finished mat; it could be carried on in the home; the necessary apparatus took up little space and could be made out of the native wood.

Before the Industrial Department took up the work, the people had always made mats for their cottages from worn-out garments; but, as the rugs produced for the Grenfell Association were to be sold, it was important that they should be hooked of entirely new materials, which must, of course, be furnished to the women.

So long as the industrial work has in it a large element of necessary educational training, so long as customs barriers continue to be erected against it, so long as transportation is expensive and rents for shops exorbitant, it is almost impossible for us as a charity to carry the unavoidable overhead for this branch of our work. Yet we realize increasingly that the really beautiful products of our clever, mechanical people are sold on their merits, and are worth every penny which is charged for them.

We can look back over twenty-five years of generous, able, and trained workers who have taken charge of this steadily developing department, beginning with Miss Jessie Luther, of Providence, who gave many years of voluntary service and brought to the work not only enthusiasm, but a trained mind and capacity. It was she who introduced the weaving of homespun, an industry which the local women had discontinued owing to the poverty of their lives and the struggle for bare existence which left no margin of strength or money. Miss Luther also started the making of pottery from our native clay, and encouraged and developed basketry from local grasses, skin-work and bead-work.

Since those early days such strides have been taken in design, colouring, and workmanship that the present mat grandchild would scarcely recognize its ancestor if it were to be placed side by side with it in one of our sales. The women are daily deriving from the industrial work an incentive to better living, cleaner homes, and a higher standard of life. We can safely say that our fisherwomen produce the best hooked mats in the world, our patterns comprising a wide range of subjects, from polar bears on icebergs to dog-teams scampering over snowy wastes. We have literally raised our

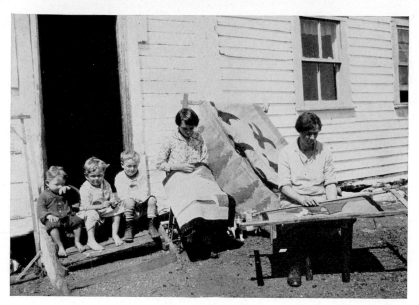

HOME INDUSTRIES

A UNIT OF THE INDUSTRIAL DEPARTMENT AT WORK

humble floor mats till today they are fit to occupy the seats of the mighty as tapestries on the walls of palaces.

The new flannelette and the jute for hooking many of our rugs still have to be imported, but more and more we are substituting for these materials the 'silk-stocking mat.' The slogan, 'When your stocking begins to run, let it run to Labrador,' has been the watchword to guide many hundreds of pairs of stockings which would otherwise have been superannuated in the waste-paper basket, to another useful lease of life on the Labrador.

The women of the Coast do the weaving also, as we have never been able to induce the men, in the long hours of enforced idleness of our winters, to follow the example of their Scotch prototypes or the Huguenot refugees at Spitalfields and take up weaving as a masculine home industry. It therefore remained for us to find a remunerative and stimulating industry for the men and boys, especially the cripples and convalescents. In the hospitals of civilization it is well recognized that physical recovery is hastened or retarded by the mental condition of the patient. In our hospitals in the North this was all the more obvious since the worry of a bread-winner over an empty cupboard and a hungry family was often a more than serious handicap to his recovery. Out of this need has grown our toy-making department. The dog-teams and animals are cut from wood and painted from nature. The komatiks which these dog-teams pull are exact models of the real sledges of the North Country. Each particular slat is lashed to the miniature runners as in the construction of a full-size komatik, for these would surely break when they hit the snow-covered rocks or snags if they were assembled with nails, whereas, when lashed, there is sufficient play to prevent snapping. The hunter and his dog trundle along on wheels; and sometimes the rôle of the hunter is reversed, and it is he who is chased by the playful polar bear.

In an attempt to utilize the local resources of the Coast in this work for the men, the ivory industry grew up; and many today look upon its products as the most interesting and beautiful our people have to offer. The ivory comes from the tusks of our walrus or narwhals, or from the fine ivory teeth of the great dentate whale, the cachelot. The teeth of all these whales which are taken on the Coast are now presented to us as a free offering by the kindly whaling companies. They thus serve as an hereditary tribute to the industrial welfare department. Bone and ivory carving can readily be done in bed with small tools and files. We feel that the apex of our ivory-work has been reached in the beautiful sets of chessmen, fantastic figures of Eskimos, seals, bears, dogs, and igloos, nothing quite like them ever having been put on the market before.

Our winter garment, locally referred to as a 'kossak' or 'dickie,' and which is made of our own special Grenfell cloth, sells even at so smart and civilized a spot as the Lake Placid Club. It has also paid a visit to the Antarctic with Admiral Byrd's Expedition, as he took with him two or three of our former volunteers as members of his crew. For lightness and warmth, for storm and rain and wind- and snow-proof qualities, for beauty and picturesqueness, with its fur trimmings and bright-coloured embroideries, this dickie does its own broadcasting.

Through the intervening years following Miss Luther's work, the department has had the splendid help of a number of able and devoted superintendents. To all of them the Coast owes more than it really understands or appreciates. The present industrial manager is a lady from Scotland. Her grasp, not only of the details, but of the broader implications of her work, is great. It seems pertinent in this connection to quote from her recent report, the title of which we have already borrowed as the heading of this chapter:

> The question has been asked whether it would not be cheaper to pay to needy people the amount now spent on payment for industrial work, and so disburse the same amount in charity while avoiding all the trouble and expense involved in the Industrial Department. Such an enquiry shows an entire misapprehension of the work that this department is endeavouring to do. As well might one ask whether it would not be cheaper to pay the funeral expenses of those who die from preventable diseases, and so avoid the trouble and expenditure of restoring them to physical health. For the work of the Industrial Department is as truly curative as the work of our hospitals, and equally fitting as a branch of a medical mission.
> The actual goods turned out for sale are in a sense only a by-

product. What we are really producing is character, individuality, independence; in a word, all that is implied in a fully developed human being.

We hear a great deal in these days about the need of adjusting the individual to his environment, and we know that when there is a lack of such adjustment, physical, moral, and mental breakdown results. Where can one find the possibility of such adjustment in the case of an individual who is physically handicapped in a community the conditions in which demand an exceptional degree of physical strength? How give hope and courage to a man whose life has taught him the futility of both? How bring beauty and colour into the life of a woman whose soul has been made barren of either by the bleak sordidness of existence?

As a community those are the life-giving qualities we lack — physical strength, courage, hope, beauty, colour. And who will deny that to restore them is a fitting task for a medical mission? Such, in brief, is our aim. 'How visionary and highfalutin!' does some one say? Let us see.

Mr. A. came to hospital as a lad suffering from a tubercular hip, very ill indeed, and not expected to live. Some years later he was alive and well — lame, it is true, but able to get about easily, earning a good wage at painting toys and able to supervise and help others. His is a useful, full life, on a self-respecting, independent basis. Without St. Anthony Hospital he would have died; without the Industrial Department he would have starved.

Mr. B., father of a large family, has a tubercular foot and a tubercular hand, and is quite unable to go fishing. Now, provided with a treadle jig-saw, he can work with his good foot, and is making toys for his livelihood. He returned to his home and family after treatment in hospital and industrial training.

C. is a very delicate boy with gastric trouble. He was unable to go fishing, and was not strong enough when he came to us to shovel coal into the furnace. In and out of the hospital, in and out of the Industrial Department, he went during two years, growing stronger steadily and earning money. Eventually restored to health, he went to Canada to a brother and is now working for himself there and doing well.

Mrs. D. is a married woman with a fisherman husband and several children. Hear what she says when told one day that there was no work for her.

'Too bad, that's two weeks now, Miss, and I never got no work.'

'So you miss it?'

'Why sure I misses it.'

'What would you do if there was not any more work ever?'

'Well, I don't know what I'd do. That's all we folks has to earn a little bit. I buys many a good thing with the money, and then again I goes in the clothing store and gets clothing for all hands home. My, Miss, if there wasn't no work, I don't know how we'd do at all.'

Scene: a living-room in a fisherman's cottage. A blizzard is raging outside. There is no sound but that of the howling wind. On the bench which runs round three sides of the wall are sitting about a dozen men, silent, listless, doing nothing because there is nothing to do. Not reading because they cannot. Not even talking, for what is there to say? This is no exception. There are many such winter days, and many such places. But happily an industrial worker is among them, also storm-stayed. She takes out of her bag some little wooden articles and hands them round. They are all things which the men are familiar with — komatiks, dogs, boats, and so on. Conversation starts, and the next stormy day there will be something to do, copying these little toys. So they join the 'stormy day brigade,' and when spring comes round many a much-needed article can be purchased with the money received from the Industrial Department in exchange for the toys. 'Do you like making them?' we asked one such man. 'Miss, I just loves it,' he answered; and the bright, interested look on his face showed the change which had taken place since we saw him last.

A visitor returning to the Coast today after an absence of years would notice a marked improvement in the clothing of the people. This, of course, is largely due to the splendid donations of good clothing sent by the many friends of Labrador; but it is the Industrial Department which has solved the problem of distributing the clothing without pauperizing the recipients. One has only to remember the severity of the sub-Arctic climate to realize the primary importance to health and efficiency of proper clothing. It is really 'mat money' which is preventing the recurrence of an incident of some years past when a child came walking barefooted over the snow to the Industrial Building because she had no shoes and stockings, with the temperature at twenty below zero. Moreover, she had no coat to wear over her cotton frock.

The Department also allows school children to come in as short-time workers during their holidays, or even for a little work in the long sub-Arctic evenings. This is arranged so that the child is allowed a reasonable amount of playtime. One little girl who had paid for her own school fees and books for two years by weaving 'on times' said to the Superintendent, 'You know, Miss, I likes to do it. It makes me feel so good.'

The area covered by the activities of the Industrial Department now stretches from Cape St. John on the east coast of Newfoundland and from Ferole on the west coast, to the most northerly part of the Island. It includes Harrington and Mutton Bay on the Canadian Labrador, and covers many hundreds of miles of coast northward along the Labrador. Naturally the larger part of the work is concentrated around our hospitals, the main centre being at St. Anthony. There are about a dozen subsidiary stations dotted along the Coast.

Gradually these products of our Industrial Department, the dog-teams, the bears, the birds, the Arctic hares, whether hooked in rugs or carved in ivory or wood, the homespuns, the dickies, the baskets, the polished Labradorite, began voyaging farther and farther afield, to the United States, Canada, and England. They were a kind of sub-polar migration. But finding purchasers for goods is perhaps the world's biggest problem today. It is being made increasingly difficult by endless tariff walls, which soon make the people on both sides the walls poorer, less able to produce, and less able to buy. On some polished blue stone which we sent to New York, one hundred per cent duty was paid. In order to try and market these products of the people, we have had to make the great venture of faith of renting a shop in New York and one in Philadelphia. Even as I write, we are having to close down the New York shop as the rental is prohibitive.

This marketing problem, however, affords another fertile challenge to service, so some of our alumnæ volunteers devised a new plan. Taking a Ford truck, they began touring the various summer resorts with our industrial goods. Through the kind coöperation of hotel-keepers and individual hostesses, they were able to hold many sales. Later, a new car was presented by the ex-Governor of Vermont, and a new Ford by that great industrialist, Mr. Henry Ford himself. In this latter Lady Grenfell and I have made several combined lecture and industrial-sale trips. Anyone can recognize the car, for in unashamed letters on the outside it is labelled 'Grenfell Labrador Industries.'

One day when Lady Grenfell was alone on an Industrial errand and alighted in a town, a small boy came up to her and enquired anxiously, 'Have you got him inside?' On another occasion, a lady passing asked who it was descending from the truck, whereupon a scornful Boy Scout piped up, 'Oh! don't you know? That's the guy who wrote "Afloat on a Dustpan."'

At the great Imperial Exhibition at Wembley, England, we had a stall, the beauty of which was that it was largely run by American volunteers. They greatly enjoyed selling dog-teams, model kayaks, and ivory carving to Her Majesty the Queen of England, who made a special visit to the stall. International, industrial coöperation is one sure road to world peace. On another occasion I had the pleasure of illustrating this to King Edward the Seventh when he asked what an unpaid magistrate like myself did for police in Labrador. 'I generally swear in an American college boy to serve Your Majesty temporarily,' I replied.

Yet another effort at marketing the Labrador and North Newfoundland goods is the Dog-Team Tavern on the Champlain Highway at Ferrisburg, Vermont. Never has a better illustration of coöperation been established. We had no money. Yet some further outlet had to be found for the articles unless we were going to throw hundreds of needy people out of the only remunerative work they had. We rented a picturesque but dilapidated old farmhouse. The grounds were a wilderness. Lady Grenfell, with her real courage, made a personal tour of the shops in Burlington, asking their coöperation, as well as that of individual well-wishers. Almost everything, including a stove for the kitchen, was freely given. I shall never forget one call, which I made with her, quaking in my shoes. The proprietor was neither of our race nor religion, nor our acquaintance; and scarcely any business was remunerative at that time. However, that proprietor was the type of man who regards all men as brothers, which is the only type which can save the world. 'You want a dozen chairs and a table? Gladly! Thank you for the opportunity.' Before we left he added, 'Later on I'll pay a visit to the Dog-Team Tavern and buy one or two of those Labrador rugs.'

The industrial work has expanded rapidly, owing to its filling a more and more important place in the life of the community. The present Industrial Building is a leaky, shaky, frame building, too small and unhygienic. As a matter of fact, it is the old orphanage, which was abandoned years

CONVALESCENTS AT WORK AT ST. ANTHONY

THE LOOM ROOM

ago after the buffetings of the storms of many winters had
made it unfit for the children to live in. We are thrown between Scylla and Charybdis — the alternative of turning
away those who desperately need the training and chance
of earning a livelihood or taking them in to work under conditions which endanger their health. The sanitation of the
building causes us constant worry. The whole plumbing
system may collapse at any moment. The heating is irregular
and uneconomical. With the slightest blizzard, the snow drifts
in at every window. The condition of the roof is so bad that
when the spring and fall rains come the rooms on the top
floor are flooded and the water leaks down the walls to the
second floor. The roof has been patched and patched until
it can be patched no more. Into this building is crowded the
preparation of all the mats for hundreds of miles of coast,
and about two thousand women 'mat hookers' who are on
the books of the Industrial Department. The weaving-rooms
are limited to thirty looms, and we have to turn girls back
to their often dreary little homes since we have no room to
give them work. The wood and ivory work is carried on in a
tiny room on the second floor, crowded with hand and electric
machinery, wood benches, wood ready to be sawn, toys in
process of construction, ivory supplies and general tools. The
toy painting is done in a room with a sloping ceiling and a
low dormer window, which does not admit proper light or
give sufficient air space for the workers.

The waiting-room to which the women of the district have
to come with their work is a small portion of the dilapidated
old kitchen. It is dark and damp, furnished with two wooden
benches, a rusty stove, a bathtub, and a sink. In another
corner of this same room all the dyeing of the materials for
the Department has been done until a summer or two ago,
when we were forced to take the boiler and tanks into the
open and pray for a long spell of dry weather! It is quite
certain that we have reached the capacity of production of
this present building for the large area and number of people
it serves. Indeed, during the winter of 1931–32 we were
obliged to close it entirely, as we could not afford to keep so
uneconomical and dangerous a plant going. The Department
has always made it its policy to put out work into the homes

of the people, rather than bringing them to a central building in any district, but there are many processes which must be done at a headquarters. We must have storage for our raw materials. Moreover, under present conditions there is no chance whatever for developing new branches of the Industrial Department, such as the polishing of our beautiful Labradorite, or making pottery from our local clay — which we were forced to discontinue owing to utter lack of space.

The Industrial Department has to stand on its own financial feet. Sales have increased, workers provided with remunerative occupation have increased in numbers very greatly; but so have our expenses and our responsibilities. We hate to think that we may not be able to continue even to try to meet the challenge of the Coast along lines of industrial and economic welfare, because our handicaps — the need for larger markets, for working capital, and for adequate central headquarters — are insurmountable.

CHAPTER XXV

LABRADOR TAKES A GLIMPSE AT THE ORIENT

In 1924, the aftermath of the 'war of civilization to end war' was already demonstrating its failure. The Western world had been in the witness box and found wanting, despite its outward show of material and scientific progress.

After thirty years in the sub-Arctic, no one could have approached a tour around the world with greater anticipation and pleasure than we did. We decided that Egypt should be our first objective. Long before the dawn of history it had evolved a civilization which, to our minds, seemed to put many of our modern ones to shame.

With deserts on each side to protect it, the barrier of the sea in front and only African natives behind, with its magnificent river, its climate, its endless man-power, it was easy to picture how Egypt, like Crete, could have remained peaceful through the centuries. Yet there, too, the uncertain element of human nature had been evidenced by the trails for their enemies which the Egyptians themselves had blazed, by their constant warlike expeditions to the north in attempts to conquer Palestine and Syria.

The water-front at Alexandria, viewed from our eyrie on the upper deck of the steamer which had borne us from Trieste, made us feel much as Moses must have felt, when with his host he clambered up the bank on the other side of the Red Sea, and saw the waters close in upon their foes, with a devout thankfulness that they were not among them.

An entry in our diary that first day reads, 'Baksheesh is the national anthem from Alexandria to the Sudan.' Every moment that we were trying to enjoy the mighty pyramids, the immortal sphinx, or the other marvels of Egypt, our ears ached from the discordant yells of men and boys fighting to extract piastres from the unfortunate. They reminded us of nothing so much as a pack of our Eskimo dogs in violent conflict over a bone. The query came to our minds whether Holy Writ had not omitted to catalogue this plague among the others which formerly afflicted the Land of the Pharaohs.

Through the kindness of Hassanein Bey, who has made such significant explorations in the Lybian Desert, we were invited by one of his friends to visit the Fayoum, truly the garden spot of Egypt. The Fayoum might be an Oriental Ireland, it is so green; while maize, cotton, oranges, figs, guavas, dates, eggplants, tomatoes, cabbages, bananas, and pears flourish luxuriantly. Whilst we were there, the Governor was kind enough to entertain us and show us many of his attempts for the advancement of his country. He has endeavoured to suit his reforms to the needs of the people; and we found such industries as a shoe factory, a technical school, an iron factory, and a cabinet-maker's shop, as well as a Farm Bureau for the instruction of the rural population.

The earliest Egyptians recorded in history are said to have been a pastoral people, as, indeed, were all the peoples of warm climates. Today, Egypt holds her future in her own hands and can yet be a mighty country if the strength of a land lies in its agriculture; but with Egypt, in spite of her wonderful river, irrigation must be the answer to her problem. During the ascent of the Nile one is struck by the constant emphasis on water. The days are punctuated by the sight of naked men toiling endlessly at pumps, by the creaking of the ever-recurrent *shadoofs*, and by the endless treading of the patient animals circumnavigating the *sakeeyahs*.

From one's armchair on the deck of Cook's Nile steamer one views a cinema which gives one the sensation of looking at one's contemporary ancestors. At dawn, when the more intrepid among us, wrapped in warm coats, would emerge on deck, the dim light revealed a few statuesque natives taking a morning dip in some back-wash of the river before saying their prayers, their faces toward Mecca. All through the days there passed down the river a kaleidoscope of picturesque *dahabeeyahs*, laden with every imaginable type of merchandise, and generally stacked so high that if it had not been for their lateen sails, they could not have functioned at all. Occasionally, a huge outrigger would drift by, innumerable clay water-pots piled on her deck; or it might be two vessels lashed together, carrying a cargo of straw sticks so that they looked like aquatic hay-pooks. We tried to live again in imagination the days when Cheops was erecting his pyramids, or the Ptolemies were rearing temples and statues in their own honour, or the times of the Arabs, the Persians, the Greeks, the Romans, and lastly the Britons, who came, saw, and conquered in this land.

At Esna, when one saw Ptolemy dancing before his god the picture was so realistic that we felt Pavlova might have been jealous; while at Denderah the horrible reproduction of the prisoners feeding the king's lions with their own right arms made one shudder as if one were looking into the arena at living victims. At Denderah also there is a huge painting on the temple wall of Cleopatra and Cæsarian, her son by Julius Cæsar. The interest of it lies in the fact that it is said to disprove the theory that she was a Negroid.

Thebes, the oldest and perhaps the greatest city in Egypt, is indeed a place to conjure up dreams. Here dwelt the god Amen Ra, the Jupiter of Egypt. It was to his temple that the great Alexander tried to find a guide at Alexandria to pilot him four hundred miles up the river, in order to cheat himself into the belief that his father was the sun god and not the great Philip of Macedon. Some say that he actually arrived at his mecca and executed what was really a keen diplomatic move, by having himself pronounced the son of Amen Ra.

In contrast, the story of King Ahknaton, who revolted against the villainy of the priests and their degrading practices, is an inspiration. Due to the influence of his mother he strove to have the people worship, not Amen Ra, the sun, but Aton Ra, the power that gives life to earth and mankind. The gory pastimes of his predecessors sickened him. Courageous as was the young king, the priestcraft of the day triumphed ultimately, and the court, which Ahknaton had moved from Thebes to Tel el Amara, returned to Thebes in the reign of his son, the now famous Tutankhamen.

Egyptology has been in the family, and one of my father's cousins, at the time he was Sirdar, had excavated some interesting tombs across the river from the town of Assuan. We christened them 'the Grenfell family vaults.' Another cousin, whilst digging up old papyri in the ancient city of Oxyrrhynchus, discovered the famous Logos, or sayings of Christ, thus contributing more to the world than if he had exhumed a baker's dozen of departed kings. We later made a pilgrimage on donkeys to the grave of another cousin, who died in a cavalry charge at Omdurman, on the relief expedition to Khartoum.

As we were anxious to miss none of the experiences of the typical tourist, we decided to risk a day's ride on a camel to the ancient Coptic Convent of Saint Simon. Once aloft on the camels, we found ourselves on a kind of tableland. We could only trust that the venerable sheepskins on which we were perched had been ascepticized by the ardent sun of Upper Egypt. The only visible means of support for the intrepid traveller were two small pummels fore and aft on the saddles. While your camel walked, you were hurled back and forth with considerable violence and with a persistency evidenced by the scraping-off of a certain portion of your anatomy on the forward swing, while the return stroke removed another area. This experience was varied when our steeds started to trot, whereupon we were bounced up and down like unwilling pistons in a cylinder, while we thought lovingly of our dog-teams in Labrador.

The manner of our exodus from the Land of Egypt did not repeat the Biblical precedent, for we accomplished the journey, which had cost Moses and the Children of Israel some forty years, on an overnight train-de-luxe running from Cairo to Jerusalem. A full moon shone brightly on us as we disembarked at Kantara, and the Canal resembled a crystal sea, with two great black ships passing like phantoms on their voyage between the deserts.

Palestine can rightly be regarded as belonging to the desert which is the former home of its people, and whose influence marks their thought and their language. Its boundaries were never defined, though today it covers an area one hundred and ten miles in length by fifty miles wide. It is still a 'parched land where no water is.' Four trains were carrying thousands of tons of Nile water up to Jerusalem each day, apparently fulfilling the ancient prophecy that the Holy City could not be conquered until the Nile flowed into it. Palestine has no rivers except the Jordan and the Kedron and singularly few wells. With the passing of centuries, its population has diminished a thousandfold. It is a mere pathway between two great cradles of the human race, the Arabian

Desert on the one hand backing up the deep valley of the Jordan, a great sea on the other, lofty mountains on the north, and the Desert of Sinai cutting it off on the south.

The too credulous visitor, with a passion for sacred sites, will be rudely disillusioned in Palestine. Jerusalem itself has been destroyed and risen out of its own ashes many times. It is a mercy of Providence that the present level of the city is forty feet above that of the time of Our Lord. Religious sites in Palestine are the prototypes of baksheesh in Egypt. Most of them are so obviously faked that they become a source of annoyance even to the gullible.

The present road to Jericho follows doubtless the same line as that traversed by the Good Samaritan. As it is the only road up to Jerusalem, Our Lord must often have come along it. In that one day's motor journey we visited the spot where Elisha struck the river with his mantle, the traditional place of Christ's Baptism, the point of the river where the Israelites passed over under the leadership of Joshua. Though we looked across into the Land of Gilead, we could distinguish none of those trees which yielded the precious pear. The legend of Saint Christopher and the Christ Child is also ascribed to this ford in Jordan, as is the healing of Naaman of his leprosy. Bathing in the Dead Sea is a unique experience, and I was delighted to find that the water was so salt that I could comfortably eat an apple and read a book while floating on my back practically on its surface.

In the Church of the Holy Sepulchre is the authentic tomb of Sir Philip d'Aubigny, a tutor in the family of King Henry the Third. One rejoices to feel that after his efforts to reach this to him most sacred resting-place, probably no one will ever dig him up. His simple tomb is a welcome contrast to the altar with the two holes drilled in its sides through which it is still alleged that sacred fire from heaven issues every Easter to light the pilgrims' candles. The most shocking fraud, however, is the Tomb of Christ, a slab about five feet long which is said to have been the covering of the entrance of 'his own new tomb' which Joseph of Arimathæa 'had hewn out in the rock.'

Fortunately, Dean Stanley points out that 'the Church of the Holy Sepulchre has not at all times been a mere battleground for its several occupants. There the traveller sees nations, with different languages, each with its own rites, worshipping in one spot. That is the unique sight through the ages — and once they all believed that this was the site of the Tomb of their common Lord.'

The upper part of the Ecce Homo Arch is in the street, while its base has been excavated below the level of the present town and is in the chapel of the Convent of the Sisters of Zion. The flagging beneath the arch is believed to be the actual pavement in front of Pilate's judgment seat — the 'Gabbatha.' The worn stones are deeply grooved in lines made by the games of the Roman soldiers. Through this very arch Christ must have passed after being condemned to be crucified.

One result of the War was a motor-car service across the Syrian Desert from Damascus to Baghdad, the capital of Mesopotamia, another 'cradle of the human race.' There was built the Tower of Babel, for thence 'it was only one step to heaven.' The ruins of Babylon are so far gone as scarcely even to suggest the height of civilization to which it had attained. The enormous thickness of its walls, on which two four-horse chariots could easily pass abreast at full speed, suggested that no effort or expense had been spared to ensure the permanence of the policies which led its monarch to exclaim that all which man could do to make for human happiness had been accomplished. The Bible account shows how great an illusion that 'master of the world' was under. Truly he believed that he had created an eternal city in this 'great Babylon that he had built'; but that very faith was itself the presage of both its and his undoing.

What might this place have been if the world of that day had awakened to the appreciation of the great illusion it was under? As a summary of our observations, I read in my diary: 'Garbage and dirt everywhere. Evil-smelling, mean streets. Not a thoroughfare through the town except one cleared by the Germans. Diseases lurking in every corner. To those who love dirty, poky corners, dark, blind alleys, suggestions to every sense of a long by-gone mediævalism, we heartily commend this city.'

We had wished to visit Russia, as she seems to be trying

out anew the old theory that man is a robot and that his happiness can be attained (if that word is applicable to a machine) by forcing him to function rightly. The experiment is a trifle belated, for determinism and materialism are now rightly discredited intellectually, and that, by far more advanced intelligentsia than Russia at the moment permits to exist. The cocksure materialism of the nineteenth century has culminated today in the necessity for the mysterious 'H factor,' either to explain phenomena or to allow advances to be made. The Russian experimenters, however, preferred at that time to let tourists get impressions second-hand and cancelled our visas. Some eight years afterwards, in 1931, in order to form her own deductions, Lady Grenfell went to Moscow and Leningrad; only to realize that one must still wait before visitors are permitted to see for themselves conditions as they really are.

As for Kish, home of kings, which four thousand years ago had rivalled Babylon itself, all the searchings of the antiquarians had only just discovered its whereabouts. The station for it was an ancient iron tank. We found the city at last, right in the centre of nowhere, with an horizon of sand on every side! When Ur of the Chaldees, also close by, was founded in 2300 B.C., palm trees covered the plain, and a far more elaborate irrigation system than that of modern Egypt enabled the people to cultivate and raise cattle and necessary vegetables, as the records unearthed recently show. The Bible tells us that some presentiment induced the 'Father of the Faithful' to leave Ur. There is reason to believe that his prophetic soul already had a vision of the great illusion.

The illusion for us was never dispelled, for when we finally sailed for India from Basrah not one vestige of all that human glory had we seen. The impression left on our minds was that we had passed over one vast ocean of flat, dried-up mud.

I was reared in an atmosphere of India. Among my earliest recollections is that of my mother's telling me stories of the beautiful land of her birth, or else clambering on to my uncle's knee to feel the bullet in his forehead which he got at Lucknow while he was helping to defend the Residency in the great Mutiny. At that time he was aide-de-camp to Sir Henry Lawrence.

It has always seemed to me that the colour prejudice which some people feel so strongly is either a convenient cover for national and racial selfishness or else an invention of one's mind. In a sense, the Indians are our blood cousins, being men of the Aryan race like ourselves.

The history of the self-government of India which stretches back four thousand years paints a picture not of peace and progress and prosperity, but of racial and religious hatreds, unspeakable butcheries and terrible wars. Women were degraded. Education was paralyzed. Gross superstitions and savageries continued to dominate the unhappy land. Today India has a population of three hundred and twenty million people, separated by nine great religions, and by over one hundred and thirty different languages. As if this were not enough to divide the country, there still exists a rigid caste system, made up of nearly two thousand exclusive castes, even more of a barrier between man and man than is the industrial class system of our Western world, since in India marriage is forbidden between members of different castes. Yet to the outside visitor a certain fascination of the country lies in this very diversity in all the aspects of her national life.

It is difficult to describe how the land impresses one, with its gorgeous, blooming trees, its picturesque villages of bizarre architecture which seems to melt into the landscape of mango orchards and palm groves. What man who has lived in our Western world, either in the crowded cities like London or New York, could fail to love the ever-changing panorama of the Indian town, which constantly reminded us of the aurora borealis of our Arctic sky? Or one like myself, who for a large portion of his life has taken his morning dip in the polar current and often between pans of ice, could fail to appreciate a bath in the lovely breakers of the Coromandel Beach?

India's vast jungles supply nearly every valuable wood in the world, while there is hardly a fruit or a vegetable which the country cannot produce. The fact that at practically no time of the year is artificial heating necessary was to us rather a drawback than otherwise; but here in Labrador one closes one's eyes and relives in memory the experience of glorious warmth and colour, which to us was a veritable dreamland compared with physical aspects of the forbidding rocks of our icebound Coast, perpetually swept by a sea of ice.

At Delhi we had the privilege of meeting Mr. Gandhi, whom we found sitting in the sun on the upper balcony of his house. We considered this interview an opportunity; for however much one may differ with him as to the political salvation of India, one cannot fail to admit that his motives are sincere and unselfish, misguided though his actions may be.

We shall never forget the impression made upon us of that stronghold of superstition and idolatry, Conjeeveram, 'the Benares of the South,' with its juggernaut cars, its idols, its religious processions, its bells to notify the gods that it was time to go to bed, its spasmodic fireworks to amuse other gods, its oil and milk poured over some of the idols and later collected by the faithful and drunk as a cure for their ills. The townspeople seemed to see nothing out of the way in the following item in the local newspaper: 'Last evening, during the course of the procession, the Diety [the spelling is the paper's, not mine] most unfortunately fell off into the drain. By the concerted efforts of the worshippers, however, he was restored to his position at eight o'clock.'

It was, however, with deep regret that we bade good-bye to India and the happy weeks which we had spent there were only a memory. We realized, as we had never been able to do before, that it is one of the most important lands on earth, not only because it possesses so large a section of the human race, but because its history shows intellectual achievements which might have made it a leader in the world today, had it not chained itself to insidious creeds and customs. India is full of capable, lovable, and honest people, but it can never develop its full potentiality by merely dropping down aerial roots from the branches overhead, any more than can its roadside banyan trees, whose descending tendrils are hidden just below the level of the earth, where the teeth of the ever-present but untouchable and sacred cow cannot reach them.

The convictions left in our minds by the various mission activities which we had visited were first that they were human, but that we heartily thanked God for them and for what they have accomplished for India and the world. We could not fail to notice that the natural and universal cooperation between the activities working for the same end is increasing rapidly, in proportion as the interest in dogmas, creeds, and human institutions is replaced by the realization that love is the only solution of the world's problems, Russia *contradicente*, and the understanding that real love in action is humble as well as heroic and must be interpreted in much the same way. We came to the conclusion that human government has been human in India as well as in Chicago, but its bias has been strongly just and would match up well, judged by their records. That it has been a blessing to India no living man can honestly doubt in the face of history.

An outstanding demonstration of what preaching by example can do in attacking prejudices and wrongs fearlessly is the great school in Srinagar, which, in the face of every possible opposition, discouragement, and danger, has made and is making new men out of the exclusive Brahmins. The Reverend Tyndal Biscoe's own modest account of his work, in a little book entitled 'Forty Years Upstream,' is as fine an antidote as I know to the discouragement caused by the present state of affairs in civilization.

The next eastward step on our rapid pilgrimage was China. Here we felt that her unwieldy size was perhaps her greatest handicap. Her population is as large as that of the United States, Italy, Spain, Belgium, Holland, and South America, all combined. Over this dense mass of humanity one finds comparatively none of the modern controls of material forces or the conservation of the marvellous natural resources. This lack spells famines, floods, poverty, misery, and human life cheap and insecure everywhere. Moreover, languages, customs, and the diversity of natural settings all make it impossible for the same laws or religion to suit the whole of China.

We took a journey of eight hundred miles up the great Yangtze Kiang, the fourth largest river in the world, passed endless cities and the teeming life of the huge stream, and thence by rail or steamer covered thousands of miles more. The fact that crises are so constantly recurrent in the history of Europe, of India, of Egypt, of China, makes one doubt whether they may not be necessary steps of evolution. Painful as they are, disturbing to peace of mind, involving loss of life and property, are they after all only evidences of that 'divine discontent' which Charles Kingsley sought to arouse in England a few years ago? Today, Kingsley is forgiven by the very section of society which so severely censured him. Probably civil wars will not last forever. The Christian foundations are laid too deep to be destroyed in the end.

The fool of the family does not find a job on the staff of a mission today, supposing that he ever did. What surprised us, perhaps, most in China was that we never got off at any city, however smelly or primeval-looking, without finding a mission hospital or school or Christian effort of some sort endeavouring to sweeten the atmosphere, many of them now staffed by splendidly capable native Chinese, highly trained in Europe or America.

We could not fail to notice, too, that old hampering customs are disappearing. For the most part even the pigtail has gone from the head of the Chinaman. The spirit walls are coming down from in front of the doors of their homes — walls built to keep evil spirits from entering since they cannot turn corners, but which literally and figuratively have kept light and air from the very homes which they were intended to protect. Today one seldom sees the scaffolding of a new house decorated with branches tied on the tops of the poles in order to deceive those evil spirits, who are trying to find an entrance, into imagining that it is only a forest. The unbinding of the feet of the women is in itself a symbol of that greater freedom which is being accorded to them; without which freedom for womanhood China or any other country can never hope to come to its own. The extraordinary skill exhibited by the Chinese men and women, so many of whom live out their whole existence on the great rivers, never failed to excite our admiration. Moreover, the calm *insouciance* of the Chinese acceptance of circumstances, which would drive the Western world to madness, keeps one on tiptoe in watching the technique of life in this anthill of a country.

Even the most sophisticated shopper would be awakened into activity by the lure of the streets of a Chinese city. You are tempted by every variety of goods. There are the caged-bird markets, the soapstone carvers, the old-clothes men singing little odes in praise of their wares, the side-shows, the medicine-men who are selling their 'cure-alls' on the principle of machine-gun artillery, charged with such a variety of explosives that some must find their mark. Dried snakes and partially ground-up bones seemed to be the favourites among the ingredients. In one place we found that our kind host had acquired no small reputation as a healer. Years before, this clergyman had been called to see a woman who had taken a lethal dose of opium, as a 'spite' against her husband. By heroic doses of mustard, hot water, and coffee, he had dragged her back to life. It is really a fearful disgrace to have your wife commit suicide against you.

When we left China for Korea and watched the countryside flitting past, far the most striking feature to us was the never-ending panorama of hillsides and valleys, glorious in a new covering of green, a fresh garment given them by the Japanese, who seem to surpass all the world in tree-planting. Korea is mountainous, rising to about nine thousand feet in places. It has an equable climate and an all-the-year-round ice-free coast-line. We carried away from the country the impression of a polite and gentle people, with qualities childlike rather than childish. One can only hope for it the happy future of a free and contented Dominion, associated with Japan as Canada is bound to the British Empire.

Cleanliness is the priceless heirloom of Japan, though the masses of her people are pathetically poor. Again in my diary I find the following, 'Although not the result of personal observation, creditable evidence convinces me that everybody in Japan takes a hot bath every day.' Certainly the cleanliness of the 'inside of the cup' does not depend upon the possession of pounds and pence.

One's vocabulary fails in attempting to depict the exquisite beauties of the country in late May, with its flowering trees, from the gorgeous plum to the famous cherry (the fluttering of whose falling leaves has been brilliantly styled 'the soul of old Japan'), the feathery bamboos among the wisteria, or the lotuses, whose hues turn the rivers, lakes, and morasses into vivid dreams of colour.

At Kamakura is the Amida Buddha, the largest on earth. He was cast in bronze about A.D. 800. To his shrine come endless pilgrims. On the day of our visit I carried my usual butterfly-net. As the demeanour of the pilgrim crowd did not suggest a place of worship, when a large and enticingly rare, black, velvety butterfly passed close by, I gave instant chase. The creature, possessed either by the Devil or by the spirit of mischief, kept just out of reach over my heretical head until the moment when it suddenly swooped downward, thus tempting me to leap after it into the air. My descent from the bound was timed exactly at the stone wall of an exceedingly sacred but equally muddy pond. Over this parapet I leaped unwittingly, and landed on all fours in the sacred slime of ages! Fellow pilgrims were doubtless amazed to see an ancient mariner select that particular moment for a mud bath. Their innate courtesy, however, prevented their showing any signs of amusement, though my Western companions were not equally reticent with their emotions.

Would that the Colony of Newfoundland had copied the Japanese example in stimulating new industries, for Japan already grows more food per acre than any other country in the world. Her fields are divided into tiny square mud plots, separated by ridges, so that they resemble exaggerated waffles. The Government of Japan is engaged in fostering every sort of trade from soap to silkworms — all the more creditable because the soul of the people is not in the market-place. The world must awake to the fact that China and Japan have come out of what to us may have seemed their long sleep. For good or ill, they must be reckoned with in the struggle for existence which mankind must increasingly face.

It is so utterly impossible to think that even the wise men of the ages have really been, and still are, victims of a great illusion, that it is little wonder that the world should remain satisfied even though the fact confronts it. We admit that it seems impious and the last word in conceit to say so. Therefore, we are told today that such deception cannot be actually true, not even of ostriches.

Yet Sir Norman Angell's prophecies have been literally fulfilled, and twentieth-century science is already questioning another 'illusion' when it admits that life after death is probable. Where can we men-in-the-street look for data on

this subject, written in the story of the conditions which produced the nations of today, and which the material development of the earth's surface teaches? How is it possible for
the average man to see the 'end results' of the old beliefs, so
proving the pudding by the eating, instead of merely listening
any longer to the babble of men, half-learned and partially
informed by what all men know is only 'current' science.

The Norsemen, Greece, Spain, France, Italy, Germany —
all the most highly civilized European powers — have attempted, and in turn temporarily succeeded, in attaining
world domination by fighting. All alike have thought that
to be the road to the greatest happiness. Each in turn has
been disillusioned. Russia is at present engaged in seeking
world happiness through physical compulsion, on the ancient
assumption that, religion notwithstanding, man is after all
only a machine. In their search for reality, some scientists
still cling to this premise, though to make progress and discoveries they must work on the basis of eternal faith to venture, which is the exactly opposite theory. Man without faith
cannot exist. That is an axiom of our human existence.

We are too prone to attribute the highest wisdom to unaided
intellect and to forget that intellectuals, like other humans,
have been known to cling to illusions which ultimately destroy.
They themselves are subject to that element of uncertainty
in things and people which has routed materialism, found
determinism of doubtful value, and in the laboratories of our
greatest thinkers today is evidencing that through the il-
limitable emotions, such as love, can truth and ultimate
reality alone be apprehended.

CHAPTER XXVI

HONOURS

As THE years have gone by, different bodies have been kind enough to confer on me various unmerited honours, every one of which, however, has been most sincerely appreciated. One need not say that each has helped in its turn to encourage one to try and do better. The players may not understand the meaning of the shouting of the crowd, but it does afford a stimulus. Long ago, one learned that, if you want to make a man do his best, trust him, even if he is Peter, or Thomas, or Judas. 'Credit,' 'trust,' mean as much in one walk of life as another, and I owe the world reparations for which I must ask a permanent moratorium.

The Royal Scottish Geographical Society, at one of their annual functions, presented me with their Livingstone Gold Medal. To be linked even in name with David Livingstone, a fellow medical man and one of my lifelong heroes, who, though passed beyond our sight, still functions as much, if not more, than during his visible stay on earth to inspire others, suggests a confidence among men we honour that does add 'power to the elbow,' which is more often needed than we always admit.

The gift from New York University (said, with its thirty-five thousand students, to be the largest in the world) was indeed a welcome new buttress in the constant argument which every man's 'persona' must have with his mechanical brain. Every thinking man wants the encouragement that comes from men of learning regarding one's faith as reasonable.

A little later, another highly prized degree was conferred on me by Berea College in far-off Kentucky, where we have sent so many students, because that college has inspired one hundred per cent of them to want to gain knowledge that they might return and give it out in help and inspiration to their less privileged neighbours. Berea, formed for the help of the 'poor white trash,' isolated by the mountains, aims not merely to inform, but primarily to inspire, its students.

It truly deserves the name of Educator, leading as it does its alumni out of themselves and into world service.

The speaker of the Convocation was the youngest president of any large college, the University of Chicago; one of the greatest in the world, Dr. Hutchins. His opening words were: 'There are many institutions of learning in this country much larger than this one, which if they dropped out tomorrow would hardly be missed in the world's economy. But if this college were to drop out, the world would be poorer.' To the last part of which we who knew the facts most fervently added, 'Amen.'

One of our former 'wops,' now Chairman of the New England Grenfell Association, beloved by everyone who knows him, and more beloved the more you know him, influenced his Alma Mater to invite me to become an honorary alumnus. They did not have to wait long for my answer. Bowdoin boys were among the first to discover the canyon of the Labrador Grand Falls, during the very year I first landed on the Coast. A narrow escape they had, a creeping fire having burned all their food, camp, boat, and outfit three hundred miles from human habitation. I always think of them as they came out of the country, barelegged and with remains of straw hats tied on their feet, as their boots had long worn out while they were coming down the turbulent river and crossing the large lakes on logs, an experience which would have tried the best metal of professional lumberjacks. Moreover, Cole and Carey had subsisted on a diet which entitled them to rank with Mr. Gandhi as professional starvation experts.

Donald MacMillan, Admiral Peary's lieutenant, is also a Bowdoin man, and has done much to help the underprivileged among the Eskimos of Northern Labrador. Only one thing was lacking — the President who gave the 'honour' has not as yet found time to visit Labrador and judge our work personally.

Yet another honour which came to me seemed one of those strange humours of experience out of which we get special satisfaction. I, who, while a university student forty years previously in England, had received from Mr. Dwight Moody, who had never himself been to any university, a spiritual

impetus which was still influencing my reactions to life, was
offered a university degree by the college at Middlebury,
Vermont, by Mr. Moody's son, who holds the position of its
widely revered President. We had, however, as is not uncommon even among 'religious' persons, one irreconcilable
difference. He was too idealistic for a Labrador doctor, and
had decided to create me a 'Doctor of Divinity,' while I
was adamant in determining to wait until — well, a little
later, when I expect to be a better authority on that 'ology.
With the grace of the Moody family, that so well fits any
protagonist for success, he deferred to my superior wisdom
in the matter, which accounts for yet another qualification
for a doctor of medicine who has never opened a book of law,
to adorn the position of an unpaid Justice of the Peace for
our Colony, with the sanctity of an eighth label — perhaps I
ought to say 'additional visa.' To receive the approbation
of any national institution is rightly or wrongly an encouragement. I was genuinely grateful to the National Academy of
Social Sciences, to the Corporation of the City of Boston,
Massachusetts, where I had residence, and to the Royal
Geographical Society of Great Britain, for their recognition.

Any man who loves courage and who saw anything of the
Canadians in France between 1914 and 1918 will realize how
honoured I felt when McGill University admitted to its
fellowship a man working in the utmost limits of Canada's
far-flung territories. More than one visitor, rightly or wrongly,
has described Canada as the most Christian country in the
world today. Be that as it may, I had known some of its
great political leaders like Sir Wilfrid Laurier, the Honourable
W. MacKenzie King, and Sir Robert Borden; and I had truly
felt, in spite of evil speaking and the too common desire to
belittle politicians, that leadership such as theirs made anyone
proud of a closer link with that great country.

When I learned that General Sir Arthur Currie, successful
man of business, even more successful military leader, and
equally praised everywhere as a great educational head, was
to confer this new token of brotherhood, I hoped it was because the men who worked in earth's centres realized how we
in the wilds need new supports to carry on effectively, and
that they would regard our acceptance of their generosity

in that light, and not as if it were taken as a new feather in a bantam's tail.

All these events are recorded here at the risk of being misunderstood; but I want to protest that the gift of the Fellowship of the Royal College of Surgeons of England, the membership of the Royal Society of Medicine, the Fellowship of the College of Surgeons of America, and other generous and infinitely appreciated honours, are of real value, of spiritual value. Those who regard life as I do, as a field of honour, do not like isolation for its own sake, any more than a sailor loves being drowned simply because he is 'accustomed to it.' These gifts all help you to help others. They bring you in touch with new personalities from whom otherwise you could never draw inspiration. Moreover, in the world as it is today, they are of immense value in securing you a hearing if you do want to say anything, and a clientèle if you write anything with a purpose. To seek to be called 'Rabbi' is one thing. To refuse to accept the gift of a real 'talent' may be only a symptom of snobbery or of fear.

Therefore, I purposely include in this record a most sincere appreciation of honours that were never sought, but which have done for me and mine exactly that which love does whenever and in whatever form it is manifested. It has brought help to me through these human expressions of goodwill, and the consciousness of a sustaining force, which I know is the greatest that the world can give anyone. Volunteer service, kindly hospitality, monetary contributions, human encouragement were all essential in proportion to our faith and courage, and are all undeniably expressions of the 'greatest thing in the world.' Such have all these red-letter days in my life been to me. I have profoundly thanked God for every one of them. Anyone who does not believe this can offer me another such opportunity, and let him see how much of a sacrifice I would be willing to make in order to come and receive it. Only when it has been physically impossible have I refused. I try to regard myself as a Christian and to that extent socialist; but bred far too deep in my flesh and blood is a respect for and appreciation of the world's intelligentsia to permit me for one moment to let anyone think I do not always look upon them as the 'men entrusted with ten talents.'

One of those days I shall always regard as particularly memorable, because, as the years have gone by since it dawned and closed, I have been able to see what it has meant to the people among whom I have lived and to the work I have set myself to achieve. It was the day when our Governor, the late Sir William Allardyce, a man I had known and learned to love and honour so well for his services to the world, the representative of His Majesty the King, was to come away down to St. Anthony to open our first modern, concrete, fire-proof, thoroughly equipped hospital in the North. This hospital is manned by a surgeon in charge, Dr. Charles Curtis, who has earned for it the A 1 rating of the American College of Surgeons. We rejoice to feel that it, like our other hospitals, gives to the fishermen that which we ourselves would demand as the best translation of love for a neighbour, in our professional line of work. How I wished that Dr. John Mason Little, of Boston, whose ashes lie in the hillside above the old hospital and whose love and skill through many years had helped so much to make it possible, could have been visibly with us to share in the happiness of that great occasion!

The twenty-fifth of July, 1927, was the day selected. His Majesty's frigate, Wistaria, was specially detailed to convey His Excellency direct from the capital. A special trip of a local steamer, the Silver City, had been arranged to bring Admiral Sir James Startin, who came from England to represent that branch of the Mission, and a number of representatives from Canada and the United States, from the nearest point of the railway a hundred and fifty miles farther south. The Newfoundland Government also sent Judge Morris to represent them.

In the Strathcona II we were to return from our first Western Labrador trip of the season, two days before the great event, in order to have plenty of time for making due arrangements. We had been at Harrington Hospital, our Canadian Hospital, near Anticosti, and were running east down the Gulf of St. Lawrence. We had collected a few patients to take back with us, amongst them an elderly blind fisherman. Dense fog shut down on us before we had picked up the one and only landmark on the hundreds of islands among which lay our next port of call. Suddenly, while I was myself at the wheel, we had that awful feeling of being pitched forward like an arrow from the bow, the horrid noise I knew only too well of 'ru-up, ru-up,' our keel glissading over the ice-smoothed top of a submerged rock — then for a moment our little craft stopped and shivered, before over she went sideways, in about five feet of water on the reef, our draft being a good nine. No bottom was to be seen. Our angle was so acute that we on the bridge were nearly pitched over the side, which lay well under water. Worst of all, we had no notion what ledge we could have struck. To save the fire-box top and bottom of the boiler, and so prevent an explosion, the engineers at once drew the fire and let the steam off as rapidly as possible. The rest of us with great difficulty got the port boat clear of the lee rigging. When the patients had been huddled into it and it was held clear of the vessel, we slid our starboard boat over the bilge of the Strathcona into the water, and hauling her round to the bow got an anchor into her and rowed it out some thirty fathoms, hoping we might perhaps haul the ship out into deep water. While the men were doing this, however, the water in the hold increased so rapidly that, when I climbed down into my own stateroom to get some papers, my bed was already under water. This made us think there must be a hole through her side; indeed we could hear the water pouring in. It seemed foolish, therefore, to try and float her off the rock and we decided to leave her where she was brought up, so that if we could find land in the fog and get back to her next day, we might at least salve some of her properties. We were forced, therefore, to give orders to abandon her, and rigging up her compass in the second boat, I told each man to salve what he could quickly and bring it along to the boat. In spite of our unfortunate plight we all had to smile, when the last man, our engineer, climbed aboard with a looking-glass and an umbrella. It was raining and he had pictured a barren rock to sit on.

The skipper's duty was to lead, so we started off due north, ordering the other boat to keep us in sight. The fog, however, was thicker than ever, and in a very few minutes we lost sight of each other. Our small foghorn brought no answer from the second boat. Suddenly, a sound broke faintly upon the stillness. Then it got louder. It was a bell ringing! At last we located the direction and thought we recognized it as the Strathcona's own bell! To our amazement, when at last the source of the noise loomed up through the darkness, we found we were not mistaken. There lay the Strathcona — afloat! To be sure, she was very deep in the water, but afloat, and our other boat alongside. It did not take us long to clamber aboard her. The mate explained that, just as the wreck was disappearing from view, he heard the bell ring. He took little notice the first time, as he knew he must be mistaken. But suddenly it rang more loudly, and longer, as if the staunch little Strathcona had made up her mind at the last moment that she could not bear to be left alone to her fate. Turning back at once, they were just in time to see a heavier sea than any of the previous waves come along and lift our beloved craft clean over the reef into deep water beyond. The surface of the rock was well ice-scrubbed and smooth, so the little steamer just slid off it, as if she were being launched again. They had begun ringing the bell again for us as soon as ever they got aboard, and already had begun bailing, armed with buckets.

It seemed like bailing the Atlantic with a teaspoon, but at last we really did begin to note progress, while we all, even the blind patient, kept at our task with an endless chain of buckets. Eventually we succeeded in so lowering the level of water in the hold that the fires could be relit and enough steam raised to drive the donkey pump. It was evident at last that the boat was leaking very little; and it subsequently turned out that the water we heard rushing in was pouring through the coal bunker lids, which were under water as she lay over on the rock. With increasing steam we were able to keep the foghorn going and to get the vessel running ahead while we worked. Suddenly, to our great joy, a large motor fishing boat with half a dozen old friends crossed our bow, having been attracted by the horn, and in less than an hour we were safely anchored between half a dozen schooners alongside our friend who had found us. He was known to us all as 'the King of the Dog Islands,' as for many years he had been regarded as the greatest fish-catcher among those dangerous shoals.

The internal economy of the Strathcona needed such drastic rearrangement that we were too busy that night to worry over what might have been. The fog held on and the chance of reaching St. Anthony in time for the opening of the hospital seemed small indeed. We were not leaking badly; and our only hope lay in putting out to sea and taking a risk. Everyone was willing to make the attempt, so with two motor boats to pilot us out, one on each bow, we wriggled out South again between the rocks, till we had a safe offing and a good clear course to steer. It was 'touch and go,' but the little boat never responded better; and having safely negotiated the northeast tip of Newfoundland, we crept alongshore on the Atlantic side and hobbled in to St. Anthony just before the Governor's arrival.

The excitement in the village was at its peak when next morning the warship anchored off our dock and we were given the standing orders for the day. Our company of Girl Guides, the most northerly in the world, was drawn up on the wharf under their able commander, to be reviewed by Lady Allardyce, who has been much interested, with her husband, in that movement in other parts of His Majesty's Dominions. The real spice of the review of all these 'troops' which the North could muster lay in the fact that His Excellency had once been Governor of the Falklands, and had himself bade good-bye to Admiral Sturdee just before he surprised and destroyed the German Pacific fleet there, and so helped to wipe out the sting to England's pride of the sinking of our own ships just previously.

Everything went well. As all the work of building and installing the equipment had been done by our own boys, we were justly proud when there was no short circuit when the lights were turned on, no leak or flooding in the plumbing, and from the moment when the front door was opened by His Excellency, no one found any flaw in any of the departments. The same day a large marble memorial to all our lads who had fallen in the War was unveiled. So beautiful a tablet, the gift of the Governor of Vermont, had never been seen by our people. When I turned back after the crowd had gone to have another look at it, I found a poor woman, mother of one of the boys who had laid down his life, silently weeping in front of it.

It is our custom each year in July to hold a memorial service on the cliff-top over the old hospital where Dr. John Little served so long. On two poles, the Flags of America and England are hauled up side by side, and then the simple service of prayer and praise is held under the open sky among the green trees, and a challenge given for all of us to profit by the memory of our friend and his ideals.

It occurred to me that it would be a help to our people to have an Admiral, who had sunk a large U-boat submarine from a fishing trawler with a little three-pounder gun when ordered to surrender, take part in the service, so when the moment came I called on him to offer the prayer. There was some slight delay before the Admiral got started, but then it was a real direct petition of a simple business-like sailor. It is not betraying any confidence to say that afterwards the Admiral told me he felt it harder to respond, when I suddenly called upon him, than if another big submarine had signalled him to come and be sunk!

It was also on this to us great occasion of the opening of our first fireproof and absolutely modern hospital by the Governor, that His Excellency told me he had received a cable from His Majesty the King, creating me a Knight Commander of the ancient Order of Saint Michael and Saint George. I had been told that in accepting any kind of a title of distinction, a dividing wall would be raised, like an international tariff, between myself and those by whom I wanted nothing better than to be considered as a brother. I have not found it so. We do not love Sir Lancelot any less for his title, or even Saint George for his even more ambitious sobriquet. Those are not the things which make or mar love. It is possible to query the value of hereditary titles, but for centuries our family have been Cornish folk, reared on Arthurian tales, and the atmosphere of the Round Table. It was as natural to accept the 'golden spurs' as it would have seemed both unpatriotic and snobbish to refuse so generous a recognition of our work by the Sovereign. As a matter of fact, it has greatly pleased our friends and our people; and if only as a testimonial to the wide knowledge and practical interest in our work on the part of one of the last of the hereditary monarchs of Europe, it will ever be the crown of the happy memories of that day, that our work was thought worthy of notice by the busy Sovereign of so vast an Empire.

A year or so later, out of the blue the morning mail brought me another undeserved temptation. It was to run as a candidate for the Lord Rectorship of Saint Andrew's, the oldest university in Scotland. In our home there was a picture which had always fascinated me. It was of a terribly religious-looking Scotch divine with a large Bible under his arm, gazing from the top of a sand-dune at two elders playing the Royal and Ancient Game on a Sunday, at Saint Andrew's. These temptable 'grown-ups,' and in Scotland at that, had often been a comfort in my moments of discouragement. This tiny link, which the picture made, had always endeared Saint Andrew's to me, though the sport, of which it is the shrine and mecca, had always in youth been too sedate a form of competition to be of much lure to me.

Anyhow, I 'fell for' this new temptation, in spite of the fact that the review of my qualifications for a rector convinced me that I was about as well fitted for it as for occupying the Papal throne. A timid inquiry as to what opponent I might expect to try to demolish settled the question. The heritage of a sporting spirit has not been silenced by the trammels of life in Labrador. My opponent was to be a peer of the realm, one of the widest known men of wealth, of action, and of philanthropy.

We have tried to make our credo, 'when two paths are open, always take the more venturesome,' so acknowledging my deep appreciation of the extraordinary honour conferred upon a Labrador general practitioner of medicine, I metaphorically forwarded my glove to be thrown into the arena, or the dunes, or Lord Melchett's back yard, or wherever the best people do throw those bouquets. Men of such great distinction as Sir James Barrie, Rudyard Kipling, Dr. Nansen, and a long line of that ilk, had been the occupants of this famous chair, and incidentally, of the actual cap and gown in which John Knox himself had first shed lustre on the office.

The ability of tomatoes to carry at least thirty per cent of their vitamines unharmed through the grilling of the canning process had long forced us in Labrador to appreciate their value. We had even had a tomato campaign and stored every year cases of them in tins for our child-welfare work, until we actually began to grow fresh ones under glass, convinced of their immense value, with cod-liver oil, for tuberculosis. An imposing letter which we received one morning revealed, however, a new service they had rendered. It informed me that I had won, by a majority of one hundred and fifty-six votes, and it was understood that overripe tomatoes had played an important part in the election, some wag hoping that I should consider it a red-letter day!

When the time came for the rectorial speech, I had not descended from the train before an avalanche, a cyclone, and a thunderstorm broke simultaneously over us and we were swept, with the Principal of the University and two representatives of the student body, into an ancient vehicle of transportation of early-Victorian vintage. The elements thereupon assumed the form of as healthy, handsome, and hilarious a crowd of youthful Highlanders as ever one could wish to see. In Labrador, the Eskimos long ago taught the settlers to harness up large dogs as motive power for the sledges; but in Saint Andrew's we discovered that it is still the custom for the students to harness themselves.

The opportunity thus to be seen driving round town with the Principal of the University reminded me vividly of a story President Hadley of Yale once told me. As he was walking down the road one day, a stranger in a dogcart stopped and offered to give him a lift. When the man had driven him to his destination by a very circuitous route, the President in thanking him asked why it was he had so kindly invited him.

'Well,' replied the stranger, 'you see, Mr. President, I owe a little money in this town.'

I wondered what would have been the effect in a Scotch town if I had needed credit!

Saint Andrew was a fisherman. He is the fishermen's saint, as well as the saint of this soundest of educational establishments, which has consistently regarded its challenge as being not merely to equip its students with up-to-date current information in all branches of learning, but primarily to send them into the world inspired men and women. It is not too much to say it has been a vital factor in maintaining all that Scotland stands for.

If the avalanche at the station overwhelmed my body, so I myself was overwhelmed by the consciousness of all that Saint Andrew's students had done for the world in the days gone by, so much so that it would have been invidious to name anyone in particular. Though a mere 'Sassenach,' I was whole-heartedly able to testify to what I had seen Scotchmen giving back to the great and needy world in its farthest-off outposts, so many of which it had been my privilege in life to visit. Truly, its alumni carry the spirit of their patron saint all over the world.

As long as the spirit of Saint Andrew's University is a guiding influence in that land, as long as Saint Andrew, the fishermen's saint, is also its real patron, no one need fear for what Scotland will continue to give the world in the days to come.

The recent magnificent improvements in the equipment and buildings of Saint Andrew's were but one more tribute to Sir James Irvine, Principal of the University, and a Fellow of the Royal Society because of his discoveries in research chemistry. These discoveries, however, had been just a side issue of his greater contributions to his day and generation through his directorship of this fine educational centre. That a great American philanthropist, Edward Harkness, should have contributed ten million dollars to be spent for Britain's benefit is remarkable in itself. That he should have chosen a Scotch University Principal to be one of the chief members of the very small administrative committee for spending the sum was in itself an indication of the well-merited esteem in which Sir James Irvine is held in the world today.

CHAPTER XXVII

SERVICE ON THE LABRADOR

BEFORE a worker comes to Labrador, we never ask him what creed he holds. I can know all that is necessary about that after he has worked on the Coast. There is no record of the Great Master asking Judas for his intellectual opinion before sending him out to preach the Gospel in service.

'Wop' is the name which the volunteers gave themselves, as a terse synonym for a worker willing to do anything, but not a past master at any particular job. It is a euphonious term, 'snappy' and modern.

Not a few of my critics have reminded me that a good many of our 'wops,' in common with the rest of humanity, have had faults. I wish someone would expend the same zeal in pointing out any human being who has not had any.

My first three 'wops' were English. One of these saved two people's lives by diving through the ice after them into the polar current, a service which nearly cost him his life. Both these lads worked hard and paid their own expenses to boot. They worked so well, indeed, that after a long winter, in spite of frost and snow, they had erected and started a steam lumber mill. After that, we did not even listen to our critics, feeling a little surer of our ground. The brother of our next 'wop' was an internationally known surgeon and had wintered on our Coast. He felt that in service for others lay his younger brother's only chance of breaking his bonds. No alcoholic beverage has ever been allowed in our work. We have difficulties enough without adding to them wittingly.

After three years of service on the Labrador Coast, this 'wop' returned to business a renewed man, except for the ineffaceable scars which the toxin of alcohol leaves. Others followed, so that our venture proved to be double-barrelled. Nervous breakdown patients, like those suffering from other forms of loss of the spirit's control over the body, responded also to the 'Labrador treatment.' One or two objected to our telling the local people of their ailments and so enlisting their help as well; but for us to be consistent that was necessary. Moreover, such candour called out valuable traits among the fishermen, who are always sympathetic.

One does not wish to convey the impression, however, that any appreciable percentage of volunteers who have been with us on the Coast have come because they felt they needed our help to master some difficulty in their lives. As a matter of fact, over fourteen hundred 'wops' have come 'down North,' while at least twice that number have had to be refused, with Labrador's grateful thanks, since we were unable to arrange for them.

These young men and young women have not despised any sort of work. They have come from every rank of society, the sons and daughters of millionaires coöperating with those who have worked their way to Labrador.

One of our nurses, when asked why she was leaving, replied quite simply, 'To earn more money in order to be able to volunteer again.' A teacher, in order to make her term of service possible, ran a private tea-shop which specialized in doughnuts; and she has remained eight years on the proceeds. To us, this seems incontrovertible evidence of the potential value of the humblest!

Many and varied have been the devices to which these young people have resorted in order to make their journey possible when the family exchequer has not been sufficiently elastic to do it for them. I particularly remember a young medical student who, when I asked him if he were going to be able to join us, said it depended on how many puppies his spaniel dog produced, as he was counting on the proceeds of the sale of these 'friends of all the world' for his journey!

Another young lady, who is on the Coast at the present moment, financed the help which she is giving to the Labrador by selling her charming paintings. She managed even in these days of depression (and I am writing in 1932) to sell enough to enable her to give us a year's voluntary service.

One is often asked, how ever we managed to persuade so many to join us when the world is in financial difficulties and there is no money remuneration to be expected. My answer is always that that in itself is the reason. If you tell the young people of today that the work is hard enough, and the circumstances of life are trying, and the food is not too good, and the journey North is apt to be terribly fatiguing, and the conditions of life are, for toughness, such as they have never experienced before, they will all jump at the chance to help. Whereas, if one were to offer them the job of rolling a perambulator down Commonwealth Avenue in Boston, even at a tempting rate of remuneration, they would be certain to refuse.

As I have recorded elsewhere, when I bought the little hospital steamer Strathcona II at Southampton, all my sceptical friends in England and in America as well told me, 'You will never be able to pay anybody to take that "rowboat" across the North Atlantic.' That might be perfectly true. But I had no intention of even trying to hire anybody, because I was certain that there were those who, perhaps, had no money to give, but could do that, and would want to do it without any payment; and such proved to be the case.

On another occasion, when in need of nurses, I went to the Massachusetts General Hospital, with many qualms as to what success I should have in luring them away from so attractive an environment. I told them the following story of one of their own nurses who had been serving with us on the Coast a year or so before.

One spring, a telegram came from a hamlet about sixty miles to the southward, asking me to come at once, as there was an outbreak in the village of a very fatal type of influenza. Unfortunately, I could not go, since I could not leave the hospital. However, one of my nurses offered to make the attempt, so we wired the village to send a team of dogs for her.

A fortnight later, an urgent telegram came from her asking for help. One of the fishermen, delirious from high fever, had escaped from his cottage in the night and gone down to his fish-stage. There he got hold of a fish-splitting knife, and, apparently finding no codfish available, had ripped himself up. (Oddly enough, he was known as a dexterous splitter.) Shortly after, sobered by his experience, he actually walked into the cottage where the nurse was, carrying his intestines, none of which he had injured with the knife.

Meantime, the rivers were all open and dog-team travel

had become impossible, while the sea-ice was so broken up that no one could make the journey from hospital to her by water. All one could do was to wire her simple directions, and urge her to 'do her best.' Six weeks later, we saw a long trap-boat forcing her way into the harbour, covered by a tent with a funnel through it, as if she were a small steamer. Out of it onto the ice climbed the nurse, followed by her patient, who was by that time on the road to recovery.

She told us that the priest had consented to help her operate, provided he gave the patient the Viaticum first. As soon as this last rite was administered, the little nurse produced the chloroform from her maternity kitbag. The good priest, who had never been present at an operation before, then gave the patient the anæsthetic, while the nurse, who, in her turn, had never performed an operation of any kind, washed out the abdominal cavity with buckets of boiled water, and having rearranged the insides the best she could, sewed the wound partially up to prevent infection. Her courage and ability, her meticulous care of the patient, together with his sound constitution, saved the man's life. He completely recovered, and that same autumn was fishing once again for the support of his family.

When I had finished recounting this story, half the nurses in the hospital wanted to go to Labrador on the next boat!

Another volunteer, though merely an undergraduate, seeing a dire need for some place in which to house our collection of derelict children, built a home at his own expense, and subsequently doubled the size of it when the need increased.

Yet another, a poor carpenter, came at his own expense all the way from Kentucky to teach us how to make looms and weaving apparatus in wood. It was just after the War, when carpenters were getting twelve to fourteen dollars a day. I had honestly never expected to see any carpenter, except Him of Galilee, make such a sacrifice willingly.

Another piece of work stands out in my mind for its high idealism. A boy had come to help me put up a small industrial centre at Seal Islands, in the middle of a group of very poor people. He was by no means a rich boy, and was rejoicing that he had been fortunate enough to secure a remunerative position for the early autumn, which he needed to help him

pay his way at the university. It was very late in the season
when I came back from the North that year, and on anchoring
in Rogues' Roost, as their harbour is called, was amazed to
find he had not gone home.

'I had not finished the job you gave me,' was his explanation. He was not being paid one penny, and he lost his post
in the States by staying so long on the Coast, but I am sure
that today he would be the first to say that he had been the
gainer by his devotion to his ideal.

Another 'wop' came and cooked for twenty-one workmen
all summer. He will, I know, forgive me for saying that we
had good reason afterwards to know that it was no special
addiction to the occupation of cooking that induced him to
give up a European trip for that experience.

Volunteers come for short or for long terms of service.
Often they have returned again and again, as they had the
time and funds. They have come from the United States,
Canada, and the British Isles, Newfoundland, from Australia
and New Zealand. They have included professors of exact
sciences, such as mathematics, surgeons, physicians and
specialists, engineers (one, a coloured skilled civil engineer
from Massachusetts Institute of Technology, came with two
white American college graduates), architects, lawyers, army
officers, librarians, industrial workers, teachers, nurses, and
'sub' and 'post' débutantes. Indeed, it would be easier to
begin at the other end, and list those, such as gangsters, boot-
leggers, or other social outlaws, as not being included in our
lists. To me, the members of this long procession of helpers
have always appeared as modern prototypes of the Canterbury Pilgrims.

As I think over the splendid help which this cross-section
of society has rendered us, I realize that it is impossible to
do justice to them by name. Perhaps that is exactly the
greatest service they could render us — the very fact that
they do not wish for any reparations or even recognition, and
instead that they have invariably insisted that they received
more than they gave.

The building of the big reservoir and laying the pipe lines
six feet deep in the rocky ground at St. Anthony for half a
mile, and the even more difficult construction of the water·

supply at Cartwright, amidst swamp, dense tuckamore above ground and roots, mud, conglomerate clay, and solid rock below ground, day after day, amidst hordes of mosquitoes and black flies, which do not even give you notice of their arrival, but charge with 'spears in rest' like mediæval knights, were both completed by 'wops' known to all of us, who successfully accomplished these and many other such 'sermons in stones.' Many buildings have been constructed, and innumerable vessels unloaded by them. On one occasion, a steamer brought us four hundred tons of coal. The skipper, who had no use for young 'missionaries,' told us we had three days to unload, and that there would be a heavy daily demurrage charge for delaying his steamer, adding, 'And I'm not giving any days on trust!' The boys determined to do it, even with their very imperfect tools; and much to the surprise of our friend the skipper, they 'put it over' with time to spare. However, they had not kept to eight or even twelve hours a day. I asked one rather delicate-looking 'wop' how he had kept awake.

'I didn't keep awake. I sat on the coal exactly under the derrick, and every time the bucket came down it hit me on the head, and I woke up and filled it, and then went to sleep again.'

This reminds me to say that they have carried their fine spirit home with them, and when I arrived once in Boston, the secretary, herself a 'woppess,' told me some Harvard boys who had been on the Coast had just finished painting the inside of the office, at a time when painters were getting twelve dollars a day.

From the alumni have come many of our directors. I shall never forget leaving Albert Gound, then a student from Bowdoin, anchored off an outside headland in the North Atlantic in a small open boat, with her only mast gone and no oars, while I went in and visited a sick man. When I returned, he had drifted away before the strong offshore breeze. He has repaid me by becoming Chairman of our New England Grenfell Association and by untold help both on the Coast and in Boston.

Then, too, all our friends know Ted Greene, whom we left when a volunteer from Amherst on the North Newfoundland

CONCRETE HOSPITAL AT ST. ANTHONY

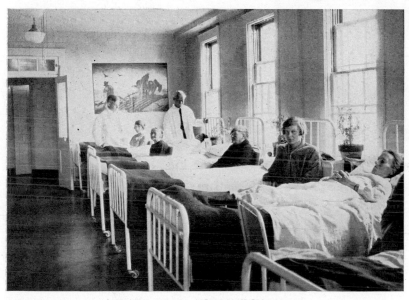

A WARD IN ST. ANTHONY HOSPITAL

coast, on the very island to which the survivors of the Viking escaped when the boat blew up in the ice-fields. Later, when he was one of the clergy at the famous Brick Church on Fifth Avenue and one of our most active directors on the International Grenfell Association, he came to Labrador to visit us on the Strathcona. We missed him by a few minutes at each rendezvous. Finally, we were obliged to leave him behind altogether. About this he made not even a mention until we discovered our terrible *faux pas;* which is only one of ten thousand little things that make one listen with more readiness to what such heroes say to us.

At Conche, a lonely little settlement on the northeast coast of Newfoundland, the nurse sent out there by the Grenfell Association lives in a room in the village. One day, at the beginning of winter, the nurse's attention was called to the plight of a man who was very ill — so ill that the nurse knew at once that the only thing that could possibly save him would be an operation. There was no doctor and no hospital nearer than St. Anthony, the headquarters of the Mission, over forty miles away. It was, at that time, impossible to reach St. Anthony by sea; and the journey by land, over high hills and across dreary stretches of snow and ice, seemed almost as impracticable. However, a 'woman box' was speedily ready, a willing band of men volunteered to draw the sledge, as it was too much of an undertaking for a dog-team, and the party set off.

The journey took five and a half days, the nurse tending the sick man whenever they stopped to take rest. Through cold, hardship, and danger the patient was brought safe and alive to St. Anthony Hospital. An operation was performed immediately and the life of that man was saved.

The thought of the return journey worried the nurse not a little. It happened that the owner of an aeroplane was in St. Anthony that day, on work connected with the seal fishery, and, hearing the story of the sick man who had been brought from Conche, he sought out the plucky little nurse and offered to take her back by air. She sent a wire to her people at Conche and, when she arrived back, it was to find all the inhabitants assembled in prayer, in the open, awaiting the return of their nurse from the sky. Her return journey had taken twenty minutes.

The 'wops' at the home end of the line also have been of immense help. They have organized sales, given lantern lectures, brought out Northern students for education, and brought in new 'wops.' Harvard, Yale, and Princeton now have their own Grenfell Alumni Associations. Boys from Yale financed, built, and support Yale School, at North-West River. Princeton boys are helping us in the same way at St. Mary's. Harvard boys have undertaken to raise the expenses of the Strathcona. That university even furnished us again last summer with a volunteer cook, a man of marvellous application and undiscourageable perseverance. We gave him his 'H' for cooking. It is a real risk to have a volunteer cook, especially when one asks him in the galley if he is cooking anything for dinner, and he replies, 'This galley is not a place for cooking. It is a place for opening tins.'

Farmington School is forever endeared to us for having given us a sailoress secretary, who is 'never never sick at sea,' and is a member of our family — Miss Eleanor Cushman, of New Bedford whaling ancestry. She is better known and loved as 'the Sphinx,' a sobriquet acquired, as she rarely stops talking! She never stops working either, and the debt which we and Labrador owe her can never be repaid.

Miss Mary Hillard and Westover School have given us magnificent helpers and help. To mention one thing only, if one were to call at many small Labrador settlements in summer, one might suppose Westover had come down in a body, so many of the young girls of the village having earned discarded uniforms of that school, in such excellent repair that the great puzzle to the recipients has always been how it is we came by them.

One famous athlete, who wore out his nether garments working on the pipe-line excavation, had to purchase some 'shorts' at the clothing store. To our great amusement, he came back with a pair of his own, which apparently his mother had included in a donation!

The Ward Belmont School in Tennessee, at Nashville, the town where Lady Grenfell's father lived and from which he went out to fight in the Civil War, sends us every year the salary of the occupational therapist. The Emma Willard School of Troy, New York, gives us the expenses of the head of the Orphanage. Several alumni keep small branches going in their neighbourhood. Two 'wops' at least have been artists, and have greatly helped us with designs, Christmas cards, and pictures.

Three of our 'wops' have brought us meritorious fame by taking part in the Byrd South Pole Expedition, Norman Vaughan and Edward Goodale driving dogs, and taking some of our Huskies, which they had driven in the North. Indeed, we were honoured by the leading dog being named 'Sir Wilfred.' Dr. Hilton Willcox went as deckhand, and in the terrible, mountainous seas south of Magellan, also carried the torch high by proving to be a fearless 'yardarm reefer' in a gale.

One of our local clergymen, who was leaving the Labrador for Japan, relieved us of a tiny new-born baby, whose mother, an Eskimo, had wandered South into one of our hospitals to die all alone in giving birth to her baby. Eskimos are Japanese or Mongolian, and when later our friend sent me a coloured photograph of the baby at five years of age in a kimono and swinging an umbrella, none of us but would have dubbed her a veritable daughter of the Land of the Rising Sun.

Many good 'woppesses' have done splendid work in child welfare, in teaching in almost every branch of work along our Coast. One has, after many summers' service, built a school of her own, and almost reared the whole colony of children of the village, she herself being a Professor and a Ph.D. Another lady came several summers to teach organized games. Another came to be a village story-teller to get people interested in taking out books from our travelling and stationary libraries.

One of our oldest and dearest friends, Miss Harriot Houghteling, married Dr. Charles Curtis, so we have her permanently on the Coast, where her presence is a bonanza. Education has been one of her chief interests; and she has added to the school, brought special teachers, provided outfit and wherewithal to teach domestic science, food preservation, and other invaluable activities.

Another volunteer, Miss Dorothy Stirling, built a most beautiful cottage which has been of great use to us ever since.

She also gave to the Grenfell Association a wonderful root cellar costing two thousand dollars, to protect all the vegetables which we must store through our winters, as well as contributing generously in money and time to numerous other activities of our work. She is still acting as voluntary head of the Chicago Grenfell Association. Another volunteer, at her own expense kept a nurse at a new nursing station, while the local people provided the nurse's board and lodging. Being a Roman Catholic village, this splendid little nurse was imported direct from Dublin and did no end of good work.

Year after year, 'woppesses' have been carrying the industrial shops with very great profit to that branch of the Labrador activities and have been doing the business and office work, and the daily round of the clothing department. Several adventuresome volunteers have commandeered trucks and driven about to various resorts in the United States, holding sales. This has been done for four summers, and one winter trip through Florida.

Long service consecutively is always hard to secure. Some seem to find the Northern climate difficult to contend with for protracted periods. Miss Murray, Miss Criswell, Miss Carlson, Miss Helen Smith have each been on the Coast to the great profit of the fishermen for many years. Miss Frances Baier, Miss Macleod, Miss Bateman, and other fine teachers have raised our chief school at St. Anthony to a position where it has been recognized by the Government of Newfoundland as offering the highest educational standards. Miss Luther, Miss Laura Young, Miss Catherine Cleveland, and Miss Pressley-Smith have a continuing memorial to their service in our fine Industrial Department.

Several of our former volunteers have joined our home offices as members of our permanent staff. Chief among these is Miss Katie Spalding, who gave us ten years of entirely voluntary service on the Labrador as head of our largest orphanage — a task so exhausting to nerves and patience that only a person with the unselfishness, the devotion, the high order of intelligence, and the saving sense of humour of Miss Spalding could possibly have coped with it for so long. When the need for opening a separate office of the International Grenfell Association in London became imperative, we realized that, in order to make this venture a success, we needed Miss Spalding vitally at that post. We asked her, therefore, if she would be willing to substitute for her work among the children on the Coast this more prosaic task of fostering a continuous progressive interest, on behalf of the Labrador fishermen, among the people of the British Isles. It was a sacrifice to ask of her, but she stepped into that breach without a murmur. For years now, she has been the volunteer head of the Grenfell Association of Great Britain and Ireland. Thanks in large measure to her, that Association has been of increasing value to the fishermen and children of the North, whom she has loved and helped for twenty years.

Our Ottawa, Boston, and New York offices all have as their guiding spirits former workers on the Coast. We always say with pardonable pride that the strongest credential of the Labrador work is the fact that its keenest protagonists are those who have the most intimate knowledge of it.

Dr. Joseph Andrews, the famous surgeon who for eighteen years came North each summer at his own expense and gave sight to more blind than are recorded in the Four Gospels, now sleeps near his beautiful California home. We like to feel that his spirit, like that of Dr. John Little, is still among the simple fishermen whom he served. It is good to remember how Dr. Andrews told us that the happiest moment of the year was that in which he received a wire from me, saying, 'The winter ice is breaking up. You can start for the Coast.'

Neither the Labrador nor I can ever hope to repay the debt which we owe to such men as Dr. Charles Curtis, whose unselfishness, high abilities, and courage in the face of the ever-recurrent problems of our biggest and most important station are beyond praise; or of Dr. Harry Paddon, whose years of untiring devotion to his most northerly section of our work at Indian Harbour and North-West River speak for themselves. The fruits of their labours, which these men see today in their districts, must be some compensation to them for the undoubted sacrifices which their lives have called for.

We rejoice that Dr. Moret, our splendid colleague at St. Mary's River, who has built up that district with the help of the Princeton boys, has this year joined forces with another of our much-loved volunteers, Miss Charlotte Cheston, who had given several summers' service on the Coast in the Industrial Department.

We sincerely miss the presence on the Coast of Mr. and Mrs. Blackburn, whose devoted services and many-sided abilities will never be forgotten in St. Anthony. It is safe to say that no one can quite fill Mrs. Blackburn's place in the hearts of the women of St. Anthony.

The loss of Varick Frissell by the explosion in the S.S. Viking, which was sunk and burned in the ice-fields, was a splendid tribute to the wop spirit. Himself a lover of his fellow men, he had helped us in a thousand ways during many years. To him we owe the Yale School at North-West River, and no small portion of the dam and water-supply at St. Anthony. He took the first moving pictures of the marvelous Grand Falls of Labrador; and also became a member of our Council. On one occasion he had driven us all over New Mexico, Arizona, Colorado, and from San Diego to Portland, Oregon. As he was driving back alone, a Mexican revolution having broken out, he secured passes from both sides in order to get pictures. He was stopped by a dozen uniformed men ten miles over the line and, showing the wrong pass, he was arrested. The soldiers crowded into the car and ordered him to drive, when without a moment's hesitation he carried them over the International line into the United States, where all were interned.

His last work was to make a film which would go out all over the world to show the public some of the hardships of our people's lives. In the spring of 1931, in the sealing steamer Viking, he was finishing the film; when one Sunday night, far out in the ice-fields off North Newfoundland, the magazine blew up, and Varick Frissell was never seen again. His dog, a large Newfoundland, always slept on his bed and used to kiss him good-night. It had accompanied him on all his journeys. When the explosion occurred, it was lying between his feet under the table. Apparently it was not killed, but some of the rescued reported that the dog was presumably unable to live without his master, for they heard it sending up a last lament, as the ship was burning.

Varick's gentle unselfishness and unstinting work for others has left behind him its lasting inspiration.

After the explosion Varick Frissell's companion, Henry Sargent, found himself, half-clad, lying in the darkness on the ice, the ship in flames. Injured men were lying all about him. From the wreckage spread around he rescued some clothing, a little food, a few pieces of the doomed ship's timber (some of it on fire), and a dozen or so matches. He himself was partially shocked, having been blown through the stern of the ship. All night and all the next day and the following night he drove out to sea on the ice-pan with his two injured men, whom he covered and cared for as best he could. At one time the mass of the floe jammed against the island five miles outside the great Cape. He did not try to save his own life by escaping to the land, but stood by his injured comrades. On the third day, when they were rescued, one of the poor fellows had gone mad, and later died. The other man lost his legs owing to severe frost-burns.

After the ship was blown up on that fateful Sunday evening, one of the master watches found himself on the ice. All his group were soon struggling to reach some islands a few miles distant. He was one of the group which, having placed two badly injured men in the shattered remains of a dory, were trying to drag them over very heavily rafted ice, to safety. The old boat broke up. Progress was impossible. All but the master watch determined to make for land over the ice, regardless of the wounded. He decided to stand by the stricken men, though the ice-field was driving out to sea away from the islands.

Next afternoon, a searching party sent out from the islands sighted them. A gallant attempt to rescue was made, but failed. Realizing the hopelessness of their situation, the rescuers strongly urged the heroic man to accompany them at least to temporary safety during the night, confident as they were that he could never save his comrades. He only replied, 'At least I can die with them.' England gave this splendid fisherman its highest reward for courage, the Albert Medal.

That same night, the steamer Beothic nosed in toward the land and sighted a man moving up and down on the ice. Though they were unable to reach him, they put a dory with two lanterns on a large ice-pan to help give him courage to hold out. When dawn broke, the master watch, having secured the dory with its beacon lights and put his wounded men in it, managed to bring them at last to safety.

For many years, it has been the custom of the volunteers in New York, Boston, and Philadelphia to hold, in the spring, reunion dinners of all our alumni. The entertainments provided at these festivities are many and varied. If it were not for Lady Grenfell and the Alumni Association officers, it would be impossible to remember the names of all the friends who share a common bond — the spirit of the lure of the Labrador.

Through the enthusiasm evoked at one of these dinners in New York, there was formed one of the strongest links in the chain which binds the Coast to the rest of the world — the Grenfell Alumni Association. A similar enterprise is just starting in England. In it all workers share in carrying on the message which they claim they learned on the Coast. To the capable hands of Dr. Theodore L. Badger, one time wop and medical assistant on the Strathcona, was entrusted the presidency. He has greatly added to the debts which Labrador owes to him by the strengthening of home ties. His contagious good-will is characteristic of all our volunteers — shall we call it 'E Pluribus Unum'?

The work of the Industrial Department has been helped enormously by years of volunteer work given by Miss Margaret Peirce. The splendid success of the shop for the sale of Labrador products in Locust Street, Philadelphia, is entirely due to her. Labrador women and children owe her a debt they never can repay.

Every branch of the work owes our dear friends Miss Emily Fowler and Mrs. Anderson Fowler gratitude for work extending over years, while to Lady Grenfell and me their devoted friendship means more than we can express. When the late Dr. Louis Stimson gave us his trans-Atlantic racing yacht, the Fleur-de-Lys, for hospital work, Mrs. Fowler came North in her, brought her doctor son, a specialist on throat work, and gave a whole season of free service to Labrador.

No more true and constant friend of any mission enterprise do we know than Mr. George Williams, of Farmington, who has visited Labrador every summer over a period of fifteen years. A sportsman, he has in his own yachts, one of which he freely presented to our work, visited every fjord in Labrador, has fished in its principal rivers, and is known as a friend and lover of all in trouble from Cape Chidley to Bonne Bay. Many a fisherman today thinks this good friend missed his vocation — 'Sure, Sir, that man should have been a fisherman.'

Once when starting for a lecture tour in England, I knew that the cost of a chauffeur and a lanternist would diminish greatly the net gain to the funds of the work. A young student of the University of Pennsylvania, Mr. Herbert Threldkeld-Edwards, who had been a volunteer on the Coast, offered his services free of expense. He drove us all over the United Kingdom. He never let us down once in his self-imposed task, and having paid his own expenses, took off his hat and said, 'Thank you'! He, like numbers of our other wops, has since seen service on our Board of Directors.

Some of our best volunteer service has still to be mentioned, however. No service has been done at more personal sacrifice than that of the 'wops,' who have come on road-making, building, driving water-supplies, building wharves, and erecting dams. When I have landed, where a crew has been working at those most exacting physical jobs in heavy boulder clays, through dense old forest roots, beset by mosquitoes and black flies innumerable, I have literally taken off my hat because I felt I was upon holy ground. I can still see the Professor of Higher Mathematics at Princeton, Professor Gillespie, stripped to the waist, directing the present head of the department of religious literature of Charles Scribner's Sons, another Princetonian, William Savage, now chairman of our invaluable executive committee, how really to get down through blue clay and gravel that had nearly become rock since it was deposited. With his 'crew,' as did Hanson Baldwin, ex-naval officer, and Bevan Pumphrey and his crowd next year, on the water-supply at Cartwright he preached a sermon in idealism and the absolute naturalness of Christian personal service and gave point to the conventional homilies that should send home to every preacher a new view of what real modernism in constructive theology stands for.

Service like this is a letting loose of the water of life itself, in the unmistakable, uncriticizable, unsectarian way in which that tap must be turned on, in deeds of love that cost the donor personal, unselfish labour, if ever it is to confer on them the joys that the new understanding of life gives, and on the recipients the assurance that the words from any pulpit anywhere, however sincere and orthodox and emotional, are any more than 'hot air.'

All our architect work has been volunteer, and the President of the Institute of Architects of America and a member of the Legion of Honour of Paris, who also has been on our Coast and on our board, is the guilty party — Mr. William A. Delano. All our marine work, and it is far from insignificant, and also our law advice ashore, have been freely given, also by well-known men, members of our Council.

Our bankers, what shall I say of them? Like every other of the services rendered, from the giving of the widow's mite to the investing and watching the funds, the responsibility of which has been entrusted by confiding friends everywhere, as their volunteer services for this work the services of the bankers are absolutely basal. All these services are of God, and to our voluntary bankers' professional services must be added hospitality, accommodation, and invaluable advice, all freely given.

I could wish that any reader of this volume whose heart is anxious for the future of our civilization, who in the dark clouds of today finds fears and discouragements for the coming of the Kingdom of God tomorrow, would read this chapter. If he still has any doubts that the spirit of Christ lives in our own environment today as much as ever it did in Galilee of old, let him write personally to me for information on any point that I can make its message clearer.

If this chapter should be read by any of my loyal helpers who fail to find in it a *personal* recognition of the debt we owe them, they must realize that these friends who are mentioned specifically are meant also as vicarious symbols, to stand for all those who have enabled me to carry each successive year what we hope is a fuller message of love to the people of the North. No one can have a keener realization than I, that, whereas the credit has come to me, but for my splendid colleagues and helpers on the Coast and off it, our work would have died of inanition years ago.

CHAPTER XXVIII

SALAAM

IT IS not unnatural to expect anyone approaching a summit to see farther over the horizon. As the end draws near, it is easier, also, to speak freely; while the truth told by grey hairs does not hurt nearly so much and the motives for speaking at all are not wrongly construed.

The word 'religion,' before Christ's day, meant collecting, or binding together. Even then it was used loosely about men's relations to the gods. After Christ's time it began definitely to connote the relation of man with God. So, as I analyze it today, a man's religion means the way in which he is related or tied to God. Moreover, looking back from my hill-top, I see more clearly that the value of a man's religion must be measured by what it has enabled him to do.

At one time, many friends told me to be sure and read Harold Begbie's 'Broken Earthenware,' and later, 'God in the Slums.' Both of these I did read with pleasure and profit. All the same, the chief reaction in my mind was, that regularly through the years I had seen exactly the same results of religion in experience; and I wondered whether the great interest in those books was a confession that such results were rare and unexpected. Are most of us so-called religious people really 'religious'— men bound to God — in any practical way?

Does this relationship, which has so marvellous a presumption as 'bound to God,' really mean the making of new men out of old ones? If so, it surely must not be necessary to go to books to find out about it. That kind of religion would be of such untold value to the individual, the home, the state, the world, that you would not be able to prevent every sane normal human being from wanting it and working to obtain it. If it does not make new men out of old, by all means scrap-heap it, and let us find something that does.

When the Kickapoo Indians came to our town with a band on the roof of their large wagon, a crowd at once gathered around them. Soon individuals like ourselves, except that they had swallowed Kickapoo pills or rubbed in Kickapoo oil, began to come out of the wagon, to throw away their crutches, and to walk off home, waving us good-bye. Nearly every man in town who was lame went and paid quite a lot to give that organization a 'try-out,' at any rate. Later on, many had to buy new crutches, but they had tried out the system.

The shelves full of patent remedies that an unfortunate druggist has to carry in stock in these days testify to the fact that men will always be interested in anything that they believe 'does things.'

Why is it that the very term 'religious life' has come to voice the popular idea that religion is altogether divorced from ordinary life? That conception is the exact opposite of Christ's teaching. The all-too-general idea is that religion has something to do with dying and the next world, but little bearing on business or pleasure in this. If religion is primarily a personal insurance ticket, which, by the way, does not even provide for those whom a man leaves behind, one would not expect much real interest in it, especially on the part of youth.

It has been my experience to be lost in a Canadian forest in stormy weather when I could not see any heavenly bodies to guide me. I have been adrift in an open motor boat on the ocean when I had carelessly left my compass at home. Thick fog came on and a field of heavy floe ice drove around my boat. I dared not move in any direction, for I might be going farther from safety. It was hours before I caught sight of the sun and so got the direction to steer. I have driven, in the dark of night, onto the rocky cliffs near Cape Bauld, which stick out into the Atlantic Ocean at the extreme northern end of Newfoundland, where the waters of the Gulf, meeting the polar current, made a most uncomfortable seaway for the broken-down motor boat I was in. A passing schooner failed to see us and left us behind. At the last minute, a young Canadian volunteer in my boat made the engine go and gave us the power without which we were lost.

I do not admit that I am an unusual fool or weakling, but my diary records are full of such physical experiences, which, even as I write, overwhelm me with proof of my own dependency through life on power and guidance outside myself in mere material matters. In a northeast gale on North Labrador I had once decided to run for a harbour called Boulter's Rock. The fog which had fallen since I left the last port had shut it entirely from sight, but the rising sea and approaching night, in that section of Coast with no lighthouse, many rocks, and none too reliable a chart, made it our best chance. We had picked up a rock which I knew and were heading for the narrow entrance when I thought I perceived the seas breaking heavily clean across the harbour mouth. What to do to save the ship I did not know when an old Newfoundland fisherman who was on the bridge with me said, 'There's an entrance not much wider than a ship under your lee. It's perfectly safe if you strike it. But you'll have to put your helm hard up instantly.' 'You take the wheel,' I said. It seemed a big venture. But he did it. I could not have saved the ship alone.

Let me give one more instance. In my little steamer I had picked up a sinking Banking schooner with twenty-three men aboard, somebodies' husbands and sons. They were pumping seven thousand strokes an hour day and night, just to keep the hull afloat. Heavy seas made it very dangerous to try to ride out the night where we were. Outside us were reefs we could not see, so that we dared not stand out from the land to get sea-room, nor could we tow her in to the land, which was totally invisible, for with that big vessel in tow, we should not be able to turn quickly enough when the cliffs were close enough for us to see them.

I ordered out a boat from each ship in the fog to try to find where we were. An hour went by. The darkness was increasing. The seas grew heavier. We became very anxious for our boats, which had disappeared instantly into the fog. There is a groove worn right into the rim of the deck-house roof by the wire which pulls our foghorn open, as a result of ceaseless blowing for those boats. At last we heard voices, and almost alongside, on the crest of a big roller, loomed up the dory with her four men in shiny oilskins rowing in perfect time, as if they were on the Thames in a racing shell. They had found an island they knew, and their cheery voices brought just what religion does when it binds man to God —

guidance, power, and joy. An hour later we lay at anchor under the shadow of a whaling station.

The tough old shell-back skipper of the Banker came aboard. 'Did you know where you were going all that time?' he asked. 'Hadn't the faintest notion. Only trying to keep her offshore.' 'I'll say you're some navigator,' he rejoined. 'You wouldn't if you knew,' had to be my reply.

Analogy is no argument, but this is true of things unseen. To say that this is what religion has meant to me may seem a negation of that very humility which is the primary essential of religion. We all lose sight of the guide and show the white feather sometimes; but what I want to insist is, that, just because we all require guidance and strength, we all need to be bound to God.

A great many of my friends have told me that emotionalism biasses judgment. They regard any such experience as that which the Bible calls 'conversion' as unworthy of a man of science. That has not seemed to me altogether fair. For the only one of the Apostles who experienced anything of the kind, so far as we know, was the most highly educated and most scientific of them all. To me it means as brave a voluntary act as a man is capable of. David speaks of men being converted. So do the great old Prophets like Isaiah. So does Christ Himself. But they never prescribed any particular process necessary for that step which binds men to God. For in this, too, one man's meat is another's poison. That is part of the price and of the glory of our individuality.

Of one thing I am convinced. Religion is the reverse of any one, cubby-holed experience. If I am not religious in the way I eat and drink, and in the way I deal with my wife, or my crew, or my students, or my customers, as the case may be, the fact that I accept all the theology ever taught does not make me so. About religious life, divorced from common sense, I believe, as Betsey Prig did about Mrs. 'Arris, 'There ain't no sich person.' How each individual keeps touch with God, I consider it impertinent on the part of any other individual to criticize. Only Christ, so far, has proved the right to say, 'Follow Me.'

I have known people who would have been saved a lot of trouble if they had had a sense of humour. A man like Will

Rogers has a real value in life. He is helping the man who
reads the papers to cultivate that saving sense. Many men
today are honestly worried because everybody does not agree
with them. Men are learning very slowly that you cannot
force even your wife to agree with you. In time, even the
infallible will see the humour of being concerned about another
man's relationship to God because he does not agree with all
their opinions, or has not 'had to go through' the same experiences to secure that companionship of the invisible Friend
and Guide which all men need. Some of us have to join a
Rotary Club or a modern Civic Club to learn how to make
any friends. As I am one of them, Rotarians will understand
that I am casting no reflection on compulsory lunches. There
is a story of an elderly bank president who joined that organization. One old member put his hand on the banker's shoulder, when, somewhat shyly, he entered the room for his first
lunch, and said, 'So glad to see you, Ted.' Ted! He had not
been called 'Ted' for forty years: — and a tear rolled down
the cheek of that 'soft-hearted old hard-shell.' No doubt
the very story shocks some people who read this. To them,
the foundations of society would be threatened by such habits.
I am inclined myself to agree that they might be, and also
that possibly we might benefit by the process. Though I am
a perfectly orthodox practitioner, I have known osteopaths
and bone-setters help to make new men out of old, sometimes.
No consulting surgeon claims to know it all. Healers of the
body know that they are not infallible, whatever others
claim to be. As I analyze experience, I would say that humility is one of the most attractive, and therefore most powerful, assets in making new men out of old ones. Obviously it is
an absolute essential of being bound to God.

In 1887, when first as a youngster from hospital I went to
the North Sea for a cruise among the deep-sea fishermen, I
knew that they were far finer sailors than I, far older and
tougher and more experienced. On the wheel of the ship was
engraved, 'Follow Me.' That was a real challenge, and I
have never since heard any other as striking. It went on,
'and I will make you fishers of men.' I knew then perfectly
well that that was my only chance anyhow; I know now that
no man can deny the truth of it. One brass wheel at least

with that inscription on it lies at the bottom of the Atlantic today, preaching to the fishes, like Saint Francis.

A few years later, when I was fitting out a ketch in Yarmouth, England, to sail around South Ireland and Greenland, to see if I could be of any service to the fishermen of the polar waters, I realized the conceit of a little general practitioner of medicine, and wondered what I should do. The best authority on such a subject that I knew was my mother. From the hilltop of her life, bound to God if ever a human being was, my mother wrote to me. 'Read Psalm one hundred and forty-three, verse ten, in the Prayer Book version.' I can still remember hurrying off to look up what David had to say about it. It read, 'Teach me to do today the thing that pleases Thee.' That was all there was to it, but I knew that a man had to be bound to God to do that.

Let me say that, in proportion as that is done, there are no divorces. We in Labrador have to come to the great centres of civilization to learn most things, but we can give civilization that, and they can try it out safely. Divorces are not a necessary corollary of modern life. It is also a certain cure for graft in Governments. That is worth thinking over. As for war — England gave a knighthood to the first man who wrote a book to show that very thing. We know absolutely now that war hurts every participant alike. Yet we still try to cure these evils by the ways which have always failed.

I once asked two of the best-known surgeons in the world what was the secret that brought hundreds of doctors from all over the earth, when they were themselves in need of help, to a village in a 'woolly western' State to get it. One reason was my friends' plain common sense. They went everywhere, studying what methods really made new men, and when they found anything that seemed helpful, they tried it out, and if it worked better for the patient than their own old ones, they threw the old methods out of the window. What a lot of time would be saved, now wasted in criticizing and arguing about methods, what strength and money would be released for better work, instead of being dissipated in bolstering up outworn 'religious' institutions and superstitions, if that plan were followed. There is nothing new about this.

There is no new way to judge the value of 'religion' any more than if it were the value of surgery or navigation. The only gauge is what it does. There is only one description of the Day of Judgment in the Bible, and Christ Himself drew the picture. Everyone was judged by his record.

A friend, while earning his living in Pittsburgh, opened a room in a factory district for services on Sundays. A crowd of operatives smashed the windows and wrecked the place. The police arrested some rioters, but, of course, my friend would not prosecute. Instead, he asked them why they did it.

'We aren't going to have you dead-beat a living out of the superstitions of our women and children.'

'But I don't get one cent for it. I merely thought it would be of help to you. If you don't need it, let's close it by all means. You do need education, however, and I'll hold a night school instead, if you like.'

Twenty-two men turned up the next night. Does it surprise anyone to learn that a little later twenty-two men were coming together on Sundays to ask God's help in their difficulties? The value and power of this venture with God is measured absolutely by how closely we tie up with Him. The testimony of their bitterest enemies to such men as ignorant John and fallible Peter was that 'they had turned the world upside down.' They put in everything they had *usque ad mortem.*

From the hill I can look back on absolute proofs of this theorem, babes and sucklings though we may be. I would add that those who have 'passed on' have only begun their influence. Carpenters and fishermen, like kings and presidents, human beings from every rank of life, still live. I do not call King David dead, or President Lincoln. I know that Livingstone and Gordon and Kingsley and my mother influence me now; and more than one 'highbrow' has told me that he got more help from an hour in a fisherman's cottage with one of those apostles of today, in duffle trousers and skin boots, than in many a big cathedral.

There is a tiny cottage at Fox Harbour in Labrador, built of logs and rough-hewn lumber. The owner could not read or write, nor did he ever have a bank account. But he was brave and honest, and he has helped to turn more than one old man into a new one. We called him 'Uncle George.' I have told his story. He still lives to us who knew him. I never go by that harbour but I thank God for 'Uncle George,' who was 'bound to God.' It is only what we put into life, or entrust to God, that He keeps for us. That is the true measure of real religion — namely, that part of life which we willingly bind to God. My failures have not been due to intellectual difficulties, but just plain unreadiness to pay the cost of following — and I believe the same is true of other men.

In Labrador we ought, in our isolation, to be able to trace causes of and reasons for events easily. Personally, however, I have long since ceased to deny things just because I could not explain them. Most 'whys' are hard to answer, anyhow, and the very first is, 'Why are we put on earth?' Is life a senseless tragedy? I know only one answer that satisfies. 'Yes. It is a senseless, cruel tragedy to a sentient, conscious mind, if there is nothing in man's being "bound to God."' But if he is, the 'why' is obvious and absolutely intelligible. It is that we are needed to make the world better. God cannot do it without us. We are not robots in an aimless drama. We are pawns on a board, but we can coöperate with the master mind of the Player, can ourselves help Him to win out. Nay, more. We are knights on a field of honour. The King Himself cannot win His battle without us, He having entrusted us with the task, ensuring victory if we 'are bound to Him.' I see no shame in admitting that this is a venture of just plain faith. So did the writers of the Bible, and so did Christ Himself. Do not forget that everything in life must always be a venture of faith, from eating breakfast to going to bed at night. It would be silly to sit up all night because you cannot be *sure* of waking.

From the hill-top of life I am trying to say that faith, 'reason grown courageous' as someone has called it, has become assurance, not because the fight is easy and we are never worsted, but because it has made life infinitely worth while, so that I want all I can get of it, every hour here, and all I can get hereafter, on the same terms. Oddly enough, this is the best proof to my mind that continuing life will be given me. None of our intuitive, reasonable longings go unsatisfied.

When the statement was made that faith could remove

mountains, it seemed unreasonable to those who did not be-
lieve it, and had no experience of it; but now we can see
through mountains, and talk through mountains; and the
'invincible' strongholds of unfaith — the nature of matter
itself, the validity of the Newtonian teachings, even whether
the mountains exist or do not — are acknowledged to be matters of faith, after all.

Many times on a Sunday morning I have looked over the
congregation in church and wondered why they spent time
and money on religion. Last Sunday, passing through a
hamlet at the hour of service, we stopped to join. This is a
habit which we both formed in childhood, thank God, and
our parents. This morning there were twenty persons between us and the clergyman, and eighteen of those twenty
were women. It was a fine morning, and we had noticed that
the golf links were crowded with men as we passed. That is
not an uncommon experience. I love to remember that Charles
Kingsley was a kinsman, if only for the common-sense apologies which he made for rest of body and mind on Sunday
which might have to take the form of golf — only it was
cricket with him on the Sands of Dee — even if it kept people
from coming to his church. I fell to wondering why those
eighteen were all women. Were the men on the golf links
wise and the women in church foolish? If so, why do we not
close up these sources of expense in these times of stringency?
Would not the country be better without them? My profession has led me to know a good many mothers, and there is a
deeper truth in 'What Every Woman Knows' than perhaps
even Sir James Barrie thought of when he wrote that clever
and wise play.

Russia has adopted the alternative. She has thrown out
and destroyed the churches. Our forefathers may have been
conventional, relics of a 'stuffy' Victorian era. Someone said
to Sandy, 'We feed oats to cattle. It is only in Scotland that
you feed them to men any longer.' Sandy looked the stranger
well up and down, drew himself up to his six feet two inches,
and replied, 'Aye, mon, but look at the men!'

Have we any need to be ashamed of those who made us and
our country? Good things in this world all seem to need
organization, from a football match to an oil company, if

the human element in them is to be efficient. Organized methods for helping us to love our neighbour are all human and fallible, but on that account they surely need our help rather than our criticism.

From a Labrador viewpoint, the women are altogether right. Judging from international efforts to improve conditions for the downtrodden, and so getting better coöperation between men, one finds that such organizations as the Red Cross, needlework guilds, or any societies for making new conditions and new men through love, owe more to churches and to women than do any other agencies. It would be ungrateful in the extreme on my part were I not to bear testimony to them from this last lap. When Mammie took in the missionary box to her master at the dinner table, he put in fifty cents. She expected more and showed it. She had given many times as much herself. 'I don't like your way of organizing, Mammie. I like to give freely just what I have to God.' Next day at dinner there was one cold potato, a few bones and remnants. When asked for an explanation, Mammie said, 'I knows, Massa, you don't like organizing, so I jes' done give you what I had, freely.'

I cannot hope to repay the debts which I owe to men either, but my considered opinion goes all with the women in their vision of values and their selfless sacrifices in life. Even a presumably increasingly intelligent electorate seems to be more and more of that persuasion.

'But what about sectarian churches?' I am often asked. Are they not only another testimony to our glorious individuality? Harvard does not necessarily hate Yale, or Oxford Cambridge, because they think they have some superiority over them, and occasionally try to show them so. Physical rivalry is a healthy stimulus to physical prowess. It is practically essential. When first we started football in Labrador, our 'unco guid' folk would not play a match without a previous agreement that neither side should win. That would be leading men into temptation. I have umpired in the early days, and have had, after allowing a goal, to wait until the other side solemnly walked down the field and kicked one to even up. From the first Sunday School which I ever entered, I was dismissed for teaching my class temperance and respect with boxing-gloves, which is the way, I think, that God teaches most of us. Every Christian, to my mind, need not be a sport, but he must be a good sportsman. That is an essential of any man 'bound to God.' To carry our analogy over, perhaps friendly spiritual rivalry is a stimulus to spiritual progress.

What of the future? Periods of prosperity and depression seem inherent in all human affairs. We are studying now the cyclic increase and diminution in fur-bearing animals. That, at least, cannot be an appanage of original sin. No Christian can be a pessimist. He knows better. God is not only on His throne, but on His earth, deeper and more ineradicably in the hearts of youth than ever I could believe, without experience had assured me of it. No man can be a Christian and regard his Master as a failure.

The future lies in the lap of the youth of today. What of them? Here again experience convinces me that never in the world's history has youth been so chivalrous as it is today, so imbued, not necessarily with a sense of 'my duty to my neighbour,' but with a real desire to help every 'neighbour' in trouble. Youth must be youth, and youth has always to learn that they do not know, and cannot grasp reality except by experience. Why worry overmuch if today they express their attitude to God or their 'neighbours' by preferring to cross the dangerous road in order to pay for the pleasure of putting a stranger in their car while they walk, or to pay the bill for a down and-out brother to eat, rather than hurrying with priest or parson to a Church Service at the capital? They need not be wrong because they do not see exactly eye to eye with us. Who would imagine, unless faith helped them to do so, that the result of asking men and women to give up holidays in Europe or in Florida, and to come and pay all their own expenses, even if they could afford it, for the pleasure of, say, digging a water-supply on the Labrador, would ever result in having to keep a special office to weed out the numbers needed and fend off more coming than, with all our widespread activities, even we can take care of? This sounds immodest, but it is true, and expresses the spirit of Christ in the youth of today better than any other way I know.

As to death — well, I keep that question in the same category, as the result of life's experience, as 'religious life' and 'Mrs. 'Arris.' Maeterlinck was a layman and a man of learning, and I see by his 'Blue Bird' that he is like-minded. The truth is, there are so many things to be done that I have not had much time to think about death, and personally yet had no experience of it. Yes, I am a surgeon; and I have seen patients paralyzed up to their necks, with their hearts still beating, and their lungs kept going by the long nerve wire which runs direct down to those bits of machinery from the brain. These people always told me they were the same personality. Why they should cease to be a person at all, because I nick through one more nerve thread, little thicker than a piece of cotton, I cannot say. Anyhow, until that last nick takes place, a magistrate will accept on oath that the person is exactly the same, though he may be 'dead' below the cervicle vertebra, which means his neck. Everyone knows that the brain is not ourselves. It is mine exactly as is my jack-knife or my boot. *I* make one side of my brain learn French. A doctor can destroy the few cells which I have educated, and I know no French. But I can go to work and educate the cells on the other side and learn French again. Everybody can know that no part of my body is 'I,' only that it and its wires and cells relate me to this material world. I have seen the accident called death of the body more than once, but I never saw any reason to believe in the death of personality. Every possible evidence of personal life after death that can come to human beings, I should say comes through other channels than the five senses that I am conscious of.

I once met Houdini, and watched him do amazing things, but I never knew how he did them, much as I wanted to. God help us not to neglect to use a thing — like faith — because we do not know why or how it works. It would be a criminal offence in a doctor not to use X-rays even if he does not know how barium chloride makes Gamma rays, or X-rays, visible. People will laugh at me when I say that I have always had great joy in seeing what the Bible has to say on any practical point. But I never knew any big life problem yet about which it did not say a wiser thing than any of the other sources available to me. Nearing the top of the hill, I have been forced to go more slowly, and shall have time, or ought to have if I do as my good advisers warn me, to devote to the problems of 'whys' and 'hows.'

To love one's neighbour as one's self is not a mere pious sentiment. It is every whit as much a law of life as fresh air is to the body. To live to one's self only is never to live at all. All the world acclaims the men who gave their lives for their country. Christ's men went farther. They were internationally minded. The world cannot finally be God's Kingdom until everyone is: and that end must be won through those individuals who are 'bound to God' and love all their brothers. Old Nehemiah was far too busy to be wasting time talking on the Plain of Ono. He had the wall of God's city to build, which would not be built unless he did it. Lots of us who go to church are not doing very much to suggest that we worry greatly whether the walls of Christ's Kingdom are strengthened; and yet there is every whit as much a piece of that wall to be built by you and by me today as there was by that splendid old Nehemiah in his day. When there are enough bits left unbuilt, enough gaps left in the line, the nation without the protection of that wall is carried into captivity as surely as was Israel, called God's people, and for exactly the same reason, unwillingness to be 'bound to God.' Herein lies the whole meaning of personality and of human life, 'It will not be built if I do not build it.'

It is absurd to philosophize further. Some people worry about my intellectual grasp of truth. We must know that our opinions are not a matter of very great moment even to our next-door neighbour, except in so far as what they lead us to do. I see no reason whatever to suppose that the Creator lays great stress on them either. Experience answers our problems — experience of faith, and common sense. For faith and common sense together make reasonable service, that service which ends by giving us the light of life, but which does not begin that way. This 'reasonable service' is what Saint Paul told us God asks for, and he wrote it as a considered judgment from his life experience, when he was 'nearing the summit' and looking to go to Rome to lay down his life. As a surgeon I have learned long ago that I must not wait to understand how many things work before I use them to save life. And so I am content to leave the comprehension of many problems until I have passed over the bar, knowing that it is to God alone that we all stand, whether it is here or beyond the horizon called death.

THE END

INDEX